Economic Development in Hawai‘i

Patricia Yu

Economic Development in Hawai'i

Building a Resilient and Innovative Island Economy

palgrave
macmillan

Patricia Yu
University of Hawai'i - West O'ahu
Honolulu, HI, USA

ISBN 978-3-032-15688-4 ISBN 978-3-032-15689-1 (eBook)
https://doi.org/10.1007/978-3-032-15689-1

This Palgrave Macmillan imprint is published by the registered company Springer Nature Switzerland AG
The registered company address is: Gewerbestrasse 11, 6330 Cham, Switzerland

Contents

CHAPTER 1

The Island Economy at a Crossroads

1 Introduction: Unpacking the Paradox

When most people think of Hawai'i, they picture paradise—crystal waters, vibrant culture, and tranquil living. But for residents, especially working families, the day-to-day experience often reflects a starkly different reality. High costs, housing insecurity, and wage stagnation persist even as the economy boasts low unemployment and robust tourism revenue. This chapter unpacks that paradox, focusing on the question: Can Hawai'i deliver quality of life and opportunity to its people?

Grounded in data and recent policy developments, this chapter examines the underlying tensions between image and infrastructure, prosperity and precarity. It explores challenges like underemployment, the ALICE (Asset Limited, Income Constrained, Employed) population's growing vulnerability, and the increasing outmigration of local talent. By drawing on state and federal labor statistics, cost-of-living benchmarks, and emerging workforce strategies, it offers a clearer and more complete understanding of Hawai'i's economic landscape. The goal is to deepen our understanding of what competition means in a place as unique—and as constrained—as Hawai'i.

P. Yu, *Economic Development in Hawai'i*,
https://doi.org/10.1007/978-3-032-15689-1_1

2 A Tale of Two Hawai'i's: Paradise and Precarity

Hawai'i boasts the lowest rates of gun violence and the highest life expectancy in the United States. It is a global symbol of relaxation, aloha spirit, and environmental beauty. But behind the postcards, nearly one in three local families live paycheck to paycheck. Young professionals, especially Native Hawaiians, are leaving the islands in record numbers, chasing more affordable lives on the continent. The State of ALICE in Hawai'i: 2025 Update on Financial Hardship documents the scale and structure of financial insecurity in Hawai'i [1]. In 2023, 10% of households were in poverty by the Federal Poverty Level (FPL), but an additional 35% were ALICE—earning above the FPL yet still unable to afford basic necessities in their county. Overall, 45% of households fell below the ALICE Threshold, placing Hawai'i 43rd among U.S. states and D.C. in financial hardship (Figure 1). Households below the threshold are found statewide

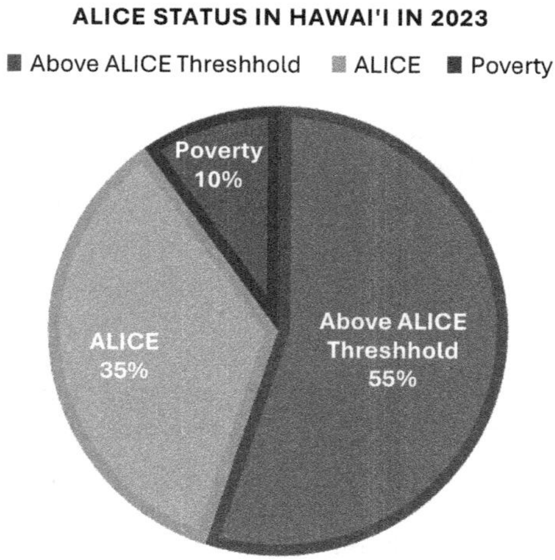

Figure 1 ALICE status in Hawai'i in 2023. This pie chart illustrates the share of Hawai'i households experiencing financial instability in 2023. According to the ALICE framework, 45% of households in the state were below the financial stability threshold. Within this group, 35% were ALICE households—those earning above the FPL but unable to afford basic necessities—and 10% were living in poverty. The remaining 55% of households were above the ALICE threshold and considered financially stable. Data sources: ALICE Threshold (2010–2023); U.S. Census Bureau, American Community Survey (2023)

and across demographic groups, and many workers in this group provide essential services such as childcare, food service, personal care, and delivery work. This report argues that the FPL substantially underestimates hardship and that ALICE measures—built from a county-level Household Survival Budget and tracked via the ALICE Essentials Index—offer a more accurate picture of local cost of living. Workers below the ALICE Threshold increasingly bear the brunt of economic change and uncertainty as the workforce shifts to incorporate new technology and automation and as employers increase reliance on non-standard work arrangements, like hourly paid work, part-time employment, and gig work. These arrangements make it easier to reduce work hours or cut employment altogether when the economy ebbs and expand them when demand increases.

This report also shows that in 2023, of the 20 most common occupations in Hawai'i as reported by the Bureau of Labor Statistics (BLS), nine still paid less than $20 per hour. And of the workers in these 20 occupations, 38% were living in households below the ALICE Threshold. Occupations with the largest share of workers in households below the threshold included waiters and waitresses (51%), laborers and movers (50%), delivery drivers/sales workers (50%), fast food/counter workers (48%), and cooks (48%) (Table 1). Despite the unemployment rate often below the national average, the underemployment and cost-burdened workforce tell a different story. The U.S. BLS (2024) provides a view of Hawai'i's labor market by presenting alternative measures of unemployment [2]. While the state's official unemployment rate (U-3)[1] was a low 3.1%, the broader U-6[2] rate, which accounts for underemployed and discouraged workers, was significantly higher at 6.4%. This divergence is critical, as it reveals that many workers are in part-time or precarious employment situations despite being counted as "employed," masking the deeper structural challenges in Hawai'i's labor market. This data is essential for understanding the gap between employment status and economic security in the state.

The Hawai'i State's Workforce Innovation and Opportunity Act (WIOA) Unified Plan (2024–2027) addresses the state's urgent workforce

[1] U-3 is the official unemployment rate reported by the U.S. Bureau of Labor Statistics (BLS). It measures the percentage of the civilian labor force that is jobless, actively seeking employment, and available to work.

[2] U-6 includes the officially unemployed (U-3) as well as discouraged workers, marginally attached workers, and those working part-time for economic reasons who would prefer full-time employment.

Table 1 Labor Characteristics and ALICE Status in Hawai‘i, 2023. This table shows the twenty most common occupations in Hawai‘i and compares total employment, median hourly wages, and the share of workers earning below the ALICE Threshold. Many of Hawai‘i’s largest occupations—such as fast-food workers, waitstaff, retail salespersons, janitors, cooks, and home health aides—have low median wages and high rates of financial hardship, with 34%–50% of workers in these roles unable to meet basic household costs. Only higher-paid occupations, such as managers and teachers, show lower levels of financial insecurity. Overall, the table reveals that a significant portion of Hawai‘i’s essential workforce earns wages insufficient to cover the state’s high cost of living

Most Common Occupations	*Total Employment*	*Percent of Workers Below ALICE Threshold*	*Median Hourly Wage*
Fast Food and Counter Workers	24,080	48%	$13.98
Janitors and Building Cleaners	20,860	38%	$20.47
Retail Salespersons	16,420	36%	$17.08
Office Clerks	16,260	41%	$19.51
Cooks	15,040	48%	$20.63
Waiters and Waitresses	14,380	51%	$13.55
Cahiers	13,230	44%	$15.82
General and Operations Managers	12,570	22%	$50.48
Registered Nurses	11,920	11%	$62.12
Maids and Housekeeping Cleaners	10,470	40%	$23.57
Office and Administrative Support Supervisors	10,330	18%	$29.17
Security Guards and Gambling Surveillance Officers	9,390	41%	$18.70
Laborers and Movers, Hand	9,180	50%	$19.35
Customer Service Representatives	8,420	44%	$18.52
Delivery Drivers/Sales Workers	8,280	50%	$22.37
Other Healthcare Support Workers	8,270	43%	$21.95
Stockers and Order Fillers	8,050	46%	$18.09
Elementary and Middle School Teachers	7,890	23%	$30.32
Food Preparation and Serving Supervisors	7,570	33%	$21.33
Secretaries and Administrative Assistants	7,520	27%	$23.05

challenges, including high living costs, low-wage service jobs, and a shrinking labor force [3]. Despite low unemployment rates, approximately 42% of Hawai'i households cannot afford necessities—a crisis driving outmigration of 10,000 residents annually. This plan outlines a strategic roadmap built on four pillars: aligning workforce development with economic growth, strengthening education and training alliances, promoting inclusivity and equity for underserved populations (including immigrants, veterans, and Native Hawaiians), and fostering cross-sector collaboration. It emphasizes leveraging federal investments, expanding sector partnerships, integrating workforce systems, and building data-driven solutions to create living-wage opportunities. It also recognizes emerging labor trends—such as remote work, AI, and the gig economy[3] and aims to prepare the workforce for high-growth sectors like health care, technology, and renewable energy. Overall, the strategy aspires to ensure every resident can thrive in a resilient and inclusive Hawai'i economy.

In Kahului, a family of four must make nearly $150,000 a year to achieve a "modest but adequate" standard of living. Yet median wages barely cross $50,000. Something does not add up. The Massachusetts Institute of Technology (2025), through its Living Wage Calculator, offers detailed estimates of the income required to meet basic needs in specific U.S. regions [4]. For Kahului-Wailuku-Lahaina, the tool estimates that a family of four (two working adults and two children) must earn nearly $150,000 annually to attain a modest yet satisfactory standard of living. This figure far exceeds the area's median household income, showing the growing disparity between wages and living costs on Maui. The paradox of prosperity versus affordability defines the economic discourse in Hawai'i. The islands are thriving in one sense, with record tourism, billion-dollar real estate, and strong military investment, but faltering in another, as local people struggle to stay rooted.

3 Isolation: Constraint or Catalyst?

Hawai'i is over 2,000 miles from the nearest continental landmass. That fact alone shapes nearly every economic decision. From fuel and food to vehicles and building materials, almost everything arrives by sea or air. This dependence leads to high prices and vulnerability to global shocks. The

[3] A labor market characterized by short-term, flexible, and freelance work, often facilitated by digital platforms or apps.

Department of Business, Economic Development & Tourism (DBEDT) (2025) provides testimony supporting legislation aimed at enhancing Hawai'i's economic self-sufficiency [5]. This document shows that Hawaii imports approximately 85% of its food and more than 90% of its energy, figures that reveal the state's heightened vulnerability to global supply chain disruptions. The testimony stresses the urgency of investing in local food production and renewable energy to build long-term economic resilience and reduce exposure to external shocks. But Hawai'i's isolation is also its innovation incubator. Faced with unique challenges, the islands have pioneered renewable energy solutions, circular agriculture systems, and climate-resilient infrastructure. Like islanders throughout history, modern Hawai'i residents are master adapters. The University of Hawai'i's research into sustainable energy grids, Pacific Islander climate change adaptation, and marine technology is a testament to how remoteness can inspire rather than restrain. One example is that University of Hawai'i (UH) is establishing the Pōʻai ke Aloha ʻĀina Center for the Ancestral Circular Economy[4] & Justice [6]. Pōʻai ke Aloha ʻĀina loosely translates to "circle of love for the land," reflecting a values-based, regenerative approach rooted in ancestral Hawaiian practices. This initiative seeks to revive Hawai'i's traditional "give, take, regenerate" model, fostering local research, advocacy, and global collaboration to inspire sustainable, community-centered circular economies worldwide.

The Hawaiʻi Natural Energy Institute (HNEI) (2024) outlines Hawai'i's progress toward achieving 100% renewable electricity and carbon neutrality by 2045 [7]. This report highlights HNEI's pivotal role in advancing innovative, cost-effective energy technologies, shaping energy policy, and facilitating collaboration between federal programs and local stakeholders. This publication is an essential resource for understanding the institutional strategies and research-driven initiatives accelerating Hawai'i's transition to a clean energy future. The 2024 Annual Report from the Pacific Islands Climate Adaptation Science Center (PI-CASC) highlights its fifth year of advancing climate adaptation research, education, and outreach across Hawai'i and the U.S.-affiliated Pacific Islands [8]. Hosted by UH, PI-CASC supported 14 university-led research projects and 22 graduate scholars working on climate resilience initiatives, including sea-level rise, invasive species, and the integration of Indigenous and cultural knowledge.

[4] An economic system designed to eliminate waste and maximize resource use by keeping materials, products, and services in circulation for as long as possible.

The consortium expanded community partnerships, hosted symposia, and developed tools like the American Samoa Sea Level Rise Viewer. Through programs like Climate Adaptation for Resource Management (CARM) and the Manager Climate Corps (MCC), PI-CASC empowered natural resource professionals and community leaders with training, mentorship, and place-based research experience. These initiatives advance locally relevant, actionable science and leadership capacity to address climate vulnerabilities and promote long-term sustainability and ecosystem stewardship in Pacific Island communities.

4 Tourism: Blessing, Curse, or Both?

Yet even the most innovative resilience strategies must contend with a defining force in Hawaiʻi's economy: tourism. As the state's most dominant industry, tourism sits at the intersection of opportunity and overdependence, shaping both environmental stress and economic survival. In 2019, over 10 million visitors came to Hawaiʻi, more than seven times the resident population. Tourism accounts for nearly 20% of Hawaiʻi's GDP and directly supports one in five jobs. But its dominance creates fragility. When the COVID-19 pandemic hit, visitor arrivals plummeted immensely. DBEDT (2021) shows the continued impact of COVID-19 on Hawaiʻi's tourism industry [9]. Travel restrictions in 2020 led to a dramatic drop in visitor arrivals, but as vaccination rates rose and the Safe Travels program eased quarantine rules in 2021, domestic tourism rebounded. Visitor arrivals by air rose to 6.78 million—up 153.1% from 2020—yet remained below pre-pandemic levels. International tourism was severely limited, with Japanese arrivals plummeting by 93.5% and other key markets such as Oceania (−87.1%) and Canada (−46.5%) also experiencing sharp declines.

Bond-Smith and Fuleky (2024) present a rigorous economic analysis of Hawaiʻi's structural dependence on tourism and the vulnerabilities it creates [10]. The authors argue that Hawaiʻi's overreliance on tourism creates both short-term vulnerability and long-term stagnation, which was made starkly visible during the COVID-19 pandemic. Their report uses the Principle of Relatedness to identify feasible diversification opportunities that build on existing regional strengths. Promising sectors include ocean-related industries such as aquaculture, boat building, and seafood processing. However, many of these industries remain underdeveloped due to infrastructure gaps and market barriers. Rather than "picking winners," the report recommends policy efforts that target and remove developmental bottlenecks, encouraging market-driven diversification to build a more resilient and sustainable economy. A more diversified economy, built on targeted and evidence-based policy, could promote long-term productivity, and reduce the risks of economic downturns tied to tourism volatility.

The Chamber of Commerce Hawai'i (2024) presents a forward-looking strategy to guide the state's economic development through 2030 [11]. This plan outlines 17 strategic actions focused on improving economic competitiveness, expanding the workforce, diversifying industry, and building local wealth. Key areas include housing, childcare affordability, regulatory reform, and targeted support for sectors like tech, agriculture, defense, and tourism. Emphasis is placed on developing local talent through STEM education, apprenticeships, and entrepreneurial ecosystems. It is significant as it reflects a coordinated vision developed by industry and policy stakeholders to shape a more sustainable and dynamic economic future for Hawai'i.

Tourism also inflates housing prices, strains infrastructure, and consumes natural resources at an unsustainable rate. Inafuku and Tyndall (2024)'s UHERO (University of Hawai'i Economic Research Organization) report that around 30,000 housing units—approximately 5% of Hawai'i's total housing stock—are short-term vacation rentals (STRs)[5], with concentrations especially high in tourist-heavy areas like West Maui and Waikīkī [12] (Figure 2). STRs remove units from the long-term housing supply, potentially raising rents and home prices in an already strained market. Drawing on peer-reviewed studies from cities such as Los Angeles, Barcelona, and London, the authors estimate that removing all STRs from O'ahu could reduce median home prices by 4%–6% and monthly rents by 2%–8%. Though not a complete solution to Hawai'i's housing crisis, regulating STRs could offer meaningful relief—especially for low- and middle-income residents. The authors emphasize that Hawai'i's unusually high share of STRs gives them outsized influence on housing affordability.

The Environmental and Energy Study Institute (2023) examines how tourism impacts Hawai'i's environment [13]. It stresses how tourism strains essential infrastructure, including wastewater systems and freshwater supplies, and contributes to habitat degradation. It also points out that

[5] Short-term rentals (STRs) in the context of Hawai'i refer to residential units—typically condos, homes, or apartments—rented to guests for a period of less than 30 consecutive days. These rentals are often listed on platforms such as Airbnb, Vrbo, and Booking.com and are popular with tourists seeking alternatives to traditional hotels.

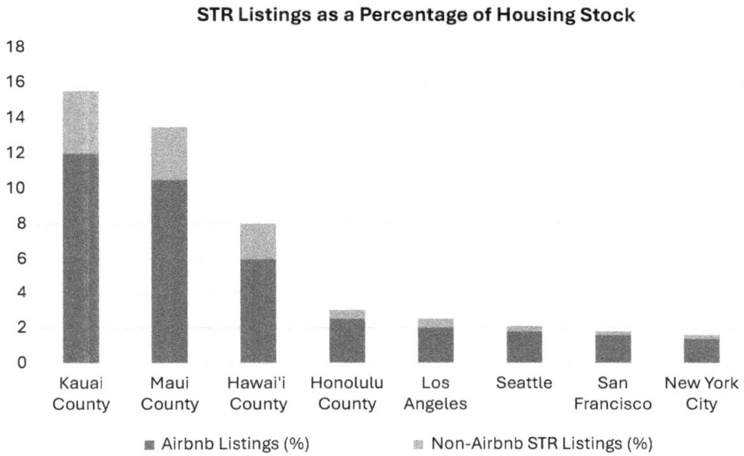

Figure 2 Short-Term Rental (STR) listings as a percentage of housing stock. This bar chart shows STR listings as a percentage of total housing stock across various counties and cities. Hawai'i's counties stand out with notably higher STR shares than major mainland U.S. cities. In 2023, Kaua'i County had the highest share, with STRs accounting for about 15.5% of all housing units—12% from Airbnb and 3.5% from non-Airbnb platforms. Maui County followed with 13.5% total STRs (10.5% Airbnb, 3% non-Airbnb), and Hawai'i County reported 8% (6% Airbnb, 2% non-Airbnb). In contrast, Honolulu County's STR share was around 3%, and large cities such as Los Angeles, Seattle, San Francisco, and New York City ranged between 1.5% and 2.5%. Source: UHERO Report, Short-Term Vacation Rentals and Housing Costs in Hawai'i, 2023, Rachel Inafuku and Justin Tyndall

tourism-related activity is responsible for roughly 25% of Hawai'i's energy sector emissions. This piece is important because it links tourism to both ecological vulnerability and climate impact, advocating for a more sustainable and community-conscious tourism model. Residents frequently express resentment, feeling like strangers in their own land. And yet, tourism is unlikely to disappear; rather, it must evolve. The rise of regenerative tourism[6] offers hope: travel that gives back more than it takes. But can

[6] A form of tourism that goes beyond sustainability by actively seeking to restore, renew, and positively impact the places, people, and ecosystems it touches. Instead of merely minimizing harm, regenerative tourism aims to leave a destination better than it was before—environmentally, socially, and culturally.

Hawai'i shift from being consumed as a product to being respected as a place? This is an economic and cultural question that will define the coming decades.

5 The Quest for Economic Diversification

As the limitations of tourism become more evident, calls for a diversified economy have grown louder. The question now is not whether diversification is needed—but how to make it real, resilient, and rooted in local strengths. For decades, Hawai'i has discussed moving "beyond tourism." But how? Agriculture faces land access and labor shortages. Tech innovation is hampered by limited venture capital and high operational costs. Manufacturing is minimal. And the Jones Act[7] raises the cost of shipping, limiting inter-island trade and external market expansion. Yet promising sectors are emerging. Renewable energy, driven by Hawai'i's ambitious 100% clean energy goal by 2045, is drawing investment and innovation. The blue economy, including aquaculture and marine biotech, is gaining momentum. Creative industries, from film production to fashion to digital media, tap into Hawai'i's unique cultural brand. The 2024 Annual Report of the Natural Energy Laboratory of Hawai'i Authority (NELHA) highlights its leadership in advancing Hawai'i's blue economy from HOST Park, a premier ocean science and technology hub located at Keāhole Point in Kailua-Kona on the Island of Hawai'i (Big Island) [14].

In 2024, NELHA supported over 55 innovative projects across aquaculture, ocean science, renewable energy, and conservation. The park generated over $140 million in economic impact and $7 million in state tax revenue (2022 figures). Key accomplishments include completing a solar-powered microgrid at the 55" Pump Station, expanding seawater infrastructure, initiating an innovation center, and enhancing community engagement through K–12 educational tours and its 50th anniversary celebration. Partnering with universities, businesses, and cultural groups, NELHA continues to diversify Hawai'i's economy by nurturing sustainability-driven startups and research. HOST Park remains a global

[7] The Jones Act, formally known as the Merchant Marine Act of 1920, is a U.S. federal law that regulates maritime commerce in U.S. waters and between U.S. ports. It requires that goods transported by water between U.S. ports be carried on ships that are built in the United States, owned by U.S. citizens, and crewed by U.S. citizens or permanent residents.

model for ocean-based innovation and environmentally responsible economic development.

The Hawai'i Creative Industries Update Report (2024) presents an in-depth analysis of the creative sector's contribution to Hawai'i's economy [15]. This report points to a 2.1% average annual job growth in film, television, and digital media from 2013 to 2023. It conveys the strategic value of Hawai'i's cultural identity in powering growth across fashion, music, and digital content, positioning the sector as a key pillar of the state's broader economic diversification efforts. Military and federal spending remain significant economic engines, especially on O'ahu. But as geopolitical dynamics shift, relying solely on military presence carries its own risks. What does a truly diversified Hawaiian economy look like? It likely blends traditional practices (like lo'i kalo farming and artisanal fishing[8]) with cutting-edge innovation. But making that leap requires coordinated policy, investment in human capital, and a cultural shift toward valuing new forms of work.

6 Human Capital: Hawai'i's Hidden Asset

People are Hawai'i's greatest strength. The islands are home to a diverse, multilingual, and often multigenerational workforce. Cultural values like community care (kuleana) and hospitality are deeply embedded. But the state suffers from a persistent brain drain[9]. Many of Hawai'i's best and brightest leave for college and never return. Others move away in search of housing, higher wages, or career advancement. DBEDT (2021) reveals that a significant number of young, educated individuals born in Hawai'i are relocating to the mainland U.S. [16]. Over 50% of Hawai'i-born adults with a bachelor's degree or higher now live outside the state. While income differences are modest, this report finds that limited high-quality job opportunities, rather than unemployment, drive this outmigration. The data suggest that the decision to leave is often influenced by career prospects and industry presence on the mainland, raising concerns about

[8] Artisanal fishing is a small-scale, traditional method of fishing that typically uses low-tech gear and practices, is labor-intensive, and is often carried out by local communities for subsistence or local markets.

[9] Brain drain is the emigration of highly educated or skilled individuals from one region or country to another, often in search of better economic opportunities, working conditions, or quality of life.

the long-term retention of local talent in Hawai‘i. To reverse this, Hawai‘i must invest in education pipelines, remote work infrastructure, and entrepreneurial ecosystems that enable residents to thrive without leaving home.

The 2023 Hawai‘i P-20 Annual Report showcases a range of initiatives designed to strengthen the education-to-career pipeline across the state, with a focus on equity and alignment with workforce needs [17]. The "Hawai‘i Graduates for Hawai‘i's Future" goal shifts emphasis toward preparing students for meaningful careers locally. A $20 million federal grant is expanding early childhood education, while regional partnerships and work-based learning (WBL) intermediaries connect high schoolers to real-world career experiences. Programs like "Finish in a Flash" and GEAR UP have improved college enrollment, especially post-pandemic. The "Stay at Home, Grow Your Own" pilot supports neighbor island students becoming teachers in their own communities. Dual credit participation continues to rise, leading to higher college attendance and completion rates. Hawai‘i P-20 also launched a new college enrollment dashboard and redesigned the College and Career Readiness Indicators (CCRI) report, which tracks trends in academic achievement, career preparedness, and postsecondary transitions to guide statewide educational strategies.

The Department of Human Resources Development (2025) evaluates the potential of expanding remote work within Hawai‘i's public sector in response to legislative direction [18]. This report identifies specific state job classifications suitable for remote or hybrid models and maps out regions where broadband improvements could unlock access to higher-wage employment. By addressing geographic disparities and infrastructure gaps, this report reinforces how remote work investments can retain local talent, support economic resilience, and reduce the need for outward migration. The growth of distance learning, telehealth, and digital entrepreneurship presents new opportunities. Can Hawai‘i become not just a paradise to visit, but also a hub for remote-first knowledge work?

7 Policy Levers and Public Will

Ultimately, whether Hawai‘i can compete depends on leadership, collaboration, and courage. Policies around housing, zoning, taxation, and education must evolve. From government agencies to grassroots organizations, all stakeholders need to work together toward shared goals. There is no silver bullet. But through bold public investment, strategic partnerships, and values-aligned governance, Hawai‘i can chart a path toward an economy that balances prosperity with equity, innovation with tradition, and growth with sustainability. This also requires transparent communication, long-term planning, and the ability to confront difficult trade-offs with integrity. This book aims to explore that path through data, storytelling, analysis, and vision. Because Hawaiʻi is not just a place to compete. It's a place to lead with intention and with aloha.

8 Conclusion: Rethinking What It Means to Compete

This chapter reveals that Hawaiʻi's challenges are systemic, structural, and deeply rooted in geography and inequality. While traditional indicators like unemployment or GDP offer surface-level reassurance, they obscure deeper vulnerabilities: underemployment, outmigration, and the growing burden faced by working families. Yet this is not a narrative of decline. Hawaiʻi has tools at its disposal: a resilient, values-driven workforce; innovative programs that align education with career pipelines; and renewed attention to equity and inclusion. If competition is redefined as the ability to retain talent, provide dignity in work, and sustain communities, then Hawaiʻi can succeed on its own terms.

This chapter urges policymakers, educators, and community leaders to ask harder questions and confront uncomfortable trade-offs. Competing as an island economy requires more than adaptation; it demands intention. And perhaps the greatest competitive advantage Hawaiʻi can claim is the willingness to pursue a model of shared prosperity, which is grounded in aloha.

References

[1]. United For ALICE. (2025). The state of ALICE in Hawaiʻi: 2025 update on financial hardship. https://www.unitedforalice.org/hawaii.

[2]. U.S. Bureau of Labor Statistics. (2024, March 6). Alternative measures of labor underutilization in Hawaii — 2024. Retrieved from https://www.bls.gov/regions/west/news-release/laborunderutilization_hawaii.htm.

[3]. Hawaii State Department of Labor and Industrial Relations. (2024). 2024–2027 Workforce Innovation and Opportunity Act (WIOA) Unified Plan. Retrieved from https://labor.hawaii.gov/wdc/files/2024/03/2024-Hawaii-Unified-Plan_FINALFINAL.pdf.

[4]. Massachusetts Institute of Technology. (2025). Living wage calculation for Kahului-Wailuku-Lahaina, HI. MIT Living Wage Calculator. Retrieved from https://livingwage.mit.edu/metros/27980.

[5]. Department of Business, Economic Development & Tourism. (2025, March 21). Testimony on HCR 209 / HR 201: Strengthening Hawaii's Economic Self-Sufficiency. Retrieved from https://capitol.hawaii.gov/sessions/session2025/Testimony/HR201_TESTIMONY_ECD_03-21-25_.PDF.
[6]. University of Hawai'i. (2024, October 14). UH revives ancestral circular economy for a sustainable future. Retrieved from https://www.hawaii.edu/news/2024/10/14/ancestral-circular-economy-sustainable-future/.
[7]. Hawai'i Natural Energy Institute. (2024). 2024 HNEI Annual Report. University of Hawai'i. Retrieved from https://www.hnei.hawaii.edu/wp-content/uploads/2024-HNEI-Annual-Report.pdf.
[8]. Pacific Islands Climate Adaptation Science Center. (2024). 2024 Annual Report. Retrieved from https://pi-casc.soest.hawaii.edu/wp-content/uploads/2024/10/2024-PI-CASC-Annual-Report-Final_ADA.pdf.
[9]. Department of Business, Economic Development & Tourism. (2021). Annual Visitor Research Report 2020. State of Hawai'i. Retrieved from https://files.hawaii.gov/dbedt/visitor/visitor-research/2021-annual-visitor.pdf.
[10]. Bond-Smith, S., & Fuleky, P. (2024, July). Potential opportunities to diversify the economy of Hawai'i. University of Hawai'i Economic Research Organization (UHERO). Retrieved from https://uhero.hawaii.edu/wp-content/uploads/2024/07/PotentialOpportunitiesToDiversifyTheEconomyOfHawaii.pdf.
[11]. Chamber of Commerce Hawai'i. (2024). Blueprint 2030: An Economic Action Plan for Hawai'i. Retrieved from https://www.cochawaii.org/wp-content/uploads/2024/10/COCH-40740_BlueprintReport_Spreads-compressed.pdf.
[12]. Inafuku, R., & Tyndall, J. (2023, April 18). Short-term vacation rentals and housing costs in Hawai'i. UHERO. Retrieved from https://uhero.hawaii.edu/short-term-vacation-rentals-and-housing-costs-in-hawai%CA%BBi/.
[13]. Environmental and Energy Study Institute. (2023, September 14). Rethinking tourism in the wake of West Maui's wildfires. Retrieved from https://www.eesi.org/articles/view/rethinking-tourism-in-the-wake-of-west-mauis-wildfires.
[14]. Natural Energy Laboratory of Hawai'i Authority (NELHA). (2025, January). Annual Report 2024. Retrieved from https://nelha.hawaii.gov/wp-content/uploads/2025/01/Annual-Report-2024-ADA-version.pdf.
[15]. Department of Business, Economic Development & Tourism (DBEDT). (2024, December). Hawai'i's Creative Industries Report 2024. Retrieved from https://files.hawaii.gov/dbedt/economic/data_reports/hawaii-creative-report/HI_Creative_Ind_2024.pdf.
[16]. Department of Business, Economic Development & Tourism. (2021). Brain drain: Characteristics of Hawai'i-born adults on the U.S. mainland. State

of Hawaiʻi. Retrieved from https://files.hawaii.gov/dbedt/economic/reports/Brain_Drain_Hawaii_Born_Population.pdf.
[17]. Hawaiʻi P–20 Partnerships for Education. (2023). 2023 Annual Report. Retrieved from https://www.hawaiip20.org/wp-content/uploads/2023/12/2023-P-20-Annual_Report_F2.pdf.
[18]. Department of Human Resources Development. (2025, January). Senate Concurrent Resolution No. 184 SD1: Remote work opportunities. Retrieved from https://dhrd.hawaii.gov/wp-content/uploads/2025/01/SCR184-2024-Remote-Work-Report.pdf.

CHAPTER 2

Measuring Productivity in the Pacific: How Does Hawai'i Compare?

1 Introduction: The Mirage of Prosperity

Hawai'i often ranks high in quality-of-life indicators: stunning natural beauty, low crime rates, and high life expectancy. But when it comes to productivity, the engine that drives economic sustainability and long-term competitiveness, the state paints a more complicated picture. Productivity, broadly defined as output per unit of input (often labor or capital), is the yardstick by which we evaluate how efficiently an economy transforms resources into goods and services. This chapter investigates Hawai'i's productivity from multiple angles: how it compares to other U.S. states and island economies, what sectors are pulling their weight, and where inefficiencies persist. The question here is: Is Hawai'i truly productive, or does its economy merely appear so due to inflated costs and tourism-driven illusions of prosperity? The answers may surprise even long-time residents.

2 The Productivity Puzzle

Productivity growth is a central measure of economic health. It enables higher wages, improves living standards, and enhances a region's ability to compete in national and global markets. Yet Hawai'i's productivity numbers often fall below U.S. averages despite high costs of living and labor.

P. Yu, *Economic Development in Hawai'i*,
https://doi.org/10.1007/978-3-032-15689-1_2

The U.S. Bureau of Labor Statistics (BLS) (2024) shows that Hawai'i's labor productivity index for the private nonfarm sector declined from 102.368 in 2022 to 99.788 in 2023 [1]. This indicates a drop in output per hour worked, signaling stagnation in economic efficiency. Given Hawai'i's high costs of labor and living, the downward trend draws attention to growing concerns about the state's productivity performance and its ability to sustain economic growth without gains in efficiency.

The U.S. Bureau of Economic Analysis (BEA) (2024) provides detailed statistics on GDP and personal income by state [2]. The 2023 data show that Hawai'i's per capita personal income was approximately $65,888—lagging behind states with similar populations and tourism-driven economies, such as Alaska ($71,309) and Oregon ($67,514). This gap shows Hawai'i's ongoing challenge—turning its high-cost economy and thriving visitor industry into real productivity gains that match those of similar states. The U.S. BEA (2024) also reports that Hawai'i has a regional price parity (RPP)[1] of 119.3, indicating that prices in the state are approximately 19.3% higher than the national average [3]. This high cost of living significantly diminishes the real purchasing power of residents, exacerbating the state's productivity gap when compared to other states with lower living costs. Labor productivity[2] also trails behind. This isn't a new trend; it has persisted for over a decade.

3 Sectoral Breakdown: Who's Pulling the Levers?

To understand why productivity in Hawai'i lags behind national trends, it is essential to examine the state's economic structure. Tourism remains the cornerstone of Hawai'i's economy. DBEDT reports on the steady recovery of Hawai'i's visitor industry through the end of 2024, particularly in the aftermath of the August 2023 Maui wildfires [4]. This report states that total visitor arrivals reached 9.69 million, while visitor expenditure totaled $20.68 billion. These figures reflect the sector's resilience and reaffirm tourism's central role in driving Hawai'i's economy, even in the face of environmental and economic disruptions. Yet despite its visibility and volume, tourism is structurally low in productivity. The industry is

[1] Regional price parity (RPP) is a measure that compares the price levels of goods and services across regions, adjusting for differences in the cost of living.

[2] Labor productivity is a measure of economic output per unit of labor input, typically expressed as output per worker or per hour worked.

labor-intensive by nature, requiring large numbers of workers to deliver guest-facing services such as housekeeping, food preparation, transportation, and recreation. This results in relatively low value-added per worker.

The U.S. BLS (2023) provides comprehensive wage data across industries in Hawai'i [5]. This report shows that the average annual wage in the Accommodation and Food Services sector—closely tied to tourism—was significantly lower than both the statewide private sector average and the national equivalent. This wage gap reveals the economic fragility of Hawai'i's tourism workforce and raises deeper questions about how long an economy built on low-wage service jobs can truly sustain itself. Compounding this challenge is the limited room for innovation within core service roles, where automation or efficiency gains have minimal impact. Although digital tools have streamlined reservations and logistics, the heart of the industry still depends heavily on manual labor. As a result, per-worker output remains low and largely stagnant.

Government and defense represent another significant portion of the state's labor market, employing nearly 18% of the workforce, with the highest density on O'ahu due to military installations and state government functions. DBEDT (2025) reports that in the fourth quarter of 2024, Hawai'i's government sector employed approximately 1.4% more workers than in the same quarter of the previous year, adding 1,800 new jobs [6]. Of those, the state government accounted for the largest increase with 1,400 jobs, followed by local government (300) and the federal government (200). With government jobs comprising about 17% of all non-agricultural wage and salary employment, the data show that the public sector continues to serve as a major source of employment across the islands. Wages in the sector tend to be stable and relatively generous, averaging over $75,000 annually—but productivity growth is inherently limited. Measuring output in public administration is difficult because services like education, law enforcement, and regulation lack clear revenue-based metrics. These institutions are also bound by procedural and budgetary constraints that limit adaptability. While government employment provides an important stabilizing effect for Hawai'i's economy, especially during downturns, it does not materially accelerate productivity at a systemwide level.

The real estate and construction sectors generate substantial income, particularly through luxury developments and foreign investment. DBEDT (2025) reports that in the fourth quarter of 2024, private building authorizations in Hawai'i increased by 87.6% compared to the same quarter in

2023, totaling $789.8 million [7]. Honolulu County led the growth, with a 135.9% increase in private building authorizations. These developments reflect the substantial income generated by the construction sector, particularly from high-value residential and commercial projects, and illustrate its significant role in driving economic activity across the state. In 2023, these sectors together accounted for roughly 15% of Hawai'i's GDP. During peak periods, the median home values reached record highs—over $1 million for single-family homes on both Maui and O'ahu. These dynamics boost certain productivity metrics in the short term, but the benefits are uneven. Much of the activity is tied to nonresident investors, and construction employment tends to fluctuate with macroeconomic conditions. Moreover, the sector faces persistent challenges: permitting delays, restrictive zoning, and skilled labor shortages have all reduced the efficiency of project delivery. Figure 3 shows that Hawai'i's median price for single family homes in 2025 is the highest in the nation. The wide gap between Hawai'i and the rest of the country suggests deep structural constraints on supply rather than merely strong demand.

Melendez (2024) examines the dual challenge facing Hawai'i's construction industry: rapid project growth alongside a critical labor shortage [8]. Despite a strong outlook fueled by projects like the Pearl Harbor Dry Dock and Lāhainā's rebuilding, the industry struggles to find enough skilled workers, with many nearing retirement—a trend dubbed the "silver tsunami[3]." The Pacific Resource Partnership (PRP) is leading recruitment efforts through expanded apprenticeships, events like Hawai'i Construction Career Days, and outreach to women, veterans, and underrepresented groups. PRP emphasizes the value of trades as debt-free, high-paying careers, and is partnering with schools, unions, and government to train the next generation. With over $10 billion in projected construction, labor shortages remain a key barrier to progress.

University of Hawai'i Economic Research Organization (UHERO) (2024) reports that Hawai'i faces a severe housing shortage, driven by high costs and regulatory barriers that hinder new development [9]. This report indicates that issues like land use constraints, infrastructure availability, and permitting delays have long been recognized as major challenges to housing affordability. These factors contribute to project delays

[3] The "silver tsunami" refers to the large wave of retirements among aging workers, particularly baby boomers, which poses challenges for workforce replacement and economic productivity.

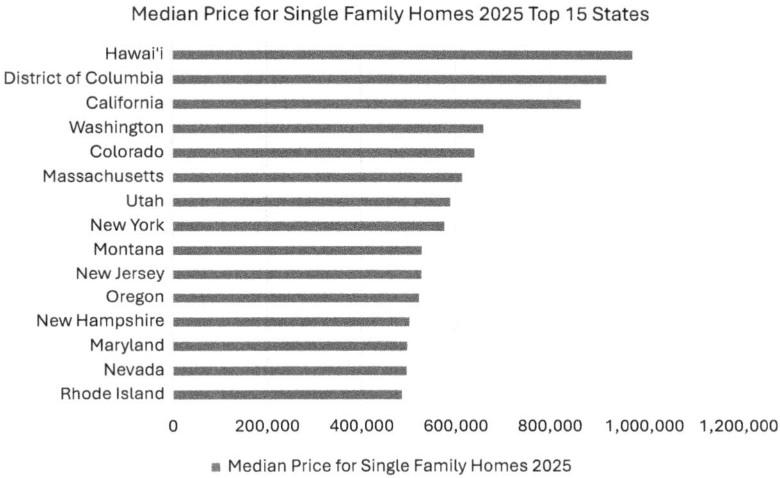

Figure 3 Median Price for Single Family Homes 2025 top 15 states. This horizontal bar chart ranks top 15 U.S. states by their median home prices in 2025, from highest to lowest. Hawai'i appears at the very top with the highest median home price ($976,000). District of Columbia ranks second ($920,000), followed by California ($866,000), Washington ($659,000), Colorado ($640,000), Massachusetts ($614,000), Utah ($589,000), New York ($576,000), Montana ($528,000), New Jersey ($527,000), Oregon ($522,000), New Hampshire ($502,000), Maryland ($497,000), Nevada ($496,000), and Rhode Island ($485,000). Source: World Population Review, 2025

and increased costs, ultimately impacting the efficiency of real estate and construction projects in the state. Real estate services also rely more on property valuations than on employee productivity, limiting their long-term contribution to output-per-worker measures. Despite its profitability, this sector does not offer the consistent productivity growth that could elevate Hawai'i's broader economy.

Health care and education continue to grow in employment share, driven by an aging population and the increasing demand for skilled services. Combined, they represent more than 17% of the workforce. However, their productivity contributions are constrained by systemic factors. These sectors are largely funded by government appropriations or insurance reimbursements, which limit wage flexibility and innovation. Salary.com (2025) reports that the average annual salary for public school teachers in Hawai'i is $55,304, with most professionals earning between $48,296 and $64,799 [10]. While this salary range may appear competitive, it often falls short when adjusted for Hawai'i's high cost of living, making it challenging for educators to afford housing and other essentials.

Trusted Health (2024) indicates that registered nurses (RN) in Hawai'i earn an average annual salary of $111,070, positioning the state as one of the highest paying for RNs [11]. Despite the seemingly substantial income, the elevated cost of living in Hawai'i can erode purchasing power, affecting nurses' ability to maintain a comfortable standard of living. World Population Review (2025) shows that Hawai'i has the highest cost of living index in the United States at 185, nearly double the national average (103.4) [12] (Figure 4). This elevated cost impacts all residents, including public school teachers and RN, whose salaries may not suffice to meet the state's high living expenses. Recruiting and retaining qualified workers remains a challenge, especially on the neighbor islands.

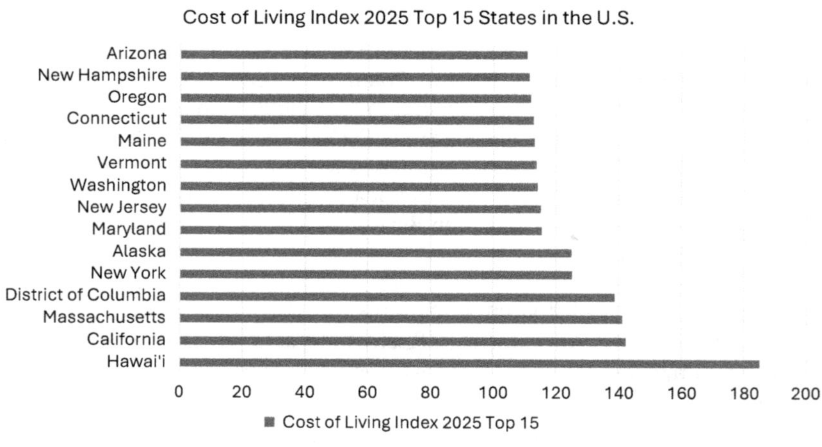

Figure 4 Cost of Living Index 2025 Top 15 states in the United States. This horizontal bar compares the cost of living across the 15 most expensive U.S. states and jurisdictions. Hawai'i ranks the highest with an index value at 185. California and Massachusetts followed at approximately 140, while the District of Columbia exceeded 130, and New York and Alaska exceeded 120. Other states such as Maryland, New Jersey, Washington, Vermont, Maine, Connecticut, and Oregon ranged between 110 and 120. Arizona had the lowest index among the top 15, just above 110. Source: World Population Review, 2025

Hawaiʻi Nursing Workforce Supply Report (2024) presents a detailed assessment of the state's nursing workforce, including licensed practical nurses (LPNs), registered nurses (RNs), and advanced practice registered nurses (APRNs) [13]. While the number of licensed nurses has grown since 2021, the percentage of nurses residing in Hawaiʻi has declined, raising concerns about long-term workforce sustainability. A key finding notes that if no significant changes occur, Hawaiʻi is projected to have only 88% of the RNs it needs by 2036 to meet healthcare demands. Despite high employment and job satisfaction rates, challenges include limited nursing education capacity, APRN financial barriers, and an acute LPN shortage. The report calls for expanded training programs, academic-practice partnerships, improved workplace wellbeing, and technological innovation to ensure a resilient and sufficient nursing workforce for the state's future healthcare needs. Meanwhile, the expansion of telehealth and distance education has potential, but its reach is hindered by infrastructure gaps, particularly in broadband access for rural communities. Both health care and education sectors are indispensable to societal well-being but offer limited contributions to measurable productivity growth due to their cost structures and funding models.

Technology and professional services, though small in employment footprint, represent some of the most promising avenues for productivity gains. Occupations in this category—ranging from software development to financial analysis and architectural consulting—routinely yield high output per worker and command wages well above $90,000 annually. Indeed (2025) reports that software engineers in Hawaiʻi earn an average annual salary of $108,389, with top earners making up to $173,152 [14]. It also reports that architects in Hawaiʻi earn an average annual salary of $119,528, with top professionals making up to $180,512 [15]. ZipRecruiter (2025) indicates that financial analysts in Hawaiʻi earn an average annual salary of $91,543, with hourly wages around $44 [16]. However, these sectors face formidable growth barriers. Capital access is limited, and Hawaiʻi's venture investment ecosystem remains underdeveloped compared to mainland innovation hubs. Furthermore, talent retention is a significant issue. Many skilled workers leave the islands for higher salaries, more expansive career pathways, and affordable housing on the mainland. The high cost of doing business, coupled with logistical challenges in shipping, staffing, and connectivity, further restricts scaling. While there are success stories—particularly in digital media, design, and boutique software firms, the sector remains too small to shift the state's aggregate productivity trends on its own. Yet it remains critical, offering a scalable model for knowledge-based growth if supported by strategic investment in broadband infrastructure, incubator programs, and workforce development.

One critical cross-cutting metric reveals the urgency of these concerns. In 2021, Hawai'i had the highest percentage of workers in low-wage sectors—defined as earning under $15 per hour—among all U.S. states. Department of Labor and Industrial Relations (DLIR) (2024) reports that 42% of Hawai'i's population is unable to afford basic necessities and secure jobs that pay a sustainable wage[4] [17]. This report emphasizes that Hawai'i is predominantly a low-skill and low-wage, service-based economy with the highest cost of living in the nation. This significant proportion reveals the challenges faced by a substantial segment of the workforce in achieving economic stability. This imbalance between wages and expenses reflects a structural misalignment between the sectors that dominate the state's economy and those that generate high value-added outputs.

4 The Cost Conundrum

Hawai'i's economy presents a persistent paradox: while the state boasts a thriving tourism industry and strong public sector employment, productivity metrics continue to underperform when compared to similarly sized or structured U.S. states. A key reason lies not in inefficiency or lack of output, but in the way high costs distort the measurement of productivity. A business in Honolulu may produce the same quantity and quality of goods or services as a comparable business in Boise, Idaho, yet face double or even triple the input costs. This imbalance makes productivity appear artificially low, even when firms are operating at peak efficiency.

Electricity is a prime example of this dynamic. Hawai'i continues to have the highest electricity rates in the United States. ElectricChoice.com (2025) provides a detailed comparison of electricity rates across all 50 states, showing that Hawai'i maintains the highest average rates in the nation [18]. Residential customers in Hawai'i in 2025 paid an average of 38.9 cents per kilowatt-hour, while commercial users paid 35 cents—more

[4]A sustainable wage is the minimum income necessary for a worker to meet basic living expenses—such as housing, food, transportation, healthcare, and childcare—without government assistance, while also allowing for modest savings and participation in community life.

than double the national averages (17.62 and 14.04 cents per kilowatt-hour respectively). These rates result in significantly higher operating costs for energy-intensive businesses, such as hotels, manufacturers, and healthcare providers. These elevated energy expenses reduce net margins and limit the capital available for reinvestment in productivity-enhancing upgrades, such as automation, employee training, or digital tools. In short, while the same level of output may be achieved as elsewhere, the cost of doing so undermines gains in measured productivity.

Housing prices further compound the problem. The Honolulu Board of REALTORS® (2025) reports that in March 2025, the median sales price for single-family homes on O'ahu rose to $1,160,000, reflecting a 5.5% increase compared to the previous year [19]. This continued upward trend reveals the island's ongoing housing affordability challenges, driven by strong demand and limited supply. The statewide average stands at $841,274. These prices are not just unaffordable for many working families; they also pose a serious challenge for employers. Companies that cannot offer wages high enough to cover housing costs struggle to attract and retain workers, particularly in essential fields such as education, health care, and public safety. The result is labor shortages, higher turnover, and elevated recruitment costs, all of which drag down operational efficiency. Even when employees are retained, long commute times from more affordable areas or the stress of housing insecurity can reduce performance and increase absenteeism.

Transportation expenses in Hawai'i also introduce inefficiencies that are rarely present on the mainland. Shipping a 40-foot container from Los Angeles to O'ahu can cost more than $13,000. These shipping costs affect all sectors, from construction to retail, and add a significant markup to the price of goods sold. Intra-island and inter-island distribution challenges further complicate the supply chain. Young Brothers (2025) outlines its request to the Hawai'i Public Utilities Commission for a general rate increase averaging 20% across most cargo categories [20]. This statement explains that proposed rate adjustments are necessary to address rising operational costs and to support capital investments in fleet maintenance and infrastructure upgrades. When companies like Young Brothers propose shipping rate increases, it directly affects input costs for local businesses and contributes to inflationary pressure across the state. High transportation costs mean that firms must spend more to receive the same materials or inventory, further reducing value-added per worker in any given industry.

A key structural barrier exacerbating these issues is the Jones Act—the federal law requiring that goods transported between U.S. ports must be carried on U.S.-built, U.S.-owned, and U.S.-crewed ships. While the law aims to support domestic maritime industries, its impact on island economies like Hawai'i is profound. By limiting competition and requiring more expensive shipping services, the Jones Act increases the cost of bringing goods to and from the islands. Newsham (2024) criticizes the Jones Act for inflating shipping costs to Hawai'i [21]. Matson purchased three new containerships from Philly Shipyard for $1 billion—over triple global prices—because the Jones Act mandates U.S.-built, -flagged, and -crewed ships for domestic routes. Though the law claims to protect national security and the U.S. maritime industry, Newsham argues it instead reduces competition and raises consumer costs. Matson, a strong defender of the Act, faces little competition, sharing market dominance with Pasha. In January 2021, Congressman Ed Case reintroduced three bills targeting the Jones Act's impact on Hawai'i's high cost of living [22]. He argues the law enables monopolistic control over domestic shipping routes to noncontiguous regions like Hawai'i, leading to inflated cargo costs that are passed on to consumers. Case's proposed legislation includes exemptions for non-contiguous areas, a cap on domestic shipping rates tied to international benchmarks, and the repeal of protections where monopolies or duopolies exist.

The implications for all these cost pressures are far-reaching. In many industries, firms spend so much just to maintain operations that little is left for innovation, employee development, or strategic expansion. Measured productivity—the value of output per unit of labor—suffers, not because workers are inefficient, but because their labor must be leveraged against far higher baseline costs. The high cost of living also influences labor dynamics more broadly. For instance, many workers in Hawai'i hold multiple jobs just to make ends meet, a trend that can reduce overall productivity due to fatigue, reduced focus, and limited availability for training or upskilling.

5 The Role of Human Capital

Hawai'i has one of the most educated workforces in the country. The University of Hawai'i system produces skilled graduates in nursing, business, engineering, and environmental science. However, many graduates leave the state, contributing to a chronic brain drain. Additionally, there is a mismatch between the skills residents possess and the industries that dominate the economy. The National Skills Coalition reports that 48%

of jobs in Hawai'i require education or training beyond high school but less than a 4-year degree, yet only 46% of the workforce has the appropriate skills or credentials [23]. Meanwhile, 29% of jobs required a 4-year degree, but 36% of workers held one, indicating an oversupply of college-educated individuals for certain roles. Additionally, 23% of jobs required only high school equivalency, while just 18% of the workforce met that criterion. This mismatch suggests that many workers lack access to the education and training needed to fill in-demand positions, particularly in areas such as healthcare, IT, and skilled trades, which can negatively affect both workers' opportunities and employers' ability to hire.

The 2023 Hawai'i Skilled Trades Workforce Analysis examines the current and projected demand for skilled trades jobs across the state, identifying 85 occupations employing over 58,000 workers [24]. This report reveals the sector's crucial role in infrastructure and clean energy, with solar photovoltaic installers showing the highest projected growth. It also explores barriers to workforce development, including lack of early exposure, transportation, and access to training. Recommendations focus on expanding apprenticeships, upskilling workers, and strengthening industry-education partnerships to build a resilient, homegrown skilled trades workforce.

Workforce development programs, including apprenticeship expansions and community college upskilling efforts, are trying to bridge the gap. For instance, the Department of Labor and Industrial Relations (DLIR) has initiated programs to connect job seekers with training and employment opportunities. DLIR (2024) reports that Hawai'i offers more than 100 registered apprenticeship programs across a wide range of occupations, combining paid on-the-job training with classroom instruction [25]. These programs are designed to build a highly skilled workforce by enabling participants to earn while they learn, ultimately achieving journey worker status. The department also promotes apprenticeship through events like Hawai'i Apprenticeship Week, aimed at expanding awareness and access statewide. This initiative plays a critical role in aligning workforce preparation with industry demands and reducing skill gaps across the islands.

The University of Hawai'i Community Colleges' Hana Career Pathways program has expanded to offer free short-term workforce training to a broader range of residents, including those currently employed [26]. Supported by over $13 million in funding from the U.S. Department of Education and local foundations, the program helps participants earn industry-recognized credentials in high-demand sectors such as healthcare, information technology, and skilled trades. Training includes Certified Nurse Aide, Pharmacy Technician, and Carpenter Pre-Apprenticeship courses. In IT, students can earn certifications like CompTIA Security+[5] and Amazon Web Services (AWS) Cloud Foundation and Solutions Architect. Most courses offer full tuition subsidies and cover costs for books and exams. Participants also receive wraparound support services including advising and job placement assistance. It aims to boost economic recovery and long-term workforce resilience by connecting residents to living-wage career pathways and helping them upskill for Hawai'i's evolving job market.

Tagami (2024) reports that Hawai'i is launching a teacher apprenticeship program to address the state's persistent educator shortage [27]. Funded by a $5 million grant from the U.S. Department of Labor, the initiative allows aspiring teachers to work full-time in public schools while earning their teaching credentials, removing financial and logistical barriers that often deter candidates. Apprentices would serve as educational assistants, gaining practical classroom experience while receiving tuition support, certification exam coverage, and mentorship. The program aims to improve recruitment and retention, particularly in high-need areas such as special education, Hawaiian language immersion, and career and technical education. State officials hope to create multiple entry points for participants at various stages of their education or experience. Despite these efforts, more targeted initiatives are necessary. Encouraging the growth of industries that require higher educational qualifications and providing incentives for graduates to remain in the state could help mitigate the brain drain. Moreover, aligning educational programs with the needs of emerging industries can ensure that the workforce is prepared for future opportunities.

6 Innovation Capacity: Seeds of Growth

In an increasingly knowledge-driven global economy, Hawai'i's long-term resilience and competitiveness hinge on its ability to cultivate and scale innovation. While the seeds of an innovative ecosystem are germinating

[5] CompTIA Security+ is a globally recognized entry-level cybersecurity certification that validates foundational skills in network security, risk management, threat analysis, and incident response. It is often required for government and private-sector IT security roles and is compliant with U.S. Department of Defense (DoD) 8570 standards.

across the islands, the system remains nascent, fragmented, and undercapitalized. Still, with intentional effort, policy support, and cross-sector collaboration, Hawai‘i can emerge as a unique hub for innovation that draws upon its cultural richness, environmental assets, and academic institutions.

At the heart of Hawai‘i's innovation efforts are the Hawai‘i Technology Development Corporation (HTDC), a state agency charged with diversifying the economy by supporting tech-based industries. HTDC offers grants, incubation spaces, and mentorship opportunities for entrepreneurs and small businesses. One of its notable programs, the SBIR (Small Business Innovation Research) matching grant, helps local companies amplify federal research dollars to scale promising technologies. The HTDC Annual Report 2024 shows significant progress in advancing innovation, economic diversification, and workforce development [28]. HTDC-supported companies generated over $900 million in revenue, while new aerospace and geothermal initiatives expanded Hawai‘i's role in space and renewable energy. The Hawai‘i Center for Advanced Transportation Technologies (HCATT) achieved a major milestone with the successful deployment of a renewable microgrid, promoting energy resiliency and cybersecurity. Through its INNOVATE Hawai‘i program, HTDC advanced smart manufacturing, textile production, and awarded over $1.79 million in grants, creating thousands of jobs. The Hawai‘i SBIR program provided $2.5 million in state matching funds to help local tech businesses secure federal research funding. Additional efforts included accelerator programs supporting over 450 companies, workforce training initiatives, and a high-demand R&D tax credit[6]. HTDC remains committed to building a sustainable, tech-driven economy for Hawai‘i's future. HTDC (2025) announced that its HCATT awarded a $1.67 million contract to Burns & McDonnell to expand the Pacific Energy Assurance Renewables Laboratory (PEARL) microgrid at Joint Base Pearl Harbor-Hickam [29]. This project enhances renewable energy integration and supports the U.S. Air Force's mission assurance goals. PEARL aims to provide resilient, cybersecure energy systems capable of operating independently during disasters. The initiative fosters collaboration between the state, Department of Defense, and private sector to reduce fossil fuel use, create high-wage energy jobs, and ensure clean, reliable energy for Hawai‘i's communities.

[6] The R&D (Research and Development) tax credit is a government incentive that allows businesses to reduce their tax liability by investing in qualified research activities aimed at developing or improving products, processes, or technologies.

Another important contributor is Blue Startups. It is a top-ranked venture accelerator based in Hawai'i, recognized by TechCrunch as one of the Top 20 in the U.S. [30]. It focuses on supporting scalable technology companies to compete globally while stimulating local economic growth. The program provides selected startups with intensive mentorship, access to over 150 business experts, product testing, pitch development, investor connections, and seed funding. As a member of the Global Accelerator Network, Blue Startups maintains a "no sales" policy to ensure mentors offer genuine guidance. Startups are selected based on team dynamics, coachability, diversity, innovation, and integrity, aiming to empower entrepreneurs with a strong moral vision.

The University of Hawai'i system also plays a role, though its efforts are uneven. Research at UH Mānoa has generated several notable commercial spin-offs. Among these is Nalu Scientific, a company that designs custom microelectronics for scientific, space, and defense applications. Founded by a UH physicist, the company illustrates how academic research can be transformed into high-value business ventures. Petranik (2021) profiles Nalu Scientific, a Hawai'i-based startup, which is developing cutting-edge electronics for global applications in space, medicine, and underwater research [31]. Since its founding in 2016, Nalu has received over $10 million in funding, including 23+ SBIR grants. The company plays a vital role in Hawai'i's innovation ecosystem by partnering with UH, employing local graduates, and allowing kama'āina (local residents) to pursue high-tech careers without leaving the islands. Its work in lidar and sensor technologies exemplifies how university-driven research can support economic diversification and job creation. Nalu's team culture emphasizes innovation, mentorship, and community impact.

University of Hawai'i News (2020) reports that the Pacific Asian Center for Entrepreneurship (PACE) awarded $40,000 in seed funding to three student-led startups—Hawai'i Innovation Lab, Manaola LLC, and Student Corner—through its Liftoff Advisors program [32]. This initiative shows UH Mānoa's active support for student entrepreneurship and demonstrates the institution's broader strategy to foster innovation by empowering students to transform their ideas into commercial ventures.

Alongside these top-down initiatives are grassroots, community-focused ventures innovating from within. Farm Link Hawai'i, for example, has introduced digital platforms that connect local farmers with consumers, schools, and restaurants. By streamlining food distribution, it enhances food security, supports small producers, and reduces the environmental footprint of imported food. Given that Hawai'i imports more than 85% of its food, such innovations are vital. Cheng (2024) profiles Farm Link Hawai'i, a local online grocer working to transform Hawai'i's food system by connecting farmers, producers, and consumers through direct-to-door delivery of locally grown and made products [33]. This company began with a mission to simplify local food distribution and support producers overwhelmed by marketing and logistics. Farm Link's offerings include poi, lychee, fresh meat, and value-added goods from across the islands. Though its sales grew to $2.8 million by 2023, this still represents just 0.3% of O'ahu's grocery market. The company faces systemic challenges such as high land and labor costs, limited infrastructure, and inconsistent supply. However, through partnerships with organizations like Kamehameha Schools and participation in programs like Da Bux[7], Farm Link is investing in supply chain development and food equity. Its work illustrates how collective efforts can build a more resilient, sustainable, and just local food system.

Another successful example is Mana Up, an accelerator funded in 2018 that helps local consumer brands scale their businesses. It is a Hawai'i-based economic development initiative aimed at growing and supporting local entrepreneurs through its intensive 6-month accelerator program [34]. The program provides mentorship, workshops, leadership training, and access to sales and distribution channels to help businesses scale globally. By 2024, 85 companies have graduated, collectively generating $84 million in annual revenue and creating 874 jobs in Hawai'i. The initiative emphasizes locally sourced ingredients, native Hawaiian culture, and community impact. Its retail arm, House of Mana Up, showcases products from program graduates online and in eight store locations. Notably, 70% of participating companies are female-led and 51% are Native Hawaiian-owned.

Despite these promising developments, Hawai'i continues to score low on national innovation indexes. TCGen Inc. (2024) reports that Hawai'i ranked 44th out of 50 states in their 2024 innovation index, scoring 1.2 out of a possible 10 [35] (Table 2). This index evaluates states based on factors such as startup activity, patent generation, and R&D investment. A major challenge is the limited availability of venture capital. Investment is heavily concentrated in places like Silicon Valley and New York.

[7] https://dabux.org/.

Table 2 TCGen[8]'s Total Innovation Rank for U.S. states in 2024. Each row lists a state and its numerical scores for the Total Innovation Rank, Financial Incentives Index, and Innovation Vitality Index. Higher numbers indicate stronger performance in innovation investment and supportive policy environments. States such as California (8.4), Massachusetts (7.3), and Washington (6.7) lead the rankings, while Hawaii (1.2), Alabama (1.1), Kentucky (0.9), Louisiana (0.9), Arkansas (0.8), West Virgina (0.4), and Mississippi (0) rank lowest

Overall Rank	*State*	*Total Innovation Rank*	*Financial Incentives Index*	*Innovation Vitality Index*
1	California	8.4	9	8
2	Massachusetts	7.3	7	8
3	Washington	6.7	5	9
4	Colorado	5.5	2	9
5	Texas	5.3	4	7
6	Utah	5.2	2	8
7	Oregon	4.9	2	8
8	New York	4.9	3	6
9	Delaware	4.6	3	6
10	Minnesota	4.5	2	7
11	Florida	4.4	3	6
12	Michigan	4.3	2	7
13	New Jersey	4.2	3	6
14	Arizona	4.0	2	6
15	New Hampshire	3.9	1	7
16	Connecticut	3.8	2	6
17	Maryland	3.8	1	6
18	Vermont	3.8	1	7
19	Nevada	3.8	1	7
20	Idaho	3.7	1	7
21	North Carolina	3.6	2	6
22	Wyoming	3.5	1	6
23	Illinois	3.5	2	5
24	Virgina	3.5	1	6
25	Missouri	3.4	1	6
26	Georgia	3.4	2	5

[8] Regenerative agriculture is an ʻāina-based approach to farming that not only produces food but also revitalizes native ecosystems, restores soil fertility, honors Indigenous practices, and strengthens community resilience by caring for both land and people.

Table 2 (Continued)

Overall Rank	*State*	*Total Innovation Rank*	*Financial Incentives Index*	*Innovation Vitality Index*
27	Indiana	3.2	1	5
28	Pennsylvania	3.1	2	5
29	Rhode Island	2.9	0	6
30	Iowa	2.8	1	5
31	Kansas	2.8	1	5
32	Ohio	2.8	2	4
33	North Dakota	2.8	0	5
34	Wisconsin	2.7	1	4
35	South Carolina	2.6	0	5
36	Nebraska	2.4	0	5
37	Montana	2.3	0	5
38	South Dakota	2.0	0	4
39	Maine	1.8	0	4
40	Oklahoma	1.8	0	3
41	New Mexico	1.7	0	3
42	Tennessee	1.7	0	3
43	Alaska	1.3	0	3
44	**Hawai'i**	**1.2**	**0**	**2**
45	Alabama	1.1	1	2
46	Kentucky	0.9	0	2
47	Louisiana	0.9	0	2
48	Arkansas	0.8	0	2
49	West Virginia	0.4	0	1
50	Mississippi	0	0	0

Table 2 shows you the TCGen's Total Innovation Rank. The Financial Incentives Index reflects per-capita investments in research and development, venture-capital funding, and Small Business Administration (SBA) loans—key indicators of a state's fiscal commitment to innovation and entrepreneurship. The Innovation Vitality Index captures non-financial factors that shape the broader innovation ecosystem, including startup formation rates, patent creation per capita, and the Consumer Technology Association's innovation-climate score. Together, these indices form the Total Innovation Rank, which categorizes states as "leaders," "in the pack," or "strugglers." Hawai'i ranks near the bottom, reflecting structural challenges such as high operational costs, limited venture-capital access, and a small-scale innovation ecosystem. Yet, this also reveals the state's potential to leverage policy-driven innovation, regional collaboration, and education-based initiatives to build greater resilience and competitiveness within the Pacific innovation landscape.

This financial bottleneck leads many to relocate to the mainland or halt operations prematurely, creating a cycle of economic leakage and lost intellectual capital. While organizations like Elemental Excelerator have helped fill the funding gap, their scope remains limited relative to the demand. Ramos (2023) highlights Elemental Excelerator, a Honolulu-based global climate-tech accelerator supporting over 150 startups that have collectively attracted more than $8 billion in funding [36]. Founded in 2012, Elemental promotes sustainability through three pillars: investing in startups, partnering with communities and leaders, and inspiring climate action. It facilitated partnerships like the Hawai'i Ulu Cooperative and Propagate to support regenerative agriculture[9]. Its Earthshot Ventures fund, launched in 2021, raised $95 million to invest in climate repair. Elemental also connects entrepreneurs with policymakers through its Policy Lab and fosters workforce diversity via its internship program. The organization continues to drive climate solutions at scale.

Running a business in Hawai'i also presents significant cost challenges. Energy expenses, commercial rent, and labor costs are among the highest in the country. Combined with a sometimes-complex regulatory landscape, these factors make it difficult for startups to survive long enough to become profitable or attract external investors. These high operational costs discourage experimentation and risk-taking, two key components of a vibrant innovation ecosystem. Talent migration is another pressing concern. Many of Hawai'i's most talented students leave the islands for college and career opportunities and do not return. Limited job options and high living expenses are frequently cited as reasons. Although recent trends in remote work have made it more feasible for professionals to live in Hawai'i while working for mainland firms, there is still a need for stronger incentives to retain and re-engage local talent. Kelleher (2020) reports on Hawaii's initiative to attract remote workers amid the pandemic as a strategy to diversify its tourism-reliant economy [37]. Through the

[9] Boomerang talent refers to individuals who leave a region or organization to gain experience elsewhere and later return, bringing back valuable skills, networks, and perspectives to their original community or employer.

"Movers & Shakas" campaign, approved participants received free round-trip tickets and were expected to contribute to local nonprofits. Remote workers from tech and software firms embraced the opportunity, enjoying Hawaii's lifestyle while maintaining mainland work hours. While some locals welcomed the economic stimulus, others raised concerns about long-term housing affordability and cultural impacts. The campaign also aimed to entice former residents to return home without economic sacrifice, leveraging Hawaii's appeal as a safe, beautiful, and connected remote work destination.

To build a more robust innovation ecosystem, Hawai'i must address these structural barriers. One approach is to develop more mission-aligned funding sources. These sources would not only seek financial returns but also prioritize social and environmental outcomes. Given Hawai'i's natural strengths in sustainability, clean energy, and indigenous knowledge, the state is well-positioned to attract impact investment. Community development financial institutions, credit unions, and philanthropic organizations could play a key role in providing early-stage capital to promising ventures. Education and workforce development must also be reimagined. Programs that link education directly with entrepreneurship, like those at PACE, should be expanded. Community colleges, vocational training programs, and mentorship networks can create clearer paths from classroom learning to startup formation. Moreover, the shift to remote work opens opportunities to draw "boomerang talent[10]" back to the islands—individuals who left Hawai'i but may now be able to return with their skills and salaries. Fostering cross-sector collaboration is equally important. Innovation does not thrive in isolation. It depends on a dynamic exchange of ideas between academia, private companies, government agencies, and nonprofit organizations. Shared goals, transparent data platforms, and cooperative pilot projects can help align stakeholders and reduce duplication of effort.

The Hawai'i Innovation Initiative, led by UH and the Hawai'i Business Roundtable, seeks to diversify the state's tourism- and military-dependent economy by building a $1 billion innovation and research enterprise by 2025 [38]. Through initiatives such as XLR8UH (Accelerate UH)[11]—a public–private partnership between Sultan Ventures and UH—the state seeks to strengthen its innovation ecosystem by transforming UH-generated

[10] https://xlr8uh.com/

[11] Konohiki refers to a traditional Hawaiian land steward or resource manager responsible for overseeing sustainable use of land and ocean resources within an ahupua'a (land division).

science, technology, and entrepreneurship into new businesses and quality jobs. This program is designed to leverage Hawai'i's regional strengths in cutting-edge research and convert them into sustainable economic growth. XLR8UH helps UH transform into a $1 billion research enterprise in partnership with various community supporters and business groups. The Maui Food Innovation Center supports value-added agriculture. Both programs received national recognition from the U.S. Small Business Administration (SBA) through its Growth Accelerator Fund. Strategic hires, new infrastructure like the i-Lab (a cutting-edge environment where students from diverse academic backgrounds can collaborate to transform design concepts into tangible prototypes), and hosting major events, including the 2016 Association of University Technology Managers (AUTM) Western Region Meeting, showcase UH's expanding innovation ecosystem.

Hawai'i should resist the temptation to replicate Silicon Valley. Instead, it can define its own approach to innovation, one that respects place, culture, and community. Areas such as climate adaptation, regenerative agriculture, sustainable tourism, and water management are all sectors where Hawai'i has a comparative advantage. By promoting itself as a global testbed for climate and cultural sustainability solutions, Hawai'i can differentiate itself on the world stage. In addition to policy and funding reform, physical infrastructure must also support innovation. High-speed internet access remains uneven, particularly on neighbor islands. Expanding broadband access is critical for equitable participation in the digital economy. Investment in co-working spaces, maker labs, and community innovation hubs can create accessible entry points for entrepreneurs from all backgrounds. UH Mānoa's new Residences for Innovative Student Entrepreneurs (RISE) is a $70 million state-of-the-art facility modeled after the University of Utah's Lassonde Studios [39]. RISE aims to foster student entrepreneurship through a unique live-learn-work environment. It includes a 10,000-square-foot innovation space with makerspaces, classrooms, and collaborative areas, and provides residential space for 374 students. Operated by the Pacific Asian Center for Entrepreneurship (PACE) in the Shidler College of Business, the center is designed to be a student-centered hub for innovation. RISE is fully privately funded through a partnership among UH, the UH Foundation, and Hunt Development Group.

Though still emerging, Hawai'i's innovation economy holds real promise. The current generation of startups, from microelectronics to food logistics to culturally grounded consumer products, demonstrates that innovation is already happening here. What remains is to ensure these efforts are not isolated or short-lived. Hawai'i must scale what is working, address what is missing, and build an inclusive, values-driven economy rooted in resilience and regeneration.

7 Toward a Localized Productivity Strategy

In Hawai'i, productivity should not be defined solely by output per worker or capital efficiency, but rather by how effectively the economy generates sustainable, inclusive, and locally meaningful value. The goal is to build a diversified economy that enhances well-being, supports community resilience, and fosters stewardship of natural and cultural resources. Traditional measures of productivity are often mismatched with the realities of island economies. Hawai'i faces structural constraints—limited land and resources, high transportation costs, geographic isolation from large markets, and a labor force deeply tied to family and 'āina (land). At the same time, the islands offer distinct comparative advantages that can support a more regenerative and self-sustaining economic model. Hawai'i has the opportunity to lead by example in reimagining productivity as quality over quantity, circular systems over linear growth, and resilience over scale.

One of Hawai'i's greatest untapped assets is its rich cultural capital. Indigenous knowledge systems contain sophisticated understandings of ecology, resource management, governance, and education that are profoundly relevant to the challenges of the twenty-first century. Revitalizing traditional land stewardship systems such as the ahupua'a framework and practices like lo'i kalo cultivation can not only restore ecological balance but also provide meaningful employment in agroecology and food sovereignty. These practices reduce dependence on imports and contribute to climate resilience while reinforcing a sense of cultural identity. Seo (2025) highlights a movement in Hawai'i to revive the traditional ahupua'a and konohiki[12] (traditional Hawaiian method of land and resource management within the ahupua'a system) systems to restore environmental balance and support community well-being [40]. Originating around A.D. 1200, ahupua'a are land divisions stretching from mountain to sea, traditionally governed by konohiki chiefs who managed resources to ensure sustainability. Amid growing concerns over water scarcity, wildfire, and food insecurity, leaders across sectors are exploring how to re-integrate

[12] Kumu hula refers to a master teacher of hula who preserves and transmits Hawaiian dance, chant, and cultural knowledge through rigorous training and lineage-based instruction.

these systems to address modern challenges. Community-led initiatives, such as He'eia fishpond restoration and Waipā Foundation stewardship, show promise. While challenges remain—such as land fragmentation and policy reform—advocates believe traditional Hawaiian values can guide a regenerative model for Hawai'i's future, rooted in mālama 'āina, or caring for the land.

Hawai'i can also reframe tourism as an educational and cultural exchange, rather than a volume-driven industry. Investing in cultural tourism—guided by community values, storytelling, and authentic experiences—can support local artisans, kumu hula[13], navigators, and cultural practitioners who preserve and transmit Indigenous knowledge. This approach elevates the role of culture in the economy and creates new revenue streams grounded in respect, learning, and sustainability. In education, integrating Native Hawaiian perspectives through 'āina-based curricula foster a deeper connection between young people and their communities, cultivating citizens who are both skilled and grounded in place-based ethics. Blanks (2022) explores the rise of 'āina-based education in Hawai'i, a movement emphasizing experiential, place-based learning rooted in cultural and environmental stewardship [41]. Programs such as Nā Kelamoku and schools like Kanu o ka 'Āina have shown success, especially for Native Hawaiian students, by integrating traditional practices with academic achievement. Educators stress the importance of building relationships with 'āina and community as foundational to learning. Supported by nonprofits, public schools, and initiatives like HĀ: Nā Hopena A'o[14], this educational model fosters identity, food security, and leadership grounded in sustainability, aiming to prepare Hawai'i's next generation for a self-sufficient future.

The islands' geographic location in the middle of the Pacific confers additional opportunities that remain underleveraged. Hawai'i is ideally positioned for observational astronomy, space surveillance, and small satellite deployment due to its clear skies and low light pollution. Expanding research capabilities in aerospace through institutions like UH can attract federal investment and support technology transfer to local businesses. The

[13] Nā Hopena A'o (HĀ) is a Department-wide framework to develop the skills, behaviors and dispositions that are reminiscent of Hawai'i's unique context, and to honor the qualities and values of the indigenous language and culture of Hawai'i. (https://hawaiipublicschools.org/about/na-hopena-a%ca%bbo-ha/.)

[14] The ARL at UH develops pioneering research and technology solutions to address challenges in defense, sustainability, and scientific discovery. (https://arl.hawaii.edu/.)

Applied Research Laboratory at UH (ARL at UH[15]) secured a $110 million, 5-year U.S. Department of Defense contract in December 2024 to support high-impact research in coastal defense, renewable energy, cybersecurity, and maritime innovation [42]. As one of only five Navy-sponsored University-Affiliated Research Centers, ARL at UH leads pioneering projects such as the Rapid Resilient Reefs for Coastal Defense (R3D), wave energy integration via the Wave Energy Test Site (WETS), and detection of underwater munitions. These efforts bolster national security and environmental sustainability while fostering student engagement in high-tech fields, reinforcing Hawai'i's leadership in innovation and defense research.

Dentons (2020) outlines development strategies for establishing a carrier-neutral cable landing station in Hawai'i to enhance broadband capacity and economic resilience [43]. Given Hawai'i's isolation and dependence on undersea cables, this report argues that a strategically located, open-access station would improve internet reliability, attract data-centric industries, and support initiatives such as cloud computing, telehealth[16], e-sports, and smart cities[17]. Three models are analyzed: private ownership, public ownership, and public-private partnerships. Dentons emphasizes the importance of stakeholder collaboration, including government agencies, utilities, and Native Hawaiian organizations, while recommending regulatory streamlining and equitable access. It positions Hawai'i as a potential Pacific hub for digital connectivity, supporting long-term diversification and innovation in the state's economy.

Hawai'i also possesses exceptional marine biodiversity and proximity to protected ocean reserves, which can support the growth of a sustainable blue economy. Investments in aquaculture, marine biotechnology, and deep-sea research can generate new industries while maintaining ecological integrity. The UH's School of Ocean and Earth Science and Technology (SOEST)[18] offers a strong research base that can be

[15] Telehealth is the use of digital technologies—such as video calls, mobile apps, and remote monitoring—to deliver healthcare services, consultations, and education outside traditional clinical settings.

[16] A smart city is an urban area that leverages technology, data analytics, and interconnected infrastructure to enhance the efficiency of services, improve quality of life, and promote sustainable development for its residents.

[17] https://www.soest.hawaii.edu/soestwp/about/

[18] The Contractor Repair Act allows contractors a right to inspect and offer to repair alleged construction defects before homeowners can pursue legal action, providing a structured process to resolve disputes efficiently and reduce costly litigation in the state's housing and construction sectors.

mobilized to support entrepreneurship and workforce development in these areas. In addition to cultural and geographic advantages, Hawai'i holds enormous renewable energy potential that remains underutilized. The state's high electricity costs and abundant solar radiation make distributed solar energy systems especially attractive. Scaling up community solar programs, particularly in low-income areas, and providing accessible financing through local credit unions or community development financial institutions can democratize energy savings. On Hawai'i island, geothermal energy presents an opportunity for base-load power production. With careful planning, environmental safeguards, and community consultation, geothermal resources could provide reliable energy while reducing reliance on imported fossil fuels. Similarly, Hawai'i's coastal waters offer potential for wave and tidal energy innovation. Pilot projects supported by the U.S. Navy's WETS can be a platform for commercial demonstration and global visibility.

Maximizing these opportunities requires enabling policy frameworks that support entrepreneurship, innovation, and inclusive development. Public policy must shift from general investment incentives to precise interventions tailored to Hawai'i's unique conditions. Tax incentives for local R&D activities, particularly in clean energy, food systems, and digital services, can reduce the cost of innovation. Startup support grants and innovation vouchers can help entrepreneurs overcome early-stage financing gaps, commonly referred to as the "valley of death," where promising ideas stall before reaching the market. Workforce development should be closely aligned with economic sectors showing growth potential and social value. Sectoral training partnerships that unite employers, community colleges, and unions can ensure that training programs are responsive to local labor market needs. For example, partnerships in renewable energy, sustainable construction, digital services, and ocean technologies can create clear pipelines from education to employment. Expanding apprenticeship programs across these sectors, modeled after successful efforts in construction and healthcare, can provide on-the-job learning while increasing access to livable-wage jobs.

Another area in need of modernization is the state's land-use and permitting systems. Regulatory delays increase costs and discourage investment in sustainable development. Gordner et al. (2025) examines how construction defect litigation exacerbates Hawai'i's housing crisis by raising costs and discouraging development [44]. While such litigation helps protect homeowners from substandard construction, it often leads to higher legal and insurance expenses and defensive building practices that inflate both hard and soft costs. Condominium projects, especially horizontal regimes, are disproportionately affected, with nearly 27% of new homes built between 2013 and 2023 involved in litigation. Critically, properties under litigation are often disqualified from financing programs backed by the Federal Housing Administration (FHA), U.S. Department of Veterans Affairs (VA), or Fannie Mae, limiting access for first-time buyers and veterans. It suggests reforming the Contractor Repair Act[19], enhancing inspections, and adopting resilient building materials to improve housing affordability and reduce litigation risk.

To support equitable innovation, it is essential to expand broadband access across the neighbor islands and underserved rural communities. Reliable internet is the foundation of remote work, distance education, telemedicine, and digital entrepreneurship[20]. Investment in broadband infrastructure—through federal grants, public-private partnerships, and local cooperative models—will enable greater participation in the knowledge economy and reduce geographic inequality. The Hawaiʻi Broadband Strategic Plan (2020) outlines a comprehensive vision for expanding broadband access and equity across the state [45]. It emphasizes broadband as critical infrastructure akin to electricity and essential for economic resilience, education, healthcare, public safety, and digital inclusion. The plan sets four strategic goals: (1) build robust infrastructure across all islands, (2) close the digital divide by promoting affordability and digital literacy, (3) develop a thriving digital economy with a dedicated Broadband and Digital Equity Office, and (4) strengthen community resilience via interconnected broadband networks. The COVID-19 pandemic exposed connectivity gaps and accelerated broadband's recognition as a public necessity. The plan also proposes partnerships, fiber investments, public Wi-Fi, and broadband zones to serve underserved and rural areas.

A persistent barrier to coordinated progress in Hawaiʻi is the fragmentation of economic development efforts. Community organizations, government agencies, and private firms often work in isolation, making it difficult to scale promising initiatives. One way to address this is through shared

[19] Digital entrepreneurship refers to the creation and operation of businesses that leverage digital technologies—such as e-commerce, apps, or online platforms—to deliver products or services, often with lower overhead and greater global reach.

[20] The Aloha+ Challenge is a statewide public-private commitment to achieve Hawaiʻi's social, economic, and environmental goals by 2030. (https://alohachallenge.hawaii.gov/.)

metrics and goals. Tools like the Aloha+ Challenge Dashboard[21] can be expanded beyond sustainability to track inclusive economic performance, workforce equity, and place-based development outcomes. Hawai'i Green Growth presents the Aloha+ Challenge Dashboard as an interactive, open-data platform designed to monitor Hawai'i's progress toward its 2030 sustainability goals [46]. Developed collaboratively across sectors, the Dashboard tracks key indicators across six priority areas, including clean energy, natural resource management, and green workforce development. Its integration of data on equity in education and job access makes it a valuable tool for assessing workforce and economic inclusivity. Localized pilot projects offer another path forward. Instead of waiting for statewide reforms, communities in places like Wai'anae, Wailuku, or Hilo can lead with their own experiments—whether in community land trusts, renewable energy co-ops, or food system revitalization. These efforts, when supported by policy, capital, and technical assistance, can demonstrate scalable models for inclusive productivity.

Underlying all of this is the need to redefine what productivity means in a Hawaiian context. In Western economic models, productivity is often measured by the volume of goods and services produced. In Hawai'i, productivity should reflect contributions to community well-being, ecological balance, and cultural continuity. Time spent caring for kupuna (elders), stewarding native forests, or teaching keiki (child) ancestral knowledge must be recognized as valuable, even if it does not show up in GDP. Productivity should be about thriving—not just growing. As Manulani Aluli Meyer reminds us, intelligence is not simply knowledge but wisdom in practice. Meyer (2013) introduces the concept of "holographic epistemology," a framework that views knowledge as an integrated expression of the physical, mental, and spiritual realms [47]. Drawing connections between Native Hawaiian worldviews and emerging ideas in quantum science, she argues that intelligence is not a purely cognitive function but a lived, embodied understanding of one's relationship to place, people, and purpose. Meyer's views challenge conventional, compartmentalized notions of knowledge and emphasizes the value of Indigenous frameworks in redefining what it means to know and to be wise. A localized productivity strategy must embody that wisdom by integrating Indigenous values,

[21] TCGen is a product development consulting firm that advises organizations on innovation strategy, project execution, and designing effective development processes.

respecting environmental limits, and building economic systems that are regenerative rather than extractive.

The challenge facing Hawai'i is how to align economic growth with justice, culture, and sustainability. The opportunity lies in building an economy that works for Hawai'i, one that draws strength from its roots and vision from its people. With targeted investments, intentional policy, and inclusive design, Hawai'i can model what a resilient, place-based economy of the future can look like. This is the essence of a localized productivity strategy: not imitation, but innovation grounded in who we are and where we are.

8 Conclusion: Redefining Productivity in Paradise

Hawai'i can't afford to be a mirage economy—beautiful on the surface, brittle underneath. Real productivity requires more than input and output; it requires a bold vision of value creation grounded in community and sustainability. Yes, Hawai'i can compete by leading with what makes it unique. The chapters that follow will delve into the sectors, policies, and stories that can bring this vision to life. From regenerative tourism and blue tech to agri-entrepreneurship and remote work hubs, this book explores how Hawai'i can build a more productive future—one that uplifts its people while caring for its land.

References

[1]. U.S. Bureau of Labor Statistics. (2024, May 31). Labor productivity for private nonfarm in Hawaii (IPUZNL000150000). Federal Reserve Bank of St. Louis. Retrieved from https://fred.stlouisfed.org/series/IPUZNL000150000.

[2]. U.S. Bureau of Economic Analysis. (2024). Gross domestic product by state and personal income by state, 2023. Retrieved from https://www.bea.gov/sites/default/files/2025-03/stgdppi4q24-a2024.pdf.

[3]. U.S. Bureau of Economic Analysis. (2024). Regional price parities by state and metro area. Retrieved from https://www.bea.gov/data/prices-inflation/regional-price-parities-state-and-metro-area.

[4]. Department of Business, Economic Development & Tourism (DBEDT). (2025, March). Visitor industry continued improvement in December 2024. Retrieved from https://dbedt.hawaii.gov/blog/25-03/.

[5]. U.S. Bureau of Labor Statistics. (2023, May). State occupational employment and wage estimates: Hawaii. Retrieved from https://www.bls.gov/oes/current/oes_hi.htm.

[6]. Department of Business, Economic Development & Tourism (DBEDT). (2025, March). Hawai'i labor market dynamics: First quarter 2025 report. Retrieved from https://dbedt.hawaii.gov/economic/qser/labor-force/?utm_source=chatgpt.com.
[7]. Department of Business, Economic Development & Tourism (DBEDT). (2025, March). Research & economic analysis: Construction. Retrieved from https://dbedt.hawaii.gov/economic/qser/construction/.
[8]. Melendez, R. (2024, November 25). Booming projects, shrinking workforce. Building Industry Hawaii. Retrieved from https://buildingindustryhawaii.com/2024/11/booming-projects-shrinking-workforce/.
[9]. University of Hawai'i Economic Research Organization (UHERO). (2024, March). Construction defect litigation, housing affordability, and homeownership in Hawai'i. Retrieved from https://uhero.hawaii.edu/wp-content/uploads/2025/03/ConstructionDefectLitigation.pdf.
[10]. Salary.com. (2025, April). Public school teacher salary in Hawaii. Retrieved from https://www.salary.com/research/salary/benchmark/public-school-teacher-salary/hi.
[11]. Trusted Health. (2024). Registered nurse salary in Hawaii. Retrieved from https://www.trustedhealth.com/nurse-salary-guide/hawaii.
[12]. World Population Review. (2025). *Cost of living index by state 2025*. Retrieved from https://worldpopulationreview.com/state-rankings/cost-of-living-index-by-state.
[13]. Hawai'i State Center for Nursing. (2023). 2023 Hawai'i nursing workforce supply report. Retrieved from https://www.hawaiicenterfornursing.org/wp-content/uploads/2024/04/2023HawaiiNursingWorkforceSupply.vFinal.pdf.
[14]. Indeed. (2025, April 10). Software engineer salary in Hawaii. Retrieved from https://www.indeed.com/career/software-engineer/salaries/HI.
[15]. Indeed. (2025, April 12). Architect salary in Hawaii. Retrieved from https://www.indeed.com/career/architect/salaries/HI.
[16]. ZipRecruiter. (2025, April). Financial analyst salary in Hawaii. Retrieved from https://www.ziprecruiter.com/Salaries/Financial-Analyst-Salary--in-Hawaii .
[17]. Department of Labor and Industrial Relations (DLIR). (2024, March). Workforce Development State Unified Plan 2024–2028. Retrieved from https://labor.hawaii.gov/wdc/files/2024/03/PRESENTATION-WORKFORCE-DEVELOPMENT-STATE-UNIFIED-PLAN-FOR-PUBLIC-MEETINGS-JAN-FEB-2024.pdf.
[18]. ElectricChoice.com. (2025, April). Electricity rates by state. Retrieved from https://www.electricchoice.com/electricity-prices-by-state/.
[19]. Honolulu Board of REALTORS®. (2025, March). O'ahu housing market gains momentum in 2025. Retrieved from https://hicentral.com/mpr/mpr-2025-03.php.

[20]. Young Brothers. (2025). Regulation – Young Brothers Hawaii. Retrieved from https://htbyb.com/regulation/.
[21]. Newsham, M. (2024, November). Matson's new vessels illustrate Jones Act's grip on Hawaii shipping. Civil Beat. Retrieved from https://www.civilbeat.org/2024/11/matsons-new-vessels-illustrate-jones-acts-grip-on-hawaii-shipping/.
[22]. Case, E. (2021, January 14). Case re-introduces bills to attack key driver of Hawai'i's high cost of living. U.S. House of Representatives. Retrieved from https://case.house.gov/news/documentsingle.aspx?DocumentID=412.
[23]. National Skills Coalition. Hawai'i skills mismatch fact sheet. Retrieved from https://nationalskillscoalition.org/wp-content/uploads/2020/12/HI-Skills-Mismatch-Fact-Sheet-2020.pdf.
[24]. SMS Research. (2023). Hawai'i skilled trades workforce analysis. Hawai'i Chamber of Commerce, Harold K.L. Castle Foundation, and The Harry and Jeanette Weinberg Foundation. https://www.cochawaii.org/wp-content/uploads/2024/10/hawaii-skilled-trades-workforce-analysis-final-report-06.01.2023.pdf.
[25]. Hawai'i Department of Labor and Industrial Relations. (2024). Apprenticeship programs. Retrieved from https://labor.hawaii.gov/wdd/job-seekers/apprenticeship/.
[26]. University of Hawai'i News. (2022, August 30). Free workforce trainings expanded to more Hawai'i residents. Retrieved from https://www.hawaii.edu/news/2022/08/30/free-workforce-trainings/.
[27]. Tagami, C. (2024, July 18). Hawai'i's latest effort to recruit teachers: Put prospective educators in classrooms sooner. Civil Beat. Retrieved from https://www.civilbeat.org/2024/07/hawaiis-latest-effort-to-recruit-teachers-put-prospective-educators-in-classrooms-sooner/.
[28]. Hawai'i Technology Development Corporation. (2024). Annual report 2024. Retrieved from https://files.hawaii.gov/dbedt/annuals/2024/2024-htdc.pdf.
[29]. Hawai'i Technology Development Corporation. (2025, April 8). HTDC awards $1.67 million contract for continued development of microgrid project at Joint Base Pearl Harbor-Hickam. Retrieved from https://www.htdc.org/htdc-awards-1-67-million-contract-for-continued-development-of-microgrid-project-at-joint-base-pearl-harbor-hickam.
[30]. Blue Startups. Blue Startups – A venture accelerator in Hawaii. The Sigmund Project. Retrieved from https://thesigmundproject.org/opportunities/blue-startups.
[31]. Petranik, S. (2021, May 4). Nalu Scientific measures the universe from Hawai'i. Hawaii Business Magazine. Retrieved from https://www.hawaiibusiness.com/nalu-scientific-measures-the-universe-from-hawaii/.

[32]. University of Hawai'i News. (2020, February 27). UH entrepreneurship program awards $40K to three student startups. Retrieved from https://manoa.hawaii.edu/news/article.php?aId=10462.
[33]. Cheng, M. (2024, September 1). Local Online Grocer Farm Link Builds Up Hawai'i's Food Systems. Honolulu Magazine. Retrieved from https://www.honolulumagazine.com/farm-link/.
[34]. Mana Up. (2024, April 8). About Mana Up Hawai'i. Retrieved from https://manauphawaii.com/blogs/news/about-mana-up-hawaii.
[35]. TCGen Inc. (2024). Most Innovative U.S. States in 2024: What Matters?. Retrieved from https://www.tcgen.com/most-innovative-us-states-ranked/.
[36]. Ramos, C. (2023, September 20). Hawai'i's sustainability heroes: Elemental Excelerator. Hawai'i Business Magazine. Retrieved from https://www.hawaiibusiness.com/hawaii-sustainability-hero-elemental-excelerator/.
[37]. Kelleher, J. S. (2020, November 22). Hawaii seeks to be seen as a remote workplace with a view. AP News. Retrieved from https://apnews.com/article/technology-us-news-coronavirus-pandemic-hawaii-honolulu-bf354466ab2c08fd860b0dfa8d5b6f6b.
[38]. University of Hawai'i. The Hawai'i Innovation Initiative. Retrieved from https://research.hawaii.edu/noelo/the-hawaii-innovation-initiative/.
[39]. University of Hawai'i News. (2023, June 4). New state-of-the-art UH Mānoa RISE center inspired by Utah's Lassonde Studios. Retrieved from https://www.hawaii.edu/news/2023/06/04/rise-inspired-by-lassonde/.
[40]. Seo, D. (2025, April 1). Can we return to ahupua'a?. HONOLULU Magazine. Retrieved from https://www.honolulumagazine.com/can-we-return-to-ahupuaa/.
[41]. Blanks, K. (2022, July 6). 'Āina-based education is the path to a sustainable future. Civil Beat. Retrieved from https://www.civilbeat.org/2022/07/keona-blanks-aina-based-education-is-the-path-to-a-sustainable-future/.
[42]. University of Hawai'i Office of the Vice President for Research and Innovation. (2024, December 13). UH lands $110M DoD contract for cutting-edge research. Retrieved from https://manoa.hawaii.edu/ovprs/uh-lands-110m-dod-contract-for-cutting-edge-research/.
[43]. Dentons & J.P. Morgan. (2020). Development options for a Hawai'i cable landing station. Retrieved from https://broadband.hawaii.gov/wp-content/uploads/2020/05/Dentons_JP-Morgan-Broadband-Report114082726_1.pdf.
[44]. Gordner, T., Tyndall, J., Burnett, K., Kim, E., Ronquilio, K., & Rhinebolt, V. (2025, March). Construction defect litigation, housing affordability, and homeownership in Hawai'i. University of Hawai'i Economic Research Organization (UHERO). Retrieved from https://uhero.hawaii.edu/wp-content/uploads/2025/03/ConstructionDefectLitigation.pdf.

[45]. State of Hawai'i. (2020). Hawai'i Broadband Strategic Plan. Retrieved from https://broadband.hawaii.gov/wp-content/uploads/2020/11/Hawaii-BB-Plan-2020-FINAL_10-23-20_v1.1.pdf.
[46]. Hawai'i Green Growth. Aloha+ Challenge Dashboard. Retrieved from https://alohachallenge.hawaii.gov/.
[47]. Meyer, M. A. (2013). Holographic epistemology: Native common sense. China Media Research, 9(2), 94–101. Retrieved from https://education.illinois.edu/docs/default-source/default-document-library/hereca256a3980b76a29a33dff4b008a8698.pdf.

CHAPTER 3

Tourism and Transformation: Reimagining Hawai'i's Economic Backbone

1 Introduction: Beyond the Postcard

For more than a century, Hawai'i has sold the image of paradise—a tranquil, sun-drenched escape framed by palm trees, hula dancers, and turquoise waters. But this glossy narrative conceals a deeper truth: tourism is both the backbone and the burden of Hawai'i's economy. The tourism sector generates billions in revenue, supports thousands of jobs, and sustains countless businesses. And yet, it also inflates housing costs, consumes precious natural resources, displaces local communities, and renders the economy vulnerable to external shocks. This chapter explores tourism's double-edged nature. It examines its economic contributions, its social and environmental costs, and the urgent calls for a more regenerative, place-based approach to travel. As we look ahead, we ask: Can tourism be part of Hawai'i's future without dominating it?

2 The Golden Goose: Tourism's Economic Footprint

In 2019, before the COVID-19 pandemic disrupted global travel, Hawai'i welcomed over 10.4 million visitors. That year, tourism generated \$17.8 billion in direct visitor spending and supported approximately 216,000 jobs—about one in every five jobs in the state. It contributed over \$2 billion in state and county tax revenues, helping to fund public

P. Yu, *Economic Development in Hawai'i*,
https://doi.org/10.1007/978-3-032-15689-1_3

infrastructure, schools, parks, and emergency services. Few other sectors in Hawai'i boast such breadth of economic influence. From hotels and airlines to restaurants, cultural institutions, and small businesses, tourism's footprint extends across virtually every corner of the economy. Indeed, the numbers speak for themselves. Visitors' expenditures directly support the hospitality industry—hotels, resorts, vacation rentals, and travel services. Indirectly, they bolster industries ranging from agriculture (through farm-to-table dining) to retail (through shopping malls, surf shops, and boutiques), and from utilities (through energy and water usage) to finance (through real estate investment). Tourism also stimulates real estate development, particularly in areas with resort zoning or oceanfront access, inflating property values and reshaping urban and rural landscapes alike.

One of tourism's most understated but essential contributions is its role in rural economic viability. In remote communities, whether it's Hāna on Maui, the north shore of Kaua'i, or Ka'ū on Hawai'i Island, tourism often serves as the main source of income for small businesses, service providers, and cultural practitioners. It enables rural residents to remain in their home communities by generating the economic activity needed to sustain basic services such as grocery stores, clinics, and schools. Without visitor spending, many of these communities would face declining economic options and increased outmigration. Baker et al. (2024) report that tourism on O'ahu's North Shore, while economically beneficial, places considerable strain on local infrastructure, residents, and natural resources [1]. Based on a comprehensive visitor survey conducted between November 2023 and March 2024, the report finds that most travelers come for Hawai'i's natural beauty, surf culture, and relaxed pace. Yet their growing presence also brings side effects—traffic congestion, overcrowding, environmental wear, and growing tension with local communities. Nearly 80% of surveyed visitors stayed outside the North Shore, intensifying day-visit pressures, particularly at iconic sites like Laniakea Beach and Waimea Bay. The study emphasizes the disconnect between visitor behavior and community well-being, revealing that residents face increased noise, reduced access to beaches, and rising housing costs partly fueled by short-term vacation rentals. Visitors often lacked awareness of culturally respectful behavior or sustainable tourism practices. To mitigate these impacts, this report recommends enhanced visitor education, stricter regulation of short-term rentals, investment in infrastructure, and promotion of regenerative tourism principles. It advocates for a place-based tourism management strategy aligned with the values of kama'āina, prioritizing community stewardship and the long-term health of both people and ʻāina (land).

Tourism also plays a critical role in fostering entrepreneurship. The ecosystem of small businesses built around visitor demand is vast: from surf instructors, cultural performers, tour guides, and massage therapists to family-owned restaurants, shave ice stands, and local artisans. For many entrepreneurs, especially Native Hawaiians and long-time residents, tourism offers a platform to share cultural knowledge, create community-based enterprises, and build generational wealth. Kamita (2025) reports that between 2019 and 2023, an annual average of 46,786 Native Hawaiians were employed in Hawaiʻi's tourism-intensive industries, accounting for just over 20% of all workers in the sector [2]. Despite a slight decline in Native Hawaiian employment in tourism since the previous reporting period, their share within the sector increased modestly. Compared to all tourism workers, Native Hawaiians tended to be younger, more likely to have only a high school education, and earned lower average wages. The most common occupations among Native Hawaiians included sales, food preparation and serving, and transportation, while higher-earning roles in areas like life sciences and healthcare had relatively lower Native Hawaiian participation. Employment was concentrated in retail trade and accommodation and food services, particularly in Honolulu County. Most Native Hawaiians were wage and salary employees, with 88% in the private sector and 6% in government roles. Full-time employment rates for Native Hawaiians in tourism were comparable to all workers, though earnings across all industries were consistently lower for Native Hawaiians. The report points to persistent gaps in education, job opportunities, and earnings, showing structural inequalities that continue to limit upward mobility. It reveals the need for policies that strengthen career pathways and increase Native Hawaiian representation across all levels of Hawaiʻi's tourism industry.

The economic benefits of tourism are neither equally distributed nor wholly retained within the state. A significant share of visitor spending flows directly to corporate hotel chains, international airlines, and off-island tour operators. These firms often repatriate profits to shareholders or reinvest elsewhere, rather than circulating them in the local economy. This phenomenon, known as economic leakage, means that while visitors may spend large sums in Hawaiʻi, the proportion that stays and stimulates local growth is more limited than raw numbers suggest. Hawaiʻi Tourism Authority (HTA) (2023) reports that strengthening governance in Hawai'i requires re-centering community voices, cultural values, and collective responsibility to build a more resilient and equitable society [3]. This report critiques traditional, top-down systems that often exclude the lived experiences of Native Hawaiians and local communities, resulting in mistrust and ineffective policy outcomes. Instead, the authors advocate for governance grounded in aloha (compassion), kuleana (responsibility), and mālama (care), where public institutions actively partner with communities to co-create solutions. It emphasizes the importance of shifting power structures to support community-led initiatives and place-based decision-making. Strategies include investing in leadership development rooted in local values, establishing participatory budgeting mechanisms, and embedding co-governance models into public processes. These approaches are designed to empower communities as active stewards of their own futures, rather than passive recipients of state programs. HTA aligns this governance transformation with the goals of the Hawai'i 2050 Sustainability Plan, particularly in achieving climate resilience, equity, and cultural preservation. It stresses that genuine change will require not only policy reform but also deep relationship-building between government and community partners. Case studies and community input illustrate that governance infused with aloha leads to more inclusive, trusted, and effective institutions. It calls for a new paradigm of governance in Hawai'i—one that honors the knowledge, agency, and aspirations of the people it serves.

Additionally, the labor structure of the tourism industry reflects duality: while it is a major source of employment, many of the jobs it creates are in the low-wage service sector. Housekeepers, kitchen staff, clerks, and maintenance workers—many of whom are Native Hawaiian or immigrant workers—earn modest incomes and often face high housing costs in resort-adjacent areas. The result is a workforce that keeps the industry afloat but struggles to achieve upward mobility or homeownership. Although unionized positions in hotels and transportation have helped raise wages and benefits in some cases, the sector overall continues to reflect wage inequality and limited career advancement opportunities. Beyond economics, tourism imposes externalities that affect infrastructure, natural resources, and community well-being. The influx of millions of visitors' places strain on roads, beaches, parks, and public utilities. Overcrowding at popular destinations such as Diamond Head, Hā'ena State Park, and Hanauma Bay has raised concerns about environmental degradation and the erosion of resident quality of life. In response, HTA and state agencies have begun implementing visitor management strategies, such as reservation systems, cultural orientation programs, and regenerative tourism frameworks. These efforts seek to shift tourism from volume-driven metrics to value-based approaches that prioritize local input and ecological balance.

Hawaiʻi has enacted its first visitor-funded "Green Fee" Signed by Governor Josh Green on March 27, 2025 [4]. Senate Bill 1396 adds a 0.75%-point surcharge to the existing Transient Accommodations Tax (TAT) on hotel rooms, short-term rentals, and cruise ships, starting January 1, 2026. The surcharge—roughly an extra $3 on a $400 room night—is projected to generate tens of millions of dollars annually. Revenues will be dedicated to climate-resilience projects such as beach restoration, wildfire prevention, hurricane resilience, coral reef recovery, flood mitigation, and invasive-species removal; local nonprofits and state agencies will compete for grants overseen by a review coalition and the Legislature to carry out these resilience projects. Leaders in Hawaiʻi's hospitality sector back the measure, arguing that transparent use of the funds can strengthen both tourism and environmental stewardship, and state officials hope the program becomes a template for other destinations. This policy reflects a growing recognition that tourism must evolve—not only to preserve Hawaiʻi's natural resources but to ensure long-term economic stability.

The COVID-19 pandemic offered a rare and dramatic pause—a moment of reflection and recalibration. When visitor numbers plummeted in 2020, the vulnerabilities of an economy overdependent on tourism were laid bare. State revenue declined, unemployment soared, and many small businesses shuttered. But amid the crisis, new conversations emerged: about diversification, sustainability, and resilience. Community leaders, cultural practitioners, and policymakers began exploring alternatives, from agriculture and technology to creative industries and circular economies. Despite the challenges, tourism is not a sector to be discarded. Rather, it is one to be reshaped. The key lies in recalibrating tourism's role in Hawaiʻi's broader economic strategy, maximizing its benefits while minimizing its harms. This includes investing in workforce development programs that help hospitality workers gain transferable skills in areas like sustainability, customer service, and digital tools. It also means expanding support for community-based tourism models that keep profits local and empower cultural stewards. Policies that encourage local ownership, whether through small business loans, tax incentives, or cooperative models, can help shift the balance of economic power. Infrastructure investments should prioritize areas of visitor-resident overlap: public transportation, parks, digital access, and workforce housing. Strengthening environmental protections and funding restoration projects through tourism-generated revenues can ensure that the natural and cultural assets that attract visitors are preserved for future generations.

Crucially, tourism policy must be informed by community voice. This means including residents, especially Native Hawaiians and long-time kama'āina (local residents), in land-use decisions, destination management, and tourism planning processes. Cultural values such as mālama 'āina (care for the land), kuleana (responsibility), and pono (righteousness) offer not only ethical guidance but practical frameworks for tourism rooted in reciprocity rather than extraction. Petranik (2017) argues that Hawai'i must radically reimagine its economic future by embracing a 100-year vision rooted in community well-being, ecological restoration, and Indigenous knowledge systems [5]. This article critiques the state's historical overreliance on extractive industries, beginning with plantations and later including tourism and military investment, and calls for a shift from reactive, short-term economic plans to proactive, long-term strategies. Perkinson advocates for a fundamental change in the way Hawai'i defines prosperity, suggesting that conventional metrics like GDP fail to reflect what truly matters to local communities. He proposes a vision anchored in aloha 'āina, a deep love for and responsibility to the land, which integrates economic development with ecological stewardship. This approach includes investing in regenerative agriculture, community-rooted education, green infrastructure, and diversified sectors such as renewable energy and digital innovation. Perkinson draws inspiration from global models and local initiatives that reflect systems thinking, collaborative governance, and place-based solutions. Central to this article is the belief that sustainable prosperity in Hawai'i must prioritize Indigenous leadership, cultural resilience, and social equity. By cultivating an economy of care rather than consumption, the state can shift away from extractive growth models that degrade both land and people. The author concludes with a call to action: to elevate civic imagination, shift institutional cultures, and build coalitions that are willing to think boldly and act for future generations.

3 Fragility Exposed: COVID-19 and the Great Reset

When COVID-19 reached Hawai'i's shores in early 2020, it arrived not only as a public health emergency but as a full-scale economic reckoning. Nowhere was this more visible than in the state's overwhelming reliance on tourism, a sector that had long been both the golden goose and the Achilles' heel of Hawai'i's economy. HTA (2020) reports that visitor arrivals to the state dropped by 99.5% in April 2020 compared to the same month in the previous year, due to statewide lockdowns and mandatory quarantines during the early stages of the COVID-19 pandemic [6]. Hotels shuttered, airlines suspended service to the islands, and unemployment soared to the highest rate in the nation that May. Hawai'i Department of Labor and Industrial Relations (DLIR) (2020) reports that the state's seasonally adjusted unemployment rate reached 22.3% in April 2020, marking a dramatic increase from just 2.4% the previous month [7]. This press release offers detailed job loss data, noting a decline of over 121,800 positions, particularly in the leisure and hospitality sector. The fragility of a single-sector economy had been laid bare.

Figure 5 corroborates the DLIR report that the state's unemployment rate surged from 2.4% in March 2020 to 22.3% in April 2020, the highest in the nation. The FRED (Federal Reserve Economic Data) graph

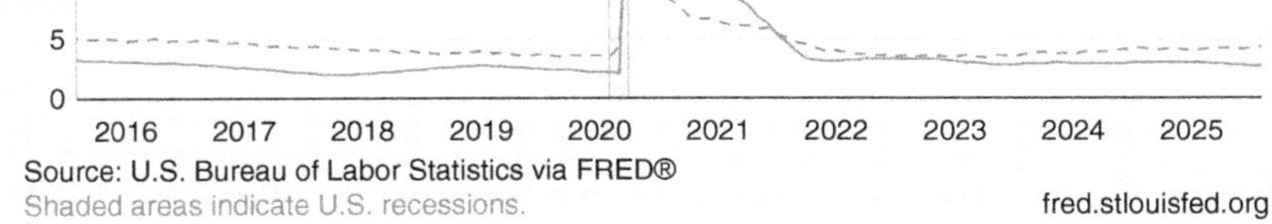

Figure 5 Unemployment Rate in Hawai'i and the United States, 2015–2025. This figure displays the seasonally adjusted unemployment rates for Hawai'i (solid blue line) and the United States (dashed green line) from 2015 to 2025. Both series remain low and stable until early 2020, when Hawai'i's unemployment rate spikes sharply to above 22%—far higher than the national peak—during the onset of the COVID-19 recession (gray shaded area). The graph shows a rapid but uneven decline over 2020–2021, with Hawai'i's labor market recovering more slowly than the nation. By 2022–2025, both rates return to pre-pandemic levels. This visual shows the extreme vulnerability of Hawai'i's economy to shocks affecting the tourism sector

clearly shows this unprecedented vertical spike, which is far steeper than the national increase. This pattern reveals the fragility of Hawai'i's highly specialized economic structure: when tourism collapsed almost overnight, the labor market suffered a catastrophic and disproportionate shock.

Tourism accounted for roughly 17% of Hawai'i's GDP and directly or indirectly supported over 216,000 jobs prior to the pandemic. Its disappearance was not a ripple but a shockwave. Restaurants, tour operators, car rental companies, and small vendors that catered to tourists found themselves without a customer base. Many closed permanently. The blow was particularly severe for Native Hawaiian and immigrant families, who disproportionately worked in front-line hospitality roles—jobs that vanished without warning or a safety net. The collapse also revealed the structural weaknesses embedded in Hawai'i's labor market. Even though Hawai'i is the only U.S. state with a prepaid healthcare coverage law—requiring employers to provide health insurance to employees working at least 20 hours a week—many workers in tourism-dependent sectors still lack consistent employer-provided healthcare or paid leave. This coverage gap reflects the prevalence of part-time, contract, and gig-based jobs that fall outside the protections of Hawai'i's Prepaid Health Care Act[1]. Before the pandemic, nearly half of all renters in Hawai'i were already struggling with housing costs, and widespread job losses pushed an already fragile situation into a full-blown crisis. Demand at food banks spiked. Calls to crisis hotlines surged. Even though federal relief—like expanded unemployment benefits and stimulus checks—offered some short-term stability, it sparked a deeper question: how can Hawai'i rebuild an economy that's not just resilient, but also equitable and rooted in local values?

While the economic pain was acute, the sudden halt to tourism offered a rare and striking counterpoint. For the first time in decades, Hawai'i's residents experienced their home islands without the pressures of mass tourism. O'ahu's North Shore, typically congested with traffic and tour buses, saw families reclaiming beaches and surfers enjoying uncrowded waves. Hanauma Bay teemed with marine life after years of overuse. The waters off Waikīkī turned visibly clearer, and reef ecosystems began to rebound. UH News (2020) reports findings from the Hawai'i Institute of Marine Biology showing that water clarity at Hanauma Bay improved

[1] The Hawai'i Prepaid Health Care Act, enacted in 1974, requires employers in the state to provide health insurance to employees who work at least 20 hours per week for four consecutive weeks and earn a monthly wage of at least 86.67 times the hourly minimum wage.

by 42% during its pandemic-related closure [8]. This study attributes this improvement to the absence of human activity, including sunscreen pollution and sediment disturbance. It provides scientific evidence of how reduced tourism pressure can result in immediate and measurable ecological recovery, offering critical insights into sustainable visitor management strategies for sensitive marine environments. Surveys conducted in 2021 revealed a shift in public sentiment. Most residents expressed support for policies that would have seemed politically risky just a few years prior—capping daily visitor numbers, implementing visitor fees to fund environmental protection, and enforcing stricter regulations on short-term rentals. HTA (2021) reports the findings of its Spring 2021 Resident Sentiment Survey [9]. It shows that a growing number of residents expressed support for stronger management policies. Key findings include that 88% of respondents favored better visitor education to encourage mālama (care for the land and community), and 76% supported action against illegal vacation rentals. It is critical for understanding the rising public demand for tourism reform grounded in sustainability and cultural respect. The pandemic pause felt like a collective wake-up call—a rare moment that revealed what Hawaiʻi might look like if the scales tipped more toward the needs of its residents than the demands of its visitors.

Economic overdependence on a single, volatile industry left the state vulnerable to external shocks. The traditional model of tourism—focused on maximizing arrivals and hotel room nights—often prioritized revenue over sustainability, leading to resource depletion, cultural commodification, and resident displacement. The term "regenerative tourism" began gaining traction. Unlike traditional sustainability frameworks, regenerative tourism emphasizes a net positive impact—where visitors give back more than they take, and where tourism supports environmental restoration, cultural revitalization, and local wealth-building. Programs such as Mālama Hawaiʻi[2] not only help to shift traveler behavior but also to reshape expectations about what a Hawaiian vacation should mean. HTA (2024) announces the launch of the Mālama Hawaiʻi Volunteer Dashboard, developed in partnership with Kanu Hawaiʻi [10]. This platform provides visitors with streamlined access to a range of volunteer

[2] Mālama Hawaiʻi is a collaborative program that encourages visitors to give back to the islands through mindful travel and volunteer activities. By engaging in acts of service, such as beach clean-ups, native tree planting, and cultural preservation projects, you become part of a virtuous circle that benefits both the land and its people. (https://www.kanuhawaii.org/malama-hawaii-visitors/.)

opportunities—such as beach clean-ups, native tree planting, and cultural restoration initiatives—across the state. It is a pivotal example of how regenerative tourism is being operationalized in Hawai'i, creating opportunities for visitors to give back while deepening their connection to local communities and ecosystems. It helps us understand how tourism policy is shifting toward more participatory and environmentally conscious models.

This reimagining has also sparked discussions around metrics. Should success continue to be measured in raw arrival numbers and hotel occupancy rates? Or should metrics such as resident satisfaction, environmental indicators, and income equity be prioritized instead? The pandemic gave policymakers a moment to consider what a high-value, low-impact tourism model might look like. From an economic perspective, diversification has long been Hawai'i's elusive aspiration. Over the past four decades, repeated efforts have sought to grow other sectors—technology, film, renewable energy, and agriculture—with limited success. Part of the challenge lies in geography and scale: Hawai'i's isolation, small market size, and high cost of living create structural barriers to industrial growth. However, COVID-19 renewed momentum for economic diversification with a sharper focus. The success of remote work during the pandemic revealed that knowledge economy jobs—particularly in IT, healthcare, and education—could be viable in Hawai'i if supported by robust broadband infrastructure and housing solutions. DBEDT (2024) announces the federal approval of the state's Digital Equity Plan, developed by the Hawai'i Broadband and Digital Equity Office [11]. This strategic framework targets long-standing disparities in internet access across the islands, particularly in rural and underserved communities. It outlines key priorities in education, workforce development, healthcare, and civic engagement, positioning Hawai'i to receive federal support for improving digital infrastructure and literacy. It also helps us understand how Hawai'i is laying the groundwork for inclusive economic participation in the digital age.

Agriculture, too, has seen renewed attention. As supply chain disruptions left grocery shelves bare, interest in local food production spiked. Community-supported agriculture (CSA) programs saw record subscriptions. Gee (2020) reports on the rising popularity of local produce delivery services like Oahu Fresh[3] and MA'O Organic Farms[4] during the COVID-19 pandemic, as Hawai'i residents sought safer and more sustainable food

[3] https://shop.oahufresh.com/.

[4] https://www.maoorganicfarms.org/.

sources [12]. Oahu Fresh, a subscription-based CSA service, saw its customer base grow fivefold as people avoided crowded grocery stores. For a small fee, subscribers could order produce bags, meal kits, and locally made foods, with the option of home delivery. The company also expanded its prepared food offerings by partnering with local caterers. MAʻO Organic Farms, which empowers underprivileged youth through agriculture, similarly experienced record demand, increasing its weekly produce boxes and adding new pickup locations. The surge in interest has been seen as a turning point for Hawaiʻi's local food systems. According to its farm manager, the spike in subscriptions not only supports local agriculture but also fosters community awareness about food origins and sustainability. Both organizations demonstrate how CSA models can strengthen Hawaiʻi's food resilience while supporting small farms and community well-being.

Terrell (2021) reports that the COVID-19 pandemic exposed deep vulnerabilities in Hawaiʻi's food system, reigniting interest in local agriculture and food security [13]. The pandemic disrupted food supply chains and revealed the fragility of relying on imports, prompting both consumers and policymakers to reconsider local food production. Small farms like Kualoa Ranch adapted by shifting from supplying restaurants to offering local food markets and direct-to-consumer models, but challenges remain. High land and labor costs, lack of processing infrastructure, limited access to affordable leases, and insufficient government support continue to hinder progress. Experts argue that food self-sufficiency in Hawaiʻi will require not only growing more staple crops like taro and ulu but also redefining sustainability to include environmental, cultural, and economic goals. This shift demands coordinated policy changes, subsidies, better infrastructure, and stronger collaborations among stakeholders. Organizations like AgHui[5] and Kamehameha Schools[6] are working to map the state's food system and identify barriers. Ultimately, Terrell emphasizes that Hawaiʻi's path forward must include systemic reform and a collective commitment to supporting local farmers, reducing dependency on imports, and restoring deeper relationships between communities and their land.

UH (2024) report that revitalizing Hawaiʻi's traditional fishponds, or loko iʻa, could significantly contribute to the state's food sustainability efforts by increasing local seafood availability [14]. These Indigenous

[5] A group of stakeholders from across the state that meets regularly to address both immediate and long-term issues in the food industry.

[6] https://www.ksbe.edu/.

aquaculture systems not only generate surplus fish within the ponds but also supplement nearby estuarine fisheries by serving as nursery grounds—something historically recognized but now demonstrated in academic literature for the first time. Loko i‘a are uniquely Hawaiian aquaculture systems that once produced nearly 2 million pounds of fish annually, managed by caretakers using a sustainable "take what you need" ethos. Although many of these systems were destroyed in the twentieth century, efforts to restore them—such as the successful revitalization of He‘eia Fishpond on Windward O‘ahu—are showing promise. Stewarded by the Native Hawaiian nonprofit Paepae o He‘eia[7], the restored fishpond provides not only a local food source but also cultural education and community healing, emphasizing the importance of linking Indigenous knowledge with contemporary environmental management. This study shows that the restoration of loko i‘a not only preserves Hawaiian cultural traditions but also connects with global movements toward sustainable aquaculture and local food security. It also marks a key step toward climate resilience, as future research by the team will examine how climate change might impact these restored systems. In essence, Hawai‘i's fishponds offer a powerful model for sustainable, culturally grounded food systems that support ecological balance and community well-being.

Salmons (2025) reports that Kaua‘i County's Office of Economic Development (OED) awarded $637,429 in Agriculture Farm Expansion Grants to 12 projects supporting local agriculture and food resilience [15]. The grants aim to enhance Kaua‘i's sustainable food system by funding infrastructure improvements, traditional farming restoration, and increased production capacity. Mālama Kaua‘i received two grants: $55,000 for the planning and design of the Olohena ‘ĀINA Center[8], an 87-acre agricultural park, and $100,000 for modernizing an aging ‘auwai irrigation system to support multi-generational kalo farmers. Wai‘oli Valley Taro Hui was also awarded funds to repair irrigation ditches and install solar-powered pumps to boost lo‘i taro production. Additional recipients include organizations focusing on agroforestry, micro-algae production, composting, pollination support, and native plant propagation. Projects emphasize community-based farming, environmental sustainability, and

[7] Paepae o He'eia is a private non-profit organization dedicated to caring for He'eia Fishpond – an ancient Hawaiian fishpond located in He'eia, Ko'olaupoko, O'ahu. (https://paepaeoheeia.org/.)

[8] https://malamakauai.org/olohena-aina-center/.

cultural restoration. OED Director Nalani Brun emphasized collaboration as central to the county's approach, recognizing the vital role farmers play in shaping a resilient, local food economy. Salmons shows how county-level investments in diverse, community-driven agricultural projects enhance local food security, sustain traditional knowledge, and position Kaua'i for a more resilient and self-sufficient future.

Policy discussions have increasingly emphasized the need to shift tourism dollars toward these kinds of enterprises. Visitor spending, if redirected to local and community-based businesses, can multiply economic benefits within the islands and reduce profit leakage to offshore investors. Strengthening this ecosystem means ensuring access to microloans, technical training, e-commerce platforms, and affordable commercial space, all of which are foundational infrastructure for inclusive economic growth. The question is no longer whether tourism should return—it already has. By 2023, visitor arrivals had rebounded to over 9 million, and economic indicators pointed toward recovery. But the pause left a lasting impression. For many in Hawai'i, the pandemic revealed a moment of clarity, a rare window to renegotiate the state's social contract. What kind of economy should Hawai'i pursue? Who benefits from growth? How can the pursuit of prosperity be balanced with cultural dignity and environmental stewardship? These are not new questions, but the pandemic has lent them new urgency. It revealed that economic resilience is not only about diversification, but also about alignment. Aligning tourism with local values. Aligning policy with lived reality. Aligning short-term recovery with long-term transformation.

4 The True Costs: Strain, Saturation, and Sustainability

Tourism has long been the economic lifeline of Hawai'i, contributing billions of dollars annually to the state's GDP and supporting hundreds of thousands of jobs. Yet, beneath the glossy veneer of aloha shirts, beach resorts, and scenic Instagram posts lies a much more complex and troubling reality—one that rarely shows up in tourism brochures or visitor surveys. The costs associated with Hawai'i's visitor industry are not evenly shared. While businesses and investors often enjoy the profits, it is kama'āina and the natural environment that pay the price. These costs take the form of strained infrastructure, environmental degradation, cultural dilution, and unsustainable housing pressures—negative externalities of an economy built on mass tourism, many of which are invisible to the average tourist.

Environmental degradation is perhaps the most immediate and visible consequence of overtourism in Hawai'i. The islands are home to some of the most unique ecosystems on the planet, including coral reefs that are biodiversity hotspots and native forests that serve as critical water sources. Yet these fragile systems are increasingly pushed to the brink. Popular destinations like Hanauma Bay and Diamond Head before the pandemic face continuous pressure from foot traffic, sunscreen pollution, and unmanaged visitor flows. The constant trampling of vegetation on trails, the anchoring of boats in reef areas, and the strain on freshwater systems from thousands of hotel rooms and vacation rentals all compound the problem. In recent years, reef bleaching events have accelerated not just due to rising ocean temperatures, but also from physical damage and chemical runoff caused by human activity. These ecological disruptions are not abstract; they directly affect local fisheries, water security, and the overall resilience of Hawai'i's environment to climate change. The problem is exacerbated by the fact that many of these environmental costs are not captured in the pricing of tourism services. A hotel near a protected marine sanctuary may market its proximity as a luxury feature yet does not bear any of the cost of reef monitoring or trail maintenance. Similarly, tourists who crowd into sacred valleys or endangered habitats often do so with little understanding of the cumulative impact of their presence. In the absence of meaningful caps, usage fees, or enforcement of conservation rules, natural sites become victims of their own popularity. The damage builds quietly, but if the state doesn't step in more decisively, its effects will ripple through Hawai'i's environment and communities for generations.

After the COVID-19 closure in 2020, Hanauma Bay Nature Preserve reopened with a tightly managed visitor flow system to protect its fragile marine ecosystem. The City and County of Honolulu introduced an online reservation system limiting daily access, requiring all visitors to watch an educational video on reef etiquette, and restricting parking to reduce congestion. As of November 1, 2025, new regulations expanded this system by partnering with Roberts Hawai'i[9] to manage a portion of nonresident entries through bundled admission-and-shuttle packages, balancing access with environmental stewardship. These measures matter because they mark a turning point—from open tourism to controlled, sustainability-centered management that protects coral health while maintaining local

[9] Roberts Hawai'i is the largest ground transportation and tour provider in Hawai'i, operating inter-island shuttle, charter, and sightseeing services since 1941.

community access. Same thing for Diamond Head, after being shut down for nearly nine months during the COVID-19 pandemic, it reopened in December 2020 with new visitor-flow controls designed to ease historic overcrowding. By May 2022, a reservation system for non-Hawai'i residents was introduced, requiring advance booking and charging entry and parking fees—changes aimed at reducing daily peaks of 3,000 + visitors to a more manageable level. These reforms matter because they shift the site from unmanaged access toward a model that prioritizes ecological preservation, resident use, and visitor experience—marking a broader transition in Hawai'i's destination-management mindset.

Cultural commodification is another deeply embedded, yet often overlooked, cost of tourism in Hawai'i. Hawaiian culture—rich in oral history, spirituality, hula, and traditional knowledge systems—has become a product to be consumed. Luaus staged for tourist consumption, performers dressed in faux-traditional garb, and superficial cultural "experiences" offered by resorts often reduce centuries of living heritage to mere spectacle. While some argue that showcasing culture helps preserve it, the reality is more complicated. The version of Hawaiian culture often presented to visitors is sanitized and simplified, stripped of its political, religious, and social meaning. It is culture without context, repackaged for entertainment value rather than authentic engagement. This process not only distorts public understanding of Native Hawaiian traditions but also marginalizes the very communities who are the bearers of this culture. Native Hawaiians are frequently underrepresented in the ownership and leadership of tourism enterprises, despite being central to the cultural appeal of the islands. The economic benefits derived from the commodification of Hawaiian identity rarely flow back into Native communities in any substantial way. Instead, cultural appropriation becomes another revenue stream for outside investors, while the real work of cultural preservation, including language revitalization, land stewardship, and intergenerational knowledge transfer, remains underfunded.

Housing pressure has reached crisis levels across the islands, and tourism plays a nontrivial role in this dynamic. The proliferation of short-term vacation rentals has dramatically altered local housing markets, especially in areas like Maui and Kaua'i where residential supply is already limited. Entire neighborhoods that once housed working families have been converted into de facto hotel districts. In some cases, absentee owners and mainland investors purchase homes solely for short-term rental income, removing them from the long-term rental pool and driving up prices for everyone else. This process has not only pushed residents out of their communities but also exacerbated homelessness and intergenerational displacement. Young people are increasingly unable to afford homes in the neighborhoods they grew up in, and multigenerational households are stretched to their limits. The irony is stark: the very people who serve the tourism industry as hotel workers, housekeepers, and restaurant staff are often those most impacted by its expansion. Many must commute long distances from more affordable areas, adding to traffic congestion and reducing their quality of life. Tourism-driven housing scarcity creates a cycle in which economic gains for property owners come at the cost of social cohesion and resident stability.

The infrastructure burden created by mass tourism is perhaps less visible than housing displacement or environmental degradation, but no less serious. Hawai'i's roads, airports, beaches, and parks were not designed to accommodate the current volume of tourists, which often exceeds 9 million annually. High visitor-to-resident ratios mean that public infrastructure experiences accelerated wear and tear, leading to costly maintenance and reduced accessibility for local communities. Restrooms at beach parks are overused and under-cleaned, hiking trails erode faster than they can be repaired, and traffic congestion during peak visitor seasons can make daily commuting a nightmare for residents. Airports, particularly Honolulu's Daniel K. Inouye International Airport, struggle to balance the needs of tourists with the efficient movement of goods and services critical to island economies. Meanwhile, state and county agencies tasked with maintaining these assets face budget constraints, often relying on tourism-related taxes that are vulnerable to market volatility. This creates a paradox in which public systems are overused by visitors but not adequately funded to manage that use. Kama'āina are left to bear the consequences, including higher taxes, longer waiting times, and diminished access to public amenities.

Environmental, cultural, economic, and infrastructural externalities are not accounted for in the typical vacation budget. They do not show up on hotel receipts, tour invoices, or airline tickets. Yet they are real and persistent, affecting the daily lives of those who call Hawai'i home. Thanks to Governor Josh Green's new "Green Fee" law, tourists will now help finance Hawai'i's climate-resilience initiatives. The true cost of tourism is not measured in dollars alone, but in the erosion of natural systems, the marginalization of Indigenous voices, and the fraying of community life. One of the core issues is that tourism, as it is currently structured, largely operates on a model of extraction. Visitors arrive, consume experiences, and depart, often with little awareness of the deeper social or environmental context. In this model, the islands become a backdrop for leisure rather than a place of living culture and ecological complexity. What is needed is a systemic shift away from this model and toward one that is grounded in reciprocity, transparency, and long-term stewardship.

Louis G. Herman's *Future Primal: How Our Wilderness Origins Show Us the Way Forward* explores humanity's disconnection from the natural world and calls for a reconnection with the ecological wisdom embedded in our ancestral roots [16]. Drawing from anthropology, philosophy, and political thought, Herman argues that sustainable futures depend on remembering our "wilderness origins"—the cooperative, reciprocal ways early societies lived in balance with their environments. He proposes that this primal consciousness can inform a new civic and ecological ethic that restores harmony between people and planet. In Hawai'i, where modern development often clashes with Indigenous stewardship values, Herman's message resonates deeply: sustainability requires not just policy reform, but a renewal of collective consciousness rooted in respect for land and the stories that shaped it. Robin Wall Kimmerer's *Braiding Sweetgrass* offers a profound framework for rethinking sustainability through reciprocity, gratitude, and balance between humans and nature [17]. Her vision—where ecological knowledge is inseparable from cultural and spiritual care—echoes Hawai'i's own ethic of mālama 'āina, the responsibility to care for the land that sustains life. Just as Kimmerer invites readers to see the Earth as a living teacher rather than a resource, Hawai'i's sustainability movement calls for a similar return to relational stewardship. Both perspectives remind us that true resilience arises not from control or consumption, but from respect, restoration, and the renewal of shared responsibility.

The O'ahu Destination Management Action Plan (DMAP), developed by HTA in partnership with the City and County of Honolulu, lays out a strategic roadmap for sustainable tourism management from 2021 to 2024 [18]. This plan was shaped through a collaborative process involving community members, government agencies, and tourism industry stakeholders. Its main goal is to "rebuild, redefine, and reset" tourism on O'ahu in a way that centers kama'āina, protects natural and cultural resources, and supports long-term economic health. The DMAP identifies three main outcomes: (1) developing respectful and collaborative relationships between the visitor industry and communities, (2) ensuring the stewardship of natural and cultural assets, and (3) improving the visitor experience through managed tourism. To achieve these outcomes, the plan outlines actions in four strategic areas: (1) managing visitor impact, (2) supporting local businesses and communities, (3) increasing communication and collaboration, and (4) repositioning O‘ahu's brand to emphasize community well-being and cultural respect. Key actions include limiting visitor numbers at hotspots, improving enforcement and signage, developing educational campaigns for tourists, supporting Native Hawaiian-owned businesses, and using real-time data to monitor visitor movement. Emphasis is placed on aligning tourism growth with community capacity, cultural integrity, and environmental sustainability. The DMAP is intended as a living document, adaptable to future needs and feedback. It represents a shift from traditional tourism growth models toward a regenerative tourism approach that places residents' quality of life at the core of tourism policy.

Still, these efforts must be scaled and sustained. Implementing impact fees for high-traffic areas, enforcing vacation rental regulations, and reinvesting tourism revenue into community priorities are all essential strategies. Moreover, more of the industry's governance and ownership should reside with local stakeholders, especially Native Hawaiian-led organizations and cooperatives. Without a rebalancing of power and profits, the current trajectory will only deepen existing inequalities. Tourism in Hawai‘i is not inherently unsustainable, but it is deeply out of alignment. Its benefits are not distributed equitably, and its burdens fall disproportionately on those who have historically had the least voice in shaping its future. To reimagine tourism in a way that honors both the land and the people require confronting its hidden costs and making them visible by pricing them into policy, practice, and planning. Only then can tourism become not a force of strain and saturation, but a contributor to sustainability, equity, and regeneration. Hawai‘i deserves nothing less.

5 Rethinking the Model: From Mass to Meaningful

Regenerative tourism is not just a shift in terminology; it represents a radical rethinking of what tourism should do and for whom it should serve. While sustainable tourism focuses on minimizing damage, essentially doing less harm, regenerative tourism goes a step further. It challenges tourism operators, visitors, and policymakers to actively improve the places they touch. The goal is not to stay neutral, but to make a difference—to build a kind of tourism that heals ecosystems, uplifts culture, and strengthens local communities. This approach demands a different set of metrics, mindsets, and mechanisms. It is about transforming tourism from an extractive industry into a participatory and place-based practice. In Hawai‘i, the stakes for such a transformation are especially high. The islands are both geographically fragile and culturally rich, making them vulnerable to the very forces that mass tourism perpetuates. Over the years, many parts of the state have seen unchecked development, traffic congestion, environmental wear and tear, and rising housing prices, all exacerbated by tourism demand. While these trends have brought financial benefits, they have also created deep imbalances. What regenerative tourism offers is a way to correct that imbalance, by making the visitor economy accountable to the place it depends on.

Regenerative tourism in Hawai‘i asks visitors to engage with the realities of the land and its people. Tourists are encouraged not just to relax, but to participate and take part in the stewardship of the islands. For example, programs now exist that allow visitors to join beach clean-ups, help restore lo‘i kalo, or plant native trees in degraded forests. These activities are not just symbolic gestures; they create tangible improvements in ecological health while also deepening the visitor's connection to the land. Equally important is the invitation to learn. Hawai‘i's history is complex and often painful, marked by colonization, the overthrow of the Hawaiian Kingdom, land loss, and ongoing struggles for sovereignty. Regenerative tourism insists that this history be acknowledged, not ignored or romanticized. Visitors are encouraged to engage with this context through museum exhibits, walking tours, storytelling events, and cultural exchanges that center Native Hawaiian voices and perspectives. This is not only an act of respect, but an opportunity for transformation. When tourism educates rather than entertains, it becomes a bridge for cross-cultural understanding and empathy.

Economic reorientation is also a critical pillar of the regenerative model. In the current system, much of the revenue generated by tourism leaves the state, flowing to off-island corporations, global hotel chains, and mainland investors. Fujii-Oride reports that nearly 30% of Hawai‘i's hotel rooms are owned by private equity firms, many of which are based outside the state [19]. These firms, known for using debt to acquire and resell properties for profit, have fueled billions in hotel renovations and increased state tax revenues. However, critics argue their focus on profit often undermines guest service, worker well-being, and community needs. Workers report understaffing, reduced benefits, and growing workloads, especially after COVID-19. Maui, particularly hard-hit by the Lahaina wildfire, has the highest concentration of private equity-owned hotels, raising concerns about the influence of absentee investors. Some firms, like locally based BlackSand Capital, have responded positively to community needs, but others, like Blackstone and Kohlberg Kravis Roberts & Co. (KKR), face lawsuits and criticism for mistreatment of workers and prioritizing profits over people. Despite these issues, industry experts say private equity will likely continue dominating hotel ownership in Hawaiʻi due to limited supply and high investor interest. Labor unions are pushing back, negotiating for better wages and conditions. The larger debate centers on whether hospitality should be driven by financial interests or by local values, sustainability, and respect for workers who are the backbone of the industry.

Regenerative tourism flips this script by prioritizing local ownership. It calls for directing visitor spending toward locally owned businesses, farms, restaurants, and tour operators. This supports a more circular economy, one in which wealth is created and recirculated within the community rather than extracted from it. It also means that economic benefits are more likely to reach Native Hawaiians and long-time kamaʻāina, many of whom have been economically marginalized despite being central to the islands' cultural identity. Regenerative tourism requires moving decision-making authority away from large corporations and into the hands of communities. It also recognizes that not all spaces are meant to be shared. Some sites hold spiritual, historical, or ceremonial significance and require special care or limited access. This perspective pushes back against the entitlement often associated with tourism—the idea that everything is available for consumption. Instead, it fosters a relationship of kuleana (responsibility). Visitors are taught to ask permission to listen, to tread lightly. This orientation cultivates humility and respect, qualities that are too often absent from tourist behavior but critical to genuine cultural exchange.

The challenges to implementing regenerative tourism are real. It requires coordination among state and county agencies, tourism boards, community organizations, and private businesses. It demands new regulatory frameworks, such as caps on visitor numbers, mandatory visitor orientation programs, and enforceable conservation protocols. It also requires sustained funding and political will, both of which are often scarce. But what is increasingly clear is that the cost of inaction is higher. Without a fundamental shift, tourism will continue to strain Hawaiʻi's infrastructure, displace its residents, degrade its ecosystems, and commercialize its culture. Regenerative tourism is not a silver bullet, but it is a path forward—one that is proactive rather than reactive, healing rather than harming. There is also a broader philosophical transformation at play. Regenerative tourism challenges us to rethink our relationship with place, not just as consumers but as co-inhabitants. It asks tourists to consider what it means to be a guest, and what responsibilities that status entails. It asks residents to imagine a future where tourism contributes to the community's goals rather than undermines them. It asks businesses to shift from growth-at-all-costs models to those rooted in care, reciprocity, and regeneration.

Education will be key. For regenerative tourism to succeed, both visitors and residents must be equipped with the knowledge and tools to participate meaningfully. This includes cultural literacy programs in schools, public media campaigns, interpretive signage at key sites, and partnerships between community groups and the visitor industry. Education also means making data transparent showing clearly how tourism revenue is distributed, how ecosystems are impacted, and how decisions are made. Only through shared knowledge can trust and accountability be built. Regenerative tourism does not seek to eliminate visitors, but to redefine their role. It is an invitation to be more than a consumer, to be a learner, a steward, and a partner. It is about quality, not quantity; relationships, not transactions. For Hawai'i, a place of extraordinary natural beauty and profound cultural depth, this model offers the opportunity to align tourism with the values of aloha, mālama 'āina, and kuleana. These are not just words, they are blueprints for a better future. In moving from mass to meaningful, Hawai'i can lead the world in demonstrating what tourism can be when it is guided by community, culture, and conscience. This is not just an economic strategy; it is a moral one. It is about restoring balance in a system that has long been out of sync and about ensuring that the islands can continue to thrive for generations to come.

6 Local Innovations and Community-Led Models

Across Hawai'i, a quiet revolution is taking place, one not led by government officials or global tourism companies, but by the communities themselves. Long relegated to the margins of the tourism industry, kama'āina, cultural practitioners, and small-scale farmers are now asserting their agency in shaping how tourism unfolds on their land. In place of the long-standing model of mass tourism characterized by unchecked access, environmental degradation, and cultural appropriation, these community-led efforts are embracing a regenerative vision: one where visitors are not passive consumers, but active participants in a reciprocal relationship with Hawai'i's land, people, and heritage. Lemarie (2025) reports that during his Fulbright research at UH Mānoa, he explored the emerging field of regenerative tourism as a community-centered and ecologically restorative alternative to mass tourism [20]. Through 30 interviews with government officials, tourism workers, nonprofit leaders, residents, and tourists, he found that while HTA has officially promoted regenerative tourism since 2019, local grassroots efforts had long embodied these principles without using the term. Lemarie shows the contrast between nonprofit organizations actively questioning commodification and environmental harm, and for-profit entities that often prioritize profitability over regeneration. He emphasizes that true regenerative tourism requires long-term collaboration, place-based knowledge, and systemic shifts beyond "greenwashing." His research suggests that bridging academic frameworks with real-world implementation, especially through inclusive policymaking and community-based planning, is key to transforming Hawai'i's tourism sector into a more resilient and equitable model.

DLNR (2021) announces the implementation of an online reservation system at Wai'ānapanapa State Park, aimed at managing visitor capacity and mitigating environmental strain [21]. This policy, effective March 1, 2021, requires all out-of-state visitors and commercial operators to book in advance and pay entrance and parking fees. This measure reflects a growing shift toward sustainable tourism strategies in Hawai'i, balancing public access with conservation and community well-being. It was not just a logistical fix; it was a philosophical statement. Limiting daily visitation and requiring advance booking gave residents the space to breathe, restored safety to local roadways, and protected vulnerable natural sites from overuse. Moreover, accompanying educational materials informed visitors of Native Hawaiian protocols, histories, and the kuleana (responsibility) that comes with entering such a storied place. The reservation system, designed with significant local input, empowered the community to reclaim agency over how tourism interacts with their home. Kate Raworth's *Doughnut Economics: Seven Ways to Think Like a 21st-Century Economist* introduces a powerful model: "The economy should serve humanity, rather than humanity serving the economy" [22]. In this framework, Raworth maps out a "safe and just space for humanity," one that lies between a social foundation ensuring everyone's basic needs are met and an ecological ceiling representing planetary boundaries. Her model challenges traditional growth-first thinking and argues that success should be measured by thriving lives and resilient ecology, not endless GDP. When we apply this to Hawai'i's tourism economy, it offers a meaningful lens: rather than maximizing visitor numbers and revenues at any cost, we should aim to "fit" the islands' development within a zone where both people and place flourish. In doing so, tourism becomes not just an industry, but a tool for regenerating cultural values, environmental health, and community well-being.

Agritourism is another frontier where community innovation is reshaping the visitor economy. UH News (2020) reports on the Hawai'i Farm Trails mobile app, developed to connect visitors and residents with agricultural experiences across the islands [23]. Spearheaded by Kaivao Farm co-founder Fa'anunu, the initiative promotes agritourism as a means of economic diversification and cultural preservation. It showcases how digital innovation can support small farms while offering visitors authentic, community-based experiences, aligning tourism with local values and sustainability. What makes agritourism so promising is its capacity to decentralize tourism. Instead of funneling all visitors into a few high-impact resorts or attractions, agritourism disperses tourism across the rural landscape, offering income to farmers and small business owners who might otherwise be left out of the economic loop. These initiatives generate revenue that stays in the community and builds resilience in sectors far removed from the traditional visitor industry. They also offer a counter-narrative to the commodified images of Hawai'i, introducing travelers to real people, real work, and real stories. Central to all these models is the concept of local control. Community-led tourism rejects the idea that experts from outside should dictate how tourism operates in Hawai'i. Instead, it posits that those with the deepest connection to the land and the culture are best positioned to determine what is appropriate, what is sustainable, and what is pono (righteous). This includes decisions about who gets to visit, when and how, what kinds of activities are encouraged, and how revenue is distributed.

Yet, even as these community-led innovations gain momentum, they face real challenges. The institutional structure of Hawai'i's tourism industry is still heavily weighted toward large-scale operators, real estate investors, and international corporations. Many communities lack the resources, legal standing, or technical expertise to fully realize their visions. Resistance from entrenched interests is common, and funding for alternative tourism models is often limited or unstable. Moreover, the burden of management frequently falls on volunteers or underpaid staff who are already stretched thin. Despite these obstacles, the progress is tangible and deeply hopeful. Community-led tourism is not a utopian ideal. It is a practical, scalable approach to creating a more equitable, resilient, and meaningful visitor economy. It acknowledges that tourism will remain a part of Hawai'i's future but insists that it must evolve to reflect local values, protect the land, and uplift the people who call these islands home. What sets these innovations apart is that they are not driven by abstract theory or imported best practices. They are born out of lived experience, cultural knowledge, and a fierce commitment to kuleana. They represent not just a change in how tourism is managed, but a change in what tourism means.

In a world increasingly aware of the harms of over-tourism, from Barcelona to Bali and from Iceland to Machu Picchu, Hawai'i's community-led models offer a path forward. They show that it is possible to welcome guests without compromising identity, to invite engagement without inviting exploitation. They remind us that true hospitality is not about offering everything on demand, but about setting boundaries, sharing wisely, and building relationships based on respect. The future of tourism in Hawai'i is already being written in taro patches restored by kupuna (elders) and keiki (children), in volunteer programs guided by local nonprofits, in reservation systems designed with cultural sensitivity, and in farms where travelers learn to plant the seeds of sustainability. It is being written not in the boardrooms of distant corporations, but in the hands of communities that have always known how to care for these islands. And if given the support they deserve, these communities will continue to lead the way toward a tourism model that is not only viable but truly just.

7 Regulatory and Policy Tools

To effectively transform tourism in Hawai'i, strategic regulatory approaches combined with innovative policy measures are essential. Tourism remains the backbone of Hawai'i's economy, but its rapid, often unchecked growth has exposed deep vulnerabilities—making it clear that stronger policy tools and thoughtful regulation are needed to secure a truly sustainable future. By harnessing the lessons from global best practices and tailoring them to Hawai'i's unique ecological, cultural, and economic contexts, a holistic strategy can emerge to guide the state's tourism industry toward a resilient and responsible future.

Green fees represent one promising approach to funding environmental conservation efforts while simultaneously moderating tourism impacts. International examples provide strong evidence supporting this method. New Zealand, for instance, has successfully implemented such fees, channeling revenues directly into environmental preservation projects that significantly benefit local ecosystems and tourism sustainability. Symons (2024) discusses New Zealand's recent decision to significantly increase the International Visitor Conservation and Tourism Levy (IVL) from NZ$35 to NZ$100 [24]. This initiative is part of the country's broader shift toward sustainable and regenerative tourism following the COVID-19 pandemic. The fee, charged to most international visitors applying for tourist visas or electronic travel authorization, supports conservation efforts such as habitat restoration, pest control, and development of sustainable infrastructure. Despite a rebound to only 84% of pre-pandemic tourist levels, New Zealand's government believes the tax hike aligns the country with global tourism standards and is necessary due to inadequate funding for environmental protection. Critics, including tourism industry stakeholders, argue that the new fee—along with simultaneous increases in visa costs—could make New Zealand prohibitively expensive and deter visitors. Nonetheless, the government asserts the increase will represent only a small portion of overall visitor expenses and is unlikely to impact demand significantly. This move reflects a global trend toward managing tourism's environmental footprint through targeted levies and investments in sustainability.

Similarly, Palau, an island nation with many ecological parallels to Hawai'i, adopted the "Palau Pledge," an innovative model where visitors pay a fee upon entry. Lin (2017) reports on Palau's groundbreaking initiative to incorporate an environmental pledge directly into its immigration process, making it the first nation globally to mandate such a visitor commitment [25]. Instead of a traditional passport stamp, tourists now receive a five-stanza pledge that commits them to protect the island's environment by promising to "tread lightly, act kindly, and explore mindfully." This effort addresses growing concerns over the environmental impact of increasing tourism, which often exceeds the local population sevenfold. The Palau Pledge is reinforced by an in-flight educational video and an arrival checklist of responsible behaviors. More than symbolic, the initiative is supported by national enforcement policies aimed at conserving the nation's fragile ecosystems. Rooted in traditional practices like bul, a historical fishing moratorium issued by village chiefs to replenish marine life, the pledge is part of a broader philosophy of sustainability and intergenerational responsibility. It aspires to instill long-term respect among tourists and strengthen community-wide conservation values. Locals hope the pledge will inspire both visitors and residents to recognize and protect Palau's unique natural resources for generations to come.

Tourism impact zones offer a critical regulatory mechanism to control visitor density in ecologically fragile and culturally significant areas. The unchecked influx of visitors has significantly strained some of Hawai'i's most iconic locations, jeopardizing their ecological health and cultural sanctity. Popular sites like Hanauma Bay on O'ahu and Haleakalā National Park on Maui already employ limited visitation quotas, providing useful templates. Expanding such mechanisms across other high-impact areas could markedly alleviate pressures while improving visitor experiences through reduced overcrowding. This measure also allows communities to reclaim greater control over the pace and scale of tourism in their regions, aligning visitor numbers with carrying capacity assessments and local preferences. Beyond managing visitor numbers, tourism impact zones could be complemented with adaptive management practices utilizing real-time data analytics. Leveraging emerging technologies, local authorities could dynamically adjust visitor limits and resource allocations based on environmental data, seasonal fluctuations, and community feedback. This approach would facilitate responsive decision-making that safeguards critical natural and cultural assets, ensures equitable distribution of economic benefits, and maintains Hawai'i's allure as a premier yet sustainable destination.

Incentivizing local ownership and control of tourism businesses is equally essential for transforming Hawai'i's tourism industry. Historically, external ownership of major hotels, resorts, and tour operators has limited the economic benefits retained locally, contributing to economic leakage and community disempowerment. Promoting Native Hawaiian and kama'āina ownership through targeted financial incentives, including tax credits, grants, and accessible financing options, can substantially shift this dynamic. These policies could enable local entrepreneurs to establish and expand culturally authentic tourism ventures that emphasize sustainability, heritage preservation, and genuine hospitality rooted in Hawaiian traditions. Increased local ownership would facilitate the circulation of tourism dollars within the community, significantly enhancing economic resilience and stability. Additionally, businesses owned and operated by kama'āina are typically more attuned to community values and ecological constraints, making them inherently better stewards of the environment and cultural heritage.

Educational mandates also represent a crucial intervention for fostering responsible visitor behavior and cultural sensitivity. Requiring hotels, airlines, and tour operators to incorporate mandatory educational programs about Hawaiian culture, history, and ecological stewardship would cultivate respect and understanding among visitors. Such initiatives could range from pre-arrival digital modules to in-flight instructional videos and hotel orientation sessions. Effective educational programs would not only minimize negative visitor impacts but also significantly enrich visitor experiences, promoting deeper engagement with Hawai'i's distinctive heritage and ecological wealth. To maximize the efficacy of educational mandates, partnerships between industry stakeholders, cultural practitioners, and educational institutions would be pivotal. Collaborative efforts could yield high-quality, culturally accurate, and engaging educational materials that resonate deeply with visitors. Moreover, integrating feedback mechanisms to continually refine educational programs would ensure ongoing relevance and effectiveness, further embedding cultural education into the core visitor experience.

Abe, Park, and Ghosh (2024) report that tourism in Hawai'i often masks deep-rooted colonial histories and social injustices, particularly the marginalization of Kānaka Maoli (Native Hawaiian) voices [26]. Their position paper introduces a prototype for a site-specific augmented reality (AR) storytelling experience designed to educate tourists through immersive, geolocated digital artifacts. The AR interface highlights themes such as historical colonialism, contemporary issues like the exclusion of Native art, and identity harm described as "cultural prostitution." By leveraging community narratives and technological tools like the 8th Wall Software Development Kit (SDK), the authors aim to amplify local voices and reframe visitor understanding of place. This work contributes to social justice by advocating responsible tourism through interactive learning and positional storytelling. Their framework serves as a model for using AR not as entertainment, but as a medium for cultural education, restoration, and empowerment in contested tourism spaces like Hawai'i.

Enhanced data sharing and inter-agency coordination represent additional policy interventions vital to transforming Hawai'i's tourism sector. Currently, fragmented data collection and limited coordination among government agencies and industry stakeholders impede timely responses to shifting tourism dynamics. Establishing robust data-sharing frameworks would enable comprehensive monitoring of visitor patterns, environmental impacts, and community sentiments. Integrating data from accommodation providers, transportation networks, attractions, and community feedback portals into a unified platform would empower stakeholders with actionable insights. Real-time data analysis and predictive modeling facilitated by such platforms could significantly enhance strategic decision-making capabilities, allowing for proactive rather than reactive responses to tourism-related challenges. For instance, advanced analytics could predict peak visitation periods, enabling preemptive implementation of visitor caps, enhanced resource deployment, and targeted educational interventions. Additionally, transparent dissemination of aggregated data to the public could foster greater community engagement, informed debate, and collective problem-solving.

Implementing these regulatory tools and policy innovations demands robust stakeholder collaboration and inclusive governance structures. Engaging diverse voices, including Native Hawaiian communities, environmental organizations, tourism industry representatives, policymakers, and residents, in participatory decision-making processes ensures broad-based buy-in and legitimacy. Inclusive governance mechanisms, such as advisory councils, participatory budgeting committees, and community consultation forums, would provide platforms for sustained dialogue, collective visioning, and consensus-building around tourism transformation strategies. Moreover, clear communication of policy rationales, transparent implementation processes, and consistent stakeholder engagement are essential to mitigate resistance and ensure successful adoption. Pilot projects and phased implementations could demonstrate tangible benefits, build confidence, and refine approaches based on experiential learning.

By strategically deploying these regulatory and policy tools, Hawai‘i can effectively address the pressing challenges posed by mass tourism. Transformative initiatives, such as green fees, tourism impact zones, local ownership incentives, educational mandates, and enhanced data sharing, collectively represent a comprehensive approach to sustainable tourism management. These policies would not only safeguard Hawai‘i's unique ecological and cultural assets but also foster a resilient, inclusive economy where tourism continues to thrive without compromising future generations' opportunities to enjoy and benefit from the islands' extraordinary resources.

8 Diversification Within Tourism

Reimagining tourism in Hawai‘i does not require its abandonment; rather, it demands a thoughtful diversification within the sector that better serves the islands' people, culture, and environment. By pivoting toward diversified, values-aligned models of tourism, Hawai‘i can retain the industry's economic benefits while mitigating its negative impacts and enriching both visitors and residents alike.

Cultural tourism represents one of the most promising avenues for diversification. Authentic, community-led storytelling can offer visitors a deeper, more respectful engagement with Hawaiian history, language, and traditions. Initiatives led by Native Hawaiian organizations, local artists, historians, and cultural practitioners can create experiences rooted in genuine heritage rather than commodified stereotypes. Cultural festivals, guided visits to sacred sites, traditional craft workshops, and Hawaiian language immersion tours are examples of offerings that can generate economic opportunities for local communities while safeguarding cultural integrity. These experiences are not only more meaningful for visitors but also foster a deeper sense of pride and stewardship among residents. By centering cultural authenticity, Hawai‘i can distinguish itself in an increasingly homogenized global tourism market and nurture a tourism economy that uplifts rather than extracts.

Tam (2025) reports that Hawai‘i's tourism industry is at a turning point, requiring a careful balance between cultural integrity and professional expertise [27]. Drawing on stakeholder input across sectors, he emphasizes that organizations like the Council for Native Hawaiian Advancement (CNHA) bring essential cultural leadership, while legacy institutions such as the Hawai‘i Visitors and Convention Bureau (HVCB) provide vital global marketing experience. Tam argues that sustainable tourism cannot rely solely on cultural alignment but must integrate proven industry relationships and accountability. He cautions against framing the future of tourism as a choice between cultural values and economic strategy. Instead, he advocates for a collaborative model where CNHA leads in destination management and HVCB strengthens marketing, guided by transparency and shared purpose. This unified approach, he concludes, is essential for ensuring Hawai‘i's tourism industry supports community well-being, economic resilience, and environmental stewardship.

Eco-tourism is another critical pillar of a reimagined, diversified tourism sector. In contrast to mass tourism's heavy environmental footprint, eco-tourism emphasizes low-impact travel experiences that prioritize conservation and environmental education. Hawai‘i's extraordinary biodiversity and fragile ecosystems, from its coral reefs to its volcanic landscapes, offer immense opportunities for eco-centric visitor experiences. Programs could include guided hikes led by conservationists, marine conservation volunteer tourism projects, and bird-watching tours in native forests. Partnering with environmental organizations and research institutions would ensure that eco-tourism initiatives are scientifically grounded and genuinely contribute to conservation goals. Revenue generated from eco-tourism could directly fund habitat restoration, invasive species management, and climate adaptation efforts. Eco-tourism also naturally attracts a segment of visitors who are more environmentally conscious and willing to pay a premium for experiences that align with their values, leading to higher per-visitor economic returns with reduced strain on natural resources.

Linnes, Agrusa, Ronzoni, and Lema (2022) report that Hawai'i's potential as a sustainable tourism destination is increasingly supported by changing visitor preferences [28]. Based on survey data, the study finds that a growing segment of tourists prioritizes environmental responsibility, showing strong interest in activities like beach cleanups, reef restoration, and educational cultural experiences. These visitors not only prefer authentic, place-based engagement, but are also willing to pay a premium for it, signaling a viable economic opportunity for the state. The authors argue that tourism planning in Hawai'i should move beyond mass-market models and instead adopt regenerative strategies that blend environmental stewardship with cultural authenticity. Their findings point out the need for destination managers to embrace a more integrated and sustainable framework that balances visitor satisfaction, ecological protection, and community well-being.

Health and wellness tourism offers a complementary avenue for diversification that is particularly well-suited to Hawai'i's natural beauty and indigenous healing traditions. Growing global interest in holistic wellness, mental health retreats, and indigenous healing practices positions Hawai'i to become a premier destination for health and wellness tourism. Traditional Hawaiian healing modalities, such as lomilomi massage, la'au lapa'au (herbal medicine), and ho'oponopono (a practice of reconciliation and forgiveness), can be authentically integrated into retreat offerings. Wellness centers could be established in collaboration with Native Hawaiian health practitioners, blending ancient wisdom with modern wellness trends in ways that respect and honor cultural traditions. The natural setting—with its pristine beaches, serene mountains, and healing ocean waters—provides an unparalleled backdrop for yoga retreats, mindfulness camps, and holistic detox programs. Not only would health and wellness tourism attract high-value, long-staying visitors, but it would also promote a model of tourism that prioritizes physical, emotional, and spiritual restoration over consumerism and exploitation.

Codinha (2025) reports that Sensei Lāna'i—an adults-only Four Seasons wellness retreat on Larry Ellison's private Hawaiian island—earns a place in Vogue's top 100 global spas [29]. The art-filled oasis blends Hawaiian calm with a Japanese ryokan aesthetic and delivers personalized longevity programs built on the "Move, Nourish, Rest" framework devised with cancer researcher Dr. David Agus. Guests undergo high-tech assessments such as heart-rate variability (HRV)[10]. And wear WHOOP[11] performance-tracking bands, screen-less wearables that log HRV, resting heart rate, sleep, and strain around the clock to guide recovery and training. A new five-night "Rest & Recovery" itinerary harnesses these metrics alongside forest bathing, yoga, and ropes-course challenges to teach high achievers the power of strategic rest. Spa treatments unfold in private hales with pools, saunas, and an onsen garden, while island sustainability efforts span electric vehicles, solar power, organic farming, and greywater irrigation.

Educational tourism represents yet another potent opportunity for Hawai'i to reimagine its visitor economy. By partnering with institutions such as the UH system, Kamehameha Schools, Bishop Museum, and various research organizations, Hawai'i can offer visitors immersive, intellectually enriching experiences. Educational tourism could include field-based programs in marine biology, volcanology, Hawaiian studies, astronomy, and climate change resilience. Programs could be designed for a wide range of audiences, from university students seeking course credit to lifelong learners interested in personal enrichment. Educational tourism also dovetails naturally with efforts to position Hawai'i as a global leader in indigenous knowledge, sustainability, and scientific research, aligning with the state's broader strategic goals. Woo et al. (2025) detail the development of an educational program by the Hawai'i Institute of Marine Biology aimed at fostering positive relationships between visitors, kama'āina, and the environment [30]. By weaving indigenous knowledge and environmental stewardship into visitor education, their program exemplifies how educational tourism in Hawai'i can simultaneously promote cultural

[10] Heart-rate variability (HRV) is the variation in time intervals between consecutive heartbeats, reflecting the balance and adaptability of the autonomic nervous system.

[11] WHOOP is a wearable fitness and health tracker designed to monitor physiological data such as heart-rate variability, sleep, recovery, strain, and other metrics to optimize athletic performance and overall well-being. (https://www.whoop.com/us/en/.)

respect, conservation, and deeper visitor engagement. This study helps us understand how indigenous knowledge can be authentically and effectively incorporated into educational tourism offerings. Moreover, visitors participating in educational tourism tend to stay longer, spend more per day, and engage more thoughtfully with the local community, resulting in a higher overall value proposition with reduced infrastructural stress.

Cultural tourism, eco-tourism, health and wellness tourism, and educational tourism each offers pathways to build a more resilient, respectful, and prosperous tourism industry for Hawai'i. They share several important attributes that align with the state's long-term needs. First, they prioritize higher-value visitors who are willing to invest in meaningful experiences rather than maximizing cheap volume. This shift from quantity to quality reduces pressure on airports, roadways, beaches, and other infrastructure, improving quality of life for residents and quality of experience for visitors. Second, these models foster deeper emotional and intellectual connections between visitors and the islands, cultivating a sense of responsibility and stewardship that endures beyond the duration of a trip. Visitors who learn about coral reef conservation, participate in a ho'oponopono ceremony, or study the Hawaiian language are more likely to become long-term advocates for Hawai'i's preservation. For example, Hanauma Bay Education Program[12] offers standards-based lessons on coral reef ecology, conservation, and Hawaiian culture to school groups visiting Hanauma Bay. By educating visitors about the importance of reef preservation and responsible behaviors, this program fosters a strong sense of stewardship and encourages participants to become long-term advocates for Hawai'i's marine ecosystems. This program exemplifies how place-based environmental education can transform visitors into lifelong supporters of preservation efforts.

Importantly, diversifying within tourism also ensures that the economic benefits are more equitably distributed. Rather than funneling most revenues to multinational hotel chains and large tour operators, these models create opportunities for local entrepreneurs, artisans, cultural practitioners, conservation organizations, educators, and health professionals. Diversification encourages the growth of small and medium-sized enterprises, strengthens the middle class, and reduces the risk of economic vulnerability that comes from overreliance on a single model of mass tourism. It aligns economic development with cultural preservation and

[12] https://seagrant.soest.hawaii.edu/hanauma-bay-education-program/hbep-school-programs/.

environmental stewardship, rather than pitting them against each other. The transition toward a diversified tourism economy will not happen automatically. It will require strategic investment, policy support, community engagement, and sustained collaboration across sectors. Public funding could prioritize infrastructure and grant programs that support cultural and eco-tourism ventures. Tax incentives could be designed to encourage wellness and educational tourism development. Marketing campaigns must be reoriented to showcase the depth and richness of Hawai'i's diversified offerings, moving beyond beach imagery to highlight authentic, regenerative experiences. Crucially, local communities must be at the center of this transformation, leading the design and delivery of new tourism products and retaining control over how their stories, lands, and traditions are shared with the world.

Educational institutions and research centers in Hawai'i have a pivotal role to play as catalysts in this diversification process. They can develop specialized programs that integrate tourism, sustainability, and indigenous knowledge, train a new generation of professionals to lead diversified tourism enterprises, and conduct research that informs policy and best practices. UH describes the Office of Indigenous Knowledge and Innovation (OIKI)[13] as a key catalyst for integrating ancestral sciences and technologies into contemporary research, education, and innovation. Through collaborations among students, faculty, and communities, OIKI works to optimize innovation while revitalizing Hawai'i's ecosystems. Its initiatives are crucial for supporting the development of specialized programs that blend indigenous knowledge, sustainability, and tourism, helping to train a new generation of professionals capable of leading diversified and culturally grounded tourism enterprises. Foundations and philanthropic organizations can further support innovation by funding pilot projects and scaling successful models that emerge from grassroots initiatives.

Hawai'i Community Foundation describes the Social Impact Investment Fund as a mechanism providing revolving, catalytic capital to nonprofit and for-profit organizations tackling critical social issues in Hawai'i [31]. By aligning investments with the foundation's CHANGE (Community & Economy, Health & Wellness, Arts & Culture, Natural Environment, Government & Civic Engagement, and Education) Framework, the fund enables pilot projects to gain the support needed for growth and scalability. This initiative is crucial for fostering innovation

[13] https://research.hawaii.edu/oiki/.

and expanding successful grassroots models, promoting sustainable development and community-driven solutions across the islands. Harold K.L. Castle Foundation presents the Ko'olau Pilina Fund as a participatory grantmaking initiative aimed at building community resilience within the Ko'olau region on O'ahu [32]. By empowering kama'āina to review and select proposals, the fund ensures that grassroots projects align with regional values and needs. This approach is vital for fostering innovation that is deeply rooted in community priorities, enabling the development and scaling of initiatives that genuinely serve and strengthen local communities.

Private sector actors, from airlines to travel platforms to hotel brands, must also evolve. Airlines can partner with universities to offer packages that combine flights with educational programs. Hotels can offer wellness packages that incorporate indigenous healing practices and eco-tourism excursions led by local guides. Tour operators can shift from volume-based sales models to premium, values-driven experiences that prioritize education, restoration, and connection. Ultimately, Hawai'i's journey to reimagine tourism through diversification is not only possible but necessary. It represents a profound opportunity to reframe the visitor economy as a tool for cultural resilience, environmental stewardship, community empowerment, and holistic well-being. Rather than measuring success by the sheer number of arrivals, Hawai'i can set a new standard: a tourism economy measured by the depth of learning, the strength of community partnerships, the health of ecosystems, and the authenticity of visitor experiences. By embracing this vision, Hawai'i can lead the world in demonstrating that tourism, when rooted in respect, stewardship, and authenticity, can be not just an economic engine, but a force for healing and renewal—for visitors and residents alike.

9 Tourism as a Bridge, Not a Crutch

Tourism has always connected Hawai'i to the broader world, serving not merely as an economic engine but as a means of cultural exchange, storytelling, and community pride. For many residents, the act of welcoming visitors is not just a transaction, but a gesture deeply rooted in the traditions of aloha and hospitality. Sharing Hawai'i's landscapes, traditions, and spirit with guests can be a source of honor. However, that sharing must be reciprocal and respectful to remain meaningful. Tourism must be built upon relationships of mutual regard, not one-sided consumption.

The future of Hawai'i's tourism industry hinges not on marketing prowess or the ability to offer luxury experiences, but on its capacity to evolve into a truly accountable sector. Genuine accountability demands that tourism benefits the places and people that sustain it. It is not enough to promote sustainability rhetorically; tourism must embed sustainability into every facet of its operations. The industry's "social license to operate" must be earned, not presumed. Communities must feel that tourism contributes to their well-being rather than detracting from it. Only through authentic partnerships with kama'āina can the tourism sector retain its legitimacy and vitality. One of the most visible dimensions of this necessary transformation is the treatment of workers. Fair wages are not optional; they are foundational. Hospitality and service workers in Hawai'i have historically been underpaid relative to the cost of living, despite the central role they play in the visitor experience. A reimagined tourism industry must commit to providing living wages, comprehensive benefits, and clear career ladders that allow employees to advance and build wealth over time. Investing in workforce development through apprenticeships, certifications, and leadership programs will not only empower individual workers but also enhance the quality of service and innovation within the industry.

Environmental stewardship must also move from a branding exercise to a core operational principle. Hawai'i's natural beauty, including its beaches, forests, coral reefs, and mountains, forms the foundation of its visitor economy. Without proactive efforts to protect these resources, tourism's very basis is at risk. This means not only minimizing harm through sustainable practices but actively investing in restoration and resilience. Hotels, tour operators, airlines, and other industry players must collaborate with conservation organizations, invest in habitat restoration, reduce carbon emissions, and support climate adaptation projects. Environmental stewardship should not be treated as philanthropy; it should be understood as an essential business investment. Moreover, tourism must be managed as a tool for broader community benefit, rather than an extractive enterprise. Revenues generated by tourism should flow back into the communities that host visitors. This can be achieved through mechanisms such as community benefit agreements, direct support for local nonprofits, and reinvestment in public infrastructure and services that improve residents' quality of life. Tour operators can prioritize locally owned businesses in their offerings. Hotels can source food, crafts, and services from local producers and artisans. Airlines can invest in community education and scholarship programs. In this way, tourism can become an amplifier of local entrepreneurship and creativity rather than a competitor against it.

When managed thoughtfully, tourism can serve as a bridge to broader economic opportunities. For instance, agritourism initiatives allow farmers to diversify their income streams by hosting farm tours, tastings, and workshops. These experiences not only support local agriculture but also educate visitors about Hawai'i's food systems and sustainability challenges. Similarly, partnerships between hotels and local artists can create pathways for artisans to showcase and sell their work, helping to sustain traditional crafts and contemporary arts alike. Education is another sector that stands to benefit from reimagined tourism. Educational tourism programs, such as cultural workshops, field-based science programs, and study abroad experiences, can drive new forms of visitor engagement that are high-value, low-impact, and mutually enriching. These programs can position Hawai'i as a global hub for learning, indigenous knowledge, and environmental leadership. Furthermore, by collaborating with universities and research centers, tourism businesses can support research initiatives that inform policy development, conservation strategies, and economic diversification efforts. Innovation, too, can be fueled by a reimagined tourism sector. Tech-enabled visitor management systems, regenerative tourism models, and sustainable infrastructure solutions are just a few areas where Hawai'i can lead. By investing in research and development, incubating startups focused on sustainability and culture, and fostering public-private partnerships, the state can transform tourism from a static sector into a dynamic catalyst for broader innovation. The visitor industry has the potential to serve as an early market for new technologies and practices that could eventually be exported beyond Hawai'i's shores.

However, realizing this vision requires a fundamental shift in mindset. Tourism must no longer be treated as an extractive industry designed to maximize short-term profits at the expense of long-term viability. It must instead be managed as a living relationship—dynamic, reciprocal, and rooted in respect. A living relationship recognizes that visitors are guests, not consumers; that residents are hosts, not service providers; and that the land and culture are not products to be sold, but gifts to be shared and stewarded. Such a relationship demands mutual accountability. Visitors must be educated about their responsibilities while in Hawai'i—to respect cultural protocols, protect natural resources, and contribute positively to the places they visit. Tourism businesses must be transparent about their environmental and social impacts and commit to continuous improvement. Government agencies must ensure that policies and regulations prioritize community well-being and environmental health over short-term economic gains. Community voice must be at the center of tourism decision-making. Residents must have real influence over how tourism is managed, where it is allowed to grow, and what forms it takes. Mechanisms such as community advisory boards, participatory budgeting processes, and public consultations should be standard practice. Trust must be rebuilt through consistent, meaningful engagement and the honoring of community priorities.

This approach is not about rejecting visitors or turning away economic opportunities. It is about recalibrating the tourism sector so that it operates in service of Hawai'i's people, culture, and environment. It is about ensuring that the benefits of tourism are widely shared, that its impacts are responsibly managed, and that its presence enriches rather than erodes the fabric of island life. In the end, tourism should not be Hawai'i's crutch, a fragile dependence that leaves the islands vulnerable to external shocks. Instead, it should be Hawai'i's bridge—a pathway to greater resilience, broader opportunity, and deeper global connection. It should be one part of a diversified, sustainable economy that honors the past, serves the present, and protects the future. Achieving this vision will not be easy. It will require courage, collaboration, and creativity. It will require confronting difficult truths and making tough choices. But the reward is profound: a Hawai'i where tourism strengthens rather than weakens, where visitors leave not only with memories but with respect and responsibility, and where the spirit of aloha thrives not just in words, but in practice.

10 Conclusion: Aloha 'Āina in Action

The Hawaiian concept of aloha 'āina, meaning love and care for the land, must be the foundation of any tourism strategy. This means asking not, "How do we get more tourists?" but "How can visitors support the well-being of these islands?" Can Hawai'i compete in global tourism? Yes. But it must choose quality over quantity, culture over commodification, and community over short-term profit. The next chapter looks at how Hawai'i can shape a more balanced and resilient economy—one where tourism remains an important thread, but not the entire fabric of our future.

References

[1]. Baker, K., Williams, D., & Puniwai, N. (2024). North Shore of O'ahu Visitor Survey and Impact Report. University of Hawai'i at Mānoa, Hawai'i Sea Grant College Program. https://files.hawaii.gov/dbedt/economic/reports/north_shore_visitors_report_final_sept_2024.pdf.

[2]. Kamita, R. (2025). Native Hawaiians in Hawai'i's tourism sector – 2025 update. Hawai'i Department of Business, Economic Development & Tourism. Retrieved from https://files.hawaii.gov/dbedt/economic/reports/Native_Hawaiians_in_Tourism_2025.pdf.

[3]. Hawai'i Tourism Authority. (2023). Governance with Aloha: Reimagining Government for a Resilient Hawai'i. Retrieved from https://www.hawaiitourismauthority.org/media/13004/handout-09-governance-with-aloha-report-final.pdf.

[4]. Collins, K. (2025, May 27). Hawai'i passes "Green Fee" law: Tourists to help fund climate resilience. KITV 4 Island News. Retrieved from https://www.kitv.com/news/hawai-i-passes-green-fee-law-tourists-to-help-fund-climate-resilience/article_66615e44-9dea-4c5a-99a7-b16709fe449e.html.

[5]. Petranik, R. (2017). A 100-year vision for Hawai'i's economy. Hawai'i Business Magazine. Retrieved from https://www.hawaiibusiness.com/100-year-visions-for-hawaii/.

[6]. Hawai'i Tourism Authority. (2020, May 28). Hawai'i visitor statistics released for April 2020. Retrieved from https://www.hawaiitourismauthority.org/news/news-releases/2020/hawaii-visitor-statistics-released-for-april-2020/.

[7]. Hawai'i Department of Labor and Industrial Relations. (2020, May 21). Hawai'i's unemployment rate at 22.3 percent in April. Retrieved from https://labor.hawaii.gov/wp-content/uploads/2020/05/20200521April-UI-Rate-PR.pdf.

[8]. University of Hawai'i News. (2020, July 20). Hanauma Bay water clarity significantly improves without visitors. Retrieved from https://www.hawaii.edu/news/2020/07/20/hanauma-bay-water-clarity/.

[9]. Hawai'i Tourism Authority. (2021, June 24). HTA releases results from 2021 resident sentiment survey. Retrieved from https://www.hawaiitourismauthority.org/news/news-releases/2021/hta-releases-results-from-2021-resident-sentiment-survey/.

[10]. Hawai'i Tourism Authority. (2024, April 5). Hawai'i Tourism Authority launches Mālama Hawai'i dashboard connecting visitors with volunteer opportunities and nonprofits. Retrieved from https://www.hawaiitourismauthority.org/news/news-releases/2024/hawai-i-tourism-authority-launches-m%C4%81lama-hawai-i-dashboard/.

[11]. Hawai'i Department of Business, Economic Development & Tourism. (2024, March 28). Hawai'i Digital Equity Plan approved by federal officials. Retrieved from https://dbedt.hawaii.gov/blog/24-20/.

[12]. Gee, P. (2020, April 6). Oahu Fresh subscription services link farms, homes. Honolulu Star-Advertiser. Retrieved from https://www.staradvertiser.com/2020/04/06/hawaii-news/oahu-fresh-subscription-services-link-farms-homes/.
[13]. Terrell, J. (2021, January 27). Hawai'i's food system is broken. Now is the time to fix it. Honolulu Civil Beat. Retrieved from https://www.civilbeat.org/2021/01/hawaiis-food-system-is-broken-now-is-the-time-to-fix-it/.
[14]. University of Hawai'i at Mānoa. (2024, April 18). Could fishponds help with Hawai'i's food sustainability? Retrieved from https://manoa.hawaii.edu/news/article.php?aId=13183.
[15]. Salmons, J. (2025, March 12). Grants awarded to Kaua'i organizations help support the island's agricultural industry. Aloha State Daily. Retrieved from https://alohastatedaily.com/2025/03/12/grants-awarded-to-these-kauai-organizations-help-support-the-islands-agricultural-industry/.
[16]. Herman, L. G. (2013). Future Primal: How Our Wilderness Origins Show Us the Way Forward. Novato, CA: New World Library.
[17]. Kimmerer, R. W. (2015). Braiding Sweetgrass: Indigenous Wisdom, Scientific Knowledge, and the Teachings of Plants. Milkweed Editions.
[18]. Hawai'i Tourism Authority. (2021, August 31). HTA publishes community-based tourism management plan for O'ahu. Retrieved from https://www.hawaiitourismauthority.org/media/7791/hta-publishes-oahu-dmap_final2.pdf.
[19]. Fujii-Oride, N. (2023, December 18). Private equity owns a big chunk of Hawai'i's hotels. Here's why that matters. Hawaii Business Magazine. Retrieved from https://www.hawaiibusiness.com/private-equity-owns-many-hawaii-hotels-why-that-matters/.
[20]. Lemarie, J. (2025). Exploring regenerative tourism in Hawai'i. Fulbright Chronicles, 3(3), 24–30. Retrieved from https://fulbright-chronicles.com/wp-content/uploads/2025/03/Article-3_Exploring-Regenerative-Tourism-in-Hawaii.pdf.
[21]. Department of Land and Natural Resources. (2021, February 13). Wai'ānapanapa State Park online reservations system beginning – Reservations required beginning March 1, 2021. Retrieved from https://dlnr.hawaii.gov/blog/2021/02/13/nr21-034/.
[22]. Raworth, K. (2017). Doughnut Economics: Seven Ways to Think Like a 21st-Century Economist. New York, NY: Random House.
[23]. University of Hawai'i News. (2020, December 4). Agritourism strategy can create sustainable Hawai'i economy. Retrieved from https://www.hawaii.edu/news/2020/12/04/faanunu-agritourism-strategy/.
[24]. Symons, A. (2024, September 4). New Zealand is tripling its visitor tax. Here's how it could impact nature and tourism. Euronews. Retrieved from https://www.euronews.com/travel/2024/09/04/new-zealand-is-tripling-its-visitor-tax-heres-how-it-could-impact-nature-and-tourism.

[25]. Lin, D. (2017, December 18). Palau becomes first country to require 'eco-pledge' upon arrival. National Geographic. Retrieved from https://www.nationalgeographic.com/travel/article/passport-stamp-ecotourism-pledge.
[26]. Abe, K., Park, J., & Ghosh, S. (2024). Revealing aspects of Hawai'i tourism using situated augmented reality. arXiv. Retrieved from https://arxiv.org/abs/2404.15610.
[27]. Tam, A (2025). Grounding Hawai'i's tourism in cultural values and professional expertise. Honolulu Civil Beat. Retrieved from https://www.civilbeat.org/2025/06/as-we-reshape-tourism-ground-it-in-both-cultural-values-and-professional-expertise/.
[28]. Linnes, C., Agrusa, J., Ronzoni, G., & Lema, J. (2022). What Tourists Want, a Sustainable Paradise. Tourism and Hospitality, 3(1), 164–183. Retrieved from https://doi.org/10.3390/tourhosp3010013.
[29]. Codinha, A. (2025, June 3). Sensei Lāna'i, A Four Seasons Resort. Vogue. Retrieved from https://www.vogue.com/article/sensei-lanai-spa.
[30]. Woo, S., Sherman, M., Villablanca, M., Luke, H., Drury, C., & Hughes, K. (2025). Building an education program to support positive relationships between visitors, kama'āina, and the environment in Hawai'i. Journal of STEM Outreach, 8(1), 1–13. https://doi.org/10.15695/jstem/v8i1.03.
[31]. Hawai'i Community Foundation. Social Impact Investment Fund. Retrieved from https://www.hawaiicommunityfoundation.org/social-impact-investing-fund.
[32]. Harold K.L. Castle Foundation. Ko'olau Pilina Fund. Retrieved from https://castlefoundation.org/pilinafund/.

CHAPTER 4

Diversify or Decline? The Search for Hawai‘i’s Next Growth Engine

1 Introduction: At the Edge of Economic Overdependence

The call to “diversify Hawai‘i’s economy” is not new. It has echoed through state legislatures, university lecture halls, and boardrooms for decades. Yet despite these repeated declarations, tourism and government spending remain the twin pillars of Hawai‘i’s economic foundation. When either pillar shakes, as with the COVID-19 pandemic or shifts in federal policy, the whole structure wobbles. This chapter explores what economic diversification actually means for an island state with limited land, high costs, and a deep cultural identity.

2 What Does Diversification Mean in Hawai‘i?

Diversification in Hawai‘i is often discussed but frequently misunderstood. It is not about abandoning the state’s largest industries, tourism and defense, which have been and will continue to be important contributors to Hawai‘i’s economy. Rather, diversification is about reducing economic vulnerability by intentionally building up complementary sectors that can thrive alongside tourism and defense, making the economy more resilient, adaptive, and sustainable over the long term. In practical terms,

P. Yu, *Economic Development in Hawai‘i*,
https://doi.org/10.1007/978-3-032-15689-1_4

diversification for Hawai'i means identifying and nurturing industries that generate high-wage, low-carbon jobs, add value to local resources, and are firmly rooted in the islands' unique place-based strengths.

Economic vulnerability in Hawai'i is largely driven by its dependence on a narrow band of activities and its geographical isolation. The COVID-19 pandemic revealed the full extent of this fragility when tourism shut down virtually overnight, triggering historic levels of unemployment and economic contraction. Diversification is a strategic response to this reality. It is about ensuring that no single industry holds disproportionate sway over the livelihoods of residents, the state's tax revenues, or the direction of economic development. A diversified economy is not only more stable; it fosters innovation, encourages entrepreneurship, and distributes benefits more broadly across different communities and demographics.

One key pillar of diversification is the creation of high-wage, low-carbon jobs. Hawai'i's future depends on industries that do not exacerbate environmental degradation or contribute heavily to climate change. Clean energy is one of the most promising sectors. Hawai'i State Energy Office outlines the Hawai'i Clean Energy Initiative (HCEI), a comprehensive plan for the state's transition to 100% renewable energy by 2045 [1]. Launched in 2008 through a partnership with the U.S. Department of Energy, HCEI serves as a strategic framework guiding the expansion of solar, wind, geothermal, and energy storage industries. It is pivotal for understanding Hawai'i's long-term energy policy direction and the collaborative efforts needed to meet its ambitious sustainability goals. Similarly, technology and digital innovation offer another pathway for job creation that aligns with Hawai'i's geographic realities. Remote work, software development, cybersecurity, and digital media are sectors that do not rely on importing large volumes of goods and can provide high-quality employment opportunities for residents. Programs that train local students and workers in tech skills, coupled with initiatives to attract and retain tech firms that are aligned with Hawai'i's values, can support the growth of this sector in ways that reinforce, rather than undermine, the islands' social and environmental priorities.

Adding value to local resources is another critical strategy for diversification. Agriculture is an obvious candidate, but it must be reimagined for the twenty-first century. Traditional large-scale export models have proven vulnerable to global commodity price fluctuations and supply chain disruptions. Instead, Hawai'i can focus on developing value-added agricultural products that command premium prices because of their quality, authenticity, and connection to place. Examples include specialty coffees, cacao, honey, taro-based products, seaweed, and artisanal food products that emphasize local ingredients and sustainable practices. Hawai'i Department of Agriculture (2023) outlines strategic goals for strengthening Hawai'i's food and agricultural systems in its Report on Sustainable Food Systems Working Group [2]. It emphasizes the necessity of a coordinated, systems-level approach to transform Hawai'i's food and agricultural landscape, especially in the face of climate change, economic inequality, and historical injustices. Key themes include strengthening regional food hubs, improving access to land and water for small farmers, building local capacity in food production, and aligning public procurement to support local agriculture. This report highlights successful pilot programs and case studies, including initiatives led by Kamehameha Schools, the Office of Hawaiian Affairs, and other Native Hawaiian organizations. These programs model collaborative land stewardship and Indigenous knowledge integration. One significant takeaway is the recommendation for Hawai'i to adopt food sovereignty principles and support regenerative agriculture. It also calls for better state-level coordination and investment, including institutional alignment across education, health, and economic development sectors to maximize impact. Overall, the working group advocates for a values-driven food system rooted in equity, sustainability, and community empowerment.

UHERO (2021) analyzes Hawai'i's agricultural economy and shows that Hawai'i's agricultural economy has faced significant shifts following the decline of large-scale sugarcane and pineapple plantations, leading to decreased total agricultural sales [3]. However, the extent of this decline varies depending on whether prices are adjusted using the Consumer or Producer Price Index[1]. The smaller increase in wholesale agricultural prices compared to consumer prices suggests a deeper decline in the economic value of Hawai'i's agricultural production than in its physical output. Despite favorable soils and climates, Hawai'i has seen slower productivity growth compared to other regions, largely due to high labor costs and low labor productivity. These issues are tied not to higher wages, but to limited mechanization caused by the small, fragmented, and geographically

[1] The Consumer Price Index (CPI) measures the average change over time in the prices paid by consumers for a basket of goods and services, reflecting the cost of living. In contrast, the Producer Price Index (PPI) tracks the average change in selling prices received by domestic producers for their output, capturing inflation at the wholesale or production level.

challenging nature of agricultural land in the state. Unlike national trends, Hawai'i's agricultural output is becoming more concentrated on smaller farms, which may further hinder productivity. A large portion of the state's cropland remains idle, presenting opportunities for high-value or niche crop production that aligns with local demand. Advances in technology such as AI and robotics could help overcome mechanization barriers, especially on small-scale farms. However, weak data collection, inconsistent metrics, and limited sampling in surveys obscure emerging trends and make policy planning difficult. Better data collection is needed to clarify the future of Hawai'i's agriculture.

Aquaculture and sustainable fisheries management also offer opportunities to add value while respecting environmental limits. With its rich ocean resources, Hawai'i is well positioned to lead in sustainable seafood production, blending traditional Hawaiian fishpond practices with modern technology to create a model of aquaculture that supports local food security and cultural revitalization. Hawai'i Sea Grant describes the Hawai'i Aquaculture Collaborative (HAC) as an initiative that integrates traditional Hawaiian fishpond practices with modern technology to advance sustainable seafood production [4]. HAC, part of the Pacific Region Aquaculture & Coastal Resource Hub, unites industry, research, and community partners to expand sustainable aquaculture and bolster Hawai'i's food security and economic diversity. Honoring 800 years of local fish- and seaweed-culture traditions, HAC leverages modern technology, shared research, and coordinated funding, such as the Center for Tropical and Subtropical Aquaculture (CTSA) grants and community-based loans, to accelerate pilot projects and workforce development. Monthly "Tech & Research Brown Bags," internships, and statewide events foster knowledge exchange and policy advocacy, while legislative tracking supports favorable aquaculture bills. Ultimately, HAC aims to build a collaborative talent pipeline, strengthen supply chains, and scale restorative, culturally rooted aquaculture across the islands.

UH News (2024) reports that UH researcher André Seale has received two Sea Grant awards totaling $315,759 to remove bottlenecks in restoring Hawaiian fishpond aquaculture [5]. Working with PhD student Tyler Goodearly, Seale is developing species-specific spawning protocols for the sea cucumber Stichopus horrens, aiming to overcome reproductive dysfunction and supply Hawaiian ponds with this high-value, sediment-cleaning species. A parallel study with graduate assistant Reilly Merlo tackles the unreliable recruitment of hatchery-raised striped mullet ('ama'ama). By exposing fingerlings to controlled salinity and temperature regimes and tracking growth, stress, and osmoregulation markers, the team seeks to "train" juveniles for better survival and growth once released into natural fishponds. Together, the projects bolster food security and offer climate-adaptive, culturally grounded strategies for sustainable aquaculture in Hawai'i.

The creative industries represent another vital avenue for diversification. Hawai'i's artists, musicians, filmmakers, designers, and storytellers have a wealth of narratives, traditions, and perspectives that are globally distinctive and highly marketable. DBEDT (2024) reports that Hawai'i's creative sector employed 55,619 workers across 5,353 establishments in 2023, accounting for 6.3 % of all civilian jobs and generating $5.6 billion in GDP (5.3 % of the state total) [6]. Jobs grew 1.1 % annually from 2013 to 2023, outpacing overall state job growth (0.7 %). Among 13 industry groups, only Film, TV, Video Production/Distribution, Cable and Media Streaming qualified as a high performing "emerging" driver. Nine groups including Business Consulting, Computer Services, and Performing Arts were "transitioning," growing locally but losing national share. Three groups (Cultural Activities, Publishing & Information, and Radio/TV Broadcasting) experienced a decline. County analysis shows Honolulu hosting 72% of creative jobs, with brisker relative growth on Hawai'i Island. The report urges deeper study of digital media, export potential, and talent-development initiatives such as Creative Lab Hawai'i to sustain sector momentum.

State Foundation on Culture and the Arts (2024) reports that Hawai'i's state arts agency managed a $26.7 million FY 2023 budget, combining general funds, a $17.5 million Bishop Museum grant, $2 million for 'Iolani Palace, and federal National Endowment for the Arts (NEA) support [7]. Core programs such as Grants & Community Arts, Art in Public Places (APP), Arts Education, and the King Kamehameha Celebration Commission advanced a vision of "a thriving and vibrant Hawai'i enriched by culture and the arts." APP oversaw 5,194 relocatable works and 309 site-specific commissions, added 71 new pieces, and dedicated the Filipino Veterans WWII monument. Capitol Modern (the rebranded State Art Museum) hosted 120 events and the sensory-friendly Under the Blue installation. Artists-in-the-Schools funded 120 residencies reaching 12,850 students, while the inaugural Hawai'i State Poet Laureate and Folk & Traditional Arts grant deepened cultural engagement statewide.

Education and research also have an integral role to play. Hawai'i's institutions of higher learning, particularly the UH system, can be leveraged to build expertise in critical fields such as marine science, astronomy, indigenous knowledge systems, and climate change adaptation. By becoming a global leader in areas where Hawai'i has natural advantages, the state can attract students, researchers, and funding from around the world, driving economic activity in a way that reinforces rather than exploits its unique environment and culture. University of Hawai'i System (2018) reports that the UH Strategic Directions 2015–2021 establishes five goals: Hawai'i Graduation Initiative (raise degree completion, targeting Native Hawaiians, low-income and rural students); Hawai'i Innovation Initiative (spark a $1 billion research-and-innovation sector); Twenty-First Century Facilities (create sustainable, digitally enabled campuses and optimize space); Mission-Focused System (become a foremost indigenous-serving, sustainability-driven university); and High Performing System (achieve efficient, transparent, financially diverse operations) [8]. Major revisions split the former High Performing Mission Driven System (HPMS) objective, embed tactics on online learning, affordability and facility utilization, and add metrics such as net-zero progress and active technology licenses to track success.

Kana'iaupuni and Ledward (2013) report that a Hawai'i Cultural Influences in Education survey of 600 teachers across 62 middle- and high-school campuses finds culture-based instruction widespread but most intensive in Hawaiian-medium and Hawaiian-focused charter schools [9]. Teachers who integrate heritage language, family/community involvement, place-based content, culturally congruent pedagogy, and authentic assessment—aligned with Center for Research on Education, Diversity and Excellence (CREDE) "best practices"—create classrooms rated higher in relevance, relationships, and rigor. Their students demonstrate greater cultural knowledge, school connectedness, community stewardship, environmental action, and academic motivation. The authors argue that teacher preparation, curriculum design, and accountability systems must embed cultural relevance to narrow Native Hawaiian achievement gaps and elevate outcomes for all learners.

Healthcare and life sciences represent another promising sector. Building on its existing healthcare infrastructure, Hawai'i could expand its capacity for biomedical research, health innovation, and telemedicine. These industries offer high-wage jobs, align with the state's aging population trends, and can be developed in ways that respect the islands' ecological and social fabrics. Withy, Joo, and Potter (2022) document Hawai'i's worst physician deficit in more than a decade: only 2,812 full-time-equivalent (FTE) physicians were practicing in 2020, versus a modeled need for 3,522 FTEs, creating a statewide shortage of 710–1,008 FTEs [10]. Primary care accounts for 412 FTEs of the gap, while specialty shortages are most acute in pulmonary/critical care, infectious disease, and colorectal surgery. Hawai'i Island faces a deficit exceeding 50%, and even O'ahu—home to most doctors—falls well below demand. The workforce is aging (mean age 54; 23% ≥ 65) and shrank during COVID-19, when 10% retired or closed practices. The authors urge rural residencies, loan-repayment incentives, and expanded telehealth to stabilize recruitment and retention.

Hawai'i Department of Health (2021) outlines the Healthy Hawai'i Strategic Plan 2030, a 10-year roadmap to prevent and reduce chronic disease statewide [11]. Chronic conditions already affect 64% of adults and, if unchecked, will cost Hawai'i an estimated $9 billion in direct medical expenses and $3.2 billion in lost productivity annually by 2030. This plan coordinates six program areas—asthma, cancer, diabetes, heart disease & stroke, physical activity & nutrition, and tobacco—across four sectors: Community Design & Access, Education, Health Care, and Worksites. Emphasis is on policy, systems, and environmental change that makes healthy choices the default. Sector-specific objectives include expanding healthy-food incentives, building low-stress walking and cycling networks, integrating health IT and team-based care, and adopting tobacco-free and breastfeeding-supportive worksite policies. Health equity is central, targeting disparities tied to income, ethnicity, geography, and social determinants.

Chang, Raethel, and Hoshide (2024) report that Hawai'i's hospitals, clinics, and long-term-care facilities listed 34,181 budgeted non-physician positions in 2024, with 4,669 vacancies—14% of the workforce [12]. Hospitals carry the largest burden (2,008 open slots), followed by skilled-nursing and long-term-care centers (992). Registered nurses (RNs) remain the most difficult to recruit, accounting for 1,043 openings, but other critical shortages persist: Certified Nurse Aides (CNAs) face 636 vacancies, Licensed Practical Nurses (LPNs) 242, and ultrasound and radiologic technologists both show double-digit vacancy rates as local training pipelines lag demand. Targeted programs are easing some gaps: specialty RN transition-to-practice residencies, CNA-to-LPN "glidepath" upskilling, and in-house surgical-tech academies have trimmed vacancy percentages in participating facilities. Nevertheless, Hawai'i's rapidly aging population and the continued exodus of younger professionals to the mainland mean the overall shortfall will likely grow without sustained investments in education capacity, rural placements, and financial incentives. This report identifies critical shortages across key professions, including nursing, primary care, and specialty fields, and stresses the urgent need for strategic investments in education, training, and recruitment. Cultivating industries rooted in Hawai'i's place-based strengths mean acknowledging that not every sector is appropriate or desirable. Industrial manufacturing, for instance, may offer economic benefits elsewhere but could be ill-suited to the ecological sensitivities and limited land base of the islands. Economic development must be selective and intentional, ensuring that new industries fit within Hawai'i's cultural, social, and environmental context.

Kaiser et al. (2019) report that conventional metrics such as GDP obscure Hawai'i's heavy dependence on "unpriced" natural capital and hence mis-signal policy priorities [13]. They propose statewide "green accounting" that tracks environmental stocks and depreciation alongside market output, using case studies to show what is at stake. In the Ko'olau watershed, a 31% loss of forest cover—driven by feral pigs, invasive miconia and urban creep—would cut Pearl Harbor Aquifer recharge by 41 million gallons per day, forcing desalination decades earlier and wiping out US $1.4–2.6 billion in present value; total deforestation could raise that bill to US $4.6–8.5 billion. The same disturbance would dump 28,000 tons of sediment annually, triggering US $26–123 million in dredging or filtration costs and further reef damage. Shoreline assets are equally critical: O'ahu's public beaches alone generate about US $700 million per year in recreational surplus and underpin an $11 billion visitor economy yet are eroding under sea-level rise and coastal armoring. The authors frame invasive species as a "silent invasion" that degrades forests, drives up public budgets and threatens biodiversity. They recommend natural-capital satellite accounts, preventive spending on biosecurity, a water-use surcharge earmarked for forest care, and proactive, ecosystem-wide planning to keep Hawaii's environment—and thus its economy—intact.

Natural Energy Laboratory of Hawai'i Authority (NELHA) describes its leadership in sustainable innovation through its operation of the Hawai'i Ocean Science and Technology Park (HOST Park) [14]. It serves as a hub for sustainable technology, ocean science, and renewable energy initiatives. HOST Park[2] fosters groundbreaking solutions to global challenges like food security, clean energy, and climate change by offering access to unique resources such as deep ocean and surface seawater. These assets

[2] https://www.hostpark.io/.

support a wide range of commercial, research, and educational ventures, including aquaculture, desalination, and clean energy development. With a diverse community of over 40 businesses and organizations, HOST Park showcases collaborative innovation through guided tours, virtual explorations, and hands-on projects. The park's scenic location and advanced infrastructure make it an attractive site for both scientific discovery and ecological stewardship. Its mission reflects Hawai'i's commitment to economic diversification, environmental responsibility, and a future shaped by sustainable development and visionary leadership.

A diversified economy will be better able to withstand external shocks, whether from global economic downturns, pandemics, geopolitical instability, or climate change. When one sector experiences a decline, others can provide stability and support recovery. Diversification also encourages a more dynamic and innovative economy, where ideas cross-pollinate between sectors, and entrepreneurship thrives. The World Bank's Economic Diversification Guidance Note stresses that countries relying on a narrow set of commodities or tourist receipts face chronic volatility, weak job creation, and "Dutch disease" pressures [15]. Diversification, defined as widening and upgrading the export basket and shifting domestic output toward higher-productivity sectors and firms, is especially urgent for resource-rich, low-income, and small-island economies such as those in the Pacific. The Note proposes a four-pillar playbook: (1) a transparent, competition-friendly incentive regime; (2) hard and soft infrastructure that slashes trade, logistics, and energy costs; (3) labor-, land-, and finance-market reforms that let capital and workers move quickly; and (4) time-bound, evidence-based industrial policies co-designed through robust public-private dialogue. Falling transport and ICT (Information and Communication Technology) costs, the rise of services trade, and entry into global value chains create new diversification pathways, particularly for women-owned enterprises, yet they also expose countries to supply-chain shocks that policy must anticipate and insure against.

World Trade Organization (2021) explores how international trade both exposes economies to shocks and equips them to withstand and recover from them [16]. The report defines economic resilience as the capacity of households, firms, and governments to prevent, prepare for, cope with, and bounce back from crises. Deep global integration means hazards such as pandemics, extreme weather, cyber-attacks, and supply-chain disruptions can propagate quickly, yet trade simultaneously provides diversification of suppliers and markets, access to critical goods, and faster post-shock growth. Analyses show merchandise trade rebounded faster than GDP after the COVID-19 collapse, while services trade lagged. Policies that aim at self-sufficiency or reshoring typically raise costs and increase domestic vulnerability; instead, resilience is best strengthened through trade diversification, streamlined customs, efficient services, and transparent rules. The report urges greater multilateral cooperation—clarifying export-restriction rules, enhancing notification requirements, deepening digital-trade work, and coordinating on risk-reduction measures—to ensure open, predictable flows that reduce volatility and foster inclusive, sustainable recovery.

Diversification does not happen automatically. It requires coordinated policy leadership, investment in infrastructure, strategic education and workforce development, and strong partnerships between government, the private sector, educational institutions, and communities. Public investment must prioritize enabling infrastructure such as broadband internet access, renewable energy grids, research facilities, and transportation networks that connect communities sustainably. Education systems must align more closely with emerging industry needs. This includes updating curricula to emphasize skills like critical thinking, digital literacy, environmental stewardship, entrepreneurship, and intercultural competence. It also means creating stronger pathways from education to employment through internships, apprenticeships, mentorships, and industry partnerships. At the same time, government policies must incentivize responsible private sector investment and innovation. Tax credits, grants, and regulatory frameworks should favor businesses that align with Hawai'i's vision for sustainable development. Similarly, procurement policies can prioritize local businesses and socially responsible enterprises, helping to grow the kinds of companies that will strengthen the economy while serving community interests.

3 Agriculture Reimagined: From Pineapples to Regenerative Food Systems

Agriculture once played a dominant role in Hawai'i's economy, shaping not only the islands' landscapes but also their communities and labor history. Sugarcane and pineapple plantations once blanketed thousands of acres across the archipelago, dominating economic output and employment. For over a century, the agricultural sector was a cornerstone of Hawai'i's identity and economy. However, with the decline of plantation agriculture in the late twentieth century, local agriculture has steadily diminished in economic importance. Today, agriculture contributes only about 0.5% to the state's GDP, a stark contrast to its historic role. Yet, despite this decline, agriculture in Hawai'i holds untapped potential to address contemporary challenges including food security, rural economic development, environmental restoration, and cultural revitalization.

In reimagining agriculture, Hawai'i must move beyond a nostalgic view of its plantation past and embrace a regenerative, diversified, and locally grounded food system. One of the most promising trends is the expansion of farm-to-school and farm-to-table programs. By building stable local markets through institutional purchasing agreements, schools, hospitals, and restaurants can become anchor customers for small and medium-sized farms. Farm-to-school programs not only create reliable demand for local produce but also educate children about healthy eating, agriculture, and sustainability. Farm-to-table movements enhance culinary tourism, create high-value markets for local farmers, and foster stronger relationships between consumers and producers.

The Hawai'i Farm to School Network (HFSN), supported by the Hawai'i Public Health Institute, is a statewide initiative that envisions a holistic education system integrating food, farming, and environmental stewardship to improve health and academic outcomes [17]. The Network focuses on building regenerative community food systems and positioning Hawai'i as a model of agro-ecological education for the Pacific region. Key goals include enhancing food education through 'āina-based learning, increasing access to locally grown food in schools and early care settings, strengthening community health, and building shared leadership across island networks. HFSN emphasizes the core elements of farm to school—education, school gardens, local food procurement, and community engagement—while highlighting documented benefits such as improved student nutrition, increased willingness to try healthy foods, and positive economic and environmental impacts. Through partnerships with schools, community organizations, and state agencies, the Network fosters collaboration across islands to create a sustainable and resilient local food system rooted in youth leadership and cultural values.

Leavitt, Yamane & Soldner (2024) shows the growth and significance of Hawaii's farm-to-table movement, emphasizing sustainable agriculture's role in preserving natural resources, supporting local economies, and promoting healthier lifestyles [18]. The movement leverages Hawaii's fertile land and climate to foster environmentally responsible farming practices, such as crop diversity, water conservation, and soil health enhancement. These practices support local economies by reducing reliance on chemical inputs, creating jobs, and retaining food dollars within the community. Sustainable farming also produces fresher, more nutritious food with lower chemical exposure. The post spotlights several prominent farm-to-table restaurants—Merriman's, The Pig and the Lady, The Mill House, Farmhouse Café, and Hale Kealoha—that source ingredients locally and prioritize community and cultural connections. It further encourages community involvement through farmers' markets, CSA, educational programs, and policy advocacy. The post concludes by urging both residents and visitors to participate in the farm-to-table movement as a pathway to a more resilient and sustainable Hawaii.

Value-added agriculture represents another significant opportunity. Hawai'i's climatic diversity allows for the production of premium crops that, when processed into higher-value products, can command premium prices on global markets. Specialty coffees from Kona and Ka'u, artisanal chocolates made from locally grown cacao, taro chips from heirloom kalo varieties, honey from native ňōhi blossoms, and breadfruit flour from 'ulu are just a few examples. By focusing on quality, authenticity, and the unique cultural narratives attached to these products, Hawai'i can create niche markets that distinguish its agricultural goods from mass-produced imports. Elevitch and Love (2017) provide practical insights into the development of value-added agricultural products in Hawai'i [19]. This guide provides practical strategies for Hawai'i farmers to improve profitability through value-added agriculture. They define value-added as any practice that differentiates a crop—through superior cultivation, harvest timing, processing, packaging, branding, customer service, or niche marketing—and captures a larger share of the retail dollar. This guide walks growers from crop and variety selection, quality-driven field and post-harvest techniques, and minimal-risk pilot processing to market research, pricing, certifications, and food-safety compliance. Case studies—Kona coffee, persimmon drying, fig preserves, lychee bagging—illustrate how careful cost-of-production analysis, creative packaging, and storytelling convert losses into sustainable profits. Detailed checklists, crop profiles, and resource lists help producers match products to site conditions, target high-value visitor and ethnic markets, and continually innovate while managing regulatory and financial risks.

Regenerative agricultural practices are essential to ensuring that Hawai'i's agricultural revival is environmentally sustainable. Regenerative farming emphasizes soil health, biodiversity, water conservation, and reduced chemical inputs. Healthy Soils Hawai'i (HSH) is a one-year pilot led by Jayme Barton (Hawai'i Agriculture Research Center) and Stephanie Mock (O'ahu Resource Conservation & Development) to show how climate-smart practices can store carbon and boost soil health statewide [20]. Five farms and ranches on O'ahu and Maui—together overseeing 41,000 acres—installed more than ten best-management practices, including multi-species cover crops, reduced/no-till, adaptive grazing, compost applications, and upgraded irrigation. Producers received flat-rate incentives plus technical assistance, and paired monitoring plots were sampled with UH's beta Hawai'i Soil Health Tool. Fields managed with Best Management Practices (BMPs) for at least two years already displayed higher organic carbon and biological activity. HSH also convened over 20 partner organizations, gave soil-health presentations at ten conferences, and surveyed islandwide producers: 87% listed soil health as a top concern, but labor, time, and up-front costs remain major barriers—especially for farms under 20 acres. The report urges larger, locally tailored incentive payments and ongoing technical support to speed soil-carbon sequestration across Hawai'i's diverse working lands.

Levin (2022) profiles a "Hawaiian Renaissance" in agriculture that weds food security to cultural revival [21]. Pioneered by Eric Enos's Ka'ala Farm in Wai'anae, community groups across the archipelago are re-creating ancestral systems—lo'i taro terraces, ahupua'a strip farms, breadfruit agroforestry, coconut groves, stone-walled fishponds—to practice aloha 'āina ("love of the land"). These projects restore kalo, 'uala, niu, and other canoe crops, teach at-risk youth, and rebuild fish stocks, all while honoring elders' protocols that link food, language, and spirituality. Landowners such as Kamehameha Schools now balance revenue with stewardship, and nonprofits like Waipā Foundation and 'Āina Momona blend farming with health and education. Advocates argue that traditional methods could again produce two-thirds of Hawai'i's food, cut imports, and improve Native Hawaiian well-being—proving that human and land "breathe life" into each other.

Agritourism provides another promising pathway for revitalizing agriculture. By offering farm tours, workshops, farm stays, and pick-your-own produce experiences, farmers can diversify their revenue streams while educating visitors about Hawai'i's agricultural heritage and contemporary food systems. Agritourism strengthens the rural economy, fosters cultural exchange, and deepens visitors' appreciation for local food and environmental stewardship. Successful examples include coffee farm tours in Kona, lavender farm visits in Upcountry Maui, and educational programs at taro farms in Hanalei Valley. GoFarm Hawai'i provides practical guidance for farmers interested in developing agritourism ventures [22]. This guide outlines a variety of agritourism activities, such as farm tours, farm-to-table meals, and pick-your-own produce experiences, revealing their potential to diversify farm income and educate visitors about local agriculture. It also addresses regulatory considerations and offers tools to assess a farm's readiness for hosting visitors, making it an essential starting point for those exploring agritourism opportunities in Hawai'i.

Swette Center for Sustainable Food Systems (2023) analyzes how agritourism can help Hawai'i's 8,000-plus small farms—66% of which operate on fewer than nine acres—diversify income while protecting fragile ecosystems and Native Hawaiian culture [23]. Through a literature review, policy scan and 17 interviews with growers, tour operators, consultants and officials, this report finds that agritourism is still practiced by only 4% of farms because of patchwork county regulations, complex permits, high liability costs and limited marketing know-how. Successful operators pair on-farm experiences (tours, tastings, farm-to-table events) with value-added products and educational narratives that honor ahupua'a land stewardship. Recommended actions include statewide online resource portals, county agritourism liaisons, grant-writing support, field surveys to gauge ecological carrying capacity, a voluntary sustainability rating for visitors, and mandatory consultation with Kānaka Maoli in planning decisions. Implemented thoughtfully, agritourism could strengthen local food security, rural economies and cultural revitalization.

However, realizing the potential of a reimagined agricultural sector requires addressing persistent and significant barriers. Land access remains a major challenge. Much of Hawai'i's agricultural land is either held by a few large landowners or has been converted to residential and commercial uses. Small farmers often struggle to secure affordable, long-term leases. Water rights are another critical constraint, particularly in areas where plantation-era irrigation infrastructure has fallen into disrepair or where competing demands for water create conflict. Intergenerational succession is a looming issue, as many existing farmers are aging without clear plans for handing down their operations to the next generation. Additionally, the high cost of inputs—seeds, fertilizers, equipment, and labor—makes farming financially precarious. Overcoming these barriers requires a coordinated, multi-pronged policy approach. State and county governments can offer tax incentives for landowners who lease land for local food production, as well as tax credits for farmers who practice regenerative agriculture. Land trusts and cooperative land ownership models can help secure affordable farmland for small farmers. Strengthening agricultural education programs, including K-12 school gardens and university-level agri-entrepreneurship courses, is essential for cultivating the next generation of farmers and food entrepreneurs. Extension services, incubator farms, and access to microloans and technical assistance can support beginning farmers in navigating the complexities of agricultural business management.

Marketing and branding are also critical components of reimagining Hawai'i's agriculture. Statewide campaigns can promote the value of buying local, connecting consumers emotionally to the people and places behind their food. Certification programs such as "Grown in Hawai'i" or regenerative agriculture labels can build consumer trust and create market premiums for local products. Storytelling that weaves together food, culture, and place can differentiate Hawai'i's agricultural products in crowded global markets, appealing to consumers seeking authenticity, sustainability, and connection. Hawai'i Department of Agriculture describes the Hawai'i Seal of Quality program, a statewide branding initiative aimed at protecting the integrity and value of Hawai'i-branded farm and value-added products [24]. By certifying products that meet strict quality standards, this program helps consumers easily identify genuine Hawai'i-grown or Hawai'i-made premium goods. This initiative is crucial for building consumer trust, enhancing brand recognition, and creating market premiums that support the growth and sustainability of Hawai'i's agricultural economy. Hawai'i Agricultural Foundation presents Localicious Hawai'i, a year-long marketing campaign aimed at promoting local agriculture and fishing industries [25]. This initiative recognizes restaurants and businesses that source local ingredients, helping to connect consumers emotionally to the people and places behind their food. By showcasing local culinary talent and agricultural products, Localicious Hawai'i strengthens relationships between consumers and producers while enhancing the visibility, value, and appeal of Hawai'i's food systems.

At the same time, it is important to acknowledge that Hawai'i's agricultural future will not look like its past. Plantation agriculture was built on monocultures, exported commodities, and exploitative labor systems. Reimagining agriculture today means embracing the diversity of crops, farm sizes, ownership models, and market channels. It means centering indigenous knowledge, environmental stewardship, community resilience, and food sovereignty. A successful agricultural sector in Hawai'i will focus less on maximizing calorie exports and more on delivering value in nutritional, cultural, ecological, and economic terms for local communities. Hawai'i's movement toward regenerative, value-added, and community-connected agriculture is already underway. Initiatives like the GoFarm Hawai'i farmer training program, the Farm to School Hui, the Hawai'i Ulu Cooperative, and the Hawai'i Good Food Alliance are laying the groundwork. Local food hubs, community-supported agriculture programs, and farmers markets are expanding access to local food. Chefs, restaurateurs, and cultural practitioners are increasingly sourcing and celebrating local ingredients. Policy momentum is building, with state-level discussions around expanding local procurement targets and investing in agricultural infrastructure.

Ultimately, agriculture reimagined in Hawai'i is about more than food production. It is about restoring relationships—to land, to culture, to community, and to future generations. It is about cultivating a sense of abundance rooted not in extraction but in reciprocity. It is about reasserting Hawai'i's capacity to feed itself, to sustain its people, and to steward its 'āina for centuries to come. Through visionary leadership, strategic investment, and deep community collaboration, agriculture can once again become a vibrant and vital part of Hawai'i's economy.

4 The Rise of the Blue Economy

The ocean defines Hawai'i in ways both visible and profound. Covering more than 99% of the state's jurisdictional area, the ocean is not simply a scenic backdrop for tourism; it is the fundamental arena in which Hawai'i's future prosperity and resilience must be shaped. As the global community turns its attention increasingly toward sustainable development and climate adaptation, the concept of the "blue economy", defined as economic activity derived from ocean resources in a way that supports ecosystem health, emerges as an essential pathway for Hawai'i's transformation. At its core, the blue economy offers Hawai'i an opportunity to pivot from a service-heavy model overly dependent on visitor arrivals to a diversified, innovation-driven economy rooted in the islands' unique strengths. Key sectors within the blue economy are already beginning to take shape, signaling substantial potential for expansion.

One of the most promising sectors is aquaculture, particularly sustainable fish and shellfish farming. Hawai'i has natural advantages in aquaculture, including abundant clean seawater, year-round favorable temperatures, and expertise developed through decades of research. Companies such as Ocean Era and Blue Ocean Mariculture are pioneering new models of offshore and nearshore aquaculture. Ocean Era[3] is advancing sustainable practices for finfish farming, with a strong emphasis on minimizing environmental impacts and supporting local food security. Miculka (2021) reports that Blue Ocean Mariculture[4], located in Kailua-Kona, operates the United States' first finfish farm certified by the Aquaculture Stewardship Council, marking a milestone in sustainable aquaculture [26]. The company raises Hawaiian Kanpachi (almaco jack) in offshore submersible pens without antibiotics or hormones, using non-GMO feed and maintaining rigorous environmental and social responsibility standards. Its certification reflects a commitment to responsible seafood production and highlights aquaculture's potential to diversify Hawai'i's economy by creating stable, local jobs while reducing ecological impact and dependence on imported seafood. These enterprises demonstrate that aquaculture, if managed responsibly, can create high-value food products, reduce pressure on wild fish stocks, and contribute to rural economic development.

McDaniel also profiles Blue Ocean Mariculture's kanpachi pens as a preview of offshore aquaculture's growth [27]. Proponents cite Hawai'i's deep, near-shore waters and food-security goals; the farm already ships 800 tons of fish a year to local and mainland restaurants. Critics warn of escapes, disease and waste, though federal agencies argue newer cage designs, strong currents and real-time monitoring minimize impacts. Innovation is moving toward integrated multi-trophic systems that pair finfish with seaweed and shellfish, like Ocean Era's planned rotating pens off 'Ewa Beach. Traditionalists such as activist Walter Ritte counter that restored Hawaiian fishponds offer a lower-risk, culturally rooted path to sustainable seafood.

Beyond food production, the marine biotechnology sector holds untapped promise. Marine organisms are a rich source of novel compounds that can be harnessed for pharmaceuticals, enzymes, cosmetics, and even biofuels. The extraordinary biodiversity found in Hawai'i's marine ecosystems offer a competitive advantage in this field. Universities and private firms can collaborate to research and commercialize discoveries such as anti-inflammatory agents from algae, anticancer compounds

[3] https://ocean-era.com/

[4] https://bofish.com/

from deep-sea organisms, and innovative biomaterials. Kumar et al. (2025) provides a comprehensive review of the biomedical potential of marine algae [28]. The authors explore how bioactive compounds such as polysaccharides and polyphenols found in marine algae can be sustainably harnessed for antiviral and anticancer therapies. They emphasize the need for interdisciplinary collaboration and environmentally responsible aquaculture practices to advance this field. This work is critical for understanding the therapeutic applications of marine algae and highlights the role of research partnerships between universities and private firms in developing next-generation biotechnologies.

The Hawai'i Institute of Marine Biology[5] (HIMB) shows its leadership in marine science research through its focus on marine biotechnology in Research [29]. HIMB's projects include the discovery and development of bioactive compounds from marine organisms, supporting advancements in pharmaceuticals and innovative biomaterials. HIMB actively engages in collaborations with private firms to translate scientific discoveries into commercial applications, fostering both economic development and environmental stewardship. HIMB's efforts exemplify how academic-industry partnerships can drive Hawai'i's blue economy forwards while honoring sustainability principles. By investing in marine biotech research and creating pathways for commercialization, Hawai'i can foster high-wage, knowledge-based jobs while maintaining a commitment to environmental stewardship.

Another critical domain is ocean data and surveillance. Advances in satellite tracking, autonomous sensor deployment, and big data analytics are reshaping how societies monitor ocean conditions, maritime activity, and environmental change. Hawai'i's geographic position in the central Pacific, coupled with existing strengths at UH in oceanography, climate science, and remote sensing, makes it a natural hub for ocean data innovation. Applications range from tracking illegal fishing and maritime trafficking to monitoring coral reef health and modeling sea-level rise. With strategic investment, Hawai'i could develop a globally recognized center for ocean intelligence, contributing not only to economic diversification but also to national and global security. Maritime workforce development is another essential piece of the puzzle. A thriving blue economy will require a skilled workforce proficient in fields such as vessel operations, marine engineering, underwater robotics, environmental monitoring, and maritime law.

[5] https://www.himb.hawaii.edu/.

Building strong educational pipelines, from high school career academies to community college certificates to advanced university degrees, will be vital. Partnerships between industry, educational institutions, and government agencies can ensure that training programs are aligned with the needs of emerging sectors. Workforce development must also prioritize inclusivity, ensuring that Native Hawaiian and local communities have access to the high-quality jobs generated by the blue economy.

The UH system stands as a critical asset in realizing this vision. With globally recognized programs in ocean sciences, marine biology, geology and geophysics, and environmental law, UH is uniquely positioned to anchor a statewide blue economy strategy. Translating research into commercial applications will require strengthening innovation hubs, supporting technology transfer offices, and fostering collaborations between academia and the private sector. Institutions such as the Hawai'i Natural Energy Institute, the School of Ocean and Earth Science and Technology (SOEST), and the Hawai'i Institute of Marine Biology can serve as engines of discovery and innovation.

Physical infrastructure must also evolve to support the blue economy. Investments are needed in ocean-friendly ports, aquaculture facilities, research vessels, satellite ground stations, and coastal resilience infrastructure. For example, expanding the capacity of the Pacific International Center for High Technology Research[6] (PICHTR) and the Natural Energy Laboratory of Hawai'i Authority[7] (NELHA) can provide spaces where startups and researchers pilot and scale new technologies. Coastal infrastructure investments must incorporate resilience to sea-level rise and extreme weather events, ensuring that the foundations of the blue economy are sustainable for future generations.

The U.S. Department of Energy (2022) outlines strategies to integrate marine renewable energy technologies into maritime markets [30]. This report emphasizes the need for investments in infrastructure such as ocean-friendly ports, aquaculture facilities, and research vessels to support the sustainable expansion of the blue economy. It provides a critical framework for understanding how energy innovations can address the unique power demands of coastal and island communities, by fostering technology innovations like wave-powered desalination, underwater charging, and offshore aquaculture. Through research, partnerships, and

[6] https://pichtr.org/.

[7] https://nelha.hawaii.gov/.

funding, this initiative supports sustainable energy solutions, ocean ecosystem health, economic resilience, and community-driven planning for climate adaptation.

The Blue Economy Strategic Plan (2021–2025), developed by the National Oceanic and Atmospheric Administration, outlines a comprehensive vision to sustainably develop ocean-related sectors while protecting marine ecosystems and supporting local communities [31]. The American Blue Economy, a vital economic sector that in 2018 contributed an estimated $373 billion to the U.S. GDP and supported 2.3 million jobs, demonstrating growth (5.8%) faster than the overall national economy (5.4%). This robust economic activity includes American seaports, which alone grew 17% from 2014–2018 to $5.4 trillion, representing nearly 26% of the national GDP. This plan acknowledges that the prosperity and security of the nation are fundamentally reliant on the understanding, health, and sustainable use of its Oceans, Coasts, and Great Lakes, particularly as 40% of the U.S. population (127 million people) resides in coastal counties. Organized around five core pillars—Marine Transportation, Ocean Exploration, Seafood Competitiveness, Tourism & Recreation, and Coastal Resilience—NOAA expands and strengthens this economy by actively leading agency-wide initiatives in these areas, along with cross-cutting internal focus areas and external opportunities. The agency achieves this by leveraging dynamic public-private partnerships, innovative Science, Technology, Engineering, and Math (STEM) education and outreach, transformative ocean science, and emerging technologies. Key efforts include the designation and expansion of National Marine Sanctuaries, the use of advanced uncrewed systems for various applications from stock assessments to hurricane forecasting, and the establishment of the Ocean Economic Satellite Account with the U.S. Bureau of Economic Analysis (BEA) to quantify the marine economy's value and inform economic recovery strategies. The plan itself was developed by the NOAA Blue Economy Executive Committee (NBEEC), which oversees its execution, ensuring alignment with national policies and a focus on accelerating contributions to a resilient and thriving economy.

The ocean economy includes jobs and businesses that rely on the ocean, like fishing, tourism, and shipping. The blue economy goes further by focusing on using the ocean in a way that protects it, helps people make a living, and supports long-term growth without harming the environment. The OECD report explores the enormous potential of ocean-based industries and their sustainable development over the coming decades

[32]. It projects that by 2030, the ocean economy could double in size, reaching over $3 trillion USD in value-added output and employing more than 40 million people globally. Major contributors to this growth include sectors such as offshore wind energy, aquaculture, maritime and coastal tourism, and seabed mining. However, this report cautions that this growth must be balanced with sustainable practices to avoid exacerbating marine pollution, overfishing, and habitat degradation. The OECD calls for improved international cooperation, enhanced ocean governance, and the integration of science, technology, and innovation in marine policy. It also reveals the role of emerging technologies, including biotechnology, robotics, and remote sensing, in improving ocean monitoring and sustainable exploitation. To ensure that the ocean economy supports inclusive and resilient development, this report recommends investing in marine education and training, creating transparent regulatory frameworks, and encouraging the private sector to adopt green innovations. The OECD emphasizes the need for ecosystem-based management and greater investment in ocean observation and research infrastructure.

Strategic policy frameworks will play a central role in guiding development. This includes updating permitting processes for aquaculture and marine energy projects to balance economic opportunity with environmental protection. It also involves creating incentives for sustainable practices, such as tax credits for ocean-friendly technologies or grants for community-based marine conservation initiatives. Regional collaborations with other Pacific Island nations and U.S. coastal states can amplify Hawai‘i's voice in shaping national and international ocean policies. Perhaps most importantly, the growth of the blue economy in Hawai‘i must be grounded in cultural respect and environmental ethics. Native Hawaiian knowledge systems, such as traditional ocean navigation, fishpond aquaculture (loko i‘a), and stewardship principles like the kapu system, offer powerful models for managing marine resources sustainably. Efforts to build the blue economy must engage and benefit Native Hawaiian communities, ensuring that economic development is not pursued at the expense of cultural integrity or environmental health.

The rise of the blue economy offers Hawai‘i a rare opportunity: to build a future where economic vitality, environmental stewardship, and cultural resilience reinforce each other rather than exist in tension. This transformation will not happen automatically. It will require visionary leadership, coordinated investments, inclusive workforce development, and a steadfast commitment to sustainability. By embracing its identity as a people of the ocean, Hawai'i can lead the world in demonstrating that prosperity and planet care are not mutually exclusive, but mutually dependent. Realizing the potential of the blue economy also means telling a new story about Hawai'i. The islands have long been portrayed primarily as a playground for tourists, an image that undervalues the deep wisdom, innovation, and resilience embedded in island communities. A thriving blue economy allows Hawai'i to redefine itself on the world stage: as a living laboratory for sustainable ocean innovation, as a custodian of precious marine ecosystems, and as a model for other coastal and island regions grappling with the challenges of the twenty-first century.

In this reimagined future, visitors to Hawai'i would not only experience the islands' natural beauty but also engage with its cutting-edge ocean technologies, tour offshore aquaculture farms, participate in coral reef restoration projects, and learn from indigenous ocean knowledge keepers. Students from around the world would come to study at Hawai'i's universities and research centers, drawn by the opportunity to learn about marine science, climate adaptation, and sustainable economies in a place where these concepts are not abstractions but daily realities. Local entrepreneurs would launch marine biotech startups, develop ocean-based renewable energy systems, and pioneer sustainable seafood brands, creating jobs that are rooted in both innovation and tradition. By aligning education, innovation, infrastructure, and policy around a shared vision of ocean-centered prosperity, Hawai'i can chart a course that honors its past while building a resilient and vibrant future.

5 Renewable Energy: Powering the Islands Sustainably

Hawai'i faces a paradox that defines both its economic vulnerabilities and its potential for leadership in sustainable development. Despite being rich in sun, wind, geothermal, and ocean energy, the islands rely on the energy resource imports, resulting in some of the highest utility rates in the United States. Hawaii State of Energy (2023) reports that the state remains heavily reliant on imported petroleum, making up over 80% of primary energy consumption and causing high energy costs [33]. While renewable energy sources are growing, they only accounted for 13.5% of consumption in 2020. This report emphasizes the importance of reducing dependence on fossil fuels to improve economic and environmental resilience. The dependence on imported fossil fuels not only strains household budgets and business costs but also exposes Hawai'i to global price volatility and supply chain disruptions. Recognizing these challenges, Hawai'i has set one of the most ambitious energy goals in the nation: achieving 100% renewable electricity by 2045. This vision reflects not only an environmental imperative but also an economic strategy for long-term resilience and prosperity.

Among the most dynamic opportunities lies in solar energy, which has seen explosive growth across the islands. Solar panels now adorn rooftops from urban Honolulu to rural Hāna, turning residential and commercial properties into decentralized power producers. Innovations in battery storage technology have accelerated this trend, enabling households and microgrids to store excess solar energy for nighttime use and grid stabilization. Community-based solar initiatives are also gaining momentum, allowing renters and multi-family dwellings to participate in the clean energy transition. By investing in distributed solar and storage, Hawai'i can not only reduce reliance on centralized fossil fuel plants but also empower communities to take control of their energy futures. Wind and geothermal energy offer additional, complementary opportunities. The open plains and ridgelines of Maui, Hawai'i Island, and Lana'i provide ideal conditions for wind energy development. Projects like the Kaheawa Wind Power facility on Maui have already demonstrated the viability of utility-scale wind power in Hawai'i's unique environment. The Kaheawa Wind 1 Project Summary outlines the continued operation of Maui's first wind farm without changes to its infrastructure [34]. It reveals the project's contributions to powering 17,000 homes annually, reducing fossil fuel dependence, and supporting Hawai'i's 100% renewable energy goal by 2045.

Geothermal energy, particularly from the volcanic heat reservoirs beneath Hawai'i Island, offers a stable and dispatchable renewable resource. The Puna Geothermal Venture (PGV), despite past setbacks, represents a critical asset in achieving baseload renewable energy generation. Gomes (2025) discusses the renewed momentum behind geothermal energy development in Hawai'i [35]. This article focuses on the PGV on Hawai'i Island, detailing state initiatives to expand geothermal production to meet renewable energy targets while addressing environmental and community concerns. It is important for understanding geothermal energy's role in diversifying Hawai'i's renewable energy portfolio and stresses the critical importance of community engagement in the expansion of such projects. Expanding wind and geothermal projects with careful environmental and cultural sensitivity can diversify Hawai'i's renewable energy portfolio and enhance grid stability.

Emerging sectors such as hydrogen and bioenergy also present promising avenues for innovation and economic diversification. Research and development initiatives at institutions like the HNEI are exploring the production of green hydrogen through electrolysis powered by renewable energy. Hydrogen can serve as a versatile energy carrier, supporting applications from transportation to long-duration energy storage. Meanwhile, bioenergy projects that utilize agricultural waste, algae, and other biomass sources can contribute to a circular economy, reducing waste streams while generating renewable power. Khanal presents the research focus of the Environment and Bioenergy Research Group at the University of Hawaiʻi at Mānoa [36]. This group's work centers on converting organic waste into bioenergy through processes such as anaerobic digestion and fermentation. Their research contributes significantly to Hawaiʻi's sustainable energy goals by promoting waste-to-energy technologies, reducing reliance on imported fuels, and advancing innovations in bioenergy systems tailored to the islands' unique environmental and economic context. The Hawaiʻi State Energy Office (2022) outlines the state's efforts to establish a Pacific Hydrogen Hub [37]. This release shows collaborative initiatives involving government agencies, research institutions, and private sector partners to leverage Hawaiʻi's renewable resources for green hydrogen production and to build supporting infrastructure. Strategic investment in these emerging technologies can position Hawaiʻi at the forefront of the global clean energy transition.

Beyond technology, renewable energy transformation offers profound workforce development opportunities. The shift to clean energy demands a new generation of skilled workers, including solar photovoltaic installers, wind turbine technicians, energy auditors, electricians, project managers, and policy analysts. Green jobs are inherently local: solar panels and wind turbines must be installed, maintained, and upgraded in the communities they serve. Workforce training programs at community colleges and technical schools, supported by partnerships with industry and government, can create pathways for residents to access these well-paying, future-oriented careers. Special attention must be given to ensuring that training programs reach historically marginalized communities, expanding economic opportunity as the energy transition unfolds. Clean energy also holds the promise of reducing cost burdens for households and businesses. High energy costs are a significant contributor to Hawaiʻi's overall high cost of living, affecting everything from housing affordability to food prices. By transitioning to locally produced renewable energy, the state can stabilize and eventually lower energy prices, providing broad-based economic benefits. However, the structure of this transition matters. If utility-scale renewable projects are developed without community input or without mechanisms to share economic benefits locally, they risk replicating existing inequalities.

Thus, balancing utility-scale renewable projects with community-based initiatives is essential. Large-scale solar and wind farms are necessary to meet statewide energy targets, but they must be developed with genuine community engagement, respect for cultural sites, and environmental stewardship. Hawaiian Electric provides an overview of the Community-Based Renewable Energy (CBRE) Program [38]. This overview explains how residents without the ability to install rooftop solar panels can subscribe to shared solar projects and receive utility bill credits. It outlines project phases, subscription steps, and the broader benefits of participation, showing the program's importance in expanding renewable energy access and promoting energy equity across diverse communities in Hawai'i. Maui Now (2023) reports on the launch of Hawai'i's first community-owned and community-designed solar projects on Moloka'i [39]. This article illustrates how local ownership and active community engagement can successfully drive renewable energy initiatives under the CBRE model. It shows the potential of shared solar projects to empower communities, promote energy self-sufficiency, and strengthen local energy resilience. Expanding CBRE programs can democratize access to clean energy and ensure that the benefits of the transition are widely distributed.

Resilience must be a central theme in all renewable energy planning. Hawai'i's geographic isolation makes grid reliability paramount. Distributed energy resources like rooftop solar, paired with microgrids and advanced energy management systems, can provide critical backup power during natural disasters or grid outages. Investing in a smarter, more decentralized grid architecture will enhance the islands' ability to withstand hurricanes, wildfires, and other climate-related threats. Equity, resilience, and innovation must work hand in hand. Indigenous knowledge and community wisdom should inform the development of renewable energy projects, ensuring that traditional land uses and cultural practices are respected. Native Hawaiian organizations and other community-based groups must be active partners, not passive stakeholders, in shaping the energy future.

Internationally, Hawai'i has the opportunity to lead by example. The state can become a model for other islands and coastal communities around the world grappling with similar energy and climate challenges. Knowledge sharing, technical exchanges, and partnerships with other Pacific Island nations and global networks focused on sustainable energy can amplify Hawai‘i's impact beyond its shores. In envisioning Hawai‘i's energy future, one sees a vibrant landscape where solar panels shimmer atop homes and schools, where offshore wind turbines gently turn beyond the horizon, where hydrogen-powered buses glide through city streets, and where microgrids keep lights on during storms. One sees a future where energy independence is not merely about technology, but about self-determination, community resilience, and living in harmony with the ‘āina.

6 Digital and Remote Work Economies

The COVID-19 pandemic fundamentally reshaped the global economy, and nowhere were the changes more visible than in the rapid normalization of remote work. For Hawai‘i, an economy historically reliant on tourism and defense spending, this shift presented an unexpected opportunity. By embracing the digital and remote work economies, Hawai‘i can diversify its economic base, retain local talent, attract knowledge workers from elsewhere, and create a more resilient, place-based economy that harmonizes with the islands' unique culture and environment.

One of the most promising trends emerging from this shift is the growth of tech entrepreneurship. Startups in sectors such as health technology, education technology, and ecommerce are sprouting across the islands, fueled by a combination of local ingenuity and the appeal of building companies in one of the world's most beautiful environments. Healthtech startups are leveraging Hawai‘i's unique demographic and geographic challenges to develop telemedicine solutions that can be exported globally. Telehealth has expanded significantly in the wake of the pandemic. With Hawai‘i's population dispersed across multiple islands and many rural communities facing limited access to specialized medical care, telehealth offers a critical solution. Remote consultations, diagnostics, and mental health services have become more commonplace, UH News (2022) shows the selection of Pear Suite, a healthcare technology startup founded by UH Mānoa [40]. Pear Suite focuses on addressing social determinants of health for older adults through a software-as-a-service platform, enhancing access to care, including telehealth services. This case exemplifies how Hawai‘i-based startups are leveraging local demographic and geographic challenges to develop scalable telemedicine solutions with national and global potential.

Blair (2023) examines the progress and remaining challenges in expanding telehealth services across Hawai'i [41]. This article reveals how telemedicine has enabled timely interventions, such as stroke care, particularly in remote and underserved communities, while stressing the ongoing need for investments in broadband access and digital equity. It is significant for understanding how telehealth addresses Hawai'i's unique healthcare delivery barriers and what is required to ensure its long-term success. Edtech ventures are responding to the need for improved distance learning infrastructure, particularly in rural and underserved areas. Ecommerce enterprises are enabling local artisans, farmers, and small businesses to reach national and international markets with products that emphasize Hawai'i's culture, craftsmanship, and sustainability. Teruya (2022) discusses the "Hawai'i Rising" initiative by showing the collaboration between Shopify and Mana Up to empower Native Hawaiian entrepreneurs through resource provisions and training to expand their online businesses [42]. This program enables local artisans and small businesses to reach broader national and international markets while emphasizing Hawai'i's culture, craftsmanship, and sustainability. It exemplifies how e-commerce platforms can support economic development and promote cultural preservation in underserved communities.

Remote learning and workforce upskilling also stand out as major opportunities, especially for residents of neighboring islands who have traditionally faced barriers to accessing higher education and professional development programs. The proliferation of online courses, boot camps, and certifications in fields such as software development, digital marketing, cybersecurity, and renewable energy has democratized access to skills training. Institutions like the UH system have expanded their online offerings, while community-based initiatives have worked to ensure that broadband access and digital literacy are not barriers to participation. By continuing to invest in remote education and training pathways, Hawai'i can cultivate a tech-savvy workforce capable of thriving in an increasingly digital global economy. Attracting digital nomads—remote workers who can live anywhere—is another strategy that has gained traction. Programs like Movers and Shakas sought to capitalize on the remote work trend by encouraging knowledge workers to relocate to Hawai'i while participating in community service and cultural immersion activities. This approach aimed not merely to attract talent, but to foster meaningful connections between newcomers and the local community. If designed carefully, such programs can help diversify Hawai'i's economy and revitalize communities, particularly in areas experiencing population decline.

However, the long-term viability of remote work attraction models depends heavily on several critical factors. Housing policy must ensure that the influx of higher-income remote workers does not exacerbate displacement pressures for kama'āina. Expanding affordable housing options, strengthening tenant protections, and promoting equitable development practices are essential to maintaining social cohesion and preventing economic stratification. Broadband access is another non-negotiable foundation for a thriving digital economy. While urban O'ahu enjoys relatively robust internet infrastructure, many rural areas and neighbor islands still face connectivity gaps. Public and private investment must prioritize universal high-speed broadband coverage, treating internet access as a basic utility rather than a luxury. Programs that subsidize broadband for low-income households and support digital literacy initiatives can help bridge the digital divide and ensure that all communities benefit from the opportunities of remote work and digital innovation.

Labor-market integration is equally important. It is not enough to attract remote workers from elsewhere; Hawai'i must also ensure that kama'āina have access to quality remote work opportunities. This includes promoting flexible work arrangements within local businesses, supporting entrepreneurship through incubators and accelerators, and fostering a culture of lifelong learning and skills adaptation. Hawaii News Now (2023) reports on the City and County of Honolulu's pilot initiative by showing how local government agencies are adopting flexible work schedules and telework options to address labor shortages and attract a more diverse workforce [43]. This initiative highlights the growing recognition of work-life balance as a critical factor in employment practices and stresses the government's role in leading efforts to promote flexible work arrangements and support broader labor-market integration in Hawai'i. Workforce development strategies should prioritize sectors where Hawai'i has a comparative advantage or can carve out a niche, such as marine sciences, renewable energy, indigenous knowledge systems, and sustainable agriculture technologies. The digital and remote work economy also offers a chance to reinforce Hawai'i's cultural strengths rather than erode them. Digital storytelling, virtual tourism, online cultural education, and e-commerce for traditional crafts can help preserve and disseminate Native Hawaiian culture and other local traditions to global audiences. Initiatives that center local voices and values in digital spaces can counterbalance homogenizing global trends and ensure that economic growth is aligned with cultural resilience.

Environmental sustainability must be a guiding principle in expanding the digital economy. Remote work reduces commuter traffic, which can lower carbon emissions and alleviate pressure on infrastructure. Smart planning of digital infrastructures such as energy-efficient data centers powered by renewable energy—can further enhance the environmental benefits of a digital economy. Hawai'i's leadership in climate resilience and renewable energy should be woven into its strategy for digital economic development. The experience of the pandemic also revealed that building social capital in a remote-first environment requires intentionality. Remote workers and digital entrepreneurs can feel isolated without deliberate efforts to foster community. Co-working spaces, hybrid professional meetups, volunteer programs, and cultural engagement opportunities can help weave remote workers into the social fabric of the islands. Encouraging a sense of kuleana—responsibility to place and community—among newcomers is critical to ensuring that remote work strengthens rather than weakens community bonds.

Policy frameworks at the state and county levels should explicitly support the growth of the digital and remote work economy. This could include tax incentives for startups and remote workers who establish roots in Hawai'i, grants for broadband expansion projects, funding for digital literacy and upskilling programs, and regulatory modernization to accommodate new forms of work and business. Public-private partnerships can play a catalytic role, pooling resources and expertise to accelerate Hawai'i's digital transformation. Metrics for success must go beyond GDP growth or the number of remote workers attracted. True success lies in creating an economy where kama'āina have access to fulfilling, well-paid work that allows them to stay rooted in their communities; where newcomers are integrated respectfully and contribute positively; and where economic growth reinforces rather than undermines cultural and environmental stewardship.

As Hawai'i looks to its economic future, the digital and remote work economies offer a promising path—not a panacea, but a powerful tool for building resilience, equity, and sustainability. The islands' isolation, once considered an economic disadvantage, can become a strength in a world where connection is increasingly virtual. Hawai'i's natural beauty, rich cultural heritage, and spirit of aloha can be the foundation of a unique, place-based digital economy that offers global connectivity without sacrificing local identity. Seizing this opportunity will require vision, collaboration, and an unwavering commitment to equity and sustainability. It will require balancing openness to new ideas and people with protection of community interests and values. And it will require recognizing that the digital economy is not separate from the land, the culture, or the people, it must be an extension of them, shaped by the islands' unique context and aspirations.

By thoughtfully cultivating its digital and remote work economies, Hawai'i can chart a new course that honors its past, embraces the present, and builds a future where economic opportunity, cultural vitality, and environmental stewardship are not competing goals but mutually reinforcing pillars of a thriving society.

7 Cultural and Creative Industries

Hawai'i's unique cultural identity is not only a source of pride but also a profound competitive advantage in an increasingly homogenized global economy. Its music, language, storytelling, and visual arts are much more than artifacts of heritage; they represent living, evolving economic assets that, when thoughtfully supported, can anchor a dynamic and sustainable sector of Hawai'i's future economy. Investing in cultural and creative industries is not just about preservation; it is about innovation, self-determination, and the creation of dignified livelihoods that are rooted in community and place.

The media production sector offers a clear example of how Hawai'i's cultural richness and natural beauty can be leveraged for economic and cultural benefit. Television shows such as "NCIS: Hawai'i" and animated films like Disney's "Moana" have showcased the islands' landscapes, stories, and local talent to global audiences. These productions generate significant economic activity, creating jobs for actors, crew members, technicians, and local businesses that support film shoots. But beyond immediate economic impacts, they also export a vision of Hawai'i to the world that, when handled respectfully, can deepen global appreciation for the islands' cultures and values. In contrast, a critical perspective emerged. Armstrong (2018) reports that despite Moana's promotion as culturally authentic, the film's music reflects Western ethnocentrism [44]. Polynesian sounds are used but are framed within Western musical styles, starting and ending with non-Polynesian music. This structure maintains control by non-Polynesian composers and reflects cultural appropriation, echoing colonial patterns of exploiting Indigenous resources for external gain.

Building a robust local media production ecosystem requires more than just being a picturesque filming location. It demands investments in training local screenwriters, directors, sound engineers, editors, and digital storytellers. It requires incentives for productions that hire local talent and authentically engage with the community. It calls for supporting independent filmmakers and emerging digital artists who can tell Hawai'i's stories on their own terms, rather than having those narratives solely filtered through mainland or international lenses. By nurturing local media production capacities, Hawai'i can ensure that its people retain control over how their stories are told and reap the economic benefits of doing so.

The global appetite for culturally rich, ethically produced fashion is growing. Consumers increasingly seek products with authenticity, sustainability, and meaning. Hawai'i is uniquely positioned to meet this demand, offering designs that are not only beautiful but deeply connected to place, history, and living culture. Supporting local fashion and design means investing in creative entrepreneurship programs, securing access to ethical manufacturing resources, and providing platforms for emerging designers to showcase their work locally and internationally. It also means protecting indigenous intellectual property rights, ensuring that cultural motifs are used with permission and reverence rather than exploited for profit. State Foundation on Culture and the Arts (2023) outlines key efforts to support Native Hawaiian art and culture [45]. This report details initiatives in funding, exhibitions, and acquisitions that aim to preserve indigenous cultural expressions. It also shows growing concerns about cultural appropriation and advocates for stronger policies to protect indigenous intellectual property rights. This document is critical for understanding how safeguarding cultural integrity supports the sustainable development of Hawai'i's fashion and design industries.

Hawai'i State Legislature (2023) affirms the protection of indigenous cultural expressions in House Concurrent Resolution 108: Supporting the Native Hawaiian Intellectual Property Working Group [46]. This resolution recognizes the collective intellectual property rights of the Native Hawaiian people, grounded in traditional cultural knowledge developed over generations. It supports the Working Group's efforts to create legal frameworks that prevent misappropriation and ensure that economic benefits derived from cultural designs are fairly shared with Native Hawaiian communities.

Beyond media and fashion, there is untapped potential in publishing, podcasting, and cultural education. Hawai'i's writers, historians, educators, and storytellers have a wealth of knowledge that can be shared with the world through books, digital media, educational materials, and online courses. The demand for authentic, place-based content is growing, especially as global conversations increasingly turn to indigenous knowledge systems, environmental stewardship, and alternative models of well-being and governance. Small publishers in Hawai'i have already begun to carve out niches, producing works that center Native Hawaiian voices, Pacific Islander perspectives, and Hawai'i-specific histories. Expanding this sector requires investment in literary arts, translation programs, distribution networks, and marketing support that connects local works to global audiences. Podcasting offers a particularly nimble and low-cost medium for cultural dissemination, allowing storytellers to reach listeners around the world without the barriers traditionally associated with publishing. Cultural education enterprises, offering everything from online 'ōlelo Hawai'i (Hawaiian language) classes to in-person cultural immersion programs for visitors and residents, also hold promise both as businesses and as vehicles for cultural revitalization.

Importantly, the development of cultural and creative industries must be community-led and culturally grounded. It is not enough to commodify culture for external consumption. True success lies in creating opportunities where cultural practitioners, artists, musicians, writers, and educators can thrive on their own terms, defining success according to their own values. This requires careful policy design that avoids the pitfalls of cultural exploitation and supports cultural practitioners not just as entertainers or service providers, but as vital stewards of knowledge and tradition. The economic benefits of investing in cultural and creative industries extend beyond the obvious. These industries tend to be more resilient during economic downturns, as they are driven by creativity, innovation, and intrinsic community demand. They generate multiplier effects, supporting a wide range of ancillary services from printing and shipping to events management and hospitality. They enhance Hawai'i's brand globally, attracting culturally mindful visitors and investors. Perhaps most importantly, they offer young people pathways to careers that do not require them to leave their communities or sacrifice their cultural identities to achieve economic success.

Hawai'i's cultural and creative industries can also intersect powerfully with other sectors prioritized for diversification. For example, tourism can be reimagined through authentic cultural tourism experiences designed and led by local communities. Sustainability initiatives can be strengthened through the revival and dissemination of indigenous land and ocean management practices. Educational exchanges can position Hawai'i as a global hub for the study of indigenous knowledge systems, arts, and languages. Every one of these possibilities rests on the vitality of local cultural practitioners and creative entrepreneurs. However, challenges remain. Housing affordability, cost of living, and limited access to capital continue to push talented artists and cultural practitioners to the margins. Infrastructure for arts education, performance spaces, and creative hubs remains underdeveloped relative to the sector's potential. Intellectual property protection for indigenous designs and knowledge is an ongoing concern. And there is a need for a more coordinated statewide strategy that recognizes cultural and creative industries as a pillar of economic development, not a peripheral concern.

Solutions will require collaboration among state and county governments, educational institutions, private investors, nonprofit organizations, and, most importantly, cultural practitioners themselves. Strategies could include tax incentives for creative enterprises, grants for emerging artists, investments in arts and cultural districts, expanded arts education in public schools, and support for international cultural exchange programs. Partnerships with universities could foster research and development in cultural entrepreneurship, helping artists build the business skills necessary to sustain their work while maintaining cultural integrity. The digital economy also opens new horizons for Hawai'i's cultural and creative sectors. Digital platforms can dramatically extend the reach of local artists and storytellers, connecting them directly with global audiences. Virtual reality experiences can immerse users around the world in Hawai'i's landscapes and stories. NFTs (non-fungible tokens) and other emerging digital tools, if used ethically and thoughtfully, could provide new avenues for indigenous artists to monetize and protect their work. Yet the same technology also brings risks of cultural appropriation and exploitation, making it all the more important that digital expansion be accompanied by strong protections and cultural protocols.

As Hawai'i looks to the future, the cultural and creative industries offer a vision of economic growth that does not sacrifice environmental sustainability or cultural integrity. They embody a model where economic success is measured not just by dollars generated but by the well-being of communities, the vibrancy of languages and traditions, and the transmission of knowledge across generations. The choice is not whether to preserve culture or to grow the economy. The real choice is whether to build an economy that uplifts culture, community, and place or to allow economic pressures to erode the very foundations that make Hawai'i unique. With thoughtful investment, collaboration, and leadership, Hawai'i's cultural and creative industries can become a cornerstone of a resilient, diversified economy that reflects the spirit of aloha not only as a value, but as a thriving, creative force in the world.

8 Health and Wellness as Export Sectors

In a world increasingly preoccupied with sustainability, well-being, and holistic approaches to health, Hawai'i stands in a uniquely advantageous position. The islands' clean environment, rich indigenous healing traditions, and the spirit of aloha, which emphasizes love, compassion, and harmony, form a natural foundation for Hawai'i to emerge as a global wellness hub. Leveraging these assets offers not just an opportunity for economic diversification but a path toward exporting values that align with the state's cultural identity. Hawai'i's existing reputation as a paradise destination already draws millions seeking rest, recovery, and inspiration. However, there is an opportunity to deepen this engagement by focusing not merely on leisure tourism, but on purpose-driven wellness experiences that integrate physical, emotional, and spiritual health. The reorientation toward health and wellness as an export sector can offer dignified, culturally grounded livelihoods for kama'āina, while attracting visitors and investment that respect and enhance the state's natural and cultural resources.

One significant area of potential is integrative medicine. Integrative medicine blends Western clinical practices with traditional and complementary healing methods, acknowledging that true health is multidimensional. In Hawai'i, lā'au lapa'au, the traditional Hawaiian practice of herbal medicine, offers a powerful and respected body of knowledge about natural healing. Practices such as lomilomi massage, ho'oponopono (conflict resolution and emotional cleansing), and traditional plant-based remedies have been passed down for generations and are now being rediscovered for their relevance to modern wellness needs. Medical centers and research institutions in Hawai'i are already beginning to explore partnerships that bridge indigenous practices with clinical care. Establishing centers for integrative health that offer both Western and Native Hawaiian approaches to healing could distinguish Hawai'i as a leader in patient-centered, culturally competent care. Integrative medicine not only meets growing consumer demand for holistic health solutions but also honors and revitalizes indigenous knowledge systems. It offers an economic model where traditional practitioners are respected as partners, not sidelined as curiosities.

Retreat tourism represents another natural extension of Hawai'i's wellness potential. The global popularity of yoga retreats, mindfulness workshops, eco-healing programs, and detox centers demonstrates that travelers are increasingly seeking more than passive vacations; they desire experiences that contribute to their physical, mental, and emotional renewal. Hawai'i's natural beauty—its forests, mountains, beaches, and ocean ecosystems—provides the ideal setting for immersive wellness experiences. Retreats that integrate Native Hawaiian values, practices, and environmental stewardship can offer uniquely transformative experiences. Programs could include forest bathing hikes in native forests, sunrise lomilomi massage sessions, lā'au lapa'au workshops, or group ho'oponopono ceremonies aimed at emotional healing. Retreat centers based on sustainability principles, using local foods, natural building materials, and low-impact design, could appeal to eco-conscious travelers seeking wellness that respect both personal health and planetary health. Such initiatives would create new opportunities for cultural practitioners, farmers, chefs, therapists, and hospitality workers, building an entire ecosystem of high-value jobs linked to wellness and culture.

Beyond tourism, there is an emerging opportunity in health research and development tailored to Hawai'i's unique environmental and demographic realities. Climate change is already affecting health patterns, bringing increased risks of heat stress, vector-borne diseases, and respiratory illnesses. Meanwhile, Hawai'i's aging population, one of the oldest in the United States, presents a laboratory for studying aging and chronic disease management in a culturally diverse context. Hawai'i also sits at the crossroads of East and West, offering a unique lens on cross-cultural approaches to aging, caregiving, and community health. Investing in research on climate-adapted therapies, interventions for aging populations, and tropical disease management could position Hawai'i as a leader in health innovation. Collaborations between the University of Hawai'i system, healthcare providers, biotech firms, and community organizations could yield new products, services, and models of care that could be exported to other coastal and island communities facing similar challenges.

Health innovation hubs, offering shared lab spaces, mentorship, and funding for startups focused on wellness, would foster an environment where new ideas can take root.

One particularly promising avenue is the intersection of mental health and climate resilience. As environmental stressors increase, so do rates of anxiety, depression, and trauma related to ecological loss. Hawai'i's indigenous concepts of well-being, which emphasize interconnectedness, balance, and relationship to place, offer frameworks for developing culturally informed approaches to mental health that could be relevant not only locally but globally. Educational programs, therapy models, and wellness technologies based on these frameworks could help address the mental health crises associated with climate change. For these sectors to flourish, partnerships will be crucial. Healthcare systems can integrate wellness programs that reduce costs and improve patient outcomes. Insurance providers may find opportunities to incentivize participation in preventive wellness programs, from nutrition coaching to stress management retreats. Universities can offer training programs in integrative health, wellness tourism management, indigenous healing practices, and health entrepreneurship. Incubators and accelerators can nurture new companies focused on wellness innovation, while impact investors can provide the capital needed to scale promising ventures.

Policies that facilitate these developments are equally important. Hawai'i can create licensing pathways for traditional healers, establish ethical guidelines for the integration of indigenous practices into commercial settings, and offer incentives for businesses that meet high standards of cultural and environmental responsibility. Protecting the intellectual property rights of Native Hawaiian cultural practitioners is essential, ensuring that traditional knowledge is respected and that economic benefits flow to the communities that have stewarded it for generations. Building a health and wellness sector rooted in Hawai'i's strengths is not without challenges. Care must be taken to avoid the commodification of culture, where sacred practices are packaged and sold without regard for their deeper meanings. Wellness offerings must be developed with and by Native Hawaiian practitioners, not merely appropriated. Affordability and access must be considered so that kama'āina are not priced out of the benefits of a growing wellness economy. If done thoughtfully, the wellness sector offers one of the most promising paths for Hawai'i's future. It aligns economic development with community health, cultural revitalization, and environmental stewardship. It appeals to a growing global consciousness that seeks more meaningful, restorative ways to live, work, and travel. It builds on Hawai'i's authentic strengths rather than forcing the islands into economic molds that have historically created dependency and vulnerability.

In a world increasingly aware of the unsustainability of business-as-usual, Hawai'i can offer a new model: a model where economy, culture, and environment are not in conflict but are mutually reinforcing. A model where visitors come not to consume a place, but to learn from it, heal with it, and contribute to its stewardship. A model where local communities thrive not by abandoning their traditions, but by living them more fully and sharing them respectfully with the world. The global wellness economy will continue to grow. The only question is whether Hawai'i will claim its rightful place within it, on its own terms. By embracing the strengths that make the islands unique, including its healing landscapes, its indigenous wisdom, and spirit of aloha, Hawai'i can not only build a healthier, more resilient economy for itself but also offer healing and hope to a world that desperately needs it.

9 The Role of Government and Policy

Diversification in Hawai'i's economy will not happen by accident. It demands thoughtful, proactive, and sustained intervention from government at multiple levels. The state's heavy dependence on tourism and defense has been decades in the making, shaped by global forces, historical patterns, and local decisions. Transitioning toward a more resilient and diversified economy will similarly require intentional strategic action. Public agencies must act not merely as regulators or funders but as catalysts and partners that shape an environment where innovation, entrepreneurship, and community-based industries can thrive. The role of government and policy is not peripheral to economic transformation; it is central.

One of the clearest ways the public sector can lead is through strategic investment. Public-private partnerships should be leveraged to build infrastructure that reduces risk for private investors while aligning with long-term sustainability goals. Innovation districts, geographic areas where research institutions, startups, investors, and community spaces are co-located, can concentrate talent and resources in ways that spark creativity and new enterprise formation. These districts could be developed near university campuses, in underutilized urban spaces, or around new green infrastructure hubs. Strategic subsidies, carefully designed, can also accelerate promising sectors like renewable energy, regenerative agriculture, aquaculture, health innovation, and the creative industries, ensuring that early-stage ventures have the support needed to scale. The alignment of education and workforce development with future economic needs is equally crucial. Curriculum reform must prioritize interdisciplinary thinking, critical problem-solving, cultural competence, and digital literacy. These skills are essential for Hawai'i's emerging industries, from clean energy and sustainable food systems to cultural tourism and marine biotechnology. Dual-credit pathways that allow high school students to earn college credit, coupled with expanded apprenticeship and internship programs, can create smoother transitions from education to employment. Special attention must be given to ensuring that opportunities are accessible to rural communities, Native Hawaiian students, and others historically underrepresented in higher-wage industries.

Apprenticeship models, particularly those developed in partnership with private industry, have shown promise in other regions for addressing labor shortages while creating career pathways. In Hawai'i, expanding registered apprenticeship programs beyond traditional trades into fields like healthcare, information technology, renewable energy installation, and sustainable agriculture could offer immediate benefits. State policy can support these efforts by providing funding incentives, simplifying program approval processes, and fostering partnerships between employers, unions, educational institutions, and community organizations. Zoning and land use reform is another indispensable lever for economic diversification. Outdated zoning laws often inhibit the development of live-work-play ecosystems that support modern entrepreneurship. For Hawai'i to foster innovation hubs, small manufacturing spaces, artist collectives, co-working centers, and affordable housing for knowledge workers, land use policy must evolve. Mixed-use zoning, adaptive reuse of existing structures, and streamlined permitting for projects aligned with community development goals are all necessary steps. Care must be taken to ensure that zoning reforms do not accelerate gentrification or displacement, particularly in Native Hawaiian communities and lower-income neighborhoods. Thoughtful land use planning should be used as a tool to build resilience and equity, not exacerbate inequality.

Reducing regulatory friction is also critical. Entrepreneurs and small businesses are often deterred by complex permitting processes, redundant paperwork, and a lack of clear guidance. Streamlining regulation, particularly for sectors like renewable energy installation, small-scale food production, and cultural tourism operations, could dramatically lower barriers to entry. Government agencies should prioritize creating a "one-stop shop" model for permitting and licensing, where businesses receive coordinated support rather than navigating a maze of disconnected offices. Clear timelines, online portals, and dedicated case managers can make a significant difference. Furthermore, regulations should be regularly reviewed to ensure they are up to date with current technologies, industry practices, and sustainability goals. Agencies such as the Department of Business, Economic Development and Tourism[8] (DBEDT), the Hawai'i Technology Development Corporation[9] (HTDC), and the Hawai'i Center for Advanced Transportation Technologies[10] (HCATT) must play coordinating roles across these initiatives. DBEDT can provide the strategic vision and policy coherence needed to align investments across sectors. HTDC can serve as the engine for technological innovation and startup development, while HCATT can drive advancements in clean transportation and renewable energy integration. These agencies must not work in silos but rather form strong partnerships with private sector leaders, educational institutions, nonprofit organizations, and community groups.

Cross-sector collaboration is not a nice-to-have; it is essential. The public sector must act as a convener, bringing together stakeholders to co-create strategies, set measurable goals, and track progress transparently. Advisory councils comprising representatives from business, labor, education, indigenous communities, and environmental organizations can ensure that diverse perspectives inform policy development. Community input must not be an afterthought but an integral part of planning processes. Policies designed without the voices of those they are intended to serve are unlikely to succeed in the long term. Financial tools can also play a catalytic role. Hawai'i can expand the use of public investment funds to support mission-aligned businesses, such as green banks for renewable energy projects, venture capital funds for local startups, and loan guarantees for regenerative agriculture enterprises. Tax incentives should be carefully targeted to reward outcomes that align with Hawai'i's broader sustainability, cultural preservation, and equity goals—not just blanket giveaways. Public procurement policies can be leveraged to support local businesses and industries, creating stable demand for emerging sectors.

[8] https://dbedt.hawaii.gov/.

[9] https://www.htdc.org/.

[10] https://www.htdc.org/programs/hcatt/.

Resilience must be woven into all aspects of economic policy. Diversification is not just about adding new industries; it is about building an economy that can weather shocks, from global recessions to pandemics to climate disasters. Investing in sectors that are inherently sustainable, locally rooted, and culturally resonant reduces Hawai'i's vulnerability to external forces. It also ensures that economic development strengthens rather than undermines the islands' social fabric and ecological foundations. Equity must also be central. A diversified economy that benefits only a privileged few will not achieve the broader social resilience Hawai'i needs. Policies should be explicitly designed to close opportunity gaps, support Native Hawaiian self-determination, and build wealth in historically marginalized communities. This may include targeted workforce development initiatives, access to capital for Native Hawaiian and locally owned businesses, and community benefits agreements for major development projects.

Communications strategies are another underappreciated element of successful diversification efforts. Public agencies must tell the story of why change is necessary, what the vision for the future is, and how specific initiatives fit into that vision. Regular updates, success stories, public dashboards, and accessible reports can build public support and trust. People are more likely to buy into bold economic shifts when they understand the rationale, see tangible benefits, and feel that their voices are heard. Chamber of Commerce Hawai'i (2024) presents a strategic roadmap for the state's future in Blueprint 2030: An Economic Action Plan for Hawai'i [47]. Drawing upon the 2023 Comprehensive Economic Development Strategy, the plan highlights Hawai'i's persistent workforce shortages, aging population, soaring housing and childcare costs, high business expenses, and heavy reliance on tourism—factors that undermine competitiveness and drive outmigration. To reverse these trends, the Blueprint proposes a coordinated set of 17 actions organized around five core goals: improving overall economic competitiveness, expanding the quantity and skills of the workforce, diversifying industry clusters beyond tourism, fostering local wealth through entrepreneurship and technical training, and establishing a collective-impact structure to ensure implementation and measurable progress. Grounded in extensive stakeholder engagement and traded-cluster analysis, this plan calls for tax and regulatory reform, housing supply expansion, youth retention programs, and a public-private leadership council equipped with shared metrics and an annual scorecard.

Its success will depend on sustained collaboration among business, government, and community leaders.

Finally, patience and persistence are required. Economic diversification is not a short-term project; it is a generational commitment. Early wins are important to build momentum, but so is sustained investment, adaptability, and learning from setbacks. Government leaders must resist the temptation to chase only the "next big thing" and instead commit to nurturing a portfolio of industries over time. They must balance the need for strategic planning with the flexibility to adjust as technologies evolve, markets shift, and communities articulate new priorities. International Monetary Fund (2024) examines strategies for economic diversification [48]. This report emphasizes that economic diversification is critical for developing economies to achieve sustainable growth, improve living standards, and enhance resilience to global market fluctuations and challenges, including climate change. It examines the impact of broad-based (horizontal) and industrial (vertical) policies. Horizontal policies, which improve the general business environment through macroeconomic stability, human capital development, infrastructure, and ease of doing business, are considered foundational. Vertical policies, or industrial policies, specifically target sectors to address market failures but demand meticulous design, effective implementation, and robust governance to be successful and cost-effective. Drawing on six country case studies (Costa Rica, Gabon, Georgia, India, Senegal, Vietnam), this paper shows that successful diversification takes a long-term commitment, often two to three decades. Key lessons include the fundamental importance of macroeconomic stability, investing in human capital, and fostering competition. While special economic zones (SEZs) can address business obstacles, tax exemptions linked to them frequently incur significant fiscal costs without always yielding clear benefits. The IMF actively advises member countries on diversification, focusing on both horizontal and, when appropriate, sector-specific vertical policies.

Hawai'i's future prosperity depends on how effectively government embraces its catalytic role. Left to the invisible hand of the market alone, diversification will remain an aspiration rather than a reality. But with visionary leadership, strategic partnerships, and unwavering commitment to equity and sustainability, Hawai'i can build an economy that honors its past, meets the needs of its people today, and ensures resilience for generations to come. The choice is not whether the government should act, but how boldly and wisely it will choose to do so.

10 Obstacles and Headwinds

The need for economic diversification in Hawai'i has become an urgent priority, but the road toward a more resilient and equitable economy is strewn with substantial obstacles and headwinds. While the promise of a diversified economy is enticing, offering greater stability, more opportunities for local communities, and alignment with sustainability values, the barriers to achieving this vision are deeply rooted and multifaceted. Meaningful change will require not just creativity and innovation, but systemic reform, bold leadership, and a sustained commitment to dismantling the structural challenges that inhibit transformation.

High costs remain one of the most formidable deterrents to new business formation in Hawai'i. Real estate prices, both commercial and residential, are among the highest in the nation. For entrepreneurs looking to start a business, securing affordable space is a monumental hurdle. Leasing or purchasing commercial property, even in secondary markets, often comes with costs that far exceed those on the continental United States. Startups and small businesses operating on narrow margins struggle to find space that allows them to scale without facing unsustainable overhead expenses. These realities not only make it difficult to incubate new industries but also limit the kinds of businesses that can survive—tilting the playing field toward capital-intensive, high-end operations that may not necessarily align with the broader goals of diversification, equity, or sustainability.

Shipping costs compound the problem. As an island chain dependent on imported goods for the majority of its basic needs, Hawai'i faces some of the highest logistical expenses in the country. The Jones Act, a century-old federal law requiring that goods transported between U.S. ports be carried on U.S.-flagged ships, adds additional cost layers to an already expensive supply chain. This affects not just consumer prices but also the cost structure for businesses that depend on mainland or international supplies, materials, or equipment. In sectors like manufacturing, agriculture, and renewable energy—key areas for diversification—the high cost of importing inputs or exporting finished goods erodes competitiveness and profitability.

Labor costs, too, while reflective of Hawai'i's high standard of living and strong worker protections, add to the challenge. Employers must offer higher wages to keep pace with the state's high cost of living, a burden that weighs heavily on small businesses and startups. While paying living wages is morally and economically just, it creates a steeper threshold for business viability, especially in industries like food production, sustainable manufacturing, and creative enterprises where profit margins are often slim. For diversification to succeed, strategies must be developed that recognize these structural cost barriers rather than assuming that market forces alone will overcome them.

Another significant challenge is fragmented governance. Hawai'i's economic development landscape is characterized by a constellation of public agencies, private organizations, nonprofit initiatives, and academic programs, each with overlapping mandates but often limited coordination. Agencies such as DBEDT, HTDC, and HCDA play critical roles but do not always operate in concert. County governments pursue their own initiatives, sometimes duplicating or conflicting with state-level efforts. While each organization may work diligently within its scope, the lack of a unified, statewide strategy for diversification leads to missed opportunities, inefficiencies, and frustration among entrepreneurs and investors seeking clear pathways. This fragmentation also makes it harder to mobilize the kind of systemic reforms needed to support emerging industries. In sectors like renewable energy, agritech, or the creative economy, businesses often must navigate a confusing array of permitting processes, incentive programs, and regulatory frameworks. Without a coordinated approach that prioritizes ease of doing business, fosters interagency collaboration, and aligns resources behind strategic goals, efforts to diversify will continue to be piecemeal and slower than they need to be.

Resistance to change presents another significant headwind. Hawai'i's current economic structure, heavily reliant on tourism and real estate development, has produced powerful vested interests that benefit from the status quo. Hotels, airlines, property developers, and associated service industries have built entrenched networks of political and economic influence over decades. Many policymakers, donors, and institutional stakeholders are closely tied to these sectors, creating an environment where bold shifts in economic strategy are often viewed with skepticism or outright opposition. In many cases, diversification is perceived as a threat to established revenue streams. Investments in tourism marketing, for example, often dwarf those allocated to nurturing new industries, reflecting a defensive posture rather than a forward-looking strategy. Public discourse can also reflect an underlying anxiety: a fear that moving too aggressively toward diversification could disrupt short-term economic stability or alienate key constituencies. Overcoming this resistance requires not only sound economic arguments but also a cultural shift in how Hawai'i defines prosperity and success—one that values long-term resilience over short-term gains, and community well-being over sectoral profits.

Access to capital remains another structural barrier, particularly for Native Hawaiian entrepreneurs, rural communities, and small businesses without established financial networks. Traditional lending institutions often view startup ventures, especially those outside of conventional sectors like tourism or retail, as too risky. Venture capital presence in Hawai'i is limited, and angel investor networks are still nascent compared to those in mainland innovation hubs. For industries like technology, regenerative agriculture, sustainable manufacturing, and cultural enterprises to flourish, there must be greater availability of patient, mission-aligned capital willing to invest in early-stage ideas and social impact ventures. Native Hawaiian and locally owned businesses often face additional barriers tied to historical disinvestment, systemic racism, and land access challenges. Without targeted support mechanisms such as low-interest loans, seed grants, technical assistance programs, and equity investments aimed specifically at underrepresented communities, economic diversification efforts risk replicating existing inequalities rather than addressing them. Building a thriving, diversified economy requires a commitment to democratizing access to capital and ensuring that the benefits of growth are widely shared.

Addressing these obstacles demands systemic reform. It is not enough to tinker at the margins or pilot a few promising programs. Comprehensive strategies are needed that tackle high costs head-on, foster governance coordination, break the political grip of entrenched interests, and expand access to capital. Policy innovation must be paired with institutional reform, streamlining processes, aligning incentives, and embedding equity and sustainability into the core of economic planning. Bold political will is equally essential. Leaders must be willing to take risks, challenge powerful interests, and invest in initiatives whose benefits may not be fully realized within a single election cycle. Visionary leadership means articulating a compelling case for diversification not just in technical economic terms, but also as a moral and cultural imperative for Hawai'i's future. It means committing to the hard, unglamorous work of reform: updating zoning codes, reforming procurement policies, modernizing tax structures, and reimagining education and workforce development systems.

Diversification will not happen quickly or easily. But by confronting the real obstacles that stand in the way and by marshaling the collective will to overcome them, Hawai'i can build a future that honors its unique cultural identity, protects its natural resources, and ensures resilience for generations to come. The headwinds are strong, but so too is the opportunity to chart a new, more sustainable course for the islands' economy.

11 Conclusion: The Future Is Plural

Hawai'i cannot and should not rely on a single industry again. Its future must be plural, a resilient weave of sectors rooted in its people, place, and values. Diversification is not about chasing trends from Silicon Valley. It is about building an economy that reflects the mana of the islands, that nourishes rather than extracts, that lifts all rather than a few. The next chapter turns to the foundation of such a transformation: Hawai'i's human capital, and how to ensure that every resident has the skills and opportunities to thrive.

References

[1]. Hawai'i State Energy Office. Hawai'i Clean Energy Initiative. Retrieved from https://energy.hawaii.gov/hawaii-clean-energy-initiative/.

[2]. Hawai'i Department of Agriculture. (2023). Report on Sustainable Food Systems Working Group. Retrieved from https://hdoa.hawaii.gov/wp-content/uploads/2023/09/AGR-SR111-Sust-Food-System-WG.pdf.

[3]. University of Hawai'i Economic Research Organization (UHERO). (2021). The Agricultural Economic Landscape in Hawai'i and the Potential for Future Growth. Retrieved from https://uhero.hawaii.edu/wp-content/uploads/2021/06/AgriculturalEconomicLandscapeInHawaii.pdf.

[4]. Hawai'i Sea Grant. Hawai'i Aquaculture Collaborative. Retrieved from https://seagrant.soest.hawaii.edu/sustainable-aquaculture/hi-aquaculture-collaborative/.

[5]. University of Hawai'i News. (2024, July 5). Multi-partner aquaculture research in support of fishpond revitalization. Retrieved from https://www.hawaii.edu/news/2024/07/05/ctahr-fishpond-revitalization/.

[6]. Department of Business, Economic Development & Tourism. (2024). Hawai'i's Creative Industries: 2024 Update Report. Retrieved from https://files.hawaii.gov/dbedt/economic/data_reports/hawaii-creative-report/HI_Creative_Ind_2024.pdf.

[7]. State Foundation on Culture and the Arts. (2024). FY2023 Annual Report. Retrieved from https://sfca.hawaii.gov/wp-content/uploads/2024/01/SFCA_FY2023_Annual-Report.pdf.

[8]. University of Hawai'i System. (2018). University of Hawai'i Strategic Directions, 2015–2021 (Version 2.0, 2018 Update). Retrieved from

https://www.hawaii.edu/wp/wp-content/uploads/2023/02/SD2.0_Revisions_2018_Update-2.pdf.
[9]. Kanaʻiaupuni, S. M., & Ledward, B. C. (2013). Hoʻopilina: The Call for Cultural Relevance in Education. Hūlili: Multidisciplinary Research on Hawaiian Well-Being, 9, 153–204. Retrieved from https://kamehamehapublishing.org/wp-content/uploads/sites/38/2020/09/Hulili_Vol9_7.pdf.
[10]. Withy, K., Joo, K., & Potter, C. (2020). Hawaiʻi Physician Workforce Assessment Project. University of Hawaiʻi John A. Burns School of Medicine. Retrieved from https://pmc.ncbi.nlm.nih.gov/articles/PMC9036453/.
[11]. Hawaiʻi Department of Health. (2021). Healthy Hawaiʻi Strategic Plan 2030. Retrieved from https://hhsp.hawaii.gov/assets/pdf/HHSP_Executive%20Summary_WEB.pdf.
[12]. Chang, K., Raethel, H., & Hoshide, N. (2024). 2024 Hawaiʻi Healthcare Workforce Initiative report. Healthcare Association of Hawaiʻi. Retrieved from https://hah.sharefile.com/share/view/s2482a25b1f8e45199adfc3bc4e96263e.
[13]. Kaiser, B., Krause, N., Mecham, D., Wooley, J., & Roumasset, J. (2019). Environmental valuation and the Hawaiian economy: Introduction and executive summary. University of Hawaiʻi Economic Research Organization (UHERO). Retrieved from https://uhero.hawaii.edu/wp-content/uploads/2019/08/HawaiiEnviroEvaluation.pdf.
[14]. Natural Energy Laboratory of Hawaiʻi Authority (NELHA). About NELHA. Retrieved from https://nelha.hawaii.gov/.
[15]. Independent Evaluation Group. (2017). Economic Diversification: Guidance Note. Retrieved from https://ieg.worldbankgroup.org/sites/default/files/Data/reports/EconomicDiversification.pdf.
[16]. World Trade Organization. (2021). World Trade Report 2021: Economic Resilience and Trade. Retrieved from https://www.wto.org/english/res_e/booksp_e/wtr21_e/01_wtr21_e.pdf.
[17]. Hawaiʻi Public Health Institute. About the Hawaiʻi Farm to School Network. Retrieved from https://www.hiphi.org/farmtoschool/.
[18]. Leavitt, Yamane & Soldner. (2024, July 24). Sustainable agriculture: Hawaii's farm-to-table movement. Retrieved from https://www.lyslaw.com/blog/2024/07/sustainable-agriculture-hawaiis-farm-to-table-movement/.
[19]. Elevitch, C., & Love, K. (2017). Adding Value to Locally Grown Crops in Hawaiʻi. GoFarm Hawaiʻi. Retrieved from https://gofarmhawaii.org/wp-content/uploads/2017/10/adding-value-hawaii-guide.pdf.
[20]. Barton, J. (2019). Healthy Soils Hawaiʻi Year 1 Final Report. Hawaiʻi Agriculture Research Center. Retrieved from https://planning.hawaii.gov/wp-content/uploads/Healthy-Soils-Hawaii-Year-1-OP-Final-Report.pdf.
[21]. Levin, A. (2022). The Breath of Life: Traditional Hawaiian Farmers are Reviving "Aloha ʻĀina," Love of the Land. Smithsonian's National Museum

of the American Indian. Retrieved from https://www.americanindianmagazine.org/story/the-breath-of-life.
[22]. GoFarm Hawai'i. Are You Considering Starting an Agri-Tourism Operation? Retrieved from https://gofarmhawaii.org/are-you-considering-starting-an-agri-tourism-operation/.
[23]. Swette Center for Sustainable Food Systems. (2023). Hawai'i agritourism: Examining how agritourism can be responsibly implemented to support small farmers and ecological and cultural preservation in the Hawaiian Islands (Capstone report). Arizona State University. Retrieved from https://globalfutures.asu.edu/food/wp-content/uploads/sites/14/2023/07/Agritourism_FINAL_4.26.23.pdf.
[24]. Hawai'i Department of Agriculture. Hawai'i Seal of Quality. Retrieved from https://hdoa.hawaii.gov/add/seals-of-quality/.
[25]. Hawai'i Agricultural Foundation. Localicious Hawai'i. Retrieved from https://localicioushawaii.org/.
[26]. Miculka, C. (2021, February 24). Big Island finfish farm hopes to lead the way in sustainable aquaculture. Honolulu Civil Beat. Retrieved from https://www.civilbeat.org/2021/02/big-island-finfish-farm-hopes-to-lead-the-way-in-sustainable-aquaculture/.
[27]. McDaniel, J. Farming the Open Ocean—Is Offshore Aquaculture in Hawai'i the Future of Seafood? University of Hawai'i Sea Grant College Program. Retrieved from https://seagrant.soest.hawaii.edu/farming-the-open-ocean/.
[28]. Kumar, A., Soratur, A., Kumar, S., & Venmathi Maran, B. A. (2025). A review of marine algae as a sustainable source of antiviral and anticancer compounds. Macromol, 5(1), 11. https://doi.org/10.3390/macromol5010011.
[29]. Hawai'i Institute of Marine Biology. Research. Retrieved from https://www.himb.hawaii.edu/research/.
[30]. U.S. Department of Energy. (2022). Powering the Blue Economy: Exploring Opportunities for Marine Renewable Energy in Maritime Markets. Retrieved from https://www.energy.gov/eere/water/powering-blue-economy.
[31]. National Oceanic and Atmospheric Administration (NOAA). (2021). NOAA Blue Economy Strategic Plan: 2021–2025. Retrieved from https://cdn.oceanservice.noaa.gov/oceanserviceprod/economy/Blue-Economy%20Strategic-Plan.pdf.
[32]. OECD. (2016). The ocean economy in 2030. OECD Publishing. Retrieved from https://doi.org/10.1787/9789264251724-en.
[33]. State of Hawaii Department of Business, Economic Development and Tourism. (2023). State of Hawaii Energy Data and Trends (April 2023). Retrieved from https://files.hawaii.gov/dbedt/economic/data_reports/reports-studies/Energy_Data_Report_2023.pdf.

[34]. Kaheawa Wind Power LLC. (2024, August). Kaheawa Wind 1 Project Summary (Proposes No Changes to Existing Facility). Retrieved from https://www.kaheawawind.com/.
[35]. Gomes, A. (2025, April 14). Geothermal power exploration building up steam. Hawai'i Tribune-Herald. Retrieved from https://www.hawaiitribune-herald.com/2025/04/14/hawaii-news/geothermal-power-exploration-building-up-steam/.
[36]. Khanal, S. K. Environment and Bioenergy Research Group. University of Hawai'i at Mānoa. Retrieved from https://www.samirkkhanal.com/.
[37]. Hawai'i State Energy Office. (2022, October 28). Integrated Hawai'i Pacific Hydrogen Hub Completes Full Application for Federal Funding. Retrieved from https://energy.hawaii.gov/integrated-hawaii-pacific-hydrogen-hub-completes-full-application-for-federal-funding/.
[38]. Hawaiian Electric. Shared Solar: Community-Based Renewable Energy (CBRE) Program. Retrieved from https://www.hawaiianelectric.com/products-and-services/smart-renewable-energy-programs/shared-solar.
[39]. Maui Now. (2023, January 12). Hawai'i's First Two Community-Owned Solar Projects Coming to Moloka'i. Retrieved from https://mauinow.com/2023/01/12/hawai%CA%BBis-first-two-community-owned-solar-projects-coming-to-moloka%CA%BBi/.
[40]. University of Hawai'i News. (2022, April 13). National accelerator picks healthcare tech startup founded by UH alumni. Retrieved from https://www.hawaii.edu/news/2022/04/13/pear-suite-techstars-la/.
[41]. Blair, C. (2023, October 30). Telehealth has improved medical service to remote areas of Hawai'i, but more is needed. Civil Beat. Retrieved from https://www.civilbeat.org/2023/10/telehealth-has-improved-medical-service-to-remote-areas-of-hawaii-but-more-is-needed/.
[42]. Teruya, C. (2022, February 23). Native Hawaiian entrepreneurs get a boost from e-commerce giant Shopify. Civil Beat. Retrieved from https://www.civilbeat.org/2022/02/native-hawaiian-entrepreneurs-get-a-boost-from-e-commerce-giant-shopify/.
[43]. Hawaii News Now. (2023, April 4). In 'hard to compete' labor market, city to test flexible work schedules and telework options. Retrieved from https://www.hawaiinewsnow.com/2023/04/04/hard-compete-labor-market-city-government-test-flexible-work-schedules-telework-options/.
[44]. Armstrong, R. (2018). Time to face the music: Musical colonization and appropriation in Disney's Moana. Social Sciences, 7(7), 113. Retrieved from https://doi.org/10.3390/socsci7070113.
[45]. State Foundation on Culture and the Arts. (2023). Report to the Legislature on Native Hawaiian Art and Culture. Retrieved from https://ags.hawaii.gov/wp-content/uploads/2023/01/SFCA-Report-to-Legislature-SCR97.pdf.

[46]. Hawai'i State Legislature. (2023). House Concurrent Resolution 108: Supporting the Native Hawaiian Intellectual Property Working Group. Retrieved from https://capitolwebsite.azurewebsites.net/sessions/session2023/bills/HCR108_.HTM.
[47]. Chamber of Commerce Hawai'i. (2024). Blueprint 2030: An Economic Action Plan for Hawai'i. Retrieved from https://www.cochawaii.org/wp-content/uploads/2024/10/COCH-40740_BlueprintReport_Spreads-compressed.pdf.
[48]. International Monetary Fund. (2024). Economic Diversification in Developing Countries: Lessons from Country Experiences with Broad-Based Growth. Retrieved from https://www.imf.org/en/Publications/Departmental-Papers-Policy-Papers/Issues/2024/07/20/Economic-Diversification-in-Developing-Countries-Lessons-from-Country-Experiences-with-532135.

CHAPTER 5

People First: Education, Talent, and the Future of Work in Hawai'i

1 Introduction: Human Capital as Hawai'i's True Superpower

Economists frequently highlight productivity, capital investment, and innovation as the pillars of economic growth. Yet these forces are not self-generating abstractions—they are the product of people: their labor, their skills, and their imagination. In Hawai'i, where natural beauty often eclipses deeper conversations about economic structure, human capital remains the most underappreciated resource. Beyond being an input on a spreadsheet, it represents a living synthesis of culture, knowledge, and resilience. It is Hawai'i's truest superpower—rooted in the aloha spirit, the multicultural fabric of its communities, and the values of stewardship and interdependence. And yet, this superpower remains precariously underleveraged.

Despite a strong tradition of education, a robust community college network, and a deep well of cultural wisdom, Hawai'i faces persistent workforce challenges. Chief among them is the so-called "brain drain"—the exodus of local talent to the mainland in search of better wages, lower housing costs, and expanded career options. This trend has hollowed out the middle of the labor force, particularly in knowledge-based industries critical to economic diversification. Compounding the problem is a persistent skills mismatch: many of the jobs available do not align with the

P. Yu, *Economic Development in Hawai'i*,
https://doi.org/10.1007/978-3-032-15689-1_5

qualifications of local workers, and many of the skills in demand are not widely taught. At the same time, the state's soaring cost of living places immense pressure on workers across the income spectrum, reducing not only disposable income but also the feasibility of staying rooted in one's home community.

If Hawai'i is to move beyond a tourism-dominated, low-wage service economy, then human capital development must be at the heart of its economic strategy. The diversification efforts explored in the previous chapter, whether in regenerative tourism, agriculture, clean energy, or digital innovation—will falter without a strong, adaptive, and locally grounded workforce to support them. This means investing not only in education and training but also in systems that allow workers to thrive: affordable housing, accessible childcare, health benefits, and career mobility pathways.

This chapter explores how Hawai'i can more deliberately cultivate, retain, and uplift its people. It begins by analyzing the educational pipeline—from K–12 to higher education and vocational training—revealing both its strengths and the gaps that hinder workforce readiness. It examines labor market dynamics, including wage trends, employment concentrations, and the growth potential of key sectors. Finally, it assesses policy levers and community-led initiatives that can bridge the divide between talent and opportunity. Whether through expanded apprenticeships, industry-education partnerships, or incentive programs to retain graduates, the goal is the same: to create an economy where kama'āina can build lives of purpose, security, and contribution—at home, not elsewhere.

In a globalized world, where talent is mobile and industries evolve rapidly, Hawai'i's competitive edge must come from within. Its people are not just a workforce, they are stewards of place, culture bearers, and innovators. Tapping into this human capital with intention, equity, and imagination is not just a strategy—it is the path to Hawai'i's economic future.

2 The Education Pipeline: Strengths and Gaps

Hawai'i's education system occupies a unique place in the American educational landscape. Unlike the decentralized education systems found in other U.S. states, the Hawai'i Department of Education (HIDOE) operates as a single, statewide district. This centralized model provides the potential for systemic coherence, equity in funding, and uniform curricular standards. It also allows for coordinated policymaking and resource allocation across all islands. However, this same structure can limit regional flexibility and responsiveness, especially in addressing the diverse educational needs of rural communities, neighbor islands, and Indigenous populations.

At the post-secondary level, the University of Hawai'i (UH) System serves as a linchpin for workforce development, higher learning, and research-driven innovation. With ten campuses across the islands—including community colleges, UH Hilo, UH West O'ahu, and the flagship UH Mānoa—the system plays a vital role in shaping the state's economic future. It offers both traditional and non-traditional students' opportunities for upward mobility, often with a strong focus on serving Native Hawaiian, Pacific Islander, and first-generation college students.

Despite formidable challenges, Hawai'i's education system has notable strengths that position it for long-term impact. One of the most encouraging indicators is the state's high school graduation rate, which is relatively high at over 85%. This figure reflects the effectiveness of high school retention strategies, student support services, and community engagement efforts. It also lays a solid foundation for post-secondary pathways, whether through college enrollment, apprenticeships, or immediate entry into the workforce. The UH community college network is another significant asset. Campuses such as Leeward, Windward, and Kaua'i Community Colleges provide accessible, affordable, and locally relevant education to thousands of students annually. These institutions offer a range of certificates and associate degree programs aligned with local labor market needs, including healthcare, early childhood education, information technology, and sustainable agriculture. The presence of robust transfer pathways between community colleges and four-year UH campuses help facilitate degree completion and career advancement.

Culturally responsive education is also a distinctive strength of Hawai'i's K-12 system. Hawaiian language immersion schools and culturally grounded charter schools integrate Indigenous knowledge, place-based learning, and community values into daily instruction. This integration not only honors the state's historical and cultural context but also improves educational engagement and outcomes for Native Hawaiian students. Programs such as Ka Papahana Kaiapuni (Hawaiian Language Immersion) and culturally grounded initiatives led by Kamehameha Schools and community-based nonprofits show how culture can serve as a vehicle for academic excellence. Kana'iaupuni, Ledward, and Jensen (2010) investigate how culture-based education (CBE) affects Native Hawaiian student outcomes [1]. Their statewide study finds that CBE enhances socio-emotional well-being, cultural identity, and academic performance. High CBE usage by teachers correlates with higher reading and math scores, especially in culturally supportive school environments.

Despite these assets, the education pipeline in Hawai‘i is marked by significant leakages that inhibit student success and economic mobility. Chief among them is the low college completion rate, particularly for Native Hawaiian, Pacific Islander, and low-income students. While high school graduation rates remain strong, the transition to and through college presents formidable obstacles. Teranishi et al. (2023) report that Native Hawaiian and Pacific Islander (NHPI) students face disproportionately low college attainment, with only 19% completing a degree and over 53% stopping out before graduation [2]. This report identifies key barriers including financial insecurity, lack of culturally responsive academic support, and the invisibility of NHPI students in institutional data and decision-making. It reveals the importance of disaggregated data and equity-centered interventions to address structural inequities. The findings call for increased institutional accountability, expanded student services, and culturally grounded practices to improve persistence and completion rates for NHPI students across higher education systems.

Financial barriers are a major contributing factor. Although the UH System offers relatively affordable tuition compared to mainland institutions, many students still face challenges in covering the full cost of attendance including housing, transportation, textbooks, and childcare. These challenges are especially acute for students from rural or outer island communities who must relocate to O‘ahu or other major campuses to pursue certain degrees. Tagami (2024) discusses the challenges Hawaii students face due to recent changes in the federal financial aid system, specifically the Free Application for Federal Student Aid (FAFSA) [3]. The delayed rollout and technical issues have led to confusion and decreased application rates, potentially exacerbating financial barriers for students, especially those from low-income and rural backgrounds who rely heavily on timely financial aid. These systemic issues threaten to deepen existing equity gaps in higher education across the islands.

Another critical challenge lies in the underfunding of public education infrastructure. Many school facilities across the state suffer from deferred maintenance, lack of modern equipment, and outdated learning environments. This physical disrepair affects both student morale and learning outcomes. In rural areas and neighbor islands, resource disparities are even more pronounced, limiting students' access to advanced coursework, extracurricular programs, and specialized teachers. UH News (2025) reports that a research brief from UH Mānoa identifies systemic underfunding as a persistent challenge in Hawai'i's public schools [4]. The analysis emphasizes how insufficient investment in facilities and instructional resources exacerbates inequities, especially for students on the neighbor islands. It calls for renewed public investment to improve infrastructure and ensure more equitable learning conditions across the state.

Academic preparedness is also a concern, particularly in the areas of STEM (science, technology, engineering, and math), entrepreneurship, and career readiness. Too many students progress through the K-12 system without sufficient exposure to high-demand fields or real-world career pathways. Early education and middle school curricula often lack robust career exploration, internships, or project-based learning opportunities that can ignite student interest and clarify post-secondary goals. DBEDT (2024) reports that Hawai'i's fashion and music industries, though culturally rich and economically promising, face major educational and workforce development challenges [5]. This report identifies a fragmented education-to-career pipeline, with gaps in technical training, access to equipment, and entrepreneurial support. It also notes the uneven availability of creative programs across islands, compounded by Hawai'i's high cost of living and limited infrastructure. DBEDT calls for strategic investments including shared hubs, enhanced partnerships with schools, and targeted tax incentives to align educational offerings with industry needs and sustain a thriving creative economy rooted in local talent and innovation.

In addition, advising and guidance services are often under-resourced and inconsistent. Many students receive minimal support in navigating complex college admissions processes, financial aid systems, and course selection. This leads to poor alignment between student aspirations and academic pathways, increasing the likelihood of dropouts and extended time-to-degree. Hawai'i Community College (2023) reports that its Counseling, Advising, and Support Services Center (CASSC) plays a vital role in guiding students through academic planning, transfer readiness, and personal development [6]. Despite its broad reach and strong satisfaction ratings, over 95% of surveyed students agreed their counselors were helpful and created a safe environment—the report also reveals gaps in consistent advising capacity. Many students, especially from special populations like veterans and returning adults, rely heavily on these services. However, limited staffing and high demand make it difficult to provide proactive, individualized guidance, a factor that may contribute to prolonged degree completion or attrition.

The cumulative effect of these challenges is a set of drop-off points that weaken the transition from high school to higher education and the workforce. For instance, a student may graduate from high school but delay or forgo college due to affordability concerns. Another may enroll in college but withdraw before completing a degree due to a lack of academic support or personal resources. These gaps are not just individual misfortunes; they are systemic inefficiencies that diminish the state's capacity to harness its most valuable asset—its people. UH (2024) discusses that by 2031, 70% of jobs in Hawai'i will require some form of postsecondary education, and 36% will demand at least a bachelor's degree [7]. This shift shows the growing importance of education and training beyond high school for securing well-paying, stable employment. This report warns against the rising skepticism toward college degrees, emphasizing that higher education remains the most reliable pathway to economic mobility. With initiatives like Hawai'i P–20 and the UH Strategic Plan, the state is working to align its education system with workforce needs to prepare students for Hawai'i's evolving job market.

To build a resilient, diversified, and inclusive economy, Hawai'i must close the gaps in its education pipeline. This requires a comprehensive approach that includes increasing funding for public schools, expanding access to culturally grounded education, and strengthening advising and support services. Additionally, curriculum reforms should emphasize STEM, entrepreneurship, and workforce readiness from an early age. Cross-sector partnerships—linking schools, universities, employers, and community organizations—can create seamless pathways from education to employment, particularly in emerging sectors like clean energy, healthcare, and digital media.

Ultimately, investing in education is not merely a social imperative but an economic strategy. By nurturing the talents, ambitions, and identities of its people, Hawai'i can transform its education system into a true engine of equity and economic resilience. The road ahead is challenging, but with coordinated effort and community-driven vision, Hawai'i's education pipeline can become a model for place-based, people-centered development.

3 Brain Drain: When Talent Leaves the Islands

Brain drain remains one of Hawai'i's most pressing challenges in building a resilient, inclusive, and forward-looking economy. Each year, hundreds of bright, talented graduates from Hawai'i's high schools head to mainland colleges and universities in search of opportunities. For many of them, that journey becomes permanent. Nearly 60% of public high school graduates who leave the islands for college do not return, contributing to a long-term outmigration trend that poses significant consequences for the state's workforce, economy, and cultural continuity. At its core, this pattern represents a fundamental disconnect between what young people want and need to build fulfilling lives, and what Hawai'i currently offers. On the mainland, they often find higher wages, greater job variety, lower housing costs, and a perception of upward mobility in fields such as technology, medicine, engineering, design, and finance. Meanwhile, back home, they encounter barriers that make returning a difficult choice: stagnant salaries, limited professional pathways, expensive real estate, and a shortage of high-skill job clusters.

Park (2025) reports that while out-migration from Hawai'i, especially among young adults, remains a concern, recent data shows a more balanced pattern [8]. In 2023, domestic and international in-migration nearly offset total outflows, with a notable return of Hawai'i-born individuals and prime working-age adults (25–44). Honolulu County attracted the most newcomers, while out-migrants primarily moved to California, Washington, and Texas. Although young people continue to leave for education and jobs, many return later in life. These trends complicate the brain drain narrative and show the importance of tailored policies to support housing, workforce development, and economic mobility for returning and resident populations. Park finds that in 2023, about 12,100 Hawai'i-born individuals moved back to the state, while approximately 6,400 moved out; which marks a reversal from pre-COVID trends, when more Hawai'i-born residents were leaving the state than returning. But still, when Hawai'i's best and brightest young people leave and do not return, the state loses more than just workers. It loses future teachers, caregivers, business owners, scientists, innovators, cultural practitioners, and civic leaders. The impact is intergenerational. Children born to these outward migrants are less likely to have ties to Hawai'i, weakening the long-term social fabric and civic life of the islands. Efforts to address brain drain often begin with nostalgia, reminding youth of their roots, their 'ohana, their kuleana to the land and community. These cultural messages are important, but insufficient on their own. What is needed is a clear, concrete value proposition for staying in Hawai'i or returning after college or military service. This means building an economy that can offer competitive wages, robust career pathways, diverse housing options, and a strong sense of purpose.

Young professionals today are not just chasing paychecks. They are seeking meaningful work, lifestyle balance, and community connection. Hawai'i already offers the latter two in abundance. The challenge is to bridge the gap on the first. Salaries in Hawai'i across a range of fields lag behind mainland counterparts. The U.S. Bureau of Labor Statistics (2024) provides detailed wage data for various occupations in Urban Honolulu [9]. It reveals that certain sectors, including computer and mathematical occupations, have mean hourly wages lower than the national average. For instance, computer and mathematical occupations in Urban Honolulu have a mean hourly wage of $47.61, compared to the national average of $56.16. Such disparities underscore Hawai'i's challenges in offering competitive wages, which can impact the state's ability to attract and retain professionals in key industries. DBEDT (2024) analyzes the performance of Hawai'i's targeted and emerging industries over a decade [10]. It shows that sectors like technology and health and wellness have experienced job growth but still face wage competitiveness issues. This report emphasizes the need for strategic investments to enhance wage structures in these sectors to prevent talent outmigration and support economic resilience. DBEDT (2023) examines occupational trends in Hawai'i over a seven-year period [11]. It identifies that many of the state's largest occupations, including those in education and healthcare support, have median hourly earnings below national averages. This report suggests that these wage gaps contribute to workforce shortages and stress the importance of aligning wages with national standards to maintain a robust labor market.

Addressing this disparity will require structural reforms. It means incentivizing industries that offer high-wage, high-skill jobs and building out ecosystems that support innovation and entrepreneurship. Programs such as accelerators, incubators, and co-working spaces are part of this strategy, but they must be coupled with mentorship, access to capital, and pathways into established sectors like renewable energy, health tech, creative industries, and sustainable agriculture.

Equally important is tackling the housing crisis. A young professional returning to Hawai'i should not be forced to live with four roommates or move back in with parents indefinitely. Developing affordable workforce housing, both rental and ownership, is critical. This means rethinking zoning, investing in mixed-use and infill development, and expanding access to down payment assistance programs for first-time homebuyers. Hawai'i Housing Finance and Development Corporation (HHFDC) (2024) reports that Hawai'i delivered over 1,000 affordable units in FY2024 and is advancing more than 9,600 additional units for future delivery, with a strong focus on addressing the workforce housing crisis [12]. In response to the Maui wildfires, HHFDC provided emergency housing for 600 families and led efforts to develop permanent housing solutions. The agency also initiated down payment and mortgage assistance programs to support first-time homebuyers, including those earning between 80% and 140% of the area median income. These efforts underscore HHFDC's strategic pivot toward affordable homeownership and workforce housing amid high interest rates and housing scarcity.

UHERO (2024) reports that Hawai'i's housing market remains in deep crisis, marked by extreme unaffordability and limited new construction [13]. In 2023, only 20% of local households could afford a mortgage on the median-priced single-family home, which held steady at $875,000. High interest rates have driven down housing transactions while keeping prices elevated, especially on Maui and O'ahu. Rental costs are also soaring, with median asking rents reaching $2,000 statewide and over $2,400 on Maui. Nearly 56% of renters are burdened by housing costs. Figure 6 shows that, in 2023, a typical three-bedroom unit commanded a rent of $3,800, and for four-bedroom units, the median was $5,200. In 2023 there were 5,600 single-family home transactions and 7,300 condominium transactions across the state. The high prices reflect an extremely limited supply of housing. Even a family that could afford these prices, there is almost no rental inventory.

Compared to 2022, single-family home transactions were down 37% and condominium transactions fell 36%. The decline in home transactions is primarily a result of high interest rates, which peaked at 7.6% in October of 2022. High interest rates lowered the demand for home purchases as mortgages became expensive. However, they also lowered the supply of housing inventory. Current owners with fixed-rate mortgages became reluctant to sell because they would be exposed to much higher interest rates when they purchase a new home themselves. Despite regulatory reforms and emergency proclamations, the new housing supply remains inadequate. Persistent affordability challenges contribute to population outmigration and rising homelessness. Maui County and Honolulu County saw the highest single-family home prices with medians at $1.05 million and $1.03 million respectively. Kaua'i and Maui saw the highest condominium prices at $800,000 and $799,000 respectively. Demand from resort, second home and short-term rental markets create strong condominium demand pressures on these islands.

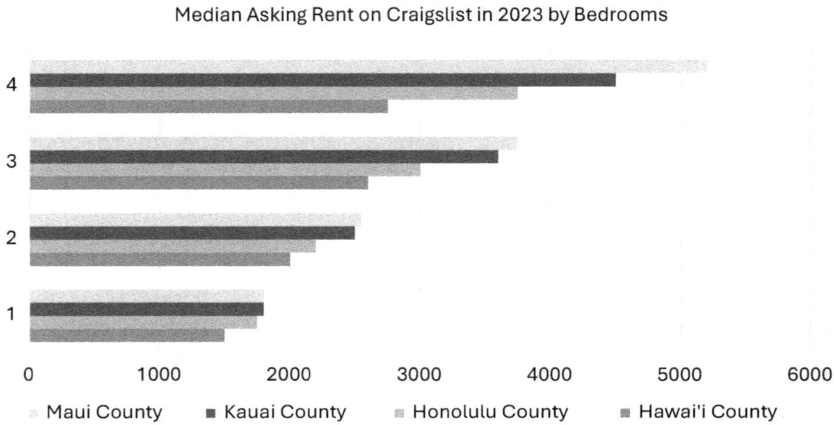

Figure 6 Median Asking Rent in Hawai'i's four counties on Craigslist in 2023 by Bedrooms. This horizontal bar chart compares rental prices across Hawai'i's four counties: Maui, Kaua'i, Honolulu, and Hawai'i County. Each county shows median asking rents for one- to four-bedroom units. One-bedroom units range from roughly $1,500 to $1,800; two-bedroom units from about $2,000 to $2,500; three-bedroom units from $2,600 to $3,800; and four-bedroom units from $2,800 to over $5,200. Maui County shows the highest rents in nearly every category, followed by Kaua'i County, Honolulu County, and Hawai'i County. Source: University of Hawai'i Economic Research Organization (UHERO), Hawai'i Housing Factbook 2024

Beyond wages and housing, young people must see a future in Hawai'i that aligns with their aspirations. This involves bolstering educational and career guidance starting in high school, expanding internship and apprenticeship programs, and strengthening alumni networks that connect students with professionals already making a difference in their home communities. Ricket, Yahn, and Bentley (2023) examine how high school internships, when grounded in community and career connected learning (CCCL), can serve as powerful tools for cultivating rural youth's social capital, career awareness, and sense of belonging [14]. Drawing on interviews with 25 alumni of internships in Appalachian Ohio, the study found that participants often reshaped their career trajectories, gained confidence, and developed a stronger connection to their rural communities. These internships—designed and facilitated by intermediary organizations Building Bridges to Careers and Rural Action—offered flexible, place-based experiences that emphasized relationships, real-world learning, and exposure to local career paths. The study argues that such models can inspire young people to imagine futures rooted in their communities, helping to combat youth outmigration and enrich local economic and civic life.

There is a role for philanthropy and community organizations in this effort. Place-based scholarships tied to a commitment to return and work in Hawaiʻi, similar to rural healthcare service obligations, could encourage more students to see college as a round-trip journey. Local businesses can also play a part by developing pipeline programs and competitive entry-level roles targeted at returning graduates. Peters (2024) outlines how sector partnerships in Hawaiʻi are helping to build skilled local talent pipelines across high-demand industries, such as healthcare, information technology, clean energy, and creative fields [15]. These partnerships, coordinated by the Chamber of Commerce Hawaii in collaboration with the Department of Labor and Industrial Relations and the UH, align employers with educators to co-create training programs, internships, and certification pathways. The model transforms employers from passive consumers to active co-creators of talent. By emphasizing career awareness, pre-apprenticeships, and transitions into employment, these programs offer scalable workforce solutions that strengthen the state's ability to retain and re-attract kamaʻāina professionals. This framework is essential for addressing local labor shortages and curbing outmigration.

The COVID-19 pandemic showed that remote work is viable and desired by many. This opens a unique window for Hawaiʻi to re-attract talent. DBEDT (2022) reports that the adoption of remote work in Hawaiʻi transforms both employer practices and employee expectations [16]. According to their extensive statewide surveys, about 59.6% of employees worked remotely at some point during the pandemic, and 32.2% of firms had employees working remotely as of August 2021. This study found that remote work boosted employee satisfaction, productivity, and flexibility, while also presenting challenges such as supervision, collaboration, and maintaining workplace culture. With strong interest in hybrid work models and the potential to reduce office space, this report stresses broadband infrastructure improvements and digital training as key to supporting a sustainable remote work ecosystem in Hawaiʻi.

Ultimately, the solution to brain drain is not about guilt or persuasion. It is about structural transformation. Hawaiʻi must become a place where its youth can envision long-term futures. Where they can build careers, raise families, buy homes, and contribute meaningfully to the well-being of their communities. Where they are not forced to choose between staying connected to their culture and pursuing economic mobility.

Data transparency is key to shaping solutions. Better tracking of graduate outcomes, job placement rates, salary benchmarks, and outmigration patterns can help policymakers and institutions design more targeted interventions. This includes expanding the state longitudinal data system to capture education-to-employment pathways and ensuring that data is disaggregated by geography, ethnicity, and income to surface equity gaps. Von Zastrow (2024) explores how statewide longitudinal data systems (SLDSs) are evolving from basic compliance tools into strategic platforms that support education-to-workforce pathways [17]. The report, published by the Education Commission of the States, draws on a 50-state comparison and emphasizes five key dimensions of SLDS effectiveness: establishment, demand, capacity, governance, and use. It shows the importance of transparency and stakeholder engagement, particularly for addressing equity gaps. By aligning data infrastructure with the needs of policymakers, educators, and learners, this report presents a roadmap for using SLDSs to inform decisions and improve outcomes. It offers a valuable framework for Hawai‘i's ongoing data modernization efforts.

Community voice must guide this work. Young people should be part of the conversation about what it will take for them to stay or return. Focus groups, design sprints, and participatory research can uncover the trade-offs that shape decisions about leaving and returning. These insights must be translated into policy and investment. Das et al. (2020) examine how graduate students in urban planning programs in Hawai‘i engaged in a participatory event, "Waipahu Talk Story", to explore and reflect on public engagement practices [18]. Through this initiative, students designed and implemented tools to involve residents in discussions around transit-oriented development (TOD). Their experiences revealed both the promise and pitfalls of participatory planning, particularly in diverse communities. This study emphasizes the importance of reflective practice and critical pedagogy in planning education, showing how such experiential learning helps future practitioners grapple with real-world complexities, community dynamics, and issues of equity and inclusion in urban planning.

Addressing brain drain is not a zero-sum game. It is not about closing the doors to the outside world or discouraging young people from exploring. It is about building a home worth coming back to—and staying in. It is about aligning values with opportunity, culture with commerce, and aspiration with access. It is about giving Hawaiʻi's next generation the tools and trust to shape the future from here, not from afar. The path forward is not simple, but it is possible. It begins with recognizing that human capital is Hawaiʻi's greatest resource. The talent, creativity, and aloha of its people, especially its youth, can be the engine of a new kind of economy: one that is locally grounded, globally relevant, and deeply rooted in shared responsibility. Retaining and reattracting that talent is not just an economic imperative. It is a moral one. It is a promise that the people of Hawaiʻi can thrive here, together, now and for generations to come.

4 Skills Mismatches: Gaps Between Education and Employment

In a state celebrated for its natural beauty and cultural richness, Hawaiʻi faces a quiet but pressing economic challenge: a persistent disconnect between the skills students acquire through education and those demanded by the state's evolving labor market. Despite Hawaiʻi having a relatively high share of residents with college degrees compared to many other states, a troubling pattern persists—many graduates end up in jobs that do not require or fully utilize their qualifications. At the same time, employers in key growth industries such as healthcare, construction, information technology, and skilled trades continue to report acute talent shortages. Strada Education Network and Burning Glass Institute (2024) report that Hawaiʻi has one of the highest underemployment rates for college graduates in the United States, with 57% of degree holders working in positions that do not require a bachelor's degree [19]. This report shows a persistent disconnect between educational outcomes and labor market demands, urging greater alignment between academic programs and real-world workforce needs. It also emphasizes the critical role of internships, apprenticeships, and other forms of work-based learning in bridging this gap and improving employment outcomes for graduates.

Chamber of Commerce Hawaiʻi (2023) reports that the state faces significant workforce gaps in the skilled trades sector, particularly in construction, electrical work, plumbing, and clean energy [20]. This analysis reveals high demand coupled with high turnover rates, skill shortages, and an aging labor force. It stresses the urgency of aligning training programs with industry needs and expanding apprenticeship and career pathway programs to build a more sustainable talent pipeline. It is crucial in guiding policy and education leaders to strengthen workforce development in critical infrastructure-related fields. This mismatch has real consequences. For workers, it means limited income mobility, underutilized talent, and frustration in trying to build meaningful careers at home. For employers, it means unfilled positions, productivity bottlenecks, and increased training costs. And for the state overall, it hampers efforts to retain local talent, diversify the economy, and ensure long-term competitiveness.

Several factors contribute to this skills mismatch. One is a lingering, outdated perception about what constitutes a "good job." For decades, the dominant narrative has emphasized four-year degrees as the singular path to economic security. While higher education remains an important engine of opportunity, this narrative can obscure the value of alternative and emerging pathways, such as industry-recognized credentials, apprenticeships, and technical certificates. In fields like heating, ventilation, and air conditioning (HVAC), cybersecurity, elder care, and sustainable agriculture, demand is rising for workers with specialized skills that may not require a bachelor's degree but still offer high wages and career advancement. Maller, Stiefvater, and Davidson (2024) report that there is significant interest among Washington State apprentices in earning educational credentials, such as associate or bachelor's degrees, particularly among apprentices of color and those in emerging industries [21]. Drawing on surveys and focus groups with over 790 current and former apprentices, this study finds that many see degrees as essential for career advancement, broader opportunities, and management roles. However, barriers such as time constraints, financial limitations, and lack of clear information persist. It stresses the value of integrating educational pathways into apprenticeship programs to align with diverse goals and promote equitable access to career mobility.

Weissman (2024) reports that a Georgetown Center on Education and the Workforce study revealed a significant misalignment between middle-skills credentials—such as associate degrees and certificates—and local labor market demands across the U.S. [22]. Analyzing 565 labor markets, this report found that in over half, the majority of credentials would need to shift to different fields to match projected job openings. With 5.8 million jobs annually expected to require sub-baccalaureate (e.g., associate degrees, certificates, technical diplomas) credentials by 2031, the current distribution of educational programs often fails to meet regional workforce needs. This report warns that students may face underemployment or be forced to relocate due to oversupply in some fields and lack of alignment in others.

Another contributing factor is the limited availability and use of real-time labor market data in curriculum design and career advising. Education systems in Hawai'i while strong in many ways often lack access to timely, localized information about emerging job trends, employer needs, and evolving skill sets. As a result, students may graduate into a labor market that looks very different from the one they were prepared for. Educators, counselors, and administrators need better tools to align instructional content with current and future economic demand. Strengthening Hawai'i's longitudinal data systems and labor market dashboards is essential for closing this information gap.

Soft skills and digital literacy also emerge as common concerns among employers. Even when technical knowledge is present, many hiring managers report gaps in communication, problem-solving, teamwork, and professionalism—attributes often referred to as employability skills. Additionally, as nearly all industries incorporate digital tools, the demand for basic and intermediate digital fluency has grown. Whether in managing patient data, using construction software, or handling remote collaboration tools, workers across sectors must be digitally competent. Ensuring that these competencies are embedded across the curriculum from K–12 through postsecondary is a foundational task for preparing students for success in the modern workforce.

To address these issues, Hawai'i must pursue more intentional alignment between educational offerings and labor market needs. A key strategy involves elevating employer engagement—not as an afterthought, but as a co-design partner in the education process. Sector partnerships, where industry leaders collaborate with educators to shape curriculum, design assessments, and offer hands-on learning opportunities, have proven successful in other states. Goger, Caves, and Salway (2024) report that stronger collaboration between employers and educators is essential to close the widening gap between workforce needs and education outcomes in the United States [23]. Their Brookings Institution report shows how today's labor market increasingly requires scalable, work-based learning opportunities such as apprenticeships and earn-and-learn models. Drawing on lessons from states like Alabama, Colorado, and Indiana, they propose systemic reforms to enable employers to co-design curriculum, offer real-time feedback on skill demands, and participate in credential development. The authors argue that a shared governance framework, streamlined infrastructure, and robust quality assurance systems are crucial for enabling broader, more equitable access to career-aligned education pathways. The

University of Hawai‘i system and its community colleges have begun to expand these partnerships through advisory councils and programmatic collaboration, but more robust and consistent structures are needed across all islands and industries.

Expanding work-based learning is another critical intervention. Internships, apprenticeships, job shadowing, and externships provide students with invaluable exposure to real-world work environments and expectations. These experiences help demystify career options, clarify student interests, and build both hard and soft skills that are difficult to teach in a classroom. For employers, work-based learning creates a pipeline of talent and an opportunity to shape potential hires early. Policymakers and employers must work together to remove barriers to participation—such as transportation, stipends, and academic credit—to ensure equitable access.

Career academies within high schools offer a promising model for early alignment. These academies, often organized around themes like health sciences, engineering, or digital media, integrate academic content with career-oriented learning and employer engagement. They provide students with coherent pathways from high school to postsecondary credentials and employment. Flack, Sludden, Hill, and Kemple (2023) report that out-of-school work-based learning programs like New York City's ExpandED STEM (Science, Technology, Engineering, and Mathematics) Options face challenges in retaining students, despite high interest levels driven by the promise of paid internships [24]. Their study reveals key barriers to participation: weak school support, long delays between application and enrollment, and conflicting demands on students' time. The most successful sites emphasized school collaboration, frequent communication, flexible scheduling, and community-building. Financial incentives and proximity to program sites were also critical for student persistence. Their findings show that sustained student engagement in work-based learning requires thoughtful design and strong institutional support.

Pistorino, Darche, and Headington (2024) report that work-based learning (WBL) connects education to career readiness by embedding real-world experiences into the curriculum [25]. Students who engage in WBL gain soft skills, social capital, and a clearer sense of purpose. This blog highlights WestEd's professional development course for community college instructors in California, which helps faculty integrate WBL into teaching. The program has reached over 10,000 students and enhanced equity, especially among underrepresented groups. WBL not only benefits learners but also employers and is crucial to bridging the gap between classroom learning and the modern workforce. In Hawai'i, schools such as Waipahu High School have demonstrated the power of this approach, with students earning industry certifications and college credits while still in high school [26]. This program's success in improving on-time graduation rates and providing cost savings for students exemplifies the potential benefits of implementing similar models in other schools, particularly in rural and neighbor island communities.

Additionally, dual credit and early college programs can help bridge the gap between high school and higher education. By earning college credits while still in high school, students gain a head start toward postsecondary credentials and reduce both the time and cost of college. These programs are particularly effective when paired with targeted advising and career exploration. They help demystify the college experience, reduce dropout rates, and provide a clearer pathway to in-demand occupations.

Beyond programmatic solutions, cultural and narrative change is also necessary. Families, educators, and community leaders play an important role in shaping perceptions about success and opportunity. Promoting local success stories whether it's a wind technician from Hilo, a chef-entrepreneur in Lāna'i, or a mobile app developer working remotely from Kaua'i can expand the imagination of what is possible. By highlighting diverse pathways and redefining what achievement looks like in Hawai'i, we can shift mindsets away from the false dichotomy between staying home and being successful. Tatiana Santiago's dissertation, E Kūlia i ka Nu'u: Striving for Excellence, explores the lived experiences and leadership strategies of Native Hawaiian leaders working in Hawaiian-serving organizations. Santiago (2022) used a phenomenological qualitative approach, conducting interviews with 13 leaders to identify values and strategies underpinning their success [27]. This study found that Hawaiian leadership is deeply rooted in cultural principles like aloha (compassion), pono (righteousness), kuleana (responsibility), 'ohana (family), and laulima (teamwork). Leaders emphasized humility, servant leadership, and collective decision-making, rather than hierarchical or individualistic approaches. Santiago developed a Native Hawaiian Leadership Development Model based on these findings, aiming to inspire culturally grounded leadership training programs and elevate Kanaka Maoli epistemologies in education, governance, and community work.

Public policy also has a role to play. Incentives for employer participation in workforce development such as tax credits, training grants, and streamlined licensing processes can accelerate alignment. State investments in regional workforce partnerships, broadband infrastructure, and micro-credentialing platforms can support more agile and inclusive training systems. Equally important is the integration of equity goals, ensuring that historically marginalized communities have access to high-growth, high-demand opportunities. Treskon, Morgan, Kumari, and Quinterno (2024) report that aligning workforce and economic development systems can improve economic outcomes for low-wage workers, particularly those from marginalized communities [28]. Traditionally, these fields have operated in silos, with workforce development focused on labor supply and economic development on business growth. However, this division has limited the effectiveness of both. This report advocates innovative, equity-centered approaches like apprenticeships, sectoral strategies, and worker voice initiatives. It emphasizes the importance of integrating local context, engaging community stakeholders, and using targeted data to ensure resources reach those most in need. The authors call for stronger connections between research, policy, and practice to foster good jobs and equitable economic opportunity across regions. They also recommend that public investments set high labor standards and that workforce and economic development efforts be coordinated at both local and federal levels to maximize impact.

Kress and Moret (2023) argue that while community colleges are central to workforce development, their potential remains underrealized due to fragmented policy support [29]. This report calls for federal and state investments to elevate community colleges as primary engines of workforce preparation, particularly through noncredit credentials and apprenticeships. It reveals successful state models like North Carolina and Virginia that align education with industry needs by improving funding formulas, streamlining program approval, and using real-time labor market data. The authors stress the need for career coaching, work-based learning opportunities, and financial support to boost access and equity, especially in rural areas. Strengthening this ecosystem can expand equitable economic opportunity nationwide.

Finally, evaluation and continuous improvement must be built into the system. Tracking graduate outcomes, job placement rates, and employer satisfaction provides feedback loops that keep programs relevant and accountable. Hawai‘i's emerging efforts to build a statewide longitudinal data system linking K–12, higher education, and labor market data offer a critical foundation for this work. Ensuring that these systems are transparent, disaggregated, and user-friendly will empower students, educators, and policymakers alike.

5 Workforce Development in Action: Success Stories

In Hawai'i, where economic transformation is both necessary and complex, localized success stories offer practical blueprints for what workforce development can look like when done right. These programs not only build skills and boost employability but also reflect the values, aspirations, and lived realities of Hawai'i's communities. While challenges remain—ranging from funding constraints to scalability, the examples below illuminate what's possible when education, industry, and community partners collaborate with intentionality and shared purpose.

The Hawai'i P–20 Partnerships for Education exemplifies this vision at a systemic level. Its 2024 annual report reveals that the state has made meaningful progress in aligning educational efforts across the K–12, postsecondary, and workforce systems through the "Hawai'i Graduates for Hawai'i's Future" initiative [30]. The initiative is guided by four major goals: expanding access to early learning, preparing all students for college and careers, improving postsecondary access and success, and training Hawai'i's residents for living-wage jobs. Despite some declines in college enrollment and degree completion post-pandemic, promising signs include increased participation in Early College programs and targeted investments in neighbor island schools. Notably, work-based learning opportunities expanded significantly, with nearly 15,000 students participating statewide. This report also highlights data dashboards to support transparency, Free Application for Federal Student Aid (FAFSA) support services, and the positive impact of Gaining Early Awareness and Readiness for Undergraduate Programs (GEAR UP) and college peer mentoring. Continued focus is placed on equity, with specific attention to historically underserved groups, such as Native Hawaiian and Pacific Islander students. These efforts aim to build a more integrated and inclusive talent pipeline statewide.

Meanwhile, on the island of Kaua'i, the Kaua'i Pathways Project demonstrates the power of regionally tailored workforce initiatives. Kaua'i Community College Office of Continuing Education and Training (OCET) (2024) reports that its workforce development programs on Kaua'i are closely aligned with local industry needs and emphasize rapid, flexible, and blended learning models [31]. Offering tuition-free training in sectors like healthcare, technology, and construction, OCET supports students with wraparound services such as childcare and transportation. This report highlights strong gains in revenue and student satisfaction, with 513 students in workforce programs and 367 certificates issued in FY 2024. Backed by partnerships like Hana Career Pathways and Good Jobs Hawai'i, OCET plays a vital role in building the island's talent pipeline and economic resilience. Graduates are connected directly with local employers, often through internships or guaranteed interviews. The impact has been significant: not only has the program increased credential attainment among low-income and rural residents, but it has also helped reverse out-migration trends by giving people compelling reasons to stay and contribute to their communities.

Social-emotional well-being is another cornerstone of workforce readiness—especially for students who face adversity. That's where the Hawai'i State Department of Education (HIDOE) program comes in. HIDOE (2022) outlines a comprehensive approach to fostering social-emotional learning (SEL) across schools through its School Social and Emotional Learning (SEL) Guide [32]. Grounded in the values of Nā Hopena A'o (HĀ), this guide encourages schools to embed SEL into every layer of the learning environment—from foundational beliefs and classroom practices to community relationships and staff development. It emphasizes creating nurturing, culturally grounded environments that support the holistic well-being of students. Key components include developing SEL teams, using data-informed practices, implementing trauma-sensitive strategies, and integrating SEL with academic instruction. It underscores that SEL is not a standalone program, but an integrated practice aligned with local values, aimed at improving student engagement, academic success, and long-term resilience

For older youth and young adults, Kupu Hawai'i offers a transformative model rooted in culture, environment, and service [33]. Established as a conservation corps, Kupu provides year-round training in environmental stewardship, natural resource management, and sustainability leadership. Participants, many of whom come from underserved or at-risk backgrounds, earn stipends, gain certifications (such as in first aid, wildfire response, or coastal restoration), and often transition into careers with organizations like the Department of Land and Natural Resources or private eco-tourism firms. Beyond skill development, Kupu's strength lies in identity formation; it helps young people see themselves as protectors of the land, empowered by a sense of kuleana (responsibility) and belonging. Its alumni have gone on to pursue advanced degrees, start businesses, or return as mentors, creating a multiplier effect that benefits the broader community.

What unites these initiatives is not just their individual success, but their embodiment of a more inclusive, relational, and place-based approach to workforce development. In contrast to one-size-fits-all models, these programs honor local context, whether that means weaving in cultural values, acknowledging trauma, or responding to specific regional labor needs. However, for such programs to reach their full potential, a few conditions must be met. First, sustained funding is essential. Many successful pilots fail to scale because they depend on short-term grants or discretionary funds that disappear after a few years. Policymakers must commit to long-term investments in these proven approaches, including line-item appropriations, bond measures, or performance-based funding models.

Second, public–private partnerships need to deepen. Employers must be more than just end-users of talent—they should be co-designers of programs, co-funders of training infrastructure, and active participants in mentorship and evaluation. At the same time, educational institutions must be responsive to labor market signals without losing sight of their broader mission to cultivate human potential.

Third, culturally grounded pedagogy must remain at the heart of Hawai'i's workforce strategies. Programs that resonate most with learners are those that affirm their identities and build on the knowledge, practices, and languages of their communities. This is especially true for Native Hawaiian youth, who are more likely to engage when education connects to 'ike kūpuna (ancestral knowledge), environmental stewardship, and community well-being.

Finally, data and storytelling must go hand in hand. Rigorous evaluation is important to assess impact and inform improvements, but so is narrative. Sharing the journeys of individuals who have benefited from these programs like a single parent who completed an apprenticeship and secured stable employment, or a high schooler who earned a credential and found her passion in healthcare, can inspire others and shift public perceptions about what success looks like in Hawai'i.

In a time of economic uncertainty and systemic inequities, these success stories offer more than inspiration, they offer direction. They show that with the right support systems, strategic collaboration, and cultural grounding, Hawai'i can grow a workforce that is not only skilled and adaptable but rooted in community and purpose. The road ahead will require vigilance, vision, and collective will. But the seeds of transformation are already planted. Programs like Hawai'i P–20, Kaua'i Pathways, and Kupu remind us that when we invest in people—especially in ways that reflect their stories and strengths—we invest in the future of Hawai'i.

6 The Role of the University of Hawai‘i System

As both an academic institution and a vital economic engine, the UH System plays an indispensable role in shaping the future of work and opportunity across the islands. With ten campuses spanning community colleges and research universities, UH is uniquely positioned to bridge education, workforce development, and community engagement. In the face of evolving labor market demands, demographic shifts, and structural economic challenges, UH must not only adapt but lead.

The UH System's potential impact can be understood across several interconnected domains: workforce innovation hubs, stackable credentials, adult re-skilling and lifelong learning, civic and cultural education, and institutional policy alignment. Each of these areas represents an opportunity to cultivate a resilient, inclusive, and future-ready economy grounded in local values and global relevance.

UH can serve as a statewide anchor for sector-based innovation hubs. By leveraging its research capacity, cross-campus collaboration, and public-private partnerships, UH can drive regional strategies around critical sectors such as climate resilience, clean energy, artificial intelligence, and cybersecurity. These hubs would function as collaborative ecosystems, bringing together students, faculty, industry leaders, and community organizations to co-create solutions, develop talent pipelines, and generate applied research. For instance, UH Mānoa's expertise in oceanography and sustainability could support innovation in blue economy initiatives, while UH Maui College might specialize in renewable energy deployment and microgrid systems. By tailoring each campus's strengths to local and statewide industry needs, the system can cultivate distributed excellence while enhancing economic self-sufficiency.

These hubs can also play a crucial role in workforce diversification by embedding inclusive design principles and prioritizing participation from historically underrepresented communities, including Native Hawaiian and Pacific Islander populations. In this way, UH can expand access to innovation while ensuring equitable representation in the industries of tomorrow. The traditional higher education pathway, a linear progression from high school to a four-year degree—no longer fits the needs of many students. In Hawai‘i, where cost of living pressures and diverse educational journeys are common, UH must continue advancing a flexible and modular credentialing system. Stackable credentials, such as industry-aligned certificates and micro-credentials, offer learners the opportunity to build skills incrementally, re-enter education as needed, and earn workforce-recognized qualifications along the way.

These credentials should align with labor market demands and be designed in collaboration with employers, ensuring that each step along the educational journey delivers immediate value. A student might begin with a six-month cybersecurity certificate, transition to a paid internship, and later return to complete an associate degree or bachelor's program, all within a seamless UH pathway. Such models recognize the realities of working learners, particularly those balancing family responsibilities, financial pressures, or rural access constraints.

Beyond entry-level employment, stackable credentials can also support advancement in sectors like healthcare, information technology, construction, and education. The UH System's ability to offer articulated, cross-campus credentialing pathways is a critical advantage that must be leveraged and scaled. UH News (2023) reports that the UH System was selected to join the national "Credential As You Go" (CAYG) 2023 cohort, a multi-state initiative focused on developing incremental credential pathways [34]. This shows UH's efforts to design stackable microcredentials that support workforce alignment, enabling students and adult learners to accumulate credentials over time without starting over. This initiative facilitates more flexible, transparent, and inclusive education-to-career transitions across the state. UH (2024) implemented Executive Policy 5.231 to guide the development and issuance of micro-credentials across its campuses [35]. This policy, shaped by extensive consultation with faculty and leadership, defines micro-credentials and outlines standards for implementation. It supports flexible, skill-based learning aligned with workforce needs and promotes lifelong learning through stackable, digitally badged credentials.

Hawai'i P-20 Partnerships for Education (2025) reports that the updated Promising Credentials in Hawai'i identifies 69 non-degree, industry-recognized credentials aligned with in-demand, living-wage occupations [36]. Through comprehensive labor market analysis and industry input, this report aims to guide job seekers, educators, and workforce development stakeholders by clarifying which credentials hold the most value for Hawai'i's economy. Key findings show a persistent gap between job openings and hires, highlighting the need for accessible, high-value credentials that can be earned locally. Recommendations include expanding training access, integrating credentials into education and career pathways, improving data systems, and strengthening alignment between education and workforce needs.

Rapid technological change and sectoral disruption are displacing workers in fields ranging from tourism to retail. Mid-career and displaced workers need accessible, accelerated opportunities to re-skill for emerging fields. UH must embrace its role as a hub for lifelong learning, where adults can return at any stage to gain new skills, earn credentials, and connect with job opportunities.

Community colleges such as Leeward and Kauaʻi CC are already models for responsive workforce training, offering short-term programs in renewable energy, early childhood education, and commercial driver licensing. Building on these foundations, the system can expand noncredit-to-credit bridges, evening and weekend formats, hybrid delivery options, and targeted support services like career coaching and childcare. Leeward Community College (LCC) (2024) reports that its workforce development programs are designed to meet local industry needs through short-term, stackable training in sectors such as commercial driving, healthcare, and technology [37]. With hybrid learning options, evening and weekend schedules, and industry certifications, LCC exemplifies flexible, accessible, and responsive education that supports both career advancement and economic resilience for Hawaiʻi's diverse learners. Kauaʻi Community College (KCC) reports that its Early Childhood Education program prepares students for careers in childcare and preschool education [38]. Designed to support both new and returning adult learners, this program offers practical training and academic instruction aligned with industry standards. It contributes to strengthening Hawaiʻi's early learning workforce in a sector essential to both child development and economic resilience.

Moreover, partnerships with labor unions, employer associations, and local chambers of commerce can enhance the relevance and reach of re-skilling efforts. Programs like the Good Jobs Hawaiʻi initiative illustrate how cross-sector collaboration can activate new learning pathways. Good Jobs Hawaiʻi is a statewide initiative offering tuition-free training in high-demand sectors such as healthcare, IT, skilled trades, and clean energy [39]. Coordinated by the University of Hawaiʻi Community Colleges and funded through federal and state support, this program targets unemployed and underemployed residents, especially Native Hawaiians and those from underserved communities. Beyond technical training, participants receive wraparound services like career coaching and job placement, aiming to support economic mobility and meet Hawaiʻi's workforce needs.

For UH, the goal is not only to respond to disruption but to proactively equip learners with adaptive capacities for a lifetime of change.

Preparing students for the workforce should not come at the expense of civic engagement and cultural knowledge. The University of Hawai'i System must continue to uphold its mission to educate leaders who are not only employable but also grounded in place, culture, and responsibility to community. This is particularly essential in a state like Hawai'i, where Indigenous values and multicultural identities shape both daily life and long-term vision. Civic learning can also include service learning, public deliberation, and leadership development. Students should graduate not only with technical know-how but with the ability to contribute thoughtfully to Hawai'i's social, environmental, and economic challenges. Embedding civic and cultural dimensions into career education reaffirms the university's role in preparing holistic, rooted citizens.

To fully realize these opportunities, the UH System must also confront its internal challenges and external responsibilities. Financial sustainability remains a pressing concern, as declining enrollment and fluctuating state appropriations strain budgets. The pandemic accelerated these trends, but demographic shifts and competition from online providers continue to exert pressure. In response, UH must modernize its administrative structures, improve cross-campus coordination, and invest in high-demand program areas. Equally important is rebuilding trust and transparency with stakeholders, including faculty, staff, students, and community partners. Clear metrics of impact, robust public engagement, and inclusive decision-making can strengthen the institution's legitimacy and alignment with public priorities.

Collaboration with employers and policymakers is not a nice-to-have; it is essential. UH must actively seek co-design opportunities with industry partners, participate in regional workforce councils, and align strategic planning with statewide goals for economic diversification and equity. The Hawai'i Workforce Development Council, DBEDT, and county-level economic agencies are key collaborators in this effort.

The UH System holds a unique position of influence in Hawai'i's economic and educational future. By embracing innovation hubs, stackable credentials, adult re-skilling, civic education, and strategic partnerships, UH can power a more agile, equitable, and community-grounded workforce ecosystem. Its success will not only be measured in degrees conferred or grants awarded, but in the tangible improvements to the lives of Hawai'i's people, their ability to stay, thrive, and lead in the place they call home.

7 Equity and Inclusion: Closing the Opportunity Gap

Any discussion of talent must confront Hawai'i's deep disparities. Native Hawaiians, Pacific Islanders, and Filipino students continue to face entrenched systemic barriers in education and employment that limit their access to opportunity. These disparities are not just statistical anomalies—they are historical and structural, compounded by legacies of colonization, land dispossession, language loss, and economic marginalization. Today, they manifest in lower postsecondary attainment rates, higher unemployment levels, and disproportionate representation in low-wage sectors.

The geographic divide further compounds these inequities. A student on Lāna'i may aspire to become a software engineer or nurse practitioner but face logistical and financial hurdles simply to access relevant education and training. Without deliberate investment and policy innovation, these gaps will persist, curtailing the full realization of Hawai'i's human capital. DBEDT (2024) outlines that updated U.S. Census Bureau definitions significantly reshaped the urban-rural classification of Hawai'i's communities, with major implications for policy and resource distribution [40]. The reclassification reduced the urban population share and expanded rural designations to include areas such as Moloka'i, Lāna'i, and parts of Hawai'i Island. These rural regions face persistent challenges including limited access to broadband internet, fewer educational and training institutions, and scarce college and career counseling resources. As a result, students and jobseekers in rural areas often encounter logistical and financial barriers when pursuing advanced coursework, degrees, or credentials. This report emphasizes that these geographic disparities require targeted strategies to avoid deepening Hawai'i's opportunity gap. Addressing rural access issues is critical for inclusive workforce development and ensuring that talent across all islands—not just in Honolulu—can thrive in an increasingly knowledge-based economy.

Equity in education requires more than equal treatment, it demands targeted strategies to meet students where they are and respond to their specific needs. Place-based learning, rooted in indigenous knowledge systems and community priorities, offers one such approach. These models connect learning to lived experience, affirming cultural identity while cultivating academic skills. For Native Hawaiian students, for instance, curricula that incorporate Hawaiian language, history, and practices such as lo'i kalo restoration or celestial navigation can foster a deeper sense of belonging and motivation. Such engagement is not a distraction from rigorous academic learning; rather, it is a catalyst.

The UH System has made meaningful progress in integrating culture-based pedagogy across its campuses, but there is room to grow. Initiatives like Hawaiian Studies pathways at UH Hilo and UH West O'ahu (UHWO) serve as exemplars. The Hawaiian-Pacific Studies concentration at UHWO offers a comprehensive curriculum focusing on the histories, languages, and cultures of Hawai'i and the Pacific Islands [41]. By integrating indigenous perspectives across various disciplines, this program exemplifies the university's dedication to culturally responsive education. The next step is expansion, ensuring that culturally relevant instruction is not confined to specific departments but embedded across disciplines. In STEM, for example, projects that explore traditional ecological knowledge can inform modern climate resilience strategies. In health sciences, training programs that center on culturally responsive care are critical to addressing health disparities among Native Hawaiian and Pacific Islander populations.

Alongside curricular reform, financial aid plays a pivotal role in access and completion. For many students from underrepresented backgrounds, the challenge is not getting into college, it's staying in. Targeted scholarships and wraparound services, including academic advising, mental health support, transportation subsidies, and childcare assistance, are essential for persistence. Programs like the UH Mānoa First-Year Programs (FYP) exemplify how integrated supports can make the difference between dropping out and graduating [42]. FYP is designed to ease students' transition into university life. With components like UNIV 110 and peer mentorship, FYP emphasizes academic readiness, student engagement, and a strong sense of community. The initiative plays a critical role in boosting retention and persistence among first-year students.

Digital equity is another cornerstone of inclusion in the twenty-first century. The pandemic underscored stark disparities in broadband access and device availability. In rural and lower-income households, students struggled to participate in remote learning, widening the achievement gap. Closing this digital divide requires sustained public investment not only in infrastructure but also in digital literacy training for students and educators.

The state's recent broadband expansion plans are promising, but implementation must prioritize the most underserved communities. DBEDT (2024) outlines Hawai'i's comprehensive strategy for achieving digital equity in its Hawai'i Digital Equity Plan [43]. Developed through extensive community engagement including 39 focus groups across the islands, this plan prioritizes expanding high-speed internet access for underserved populations, particularly those in rural, low-income, and Native Hawaiian communities. It identifies barriers to digital inclusion, such as affordability, device access, and digital literacy, and presents targeted strategies to overcome them. By focusing on community-informed solutions and sustainable implementation, this plan serves as a foundational roadmap to guide state agencies, educators, employers, and nonprofit partners in narrowing the digital divide and promoting statewide economic opportunity through connectivity. Office of the Governor in State of Hawaiʻi (2024) releases that Governor Josh Green has approved $33 million in state funding to complement federal investments through the Broadband Equity Access and Development (BEAD) program [44]. This initiative focuses on building broadband infrastructure to extend "last mile" connections, particularly in Hawaiʻi's unserved and underserved areas. It marks a significant step toward digital equity and inclusion across the islands.

Equity is not only a moral imperative but an economic one. When entire segments of the population are left behind, the state loses out on talent, innovation, and productivity. A truly inclusive workforce strategy must lift all communities, not just the privileged few. This means creating accessible on-ramps to quality employment, supporting entrepreneurship in historically marginalized communities, and ensuring that labor protections and benefits reach those in gig work or low-wage sectors where many Pacific Islander and Filipino workers are overrepresented.

Community partnerships are key. Local nonprofits, cultural organizations, and faith-based groups often have deep trust and reach within their communities. Their involvement in co-designing educational programs, mentorship initiatives, and job training pathways enhances cultural resonance and effectiveness. For instance, organizations like Kamehameha Schools and the Council for Native Hawaiian Advancement (CNHA) have long demonstrated how community-rooted institutions can drive systemic change through policy advocacy, capacity-building, and direct service. Kamehameha Schools (2024) introduces a new partnership with Arizona State University called Ke Ala I Ka Palapala Laepua—Pathway to Bachelor's, which enables high school students to earn up to 60 college credits before graduation [45]. This program reduces post-secondary costs and boosts academic preparation. By integrating culturally grounded pedagogy, it supports Native Hawaiian students with learning that honors their identity, fostering both engagement and long-term achievement. CNHA introduces the Hawaiian Trades Academy, an initiative offering accelerated training in fields such as commercial driver licensing and Occupational Safety and Health Administration (OSHA) certifications

[46]. This program uniquely integrates financial literacy and Hawaiian cultural values, creating a holistic workforce development model. This culturally responsive approach empowers Native Hawaiians with both market-relevant skills and a strong sense of identity, contributing to lasting employment and community impact.

Measuring progress is equally important. Disaggregated data by race, ethnicity, geography, and income is essential to uncovering inequities and guiding resource allocation. Hawaiʻi must strengthen its longitudinal data systems to track educational and employment outcomes across student populations. Transparency and accountability will allow policymakers, educators, and community leaders to assess what's working, identify gaps, and make evidence-based improvements.

Ultimately, equity and inclusion must be woven into the fabric of all policies, practices, and partnerships across the education-to-employment continuum. From how curricula are designed and faculty are hired, to how financial aid is distributed and broadband networks are built, every decision must consider who benefits and who might be left behind. By honoring the histories and aspirations of all its people, Hawaiʻi can cultivate a workforce that is not only highly skilled, but also deeply rooted in the values of justice, community, and aloha.

8 Remote Work and the Diaspora Connection

The rise of remote work presents Hawaiʻi with a transformative opportunity to address one of its most persistent challenges: the outmigration of skilled residents. For decades, high housing costs, limited career prospects, and relatively lower wages have pushed many kamaʻāina, especially young, educated professionals, to seek opportunities on the continent or abroad. This phenomenon has not only weakened the local economy but has also strained communities, families, and cultural continuity.

Remote work alters this landscape. With the normalization of location-independent employment, Hawaiʻi now has a unique opening to bring back members of its diaspora who left in search of professional opportunities. Today, a kamaʻāina working for a global firm in Seattle or San Francisco can realistically relocate to Hilo, Wailuku, or Kailua and continue contributing to the same company, all while living in the islands and re-engaging with local life. Washington Post (2024) reports that there has been a significant rise in Native Hawaiians holding management and professional positions over the past decade [47]. This upward trend is attributed in part to the expansion of remote work, which enables professionals to reside in Hawai'i while maintaining employment with firms located outside the state. It shows how this shift is helping to reverse decades of outmigration and underrepresentation, marking a potentially transformative moment for the Native Hawaiian community in both economic and cultural terms.

To capitalize on this shift, state and county governments can pursue proactive policies that welcome returnees while aligning their relocation with broader workforce needs. For example, offering targeted tax credits or housing assistance for returning professionals in high-demand sectors like education, healthcare, STEM, and public service could help reverse talent loss in critical areas. Hawai'i Department of Taxation (2021) outlines the state's Low-Income Housing Tax Credit (LIHTC) program, which incentivizes developers to build affordable housing through targeted tax benefits [48]. Although this program is not specifically designed for returning professionals, it serves as a model of how Hawai'i leverages fiscal policy to address housing challenges. With strategic adaptation, similar tax credit frameworks could be extended to support returnees in high-demand sectors such as healthcare, education, and STEM, thereby aligning housing policy with workforce development goals. While such incentives require investment, the long-term returns in the form of a more skilled, place-committed workforce could be substantial. Other states, such as Vermont, have pioneered similar strategies, providing a potential blueprint for a Hawai'i-specific model rooted in cultural connection and sectoral need. Vermont legislative report (2021) evaluates worker relocation incentive programs, finding they generated substantial economic returns up to $93.88 per tax dollar spent [49]. It shows that well-designed incentives, especially when paired with housing and childcare support, can attract skilled workers, offering a compelling model for Hawai'i's long-term workforce development.

In addition to easing the return of diaspora professionals, building infrastructure that supports remote workers within Hawai'i is essential, especially in rural communities. Remote work hubs can play a vital role here. These shared spaces, equipped with high-speed internet, co-working areas, childcare services, and networking events, could serve as catalysts for rural economic revitalization. They offer more than just desks and Wi-Fi; they provide remote workers with professional community, mentoring opportunities, and pathways to engage in local initiatives. In communities where economic activity has stagnated, such hubs could reenergize commerce, create jobs in supportive industries, and attract a new wave of residents committed to staying.

Meanwhile, universities and high schools across the islands have an important role to play in reconnecting with their alumni. These institutions have access to robust networks of graduates who have gone on to build impressive careers elsewhere. With coordinated outreach, these alumni networks can serve as strategic talent pipelines. "Return to Hawai'i" campaigns featuring digital outreach, career fairs, and storytelling from those who have made the move back could inspire and inform those contemplating a return. While salary disparities between Hawai'i and the continent still exist, remote work removes much of that barrier, allowing people to earn global wages while living locally.

Equally important is the opportunity to retain local youth before they feel compelled to leave. For too long, the implicit message has been that career success means moving away. But remote work challenges that narrative. A student graduating from the University of Hawai'i can now realistically pursue a tech, design, writing, or policy career from their hometown. To make this viable, the state must invest in digital infrastructure, broadband equity, and curriculum reform. Teaching students how to collaborate across time zones, manage projects remotely, and use digital tools effectively is as essential as teaching them to code or write. This is not just a workforce development strategy; it's a way to preserve community integrity. When young people stay, they strengthen families, enrich schools, and contribute to local governance and volunteerism. If the best and brightest no longer feel compelled to leave, entire communities become more resilient. And if they do leave for a time, they do so knowing that they can come back without sacrificing their professional goals.

As promising as remote work is, its expansion must be pursued thoughtfully, with clear attention to equity. The influx of remote workers, especially those with high salaries, has already been linked to rising housing prices in various parts of the U.S. mainland. In Hawai'i, where housing costs are already among the highest in the nation, policies must avoid exacerbating displacement and gentrification. Any incentive designed to attract remote workers or returnees should be coupled with investments in affordable housing, rental assistance, and protections for long-term residents. Community benefit should be at the center of these efforts—not an afterthought.

Cultural sensitivity must also guide this movement. Hawai'i is not merely a scenic backdrop for Zoom calls—it is a homeland with a rich indigenous history and a deep sense of place. Remote workers, whether returnees or newcomers, must be encouraged to engage respectfully with the land and its people. Volunteerism, participation in cultural events, and partnerships with local organizations can help foster reciprocal relationships. Returnees have an opportunity, and arguably a responsibility, to serve as bridges between global professional networks and local needs.

The broader economic benefits of expanding remote work are considerable. Remote workers spend money in local economies. They rent homes, buy groceries, frequent restaurants and cafes, and often enroll their children in local schools. Over time, this contributes to a more diversified and stable economic base, particularly in areas overly dependent on tourism or government employment. For rural towns that have seen population decline, remote work could bring new life and vitality.

Moreover, the integration of remote work into Hawai‘i's economic strategy would support broader sustainability goals. DBEDT (2022) reports that remote work in Hawai‘i, accelerated by the COVID-19 pandemic, significantly reshaped employer and employee behavior, revealing long-term benefits such as increased job satisfaction, reduced operational costs, and enhanced access to talent [50]. This report highlights that remote work mitigates outmigration by enabling kama‘āina to stay or return, lowers commuting-related emissions, and fosters economic diversification by integrating Hawai‘i into the global digital economy. With sustained investment in broadband and digital equity, remote work can be a central strategy for the state's sustainable economic future.

Taken together, these possibilities point toward a future in which Hawai‘i's economic and cultural resilience are strengthened through the intentional integration of remote work. Reconnecting with the diaspora, retaining local youth, and welcoming professionals who respect and contribute to the community can help Hawai‘i move beyond reactive strategies and toward a vision of economic development rooted in equity, place, and belonging. If pursued thoughtfully, remote work will not be a temporary trend, but a cornerstone of a more inclusive, sustainable, and self-determined Hawai‘i.

9 Forecasting the Future of Work in Hawai‘i

As the global economy continues to evolve, Hawai‘i faces both urgent challenges and unprecedented opportunities in preparing its workforce for the future. Demographic shifts, technological advances, climate change, and cultural values are converging to reshape what work looks like, who performs it, and where it takes place. Against this backdrop, forecasting the future of work is no longer a speculative exercise, it is a strategic imperative. For Hawai'i, an island economy with distinctive vulnerabilities and strengths, the ability to anticipate and adapt to change will determine not only economic resilience, but also the well-being of future generations. To stay competitive and inclusive, Hawai'i must cultivate a nimble, anticipatory workforce development system that aligns emerging labor market needs with the unique aspirations and capabilities of its people. This requires the use of advanced forecasting tools, robust public–private-academic collaboration, and a renewed investment in lifelong learning. The following analysis identifies four critical labor market trends shaping the future of work in Hawai'i: automation, the rise of green jobs, the expansion of the care economy, and the emergence of a creative digital economy. Each trend presents both risks of disruption and pathways for innovation, particularly when grounded in Hawai'i's values of equity, sustainability, and cultural integrity.

Across the globe, automation continues to displace routine and repetitive jobs, particularly in sectors like retail, logistics, and hospitality, three of Hawai'i's largest employment categories. Self-checkout kiosks, automated inventory systems, contactless hotel check-ins, and delivery drones are already changing the structure of service-related occupations. In a state heavily reliant on tourism and service industries, this shift is particularly consequential. Many entry-level positions that traditionally served as on-ramps for younger or less formally educated workers are at risk of being replaced or radically transformed.

However, automation is not purely a threat; it also creates new economic possibilities. Emerging roles in data analytics, robotics maintenance, artificial intelligence training, and cybersecurity are growing in demand. These jobs often pay higher wages and offer more career mobility. For Hawai'i to capture this upside, there must be intentional investment in retraining displaced workers, integrating digital literacy into K–12 and postsecondary curricula, and forming industry-aligned training programs in automation-resilient sectors. Community colleges can serve as agile hubs for re-skilling, particularly if paired with industry partnerships and real-time labor market data.

As Hawai'i confronts the realities of climate change from sea-level rise and coastal erosion to extreme weather events and invasive species, the need for a green economy has never been more urgent. Fortunately, the transition to sustainability is also a powerful engine for job creation. The 2024 Characterizing Hawai'i's Natural Resources Management Sector report documents a 6.3% growth in natural resource management (NRM) employment since 2018, with nearly 5,000 full-time positions reported across state, federal, nonprofit, academic, and private organizations [51]. Key roles include administrative support, field technicians, conservation scientists, and cultural practitioners. This report highlights rising starting salaries, increased demand for college majors in environmental and Hawaiian studies, and growing availability of paid internships and fellowships. These findings demonstrate the expanding potential of green jobs in Hawai'i, particularly as the state moves toward its 100% renewable energy goal by 2045. It stresses how investment in environmental stewardship not only conserves natural resources but also drives sustainable job creation, advancing Hawai'i's economic resilience and climate adaptation priorities.

Moreover, Hawai'i's unique island ecosystems and cultural reverence for nature position it to lead in regenerative land and ocean-based practices. The expansion of careers in marine biology, sustainable agriculture, native forest restoration, and invasive species management is both economically viable and culturally rooted. These jobs not only align with climate goals but can also promote place-based education and intergenerational learning by integrating traditional ecological knowledge. To unlock the full potential of green jobs, workforce systems must ensure equitable access to training programs in both urban and rural areas, especially in historically underserved communities. Policies that align workforce incentives with clean energy development, conservation initiatives, and climate resilience planning will be crucial to ensuring that green jobs are accessible, dignified, and stable.

Hawai'i's rapidly aging population, combined with the emotional and educational needs of younger generations, underscores the growing importance of the care economy. This sector encompasses a wide array of jobs, including home health aids, nursing assistants, mental health counselors, early childhood educators, and community health workers. These are essential professions that uphold the well-being of families and communities, yet they are often underpaid and undervalued.

UHERO (2024) projects that by 2035, one in four Hawai'i residents will be 65 or older, signaling a profound demographic shift [52]. This report warns that without increased investment in elder care, education, and healthcare infrastructure, the state's economic and generational equity will deteriorate. Aging kūpuna, particularly those over 75, face high consumption needs but limited labor income, placing strain on public resources like Medicare and Social Security. Simultaneously, declining fertility and stagnant investments in youth deepen long-term economic risks. The findings emphasize that supporting both young children and kūpuna is essential not only for moral reasons, but as a strategic economic imperative—making the case for bold investment in Hawai'i's care economy to preserve social cohesion and economic sustainability.

Expanding and professionalizing the care workforce involves more than increasing wages; it includes credentialing pathways, stackable certificates, and strong wraparound supports such as tuition assistance, housing stipends, and transportation subsidies. Workforce development programs should also center culturally relevant caregiving practices and bilingual service delivery, reflecting the diversity of Hawai'i's families. Additionally, expanding public-private partnerships in the care economy such as employer-sponsored childcare or school-based health services can relieve workforce bottlenecks and support the dual goals of productivity and care. Ultimately, strengthening human infrastructure is foundational to building a resilient and equitable economy.

The convergence of digital technology and creative expression is generating new markets and career paths, particularly for younger generations. Fields like graphic design, video editing, virtual reality (VR), gaming, augmented reality (AR), and social media content creation are thriving in the decentralized digital economy. These sectors rely less on geographic proximity and more on connectivity, creativity, and access to tools—making them ideal for Hawai'i's remote workforce strategy.

The state's rich cultural assets—language, storytelling, music, and visual arts—can be reimagined and scaled through digital platforms. Hawaiian mo'olelo (oral histories), for instance, can become immersive educational VR experiences or animated digital series. Gaming companies can collaborate with Native Hawaiian artists to create culturally grounded environments. Influencers and content creators who work from Hawai'i contribute to the global digital landscape while generating income and preserving local identity. However, the digital divide remains a barrier. Many aspiring creatives lack access to software, hardware, mentorship, and platforms for exposure. Addressing this requires both infrastructure investments and community-based training hubs where youth and emerging creatives can experiment, learn, and collaborate. Public libraries, schools, and neighborhood centers can serve as launchpads for this work.

Building partnerships between the tech industry, media organizations, and educational institutions can further develop this talent pipeline. Programs such as hackathons, pitch competitions, and creator incubators can spotlight Hawai'i's creative potential while connecting local talent to global opportunities. Kurosu (2024) reports that students from the University of Hawai'i at Mānoa's Pacific Asian Center for Entrepreneurship (PACE) program won $4,000 in prizes at the 2024 Honolulu Tech Week Community Hackathon for projects tackling real-world problems [53]. Innovations included MopedSafe, a Bluetooth-based anti-theft system; WriteLevel, an AI tool for automated essay grading; and AquaHealth, an AI platform diagnosing fish diseases. This event showcased how PACE's entrepreneurial training empowers students to build practical solutions and connect academic research to market applications.

To navigate these intersecting trends, Hawai'i must shift from reactive planning to proactive strategy. Workforce forecasting tools—such as labor market analytics, scenario modeling, and employer needs assessments—can help educators and policymakers better anticipate demand and align curriculum and credentials accordingly. Data transparency and alignment across education, economic development, and labor departments are essential. Cross-sector collaboration will also be key. Workforce development cannot fall solely on government or schools. Industry leaders, labor unions, community organizations, and indigenous practitioners all have essential roles to play. Convening sector-specific working groups, coordinating apprenticeships, and incentivizing work-based learning can accelerate the adaptation process.

Finally, a culture of lifelong learning must be embedded in Hawai'i's economic fabric. With the half-life of skills shrinking, workers at every stage of life must have access to affordable, relevant, and flexible learning opportunities, whether through community colleges, microcredentials, online platforms, or employer-sponsored training. Forecasting the future of work in Hawai'i is not about predicting one fixed outcome; it is about building the capacity to respond to change with agility, inclusion, and foresight. As automation, climate change, caregiving needs, and digital innovation reshape the labor market, Hawai'i has an opportunity to lead with intention. By investing in its people—across age, sector, and island—the state can chart a course toward an economy that is resilient, equitable, and uniquely grounded in aloha.

10 Conclusion: Investing in Hawai‘i’s Greatest Resource

Hawai‘i’s future competitiveness will not be determined by land or capital, but by its people. Investing in human potential is the most strategic, equitable, and culturally grounded economic policy available. That means making education joyful, relevant, and rigorous. It means valuing all forms of work—from science to storytelling, from caregiving to coding. And it means creating pathways home for those who left and ladders up for those still climbing. The next chapter explores the infrastructure and regulatory systems that support (or stifle) Hawai‘i’s economic ambitions—from permitting to shipping, housing to broadband.

References

[1]. Kana‘iaupuni, S. M., Ledward, B., & Jensen, U. (2010). Culture-Based Education and Its Relationship to Student Outcomes. Kamehameha Schools Research & Evaluation. Retrieved from https://www.ksbe.edu/assets/research/collection/10_0117_kanaiaupuni.pdf.

[2]. Teranishi, R., Gutierrez, R. A. E., Gogue, D. T.-L., Le, A., & Hafoka, ‘I. (2023). Native Hawaiians & Pacific Islanders in higher education: A collection of campus research to inform student success. Institute for Immigration, Globalization, and Education, UCLA. Retrieved from https://apiascholars.org/wp-content/uploads/2023/03/NHPI_2023_CampusResearch_FINAL_R2.pdf.

[3]. Tagami, M. (2024, January 7). Financial aid changes are creating ‘new levels of frustration’ for Hawaii students. Honolulu Civil Beat. Retrieved from https://www.civilbeat.org/2024/01/financial-aid-changes-are-creating-new-levels-of-frustration-for-hawaii-students/.

[4]. University of Hawai‘i News. (2025, January 29). Hawai‘i schools facing chronic underfunding, report reveals. Retrieved from https://www.hawaii.edu/news/2025/01/29/underfunding-hawaii-public-schools/.

[5]. Department of Business, Economic Development and Tourism. (2024, December). A report to the Hawai‘i State Legislature pursuant to HCR 184. Retrieved from https://files.hawaii.gov/dbedt/annuals/2024/2024-cid-act184.pdf.

[6]. Hawai‘i Community College. (2023). 2023 Annual Review of Program Data: Counseling, Advising, and Support Services Center. Retrieved from https://hawaii.hawaii.edu/files/program-unit-review/docs/2023-cassc-aur.pdf.

[7]. University of Hawai'i. (2024, February 19). Hawai'i's future jobs: 70% require postsecondary education by 2031. University of Hawai'i News. Retrieved from https://manoa.hawaii.edu/news/article.php?aId=13081.
[8]. Park, J. Y. (2025, January 18). Migration in Hawai'i: Who's moving and why it matters. University of Hawai'i Economic Research Organization (UHERO). Retrieved from https://uhero.hawaii.edu/who-is-moving-in-and-out-understanding-migration-trends-in-hawaii/.
[9]. U.S. Bureau of Labor Statistics. (2024, May). Occupational Employment and Wages in Urban Honolulu — May 2024. Retrieved from https://www.bls.gov/regions/west/news-release/occupationalemploymentandwages_honolulu.htm.
[10]. Department of Business, Economic Development & Tourism. (2024, November). Hawai'i's Targeted & Emerging Industries. Retrieved from https://files.hawaii.gov/dbedt/annuals/2024/2024-read-emerging-industry-report.pdf.
[11]. Department of Business, Economic Development & Tourism. (2023, December). Top Occupations in Hawai'i 2016 to 2023. Retrieved from https://files.hawaii.gov/dbedt/economic/reports/Top20_Occupations_Hawaii_2023.pdf.
[12]. Hawai'i Housing Finance & Development Corporation. (2024). 2024 HHFDC Annual Report. Retrieved from https://dbedt.hawaii.gov/hhfdc/files/2025/02/2024-HHFDC-Annual-Report-only.pdf.
[13]. University of Hawai'i Economic Research Organization. (2024). The Hawai'i Housing Factbook 2024. Retrieved from https://uhero.hawaii.edu/wp-content/uploads/2024/05/HawaiiHousingFactbook2024.pdf.
[14]. Ricket, A. L., Yahn, J., & Bentley, E. (2023). Rural community and career connected learning: Impacts of high school internships prioritizing people and place. Journal of Research in Rural Education, 39(3). https://doi.org/10.26209/JRRE3903.
[15]. Peters, K. (2024, February 15). Workforce development: Building local, skilled talent pipelines for Hawaii's growth industries [Presentation]. Chamber of Commerce Hawaii. Retrieved from https://labor.hawaii.gov/wdc/files/2024/03/Presentation-Sector-Partnerships-Workforce-Development-Buildling-Local-Skilled-Talent-Pipelines-K.Peters.pdf.
[16]. Department of Business, Economic Development & Tourism. (2022). Remote work in Hawai'i: Effects of the COVID-19 pandemic on Hawai'i's remote work marketplace. Retrieved from https://files.hawaii.gov/dbedt/economic/reports/DBEDT_REMOTE%20WORK_FULL%20REPORT_FINAL_REV220311.pdf.
[17]. Von Zastrow, C. (2024). The statewide longitudinal data system landscape. Education Commission of the States. Retrieved from https://www.ecs.org/50-state-comparison-statewide-longitudinal-data-systems-2024/.

[18]. Das, P., Tadj, Y., Cloudwatcher, S., & Ho-Schar, C. (2020). Future planning practitioners and the "Waipahu Talk Story": Learning from and reflecting on participation. Journal of Planning Education and Research, 44(1), 469–483. Retrieved from https://doi.org/10.1177/0739456X20954536.
[19]. Strada Education Network & Burning Glass Institute. (2024). Talent Disrupted: College Graduates, Underemployment, and the Way Forward. Retrieved from https://cdn.prod.website-files.com/6777c52f82e5471a3732ea25/679a6fadfda4220bbac585d7_Talent-Disrupted-2.pdf.
[20]. Chamber of Commerce Hawai'i. (2023). Hawai'i Skilled Trades Workforce Analysis. Retrieved from https://www.cochawaii.org/wp-content/uploads/2024/10/hawaii-skilled-trades-workforce-analysis-final-report-06.01.2023.pdf.
[21]. Maller, R., Stiefvater, E., & Davidson, S. (2024). Demand for degrees: Perspectives from apprentices. Education Northwest. Retrieved from https://wpcdn.web.wsu.edu/wp-wsucahnrs/uploads/sites/2180/2024/12/Appendix-D-EDNW_Demand-for-Degrees.pdf.
[22]. Weissman, S. (2024, May 29). A 'Great Misalignment' Between Credentials and Jobs. Inside Higher Ed. Retrieved from https://www.insidehighered.com/news/tech-innovation/alternative-credentials/2024/05/29/report-finds-misalignment-between.
[23]. Goger, A., Caves, K., & Salway, H. (2024). How U.S. employers and educators can build a more nimble education system with multiple paths to success. Brookings Institution. Retrieved from https://www.brookings.edu/articles/how-us-employers-and-educators-can-build-a-more-nimble-education-system-with-multiple-paths-to-success/?utm_source=chatgpt.com.
[24]. Flack, C., Sludden, J., Hill, J., & Kemple, J. J. (2023, November 14). ExpandED Options: Lessons from the First Year of a Citywide Career-Connected Learning Program. Research Alliance for New York City Schools. Retrieved from https://steinhardt.nyu.edu/sites/default/files/2023-11/ES%20Options%20Final%2011.14.23.pdf.
[25]. Pistorino, P., Darche, S., & Headington, K. S. (2024, April 30). Work-based learning: Creating real-world relevance in education. WestEd. Retrieved from https://www.wested.org/blog/work-based-learning-creating-real-world-relevance-in-education/.
[26]. Waipahu High School. (2023). The McInerny Foundation Early College 3.0 Program. Retrieved from https://www.waipahuhigh.org/apps/pages/index.jsp?pREC_ID=1064039&termREC_ID=&type=d&uREC_ID=555404.
[27]. Santiago, T. (2022). E KŪLia I Ka NU'U: Striving for Excellence: Successful Strategies of Leaders in Hawai'i. Retrieved from https://search.proquest.com/openview/765995628cfbd2996c5676679e4606c1/1?cbl=18750&diss=y&pq-origsite=gscholar.

[28]. Treskon, M., Morgan, C., Kumari, M., & Quinterno, J. (2024). Aligning workforce and economic development to benefit workers: Intersections of research and practice. Urban Institute. Retrieved from https://www.workrisenetwork.org/sites/default/files/2024-06/aligning-workforce-and-economic-development-benefit-workersintersections-research-and-practice.pdf.
[29]. Kress, A. M., & Moret, S. (2023). Creating a policy environment to unleash the workforce development potential of America's community colleges. American Enterprise Institute. Retrieved from https://www.aei.org/wp-content/uploads/2023/12/Creating-a-Policy-Environment-to-Unleash-the-Workforce-Development-Potential-of-Americas-Community-Colleges.pdf?x85095.
[30]. Hawai'i P-20 Partnerships for Education. (2024). Annual Report 2024. Retrieved from https://www.hawaiip20.org/wp-content/uploads/2024/09/Annual_Report_2024F2.pdf.
[31]. Kaua'i Community College. (2024). Annual Report of Program Data: Office of Continuing Education and Training (OCET). Retrieved from: https://www.kauai.hawaii.edu/sites/www.kauai.hawaii.edu/files/pdf/IE/APRU-CPR-2024/APRU_OCET2024.pdf.
[32]. Hawai'i State Department of Education. (2022). School Social and Emotional Learning (SEL) Guide. Retrieved from: https://www.hawaiipublicschools.org/DOE%20Forms/OSSS/HIDOE%20School%20Social%20and%20Emotional%20Learning%20Guide.pdf.
[33]. Kupu. (2023). Annual Impact Report 2023. Retrieved from https://www.kupuhawaii.org/annual-report-2023.
[34]. University of Hawai'i System. (2023, January 24). UH System selected to national cohort on incremental credentials. University of Hawai'i News. Retrieved from https://www.hawaii.edu/news/2023/01/24/uh-system-incremental-credentials-cohort/.
[35]. University of Hawai'i System. UH Micro-Credentials. Retrieved from https://www.hawaii.edu/offices/vp-academic-strategy/uh-microcredentials/.
[36]. Hawai'i P-20 Partnerships for Education. (2025, February). Promising credentials in Hawai'i: February 2025 update. Retrieved from https://www.hawaiip20.org/wp-content/uploads/2025/04/Promising-Credentials-in-Hawaii-2023-February-2025-Update.pdf.
[37]. Leeward Community College. (2024). Workforce Development. Retrieved from https://www.leeward.hawaii.edu/wfdev/.
[38]. Kaua'i Community College. Early Childhood Education Program. Retrieved from https://www.kauai.hawaii.edu/early-childhood-education.
[39]. University of Hawai'i Community Colleges. (2023). Good Jobs Hawai'i overview flyer. Retrieved from https://uhcc.hawaii.edu/goodjobshaw

aii/downloads/Good%20Jobs%20Hawaii%20Overview%20Flyer_012023.pdf.
[40]. Hawai'i State Department of Business, Economic Development & Tourism. (2023). Urban and Rural Areas in the State of Hawai'i: 2020. Retrieved from https://files.hawaii.gov/dbedt/census/census_2020/data/reports/HI_Urban-Rural_2020.pdf.
[41]. University of Hawai'i–West O'ahu. Hawaiian-Pacific Studies. Retrieved from https://westoahu.hawaii.edu/academics/degrees/humanities/hawaiian-pacific-studies/.
[42]. University of Hawai'i at Mānoa. (2023). First-Year Programs: About FYP. Retrieved from https://manoa.hawaii.edu/undergrad/freshman/our-mission/.
[43]. Hawai'i Department of Business, Economic Development & Tourism. (2024, March 26). Hawai'i Digital Equity Plan. Retrieved from https://broadband.hawaii.gov/digitalequityplan/.
[44]. Office of the Governor, State of Hawai'i. (2024, April 26). Gov. Green approves Broadband Equity Access and Development State Match Plan. Retrieved from https://governor.hawaii.gov/newsroom/office-of-the-governor-news-release-gov-green-approves-broadband-equity-access-and-development-state-match-plan/.
[45]. Kamehameha Schools. (2024). Ke Ala I Ka Palapala Laepua – Pathway to Bachelor's. Retrieved from https://www.ksbe.edu/article/a-new-partnership-creates-a-pathway-for-students-to-earn-their-college-degree-early.
[46]. Council for Native Hawaiian Advancement. Hawaiian Trades Academy. Retrieved from https://www.hawaiiancouncil.org/programs/trades/.
[47]. Washington Post. (2024, August 30). Are Native Hawaiians finally getting ahead professionally? Retrieved from https://www.washingtonpost.com/business/2024/08/30/native-hawaiians-professional-success/.
[48]. Hawai'i Department of Taxation. (2021). Tax Facts 99-2: Tax Credits for Low-Income Housing. Retrieved from https://files.hawaii.gov/tax/legal/taxfacts/tf99-2.pdf.
[49]. Vermont Agency of Commerce and Community Development. (2025). Relocation Incentives. Retrieved from https://accd.vermont.gov/economic-development/newrelocatingworkergrant/reports.
[50]. Department of Business, Economic Development and Tourism. (2022). Remote Work in Hawai'i: Effects of the COVID-19 Pandemic on Hawai'i's Remote Work Marketplace. Retrieved from https://files.hawaii.gov/dbedt/economic/reports/DBEDT_REMOTE%20WORK_FULL%20REPORT_FINAL_REV220311.pdf.
[51]. Hau'oli Mau Loa Foundation. (2024). Green Jobs Report – March 2024. Retrieved from https://www.hauolimauloa.org/images/news/HML-Report-FINAL-rev.-6.6.24.pdf.

[52]. Mason, A. (2024). Aging and Hawai‘i’s generational economy. University of Hawai‘i Economic Research Organization (UHERO). Retrieved from https://uhero.hawaii.edu/wp-content/uploads/2024/12/HawaiisGenerationalEconomy.pdf.

[53]. Kurosu, M. (2024, December 17). PACE leaders earn top awards at 2024 Honolulu Tech Week hackathon. University of Hawai‘i News. Retrieved from https://www.hawaii.edu/news/2024/12/17/pace-leaders-2024-honolulu-tech-week-hackathon/.

CHAPTER 6

Building Smart: Infrastructure, Regulation, and the Cost of Getting Things Done in Hawai‘i

1 Introduction: Why It Takes So Long (and Costs So Much)

In Hawai‘i, the time between idea and implementation can feel like an eternity. Whether it's building affordable housing, launching a new farm, or upgrading an airport terminal, the process is often slow, expensive, and encumbered by a labyrinth of regulations and logistical hurdles. These delays are not merely inconvenient; they are economically costly. When projects stall, jobs are delayed, costs rise, and communities suffer. This chapter investigates the structural bottlenecks in Hawai‘i's infrastructure development and regulatory environment. It explores the true cost of "getting things done," from shipping to permitting, and consider how smarter planning, policy reform, and innovation can build a foundation for sustainable growth.

2 The High Cost of Place: Hawai‘i's Geographic Premium

Hawai‘i's geographic location defines not only its natural beauty and cultural uniqueness but also its economic reality. This geographic separation has created what many economists refer to as a "geographic premium", a persistent, structural elevation in the cost of living, doing business, and

P. Yu, *Economic Development in Hawai‘i*,
https://doi.org/10.1007/978-3-032-15689-1_6

building infrastructure. It is a feature of place that affects virtually every sector, from construction and agriculture to education and healthcare. While this premium is often acknowledged in passing, its true scale and impact warrant a more serious, strategic reckoning. If Hawai‘i is to chart a path toward economic resilience and equity, it must contend directly with the systemic cost burdens imposed by its geography.

The effects of Hawai‘i's isolation are most starkly seen in the logistics of material goods. Nearly everything consumed, used, or built in the islands must be shipped in, whether it be food, fuel, vehicles, building supplies, or consumer electronics. The result is a cascading effect of costs that begins with transportation and ripples through every layer of the economy. The Marine Cargo and Waterborne Commerce in Hawai‘i's Economy report (March 2024) shows Hawai‘i's overwhelming dependence on maritime imports, with 88.4% of its 12.4 million annual cargo tons arriving from outside the state [1]. Key inbound goods include petroleum products, construction materials, food, chemicals, and manufactured items. This imbalance, 11.6% of goods are outbound—illustrates the state's logistical vulnerability and import reliance. It also notes Hawai‘i's limited local production and lack of outbound cargo to balance return trips, which further raises freight costs.

Central to this challenge is the Jones Act, which is a century-old federal maritime law that requires all goods shipped between U.S. ports to be transported on vessels that are built in the United States, owned by U.S. companies, and crewed by U.S. citizens or permanent residents. While the Jones Act was originally enacted to ensure a robust domestic maritime industry and national defense capability, its unintended consequences have disproportionately affected non-contiguous states like Hawai‘i. Because foreign-built or operated ships cannot be used to transport goods from Los Angeles to Honolulu, for instance, there are fewer options for shippers, less competition, and higher prices. These elevated costs are passed on to consumers and businesses, inflating the price of everyday goods and services.

The Jones Act also impacts inter-island shipping within Hawai‘i, further complicating logistics for small businesses and agricultural producers. Farmers on Moloka‘i or ranchers on Hawai‘i Island, for example, may face exorbitant costs to get their products to urban markets on O‘ahu. This limits economies of scale, discourages local food production, and exacerbates the state's dependence on imports. Derr (2025) reports on a lawsuit by Hawai‘i's Kōloa Rum Company challenging the constitutionality of the Jones Act under the Port Preference Clause [2]. The lawsuit claims the act unfairly raises shipping costs for Hawai‘i by favoring mainland ports, harming consumers and local businesses. This article outlines legal interpretations of the clause, historical context, and the act's economic impacts. Research from the Grassroot Institute suggests the Jones Act adds hundreds of dollars annually to household expenses in Hawai‘i. While calls for Jones Act reform have circulated for decades, political resistance from maritime unions and national security advocates has stalled any meaningful change. Newsham (2025) reports that U.S. Rep. Ed Case is advocating for major reforms to the Jones Act, which he argues unfairly burdens Hawai‘i by raising shipping costs and enabling monopolistic control over the state's supply chains [3]. In a series of town hall meetings and a Congressional statement, Case introduced three bills aimed at reducing the Act's impact on noncontiguous regions like Hawai‘i. He pointed out that the law adds nearly $1,800 a year to household costs and creates logistical challenges—issues that became especially clear during the Red Hill fuel crisis. Case stressed the urgent need for policy reform to make life more affordable and foster real competition for Hawai‘i's residents.

Beyond shipping costs, Hawai‘i's geographic premium manifests in time delays and planning uncertainty. Unlike in most mainland states, a simple supply chain disruption such as a port labor strike, a global container shortage, or a natural disaster can cause cascading effects in Hawai‘i's tightly coupled logistics system. A delayed shipment of construction materials might stall a project for weeks, triggering budget overruns, missed contract deadlines, and broader economic ripple effects. These challenges are especially acute in infrastructure development, where even small delays can derail public timelines and increase taxpayer burden. The state must plan not just for cost, but for volatility, a reality that places unique demands on public agencies, contractors, and community stakeholders.

However, geography should not be used as an excuse. Rather, it should be treated as a defining parameter that shapes how solutions are conceived, implemented, and evaluated. Hawai‘i's policy and planning frameworks must integrate this geographic premium into cost models, procurement protocols, and budgeting assumptions. Too often, mainland benchmarks are applied uncritically to Hawai‘i, leading to underfunded projects, unrealistic timelines, and policy failure. A school built in Arkansas cannot serve as the cost baseline for one built in Hilo or Lāna‘i. Nor can a food security program, designed in Iowa, function effectively without considering the shipping constraints, land availability, and cultural context of the islands.

Tailored solutions begin with smarter supply chain management. Diversifying shipping partners, investing in local barge infrastructure, and creating buffer stock systems for critical supplies can reduce vulnerability. Hawai'i could also pursue targeted exemptions or waivers from federal maritime laws for specific goods or routes, focusing on agricultural produce, renewable energy components, or disaster preparedness stockpiles. Investing in strategic warehousing and adopting modular or prefabricated construction methods could help ease some of the high costs and long delays that come with building in Hawai'i. In this context, technology becomes a critical enabler as it allows planners to forecast supply chain risks, manage inventory flows, and design resilient infrastructure systems attuned to island realities.

Public procurement reform is also essential. State and county governments must recognize the true cost of doing business in Hawai'i when issuing contracts and setting budgets. Procurement processes that penalize cost overruns without accounting for the unique risk environment in the islands are likely to discourage qualified bidders or incentivize corner-cutting. Instead, procurement models should reward risk management, logistical foresight, and local sourcing. Kapalama Container Terminal (2023) documents one of Hawai'i's most significant infrastructure projects aimed at improving interisland cargo flow [4]. This project points out that public works in the islands need to be designed with phased implementation, built-in risk buffers, and the use of modern logistics technologies. It provides a valuable example for procurement reform advocates seeking to structure contracts that reward logistical foresight, strategic resilience, and local adaptability, which are key considerations in Hawai'i's high-cost, high-risk operating environment.

Furthermore, investment in local industries must be viewed not just as economic development, but as supply chain resilience. Encouraging the growth of local manufacturing, whether in concrete batching, agricultural processing, or renewable energy assembly, can reduce dependence on imports and cushion the economy from global disruptions. Workforce training programs aligned with these sectors would multiply the benefits, providing skilled jobs while fortifying Hawai'i's productive base. Such investments are not just about economics, they are about sovereignty, sustainability, and community resilience.

Energy infrastructure deserves particular attention. Hawai'i's reliance on imported fossil fuels has long made its energy prices among the highest in the nation. Hawaii State Energy Profile (2024) reports that Hawai'i consumes nearly nine times more energy than it produces, with over 80% of its energy coming from imported petroleum, the highest share among U.S. states [5]. The state's geographic isolation, lack of inter-island grids, and dependence on ocean freight contribute to the nation's highest electricity prices. While transportation is the largest energy-consuming sector, Hawai'i is rapidly shifting toward renewables like solar and wind. However, supply chain challenges, high infrastructure costs, and reliance on international imports for renewable technology components highlight the need for localized solutions, inter-agency coordination, and sustained federal investment to ensure energy security. Without a clear strategy to localize at least parts of this supply chain through assembly, recycling, or innovation hubs, the promise of energy independence may be undermined by the same geographic constraints that plague other sectors. Here again, strategic planning, inter-agency coordination, and federal advocacy are key.

In the end, addressing Hawai'i's geographic premium requires a mindset shift: moving from lamenting its costs to designing for its reality. Geography will never change. But policies, processes, and partnerships can. By integrating geographic awareness into every layer of economic planning, from school construction to climate adaptation, Hawai'i can turn its isolation from a liability into a source of innovation. It can become a global model for how small, remote economies navigate complexity with creativity, equity, and foresight. And in doing so, it can ensure that the high cost of place is met not with resignation, but with resilience.

3 Permitting Paralysis: The Regulatory Bottleneck

In Hawai'i, the road from project conception to construction completion is often an arduous one. While delays in major developments are not unique to the islands, the extent, duration, and cost of permitting in Hawai'i are among the most prohibitive in the United States. Behind the delays lies a complex, multilayered permitting process that is rooted in well-intentioned policies but often results in regulatory paralysis.

Zoning approvals, environmental impact assessments (EIS), historic preservation reviews, community input processes, and overlapping approvals from county, state, and federal agencies create a bureaucratic labyrinth for developers to navigate. These layers are meant to uphold environmental stewardship, cultural respect, and community voice. However, when mismanaged or left uncoordinated, they become major barriers to timely and affordable development, especially in sectors such as housing, renewable energy, and infrastructure.

The cumulative effect is staggering. UHERO (2025) reveals that the state's housing development is hampered by exceptionally long and complex permitting processes, which align with concerns that a single project often requires more than 20 separate approvals across multiple agencies [6]. The median permit processing time for single-family homes in 2024 ranged from 172 days in Hawai'i County to an astonishing 393 days in Honolulu County. Multifamily projects faced even longer delays, up to 554 days in some cases. These extended timelines can stretch over several years, increasing development costs and reducing the financial viability of needed housing projects. While some of the delays are attributed to incomplete applications, the broader issue stems from fragmented agency coordination, differing local procedures, and resource shortages. For developers, this extended timeline introduces uncertainty, inflates costs, and often renders marginally feasible projects financially unviable. For residents, it worsens housing shortages, slows down infrastructure modernization, and frustrates attempts at economic diversification. UHERO estimates that just a 10% reduction in permitting times could generate an additional $6 million in annual property tax revenue statewide, highlighting both the economic costs of delays and the opportunity for reform.

Several underlying issues contribute to this gridlock. First is the lack of inter-agency coordination. Many permits require similar information and assess overlapping risks, such as environmental, archaeological, and land-use concerns, but agencies often operate in silos. This leads to duplication of effort, inconsistent interpretations, and conflicting requirements. For example, a developer may clear an environmental review at the county level, only to be asked for redundant documentation by a state or federal agency. Even when agencies agree in principle, asynchronous review timelines mean that approvals are not aligned, forcing developers into a holding pattern while one agency catches up with the others.

Second is the duplication of review processes. Environmental impact assessments are an area where redundancy can be excessive. Hawai'i's Chapter 343 environmental review law mandates EIS filings for many public and private projects, but these often replicate federal NEPA (National Environmental Policy Act) assessments. Despite calls for better harmonization of state and federal environmental processes, there remains no unified framework to conduct a single review that satisfies both sets of requirements. This not only burdens applicants but also overwhelms reviewing agencies, contributing to long delays. Inafuku, Tyndall, and Bonham (2022) provide strong evidence that Hawai'i's housing market is among the most regulated in the nation [7]. Drawing on the Wharton Residential Land Use Regulatory Index, they show that all four counties in Hawai'i score well above the U.S. average, with Hawai'i County ranking in the top 1% nationally for regulatory restrictiveness. This report details approval delays averaging 14 to 18 months, extensive political and legal involvement, and stringent affordable housing mandates. It demonstrates how fragmented, overlapping regulations discourage housing production, especially from small developers, and contribute significantly to high housing costs and supply constraints. It calls for smarter, more coordinated regulatory reform to reduce bottlenecks and make housing development more feasible across the state.

The FRED graph compares the All-Transactions House Price Index for Hawai'i (solid line) with the U.S. national index (dashed line) from 1975 to 2025 (Figure 7). Several patterns in the graph strongly support the argument that Hawai'i's highly restrictive land-use regulations contribute to both elevated and more volatile housing prices. Hawai'i's index consistently remains far above the national average over the entire 50-year period, indicating a persistent structural imbalance between housing demand and constrained supply. Periods of rapid price acceleration—such as the spikes in the late 1980s, mid-2000s, and post-2020—are also noticeably sharper in Hawai'i than in the U.S. overall, suggesting that limited developable

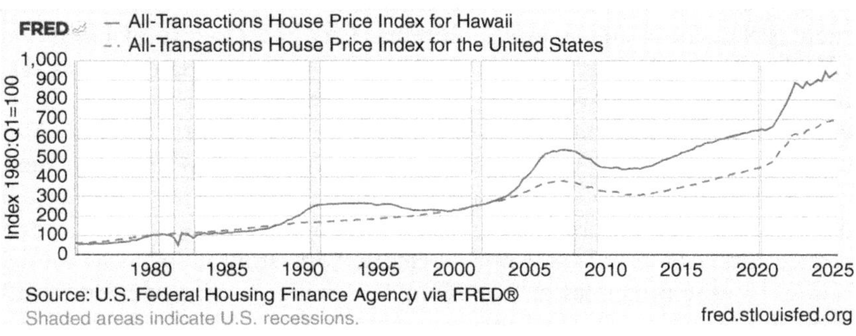

Figure 7 Hawai'i and U.S. All-Transactions House Price Indices, 1975–2025 (1980 = 100). Hawai'i's index (solid line) consistently exceeds the U.S. index (dashed line), with pronounced peaks during housing booms. Gray shading marks recessions

land and strict zoning intensify price responses to economic cycles. Even during national downturns, Hawai'i's prices exhibit shallower declines and quicker rebounds, further showing how supply restrictions insulate the market from downward adjustments.

Third is the lack of clear timelines and accountability. Many agencies are under-resourced, with insufficient staff or technology systems to handle permit applications in a timely manner. Review periods can be vague or extendable without limit, leaving applicants with little recourse. Moreover, few agencies are held accountable for delays. Developers are often left in limbo, unable to secure financing or commit to schedules while waiting months, or even years, for a single agency response. Fourth is community opposition, which, while a vital part of democratic governance, is increasingly shaped by misinformation, mistrust, and NIMBY (Not In My Backyard) attitudes. Public comment periods and community consultations are essential safeguards. However, they can be manipulated by interest groups or derailed by emotionally charged opposition, often disconnected from factual analysis. In some cases, this results in projects being delayed indefinitely or abandoned altogether, even if they have substantial public benefit or meet all regulatory criteria.

These problems are not new, nor are they unsolvable. But addressing them requires a multifaceted and politically courageous approach. First, inter-agency coordination must be institutionalized. One model is the "one-stop shop" permitting system, where a centralized office coordinates all necessary reviews and communicates with developers through a single point of contact. This model has been adopted with success in jurisdictions such as Singapore and British Columbia. City and County of Honolulu (2025) reports that its 2025–2028 Strategic Housing Plan outlines significant steps toward reducing permitting delays and improving coordination in the housing development process [8]. Central to this effort is the creation of the Department of Housing and Land Management (DHLM), which aims to consolidate planning, permitting, finance, and policy under one umbrella to improve inter-agency communication and reduce inefficiencies. While not labeled a "one-stop shop," this model echoes its core principles by providing a centralized point of contact and oversight. Additionally, the City is investing in digital platforms like Clariti and ProjectDox to increase transparency, track application progress, and accelerate review times. The plan also targets transit-oriented development zones for focused housing initiatives, beginning with the Kūwili Station Redevelopment Area. These combined efforts reflect Honolulu's recognition that fragmented permitting processes hinder timely housing delivery and that a more integrated, tech-enabled approach is essential to breaking the bottleneck.

Second, the state should implement parallel, rather than sequential, review processes. Too often, agencies require that one step be completed before another can begin, even when the steps do not depend on each other. Allowing agencies to conduct their reviews in parallel would compress timelines significantly and reduce uncertainty.

Third, legislation should establish firm timelines for agency reviews, with automatic approvals or escalations to higher authority if deadlines are missed without justified cause. The Goldilocks Zone Permitting Reform report by the Bipartisan Policy Center (2023) underscores the growing bipartisan momentum for improving federal permitting systems, particularly through enforceable timelines, often referred to as "shot clocks" [9]. These frameworks, already part of federal initiatives such as FAST-41, encourage timely and transparent agency reviews. While automatic approvals were discussed, most participants favored transparency and reporting mechanisms over blanket approvals. This report emphasizes the importance of agencies reporting missed deadlines to Congress and supports judicial recourse for project sponsors. This model resonates with the push for similar permitting reforms in Hawai'i, where projects frequently face indefinite delays. The Grassroot Institute of Hawaii (2025) supports SB66 SD1, which proposes a 60-day "shot clock" for issuing housing permits certified by licensed professionals [10]. This bill addresses excessive delays, which average 161 days in Hawai'i, and aims to create predictability for applicants. The Institute cites Florida's 2021 law as a successful example of reducing permit wait times. It also emphasizes the importance of automatic approvals after 60 days and recommends third-party review options to ensure timely permitting without overburdening county staff.

Fourth, digital permitting platforms should be expanded. Too many agencies still rely on paper submissions and fragmented databases. A unified digital system for tracking, managing, and reviewing permit applications would streamline communication, flag conflicts early, and improve transparency. It would also enable performance monitoring and accountability, allowing policymakers and the public to assess where bottlenecks persist. The 2004 City Auditor's report evaluates the effectiveness of Honolulu's Department of Planning and Permitting's (DPP) One-Stop Permit Centers [11]. These centers aimed to improve customer service and streamline building permit processes by consolidating approval functions and implementing

POSSE, short for Public One-Stop ServicE, a digital permit tracking and management system developed by Computronix. POSSE was designed to centralize permit data, track application progress electronically, integrate with GIS data, and enhance interagency communication. Despite its potential, this report found the system underutilized due to insufficient staffing, inadequate training, and poor implementation planning. Many of POSSE's key capabilities, such as online filing, payment processing, and integration with all permitting agencies, remained dormant or only partially deployed. As a result, permit applicants still encountered delays, fragmented procedures, and had to navigate multiple locations. This report concluded that, without full digital adoption and systemic reforms, the intended efficiency gains of the One-Stop Permit Centers would not be realized.

Bauer (2024) reports that Honolulu's Department of Planning and Permitting is replacing its outdated POSSE system with Clariti[1], a modern, cloud-based platform designed to streamline permit processing, improve transparency, and reduce delays [12]. Funded by federal recovery dollars, the $5.6 million upgrade includes ProjectDox enhancements and a pilot program with CivCheck, an AI tool for residential plan reviews. These innovations aim to reduce review cycles and improve submission quality. While residential pre-screening wait times have dropped dramatically from months to days, Bauer notes that commercial permitting and staffing shortages remain persistent challenges. Jedra (2025) reports that Honolulu's $7.3 million Clariti permitting system—built on Salesforce and launched in August 2025—has been widely regarded by staff as a "complete failure" [13]. In an anonymous survey of over 150 employees, workers said the new platform slowed processing times, lost essential data, lacked security logs, and even allowed certain safety reviews to be bypassed. Designed as an "off-the-shelf" solution rather than a customized system, Clariti proved ill-suited to Honolulu's complex regulatory environment, undermining confidence in construction safety and delaying permits even further instead of streamlining them. Clariti could be improved by rebuilding locally tailored workflows that reflect Honolulu's regulatory structure rather than relying on generic templates. The city should also restore full audit tracking and non-bypassable safety reviews to strengthen accountability. Finally, streamlined user interfaces, staff training, and transparent performance monitoring would help rebuild efficiency and trust in the permitting system.

[1] https://honolulu.my.site.com/s/.

Fifth, community engagement should be modernized and depoliticized. Rather than relying solely on large public hearings, where the loudest voices often dominate, agencies could use deliberative polling, online platforms, and localized consultation models that better reflect community sentiment. Clear, accessible public information campaigns can also counteract misinformation and build trust. Importantly, mechanisms should differentiate between valid concerns and obstructionist opposition, ensuring that the public voice is heard, but not weaponized against the public interest. The Final Report on Virtual Public Engagement in Agency Rulemaking (2023) from the Administrative Conference of the United States advocates for agencies to modernize community engagement using virtual and hybrid formats [14]. It identifies best practices in structuring online meetings, expanding outreach, increasing accessibility, and improving transparency. It recommends separating educational sessions from public input sessions, leveraging user-friendly platforms, and using targeted outreach to reach underrepresented communities. This aligns with the push for deliberative polling, localized consultation, and digital engagement tools to better reflect community sentiment, shifting away from traditional public hearings dominated by the loudest voices toward inclusive and representative participation.

Finally, Hawai‘i must recognize the cost of inaction. Permitting paralysis is not merely a bureaucratic annoyance, it is a driver of economic stagnation and social inequity. The housing crisis, for example, is partly a regulatory crisis. When it takes a decade to permit a modest apartment building, and millions of dollars in compliance costs must be passed on to buyers or renters, the result is unaffordable homes and increased homelessness. The state's ambitious climate and energy goals similarly hinge on the ability to permit solar farms, battery storage facilities, and transmission upgrades in a timely way. Delays here have real consequences for grid stability, climate resilience, and long-term cost savings.

Permitting reform is not a call to deregulate. Hawai‘i's environment, culture, and communities deserve protection. But stewardship and progress must be balanced. It is possible to protect sacred sites, assess environmental impacts, and honor community voice while also building the homes, schools, clinics, and renewable energy systems that Hawai‘i urgently needs. In short, reform must be about smarter regulation, not less regulation. A regulatory framework that fosters trust, transparency, and timeliness will do more to protect Hawai‘i's values than one that simply stifles them under the weight of inaction. Achieving that vision will require not just technical fixes, but political leadership, agency culture change, and a shared commitment to unlocking Hawai‘i's potential. The cost of doing nothing is far greater than the cost of change.

4 Housing as a Case Study in Infrastructure Gridlock

Hawai‘i is at a critical juncture. The state faces one of the most severe housing shortages in the United States, a crisis that has reached breaking point on O‘ahu, where the median price for a single-family home now regularly exceeds $1 million. Despite growing demand, the pace of new housing construction remains anemic. A range of structural, regulatory, and social factors has created a bottleneck in the housing pipeline, revealing a broader infrastructure gridlock that threatens Hawai‘i's long-term economic and social sustainability. Several interlocking causes underlie Hawai‘i's housing paralysis. The process of obtaining building permits in Hawai‘i is notoriously slow and complex. Developers must navigate multiple layers of regulation from state, county, and occasionally federal authorities. Permits can take months or even years to secure, deterring developers and adding uncertainty and cost to projects. Even recent technological upgrades, such as the shift to Clariti permitting software and AI-assisted reviews, require time to take full effect.

Nearly half of the land in Hawai‘i is owned by government or large trusts, and a significant portion is classified as conservation or agricultural land. Strict zoning codes and land use designations further constrain the availability of land for residential development. These rules, originally designed to preserve the natural beauty and cultural heritage of the islands, now contribute to a severe shortage of buildable urban land, especially near employment centers. Higa (2024) identifies five urgent reforms to address Hawai‘i's deepening housing crisis, which stems from decades of underbuilding, restrictive zoning, high development costs, and infrastructure shortfalls [15]. He recommends encouraging dense, mixed-use development near job centers, accelerating approvals through "by-right" entitlement where projects that meet existing zoning and code requirements receive automatic approval without discretionary review, and promoting adaptive reuse of vacant commercial properties. Higa also advocates for innovative financing models like community land trusts and housing conservancies, as well as sustained investments in infrastructure that support long-term growth. He warns that continued population decline, economic stagnation, and rising housing costs demand a paradigm shift, calling on public and private sectors to act decisively to preserve affordability and opportunity for future generations.

Hawai'i's remote location in the Pacific dramatically increases the cost of importing construction materials. In addition, the state's labor market suffers from a shortage of skilled construction workers, a problem exacerbated by an aging workforce and outmigration. As a result, the cost of building housing units is often prohibitively high, particularly for projects that are not aimed at luxury markets. Dayton (2024) reports that Hawai'i's construction industry is poised for a significant boom driven by federal investments, including $4 billion at Pearl Harbor and funds for wildfire recovery [16]. However, due to a declining population and shrinking labor force, the state will need to import skilled workers from the mainland. This shortage may cause delays and raise project costs. While concerning, the situation also presents opportunities to invest in training kama'āina for construction careers and strengthen Hawai'i's long-term workforce capacity.

Local opposition to new housing developments, often referred to as "Not In My Backyard" or NIMBYism, presents a significant barrier. Even well-intentioned projects aimed at increasing affordable housing stock frequently encounter resistance from community members concerned about traffic, school overcrowding, environmental degradation, or changes to neighborhood character. While public participation is vital, current processes often empower the loudest and most resistant voices rather than reflecting broad community sentiment. Spangler (2022) reports that NIMBYism, or "Not in My Backyard" opposition, continues to obstruct affordable housing development across Hawai'i [17]. Despite efforts from Honolulu's administration to distribute project-based housing vouchers and support federal and local investments, community resistance, particularly from affluent neighborhoods, delays approvals and raises development costs. Experts like UHERO's Philip Garboden and Honolulu officials warn that opposition based on traffic, environmental, or aesthetic concerns often disguises a resistance to change that exacerbates segregation and inequality. These dynamics hinder housing distribution and undercut projects aimed at alleviating homelessness, supporting local families, and promoting economic diversity. Spangler emphasizes that overcoming these social and political barriers is critical if Hawai'i hopes to address its housing crisis meaningfully.

The social and economic repercussions of Hawai'i's housing gridlock are widespread and intensifying. The median household income in Hawai'i cannot support the cost of homeownership in many areas, forcing residents to allocate unsustainable portions of their income to rent or mortgages. Even for renters, Hawai'i's housing costs are out of reach, with a $17.46/hour gap between required and actual average wages. Many families are doubling up, commuting long distances, or abandoning the prospect of owning a home altogether. The 2024 Hawai'i Housing Planning Study, commissioned by the Hawai'i Housing Finance and Development Corporation, highlights a deepening statewide housing crisis [18]. This report estimates a shortfall of 64,490 housing units by 2027, with the greatest need among households earning 80% or less of the area median income (AMI)[2]. It emphasizes that housing demand is not only about quantity but affordability and accessibility. Nearly half of all renters are housing cost-burdened, and overcrowding is especially prevalent among Native Hawaiian households. High development costs, short-term rentals, and income stagnation further exacerbate these challenges. This study urges greater coordination between public agencies and private stakeholders to expand affordable housing production and mitigate the displacement of local families, particularly Native Hawaiians and other underserved populations.

Increasing numbers of young, educated residents are leaving Hawai'i for mainland cities where housing is more affordable and economic opportunities more diverse. This brain drain undermines the state's future workforce and weakens its ability to compete in knowledge-based industries. The lack of affordable housing exacerbates homelessness, with Hawai'i consistently ranking among states with the highest per capita rates of homelessness (Table 3). Meanwhile, many residents live in overcrowded or substandard housing conditions, further impacting public health and educational outcomes.

Table 3 shows that homelessness has increased significantly in many high-cost regions, with Hawai'i's 2024 homeless rate—81 per 10,000 residents—among the highest in the nation [19]. The data reveal a stark contrast between states that have reduced homelessness, such as Michigan (−65.6%), Georgia (−37.4%), Florida (−34.8%), and Texas (−29.7%), and those like New York (81%) and Hawai'i (81%), where housing shortages, rising rents, and limited mental-health infrastructure continue to drive upward trends. These findings reveal that housing insecurity in Hawai'i is not an isolated problem but part of a broader national crisis tied to affordability and access to social support systems. Without decisive action, Hawai'i's housing crisis will continue to deepen, with far-reaching consequences for economic

[2] Area Median Income (AMI) is the midpoint income for a specific geographic area, where half of the households earn more and half earn less.

Table 3 Homeless Population by State 2024. Table 3 summarizes the 2024 homeless population and rate by U.S. state, including the percentage change since 2007. It shows that homelessness remains heavily concentrated in urbanized, high-cost states such as District of Columbia (5,616 people, 83 per 10,000), New York (158,019, 81 per 10,000), and Hawai'i (11,637, 81 per 10,000)—placing Hawai'i among the top three states with the highest homelessness rates nationwide. Source: World Population Review, 2025

State	*Total Homeless 2024*	*Homeless rate 2024*	*% Change from 2007 to 2024*
District of Columbia	5,616	83	5.60%
New York	158,019	81	152.40%
Hawai''i	**11,637**	**81**	**91.7%**
Oregon	22,875	54	30%
Vermont	3,458	53	234.10%
California	187,084	48	34.60%
Massachusetts	29,360	42	94.10%
Washington	31,554	40	35%
Alaska	2,686	37	63.60%
Colorado	18,715	32	31.60%
Nevada	10,106	32	16.90%
New Mexico	4,631	22	53.60%
Rhode Island	2,442	22	78%
Illinois	25,832	21	66.80%
Arizona	14,737	20	0.60%
Maine	2,702	19	2.40%
Montana	2,008	18	74.60%
Minnesota	9,201	16	25.60%
New Hampshire	2,245	16	-0.10%
South Dakota	1,338	15	131.10%
Florida	31,362	14	-34.80%
New Jersey	12,762	14	-26.30%
Idaho	2,750	14	57.20%
Nebraska	2,720	14	-23%
Oklahoma	5,467	13	29.50%
Delaware	1,358	13	28%
Tennessee	8,280	12	-26.10%
Missouri	7,312	12	17%
Kentucky	5,231	12	-35.10%
Pennsylvania	14,088	11	-13.10%

Table 3 (Continued)

State	*Total Homeless 2024*	*Homeless rate 2024*	*% Change from 2007 to 2024*
Georgia	12,290	11	-37.40%
North Carolina	11,626	11	-1.50%
Utah	3,869	11	28.50%
North Dakota	865	11	36%
Ohio	11,579	10	4.40%
Michigan	9,739	10	-65.60%
Maryland	6,069	10	-37%
West Virginia	1,779	10	-26.20%
Texas	27,987	9	-29.70%
Indiana	6,285	9	-14.60%
Wisconsin	5,049	9	-10.60%
Alabama	4,601	9	-15.60%
South Carolina	4,593	9	-18.90%
Connecticut	3,410	9	-23.90%
Kansas	2,793	9	32.30%
Arkansas	2,783	9	-27.50%
Wyoming	501	9	-6.70%
Virginia	7,141	8	-26.70%
Louisiana	3,469	8	-36.90%
Iowa	2,631	8	-3.80%
Mississippi	1,041	4	-24.40%

resilience, social cohesion, and generational equity. Addressing housing as infrastructure means treating it as a public good, worthy of strategic planning, sustained investment, and inclusive governance. It also means overcoming institutional inertia and political gridlock to make room for the homes our communities need to thrive. By unlocking the housing pipeline, Hawai‘i can chart a more inclusive, vibrant, and sustainable future.

5 Transportation and Mobility

Transit-oriented development has emerged as a vital strategy for reconciling housing policy with the imperatives of sustainability, density, and urban livability. In Hawai‘i, where the geography is constrained, the population centers are concentrated, and housing affordability is in crisis, this approach offers not just convenience but necessity. Central to this strategy is the potential for upzoning parcels near major public transit routes, which can facilitate the development of mid-rise and mixed-use communities that reduce car dependency, improve walkability, and align urban growth with climate and equity goals. As Honolulu advances its Skyline rail project, there is a timely and critical opportunity to integrate infrastructure investment with bold housing reform.

Transit-oriented development (TOD) capitalizes on land value uplift near transit hubs to support higher density development, making more efficient use of limited urban land. Rather than continuing low-density suburban sprawl, which strains road networks and inflates carbon footprints, TOD can deliver compact, pedestrian-friendly neighborhoods where people live, work, and access services without reliance on personal vehicles. This framework is particularly suited to O'ahu, where traffic congestion, high housing costs, and land scarcity intersect. The state's adoption of TOD principles is not merely a land-use experiment; it is a structural response to decades of fragmented planning and housing undersupply.

Recent literature has reinforced the practical and policy dimensions of TOD in Hawai'i and beyond. The Honolulu Strategic Housing Plan 2025–2028 outlines the City and County of Honolulu's multi-pronged strategy to address O'ahu's housing crisis by integrating land use, housing, and transit planning [20]. A central pillar is driving TOD, particularly around the new Skyline rail system. This plan includes targeted redevelopment at Kūwili Station, use of city-owned land for affordable housing, zoning reforms, and leveraging public-private partnerships. Innovative financing models such as private activity bonds and multifamily revenue bonds are emphasized. It also proposes reorganizing city housing functions and modernizing permitting processes through technology. Collectively, these measures aim to increase housing supply, support equitable growth, and reduce outmigration driven by housing unaffordability.

Bhagwati and Kumar (2024) examine global TOD practices, drawing lessons from cities like Hong Kong, Singapore, London, Washington D.C., and Mexico City [21]. This paper identifies key TOD success factors: mixed land use, high density, walkability, and especially strong financial frameworks like land value capture and public-private partnerships. While planning frameworks are widely adopted, financial mechanisms are crucial to implementation. It provides a comparative model for developing sustainable TOD strategies in emerging and established urban regions.

The experience of these global cities also highlights potential pitfalls. TOD is not immune to the risks of gentrification and displacement, especially when new development targets higher-income residents or attracts outside investment. To counter these effects, successful TOD strategies incorporate anti-displacement measures such as inclusionary zoning (requiring a share of new units to be affordable), community land trusts, and housing trust funds. In Hawai'i, the preservation of local culture and the protection of Native Hawaiian communities from displacement are particularly important. TOD plans must be developed in partnership with affected communities, ensuring that benefits are equitably distributed and that new development strengthens, rather than erodes, local identity.

Financing is another crucial piece of the puzzle. Hawai'i's high construction costs, driven by imported materials and a limited local workforce, can make TOD projects financially challenging. The city and state have responded by layering funding sources, including low-income housing tax credits, bonds, and state revolving funds. Public land assembly and land swaps have been used to lower development costs and increase the feasibility of affordable housing. U.S. Environmental Protection Agency (2013) provides a comprehensive review of funding and financing mechanisms that local governments can use to support infrastructure investments necessary for successful TOD implementation [22]. It outlines traditional tools like user fees and bonds, as well as innovative strategies including land banking, anchor institution partnerships, and district energy systems. It categorizes strategies into the station area, district-level, corridor-wide, and regional financing plans. The report emphasizes that financing TOD requires creativity, flexible planning, and public-private coordination, especially for projects involving non-revenue-generating infrastructure like sidewalks and parks. This guide is especially useful for municipalities like Honolulu navigating TOD amidst high construction costs and limited local revenue.

Edmonds (2018) explores the Denver Regional TOD Fund as an innovative financing tool designed to support affordable housing and community infrastructure near transit lines [23]. Managed by Community Development Financial Institutions (CDFIs), the fund combines public, private, and philanthropic capital to provide below-market acquisition loans for projects within a half mile of transit. The fund emphasizes speed, flexibility, and community preservation, offering a model that mitigates displacement risks while promoting mixed-use, equitable development. Edmonds highlights how the Denver TOD Fund aligns financial tools with planning goals, serving as a blueprint for cities like Honolulu facing high costs and equity challenges.

Sustainability and resilience are also central to TOD's appeal. By focusing growth in areas already served by transit, utilities, and emergency services, Honolulu can minimize sprawl into sensitive environmental areas. TOD can support the state's climate adaptation goals by promoting energy-efficient buildings, reducing vehicle miles traveled, and creating urban green spaces that mitigate heat and manage stormwater. For an island state facing rising sea levels and extreme weather, these co-benefits are not just desirable but essential. The 2025 Annual Sustainability Report of the City and County of Honolulu highlights progress toward creating a clean, integrated, and affordable multi-modal transportation system [24]. Recent milestones include the launch of the city's first Vision Zero Action Plan to eliminate traffic fatalities, expanded bike and bus infrastructure, and increased electric vehicle charging stations. The Kūhiō Avenue bus-only lane and investments in bike facilities have improved safety and reduced carbon emissions. The city's Transportation Emissions Reduction Plan lays out strategies for lowering vehicle emissions and boosting alternative transit options. Honolulu aims for 100% renewable ground transportation by 2045 and a safer, more equitable system.

The social impact of TOD extends beyond housing. Well-executed TOD can enhance public health by encouraging active transportation such as walking, cycling, and transit use, while also helping to reduce air pollution. It can also strengthen economic resilience by supporting small businesses, expanding job access, and attracting investment to previously underutilized neighborhoods. Perhaps most importantly, it can help restore the sense of community that is the hallmark of island life, as public spaces and mixed-use environments foster social interaction and cultural exchange. Frank et al. (2022) develop the San Diego Public Health Assessment Model (SD-PHAM), a quantitative health impact assessment tool that evaluates the health effects of TOD [25]. Applied to the Palomar Gateway District, this model estimates improvements in physical activity, park visitation, and reductions in chronic conditions like diabetes and high blood pressure, while also identifying potential risks such as increased asthma rates due to traffic exposure. It demonstrates the importance of integrating health metrics into transportation planning and offers a replicable framework for evidence-based urban development.

Yet, TOD is not a silver bullet. It requires careful design, robust policy support, and vigilant monitoring to ensure that it achieves its goals without unintended consequences. There must be an ongoing commitment to affordable housing production, tenant protections, and transparent governance. Community engagement is essential throughout the process, from visioning and planning to implementation and evaluation. Looking ahead, the integration of transit, housing, and land use through TOD is set to define the next era of urban growth in Honolulu and across Hawai'i. The combination of strategic upzoning, investment in transit infrastructure, and a focus on affordability and equity provides a roadmap for addressing the state's intertwined housing, transportation, and climate challenges. As the Skyline rail comes online and TOD plans move from paper to construction, Hawai'i has the opportunity to lead the nation in showing how thoughtful, inclusive, and resilient urban development can work in practice.

6 Energy Infrastructure: Toward a Renewable Grid

Hawai'i stands at the forefront of the global transition to clean energy, having committed to achieving 100% renewable electricity generation by 2045. This ambitious goal is not just about replacing fossil fuels with renewables; it requires the complete reimagining and upgrading of the state's energy infrastructure. In a geographically isolated, resource-constrained, and culturally unique setting, this transformation is both more challenging and more consequential than in many other jurisdictions. Achieving a renewable-powered grid in Hawai'i involves addressing technical, regulatory, social, and environmental challenges, all while ensuring energy equity and system reliability.

A central issue in Hawai'i's energy transition is the management of intermittency inherent to renewable sources such as solar and wind. Unlike fossil fuels, which can be dispatched on demand, solar and wind are variable and dependent on weather conditions. Solar production, for example, peaks during the day and drops to zero at night, requiring a robust system to manage these fluctuations. To maintain grid stability and meet energy demand consistently, Hawai'i must invest in advanced forecasting tools, demand response programs, and a modernized grid capable of absorbing these fluctuations without compromising reliability.

The expansion of storage capacity is vital to address this intermittency. Battery storage technologies, especially lithium-ion batteries, have become more cost-effective and are being deployed across the islands to store excess solar energy for use during peak demand or nighttime hours.

In addition to batteries, the state is exploring pumped hydroelectric storage and other long-duration storage solutions that can provide grid-scale reliability. Energy storage not only balances supply and demand but also enhances resilience during grid disturbances or extreme weather events.

Resilience is another key priority, particularly as Hawai'i faces increasing climate-related threats such as hurricanes, wildfires, and rising sea levels. Hardening the grid against these threats involves both physical infrastructure improvements and smart grid technologies. Undergrounding power lines, diversifying energy sources, and deploying microgrids in vulnerable or remote communities can all enhance system resilience. Microgrids, especially when powered by renewable energy, can operate independently during outages, offering a lifeline to communities during natural disasters.

One of the most transformative ideas in Hawai'i's energy strategy is the development of an inter-island grid. Currently, each island operates its own standalone electric system, which limits economies of scale and resource optimization. An inter-island cable system would enable resource sharing, balancing wind energy from one island with solar from another, and reducing the need for each island to maintain redundant reserves. The Hawai'i Clean Energy Final Programmatic Environmental Impact Statement (PEIS) prepared by the U.S. Department of Energy evaluates 31 clean energy technologies across five categories to help the state meet its ambitious renewable energy goals [26]. A critical component analyzed is electrical transmission, particularly the feasibility of undersea cables to support an inter-island grid. This infrastructure would allow for resource sharing across islands, enhancing grid resilience, efficiency, and renewable energy integration. The PEIS informs decision-makers about environmental impacts and best practices, supporting smarter planning and streamlined permitting processes aligned with Hawai'i's energy transformation goals.

Hawai'i has already made substantial progress toward its renewable energy goals. Utility-scale solar and wind farms are operational on several islands, contributing significantly to the renewable portfolio. These projects are often developed through Power Purchase Agreements (PPAs) with independent power producers, allowing utilities to procure clean energy at competitive prices. The growth of Community-Based Renewable Energy (CBRE) programs has further democratized access to clean power, allowing renters, apartment dwellers, and others who cannot install their own systems to benefit from shared renewable projects. The Hawai'i Public Utilities Commission's FY 2023 Annual Report details the significant expansion and progress of the state's CBRE program [27]. During FY 2023, Phase 2 of the CBRE program was implemented, increasing total capacity from 8 MW to 235 MW. This phase aims to provide broader access to renewable energy, particularly benefiting renters, residents in shared buildings, and low-to-moderate-income households. It highlights community engagement efforts across islands, including meetings to discuss project locations, benefits, and customer education. Additionally, Hawaiian Electric issued new request for proposals (RFPs) for Moloka‘i, Lāna‘i, and low-income-targeted projects. These developments reflect the state's strategy to democratize clean energy access while advancing its 100% renewable energy goal. The CBRE program directly supports the values of equity and sustainability and plays a crucial role in Hawai‘i's transition away from fossil fuels, particularly for communities that cannot install on-site systems.

Beyond solar and wind, Hawai‘i is exploring other renewable resources suited to its unique geography. Geothermal energy, especially on Hawai‘i Island, provides a stable and dispatchable power source that can complement variable renewables. Efforts are also underway to assess the potential of ocean energy technologies, including wave and tidal power. While these technologies are still in the pilot stage, they represent promising additions to Hawai‘i's energy mix given its oceanic setting. Despite these successes, several barriers continue to impede Hawai‘i's clean energy transition. Permitting delays are a significant bottleneck, particularly for large-scale renewable projects. The current permitting process often involves multiple agencies and lengthy environmental and cultural reviews, which, while necessary, can slow down urgently needed development. Streamlining these processes without compromising environmental or cultural protections is essential.

Another major challenge is ensuring equitable grid access for independent power producers. Smaller developers and community organizations often struggle to connect their projects to the grid due to high interconnection costs and technical constraints. Ensuring that Hawai‘i's grid is open, fair, and technologically capable of integrating distributed energy resources is vital for fostering innovation and participation across all communities. Siting conflicts also pose complex challenges. Renewable energy projects may be located in areas with high cultural, historical, or ecological value, leading to opposition from local communities and Native Hawaiian groups. These conflicts highlight the need for early and meaningful community engagement, culturally sensitive planning, and the integration of Indigenous knowledge in energy development.

To accelerate the clean energy transition, Hawai'i must embrace integrated planning that aligns energy development with land use, transportation, housing, and climate resilience efforts. This means breaking down silos between agencies and disciplines and developing cross-sector strategies that recognize the interconnectedness of energy with other aspects of daily life and infrastructure. For example, pairing energy upgrades with affordable housing developments or aligning solar deployment with public transportation corridors can maximize public benefits and improve cost-effectiveness.

Public buy-in is equally essential. Achieving 100% renewable energy is not just a technical challenge but a societal one. It requires public understanding, trust, and participation. Transparent communication, education campaigns, and inclusive decision-making processes help build community support. Programs that directly benefit ratepayers, like bill credits for shared solar or job training in renewable sectors, can improve equity and foster broader public investment in the clean energy transition.

Finally, regulatory modernization is a cornerstone of success. Hawai'i's Public Utilities Commission (PUC) plays a critical role in shaping utility behavior, approving new technologies, and guiding the evolution of the energy market. Forward-thinking regulatory reforms can incentivize utilities to adopt performance-based models, support innovation, and ensure that the benefits of clean energy are equitably distributed. The Hawaii PUC's Decision and Order No. 37507 (2020) establish a comprehensive Performance-Based Regulation (PBR) framework for the Hawaiian Electric Companies [28]. This framework shifts utility incentives from traditional cost-of-service models to performance-driven metrics that align with state policy goals, including decarbonization, customer engagement, and grid modernization. Key mechanisms include revenue adjustment, performance incentive mechanisms (PIMs), and safeguards like earnings sharing. This order was developed through multi-stakeholder collaboration and sets a foundation for evolving regulation as Hawaii moves toward a resilient, clean energy future.

McCoy (2021) discusses Hawai'i's pioneering shift to PBR through an interview with Isaac Moriwake of Earthjustice [29]. This episode explains how the Hawai'i PUC replaced the outdated "cost-plus" utility model with a 5-year revenue cap for Hawaiian Electric, incentivizing efficiency and innovation over excessive capital spending. PIMs were introduced to ensure reliability, support low-income customers, and promote clean energy adoption. This regulatory reform realigns utility profit motives with public interest goals such as decarbonization, cost control, and equity, offering a national model for transforming monopoly utilities into clean energy partners.

Hawai'i's journey toward a 100% renewable electricity grid is both a test case and an inspiration for other island and coastal communities around the world. The state's experience demonstrates that the path to sustainability is as much about governance, culture, and equity as it is about technology. With continued leadership, investment, and collaboration, Hawai'i can show the world how to build an energy system that is not only clean and reliable, but also resilient, inclusive, and deeply rooted in the values of place and community.

7 Digital Infrastructure: Broadband as a Basic Utility

Access to fast, reliable internet is no longer a luxury, it is a basic utility essential to modern life. In Hawai'i, the internet underpins access to education, health care, economic opportunity, and democratic participation. A well-connected digital infrastructure is foundational for everything from telemedicine and remote learning to e-commerce and online civic engagement. Yet, despite its vital role, the state's broadband access remains uneven and inequitable.

The digital divide in Hawai'i is particularly stark in rural areas, where connectivity is often inadequate or nonexistent. Communities on Moloka'i, Lana'i, and parts of Hawai'i Island face disproportionately high rates of under-service, resulting in limited access to telehealth services, online education, and job opportunities. During the COVID-19 pandemic, these gaps became even more apparent, as students struggled to connect to virtual classrooms and patients were unable to reach medical providers through digital platforms. Without reliable internet, entire communities are left behind in the digital economy.

Affordability is another barrier. Broadband costs in Hawai'i are higher than the national average, due to the state's geographic isolation, smaller market size, and the significant capital investments required to build infrastructure across island terrain. Households with lower incomes, particularly in Native Hawaiian, Pacific Islander, and immigrant communities, may be forced to choose between internet access and other basic needs. These cost burdens perpetuate systemic inequalities and stifle upward mobility.

Beyond physical infrastructure and affordability, digital literacy presents a subtler but equally significant challenge. Some community members, particularly kūpuna (elders), non-English speakers, and those with limited formal education, may lack the skills or confidence to navigate the digital world. Even when broadband is available and affordable, it cannot be fully utilized without training, culturally relevant support, and community-based guidance. The Kūpuna Digital Inclusion Roadmap highlights the critical need to close the digital divide for older adults (kūpuna) in Hawai'i [30]. This report documents barriers such as lack of digital literacy, cost, internet access, and fear of technology. It identifies enabling factors like family support, tailored training, and social connection. It also presents actionable recommendations at state, county, and community levels—especially as broadband becomes essential for telehealth, social engagement, and services post-COVID. This roadmap leverages funding opportunities under the Infrastructure Investment and Jobs Act to prioritize equitable digital access.

Bridging this multifaceted digital divide requires a holistic, place-based strategy. Hawai'i must view broadband as critical infrastructure and invest accordingly. Public–private partnerships are a powerful mechanism for accelerating broadband deployment, especially in underserved areas where market incentives are weak. State and county governments can coordinate with internet service providers (ISPs), utilities, and technology firms to extend fiber optic and wireless networks into rural communities. Federal programs, such as the Broadband Equity, Access, and Deployment (BEAD) Program and the Infrastructure Investment and Jobs Act, offer unprecedented opportunities to leverage federal dollars for local deployment. There are federal resources providing detailed guidance on the BEAD Program, including eligibility, priorities, and funding processes for broadband expansion [31]. It outlines how states can access historic levels of funding to support fiber and wireless deployment in unserved and underserved areas. This is essential reading for understanding the federal-state partnership model that underpins current broadband infrastructure investment.

These efforts should be guided by data and community needs. Hawai'i can build on recent mapping initiatives that identify broadband availability and service quality at the census block level. By grounding investment in real-time, community-informed data, policymakers can ensure that funding targets the areas of greatest need and addresses not only availability, but also reliability, speed, and latency. Affordability must be tackled head-on through subsidies and pricing reforms. Programs such as the Federal Communications Commission's Affordable Connectivity Program (ACP) help offset monthly broadband costs for low-income households. The official Federal Communications Commission (FCC) page provides an overview of the ACP, which offers eligible low-income households a discount on monthly broadband service and a one-time discount on a device [32]. It outlines eligibility, benefits, and enrollment procedures. This source is foundational for understanding the scope and structure of the program and how states like Hawaiʻi can use it as a springboard for broader digital equity efforts. Hawaiʻi can complement this federal support with local assistance programs, targeted outreach to eligible households, and streamlined enrollment systems that minimize administrative burden. Ensuring that affordability initiatives are easy to access, multilingual, and integrated with other social service programs will improve uptake and impact.

Digital equity also hinges on robust support systems to help residents navigate the online world. The deployment of "digital navigators", trained individuals who provide one-on-one assistance with internet setup, device use, and accessing online resources, is one promising model. National Digital Inclusion Alliance (NDIA) (2021) introduces the Digital Navigator model as a community-centered approach to bridging the digital divide [33]. Digital navigators are trusted individuals, often based in schools, libraries, clinics, or nonprofits, who provide personalized assistance with internet access, device setup, and digital literacy. NDIA developed standards, toolkits, and training materials to help organizations launch and scale digital navigator programs, with a focus on equity, flexibility, and cultural responsiveness. These navigators help clients achieve both immediate and long-term digital goals, and specialized support can be provided for seniors, caregivers, disabled individuals, and other vulnerable populations. NDIA's ongoing efforts include support for rural and Tribal communities through the National Digital Navigator Corps.

In addition to personalized assistance, Hawaiʻi must invest in ongoing digital literacy education. Community-based training programs should offer courses on basic computer skills, cybersecurity, online job applications, and telehealth navigation. These programs must be tailored to meet the linguistic and cultural needs of diverse populations. Gevelber (2025) reports that Google is addressing the digital divide in Hawaiʻi and the Pacific by expanding language access, improving connectivity, and offering workforce development tools [34]. Through the Pacific Connect initiative, Google introduced new subsea cables to strengthen internet infrastructure across Pacific islands. Additionally, Google partnered with the University of Hawaiʻi to provide students across all campuses access to Google Career

Certificates and AI Essentials courses, supporting skills development in fields like cybersecurity and data analytics. More than 46,000 Hawai‘i residents have benefited from Google’s digital training efforts, empowering communities to participate more fully in the digital economy.

Digital inclusion is not merely a technical issue; it is a social and economic imperative. For the neighbor islands, closing the digital gap is essential to long-term workforce development. As Hawai‘i diversifies its economy beyond tourism, remote work opportunities and digital entrepreneurship offer new pathways for residents to earn a living without relocating to urban centers. High-speed internet can also facilitate access to telehealth, allowing rural residents to receive care from specialists without costly inter-island travel.

Furthermore, digital infrastructure supports climate resilience and emergency response. Real-time weather updates, emergency alerts, and online coordination tools are lifelines during hurricanes, wildfires, and other disasters. Ensuring that all communities are connected is a matter of safety as well as inclusion. The World Economic Forum (2025) emphasizes that equitable access to technology is foundational to community resilience [35]. As global disruptions intensify, communities with secure digital infrastructure are better positioned to adapt and thrive. Cisco’s Resilient Ecosystems Framework illustrates how technology, when integrated with social, governmental, economic, and environmental systems, can transform adversity into opportunity. However, nearly 2.6 billion people remain disconnected, limiting participation in society, education, and emergency response. Cisco aims to close this gap by expanding digital access and investing in 40 global communities through partnerships, skilling initiatives, and infrastructure. True resilience, this report argues, depends on inclusive digital empowerment and long-term systems change.

To institutionalize progress, Hawai‘i should adopt a statewide digital equity plan that sets measurable goals, identifies accountability mechanisms, and outlines sustained funding streams. Such a plan must be developed in partnership with local communities, especially those most impacted by digital exclusion. Native Hawaiian organizations, rural health providers, public housing agencies, and youth-led initiatives should be at the table from the outset. DBEDT (2023) shows the launch of Hawai‘i’s digital equity planning process [36]. It reflects the state’s deeper effort to bring local voices—especially kūpuna, Native Hawaiian organizations, and public housing residents—into shaping a 5-year roadmap that makes digital inclusion both equitable and community-driven. This is essential for grounding academic or policy work in the most recent, place-based initiative Hawai'i is pursuing on digital equity.

Finally, Hawai'i must recognize that digital inclusion is a matter of justice. Equitable access to the internet is inseparable from the right to education, health, economic opportunity, and civic participation. Addressing the digital divide with urgency, creativity, and compassion will help build a future in which every resident can thrive, fully connected, empowered, and included.

8 Resilience and Climate-Ready Infrastructure

Hawai'i stands at the front lines of the global climate crisis. Rising sea levels, intensifying storms, coastal erosion, and prolonged droughts pose existential threats to the state's ecosystems, infrastructure, and communities. For an island chain already grappling with a high cost of living and geographic isolation, the urgency to invest in climate-ready infrastructure is not simply a matter of environmental stewardship, it is central to economic stability, social equity, and long-term resilience. A forward-looking approach to infrastructure in Hawai'i must integrate climate science, indigenous knowledge, engineering innovation, and inclusive governance to safeguard the state's future.

One of the most visible impacts of climate change in Hawai'i is coastal erosion, which has already damaged roads, utilities, and homes along vulnerable shorelines. Fletcher et al. (2012) report that approximately 70% of beaches in the Hawaiian Islands are undergoing long-term erosion, with Maui experiencing the most severe retreat [37]. Their analysis, based on over a century of aerial photographs and topographic data, reveals that nearly 22 kilometers of beach have been lost, primarily due to chronic shoreline retreat. This study points to the growing risks facing Hawai'i's coastal infrastructure, ecosystems, and communities—and underscores why proactive planning and stronger policy action are essential to safeguard them. As sea levels continue to rise, the findings reveal the pressing need to invest in climate-resilient infrastructure and to seriously consider managed retreat as a strategy to reduce long-term risks and protect vulnerable communities.

Hawai'i State Climate Commission (2022) reports that sea level rise is occurring faster than previously anticipated, with a mid-range projection of 3.9 feet by 2100 and up to 6 feet for critical infrastructure planning [38]. It documents how coastal erosion and chronic flooding are already threatening roads, homes, and public utilities across the islands. It shows progress in local adaptation efforts, such as the adoption of updated shoreline setback ordinances, integration of sea level rise exposure data into planning documents, and increased discussion of managed retreat strategies. However, it also identifies major gaps—including a need for more coordinated governance, equitable adaptation, and resilient infrastructure investment. The Commission urges state and county governments to plan for 4 feet of sea level rise in most land-use decisions and 6 feet when addressing long-term infrastructure. In response, state and county governments are weighing options between shoreline hardening—the construction of seawalls, revetments, and other barriers—and managed retreat, a strategy that involves relocating infrastructure and development away from high-risk areas. While shoreline hardening offers immediate protection, it can exacerbate erosion downstream and damage coastal ecosystems such as coral reefs and native wetlands. Managed retreat, though politically and logistically challenging, can provide more sustainable outcomes by restoring natural buffers and minimizing long-term exposure.

Hawai'i State Office of Planning (2022) reports that managed retreat—shifting development inland from the coast—is a necessary but complex adaptation strategy for Hawai'i in the face of sea level rise and chronic coastal hazards [39]. This report emphasizes that accommodation and protection measures like seawalls may not suffice. Through scenario modeling, stakeholder interviews, and case studies from New Jersey to Ventura, the assessment identifies legal, financial, social, and political barriers that complicate managed retreat in Hawai'i, including property rights, cultural sensitivities, and economic implications. While a universal retreat strategy remains unfeasible at this stage, the report calls for further exploration of policy tools such as buyout programs and land use reforms. Importantly, it stresses that managed retreat requires long-term vision, cross-sector collaboration, and community trust to be viable.

To enhance climate resilience in urban and rural areas alike, Hawai'i is increasingly turning to green infrastructure. Unlike traditional grey infrastructure, which focuses on engineered solutions such as storm drains and concrete channels, green infrastructure leverages natural systems to absorb and filter water. Rain gardens, bioswales, green roofs, and permeable pavements reduce flooding, improve water quality, and create habitat for native species. These nature-based solutions are especially vital in areas prone to flash floods and urban heat, and they align with Native Hawaiian principles of living in harmony with the 'āina (land). Incorporating green infrastructure into building codes, capital improvement projects, and school grounds can multiply benefits across public health, education, and environmental conservation.

Transportation and utility systems also require major upgrades to withstand the changing climate. Roads on low-lying coastal corridors, such as Kamehameha Highway on O'ahu's North Shore or Honoapi'ilani Highway on Maui, are already experiencing chronic flooding. Resilient roadways must be elevated, relocated, or retrofitted with culverts and absorptive landscaping to remain passable during extreme weather. Similarly, utility infrastructure—from water pipelines to electric grids—must be reinforced against high winds, saltwater intrusion, and heat stress. Distributed energy systems, such as microgrids powered by solar and battery storage, offer greater reliability during outages and enhance emergency preparedness in remote communities. Water utilities must also prepare for drier conditions and saltwater intrusion by investing in leak detection, stormwater capture, and alternative supply sources.

Emergency response infrastructure is another linchpin of resilience. As wildfires, hurricanes, and tsunamis become more frequent and severe, Hawai'i must modernize its emergency operations centers, evacuation routes, and communication systems. Investments in early warning technologies, resilient broadband, and redundant power supplies ensure that residents can receive timely alerts and access critical services when disasters strike. The State of Hawai'i 2018 Hazard Mitigation Plan is a foundational document that guides statewide efforts to reduce vulnerability to natural disasters and climate-related hazards [40]. Developed by the Hawai'i Emergency Management Agency (HI-EMA), this plan identifies the primary risks facing the islands such as hurricanes, tsunamis, coastal erosion, flooding, landslides, wildfires, drought, and sea level rise, and outlines strategies to minimize their impact on people, infrastructure, and the environment. It emphasizes the modernization of emergency response infrastructure, recognizing that population growth, urbanization, and climate change are increasing the state's exposure to disasters. Key recommendations include upgrading emergency operations centers, improving evacuation routes, and investing in resilient communication systems and early warning technologies. These upgrades are especially crucial for rural and geographically isolated communities where access to critical services during a disaster can be severely delayed. This plan advocates redundant power supplies, resilient broadband networks, and renewable energy installations, particularly in community-based shelters like schools and churches, to ensure continuity of services during and after extreme events.

Institutionally, the Hawai‘i Climate Commission and county-level resilience offices play central roles in coordinating policy, planning, and funding. These bodies develop climate adaptation strategies, convene cross-sector stakeholders, and guide the integration of resilience into zoning codes, building standards, and capital improvement programs. However, institutional fragmentation and inconsistent funding streams hinder the pace and scale of implementation. A state-wide resilience framework with clear authority, dedicated funding mechanisms, and performance metrics is essential to overcome silos and accelerate action. This framework should prioritize equity, ensuring that frontline communities such as Native Hawaiians, rural residents, and low-income families receive targeted investments in resilience.

From an economic standpoint, the case for resilience is compelling. Studies by the National Institute of Building Sciences show that every dollar spent on disaster preparedness yields an average of $6 in recovery savings. Federal Emergency Management Agency (FEMA)'s Building Codes Save: Fire Hazards Pilot Study (2024) quantifies the economic and safety benefits of modern building codes in California and Colorado [41]. Over a 75-year building lifespan, updated fire codes could prevent billions in property losses and hundreds of injuries and fatalities. This study emphasizes that investment in resilient infrastructure dramatically reduces disaster recovery costs. In Hawai‘i, where the costs of post-disaster rebuilding are amplified by logistical constraints and limited labor pools, proactive investments in resilient infrastructure are fiscally prudent. Moreover, these investments generate jobs in construction, engineering, environmental restoration, and clean energy—sectors aligned with a sustainable economic future. Resilience also protects tourism, the state's economic engine, by preserving natural attractions and ensuring operational continuity in the face of disruptions.

Culturally, climate-ready infrastructure offers an opportunity to reconnect with ancestral wisdom and traditional practices. Native Hawaiian approaches to land and water management, including the ahupua‘a system, emphasize sustainability, interdependence, and adaptation to natural cycles. Reviving lo‘i kalo (taro patches), loko i‘a (fishponds), and traditional irrigation networks can enhance food and water security while fostering environmental stewardship. These practices can be integrated into modern resilience strategies through co-management agreements, educational programs, and planning processes that respect cultural protocols and intellectual sovereignty. McMillen et al. (2023) report that the concept of Urban ʻĀina offers an Indigenous, biocultural framework to transform urban environments in Hawaiʻi by centering ancestral knowledge and reciprocal relationships with land [42]. Drawing from Hawaiian cultural values, the authors introduce the Pewa Framework, a metaphor based on the wooden butterfly joint (pewa) traditionally used in Hawaiian woodworking to mend and strengthen cracks. This framework symbolizes how Indigenous knowledge can bind fragmented landscapes, communities, and ecosystems together. Through community-led stewardship of places like Kalauao on Oʻahu, this paper highlights how restoring loʻi kalo and other traditional practices fosters food security, ecological resilience, and cultural regeneration.

Resilience must also be reflected in governance. Public engagement, transparency, and co-design are essential to building infrastructure that meets community needs and earns lasting support. Planners and engineers must work alongside residents to identify risks, set priorities, and evaluate tradeoffs. This participatory approach ensures that resilience is not imposed from above but cultivated from within, an ethic consistent with Hawaiʻi's values of aloha, kuleana, and laulima (teamwork or cooperation).

As climate risks intensify, the urgency for transformative infrastructure investment becomes clearer. Hawaiʻi cannot afford to wait until the next disaster to act. It must lead by example, weaving resilience into every aspect of its built environment, economic planning, and community life. The choice is not between adaptation and development, but between sustainable growth and mounting vulnerability. By embracing climate-ready infrastructure, Hawaiʻi has the chance to become a global model of island resilience—protecting its people, lands, and future generations through proactive vision, collaborative spirit, and unwavering commitment.

9 Institutional Innovations: Building Better, Smarter, Faster

Hawaiʻi faces urgent challenges in overcoming infrastructure and regulatory bottlenecks, but it also has unique opportunities to turn these constraints into catalysts for innovation. Institutional innovation is the key to unlocking better, smarter, and faster infrastructure development that supports economic resilience, climate adaptation, and equitable community outcomes.

One of the most impactful strategies is the establishment of one-stop permitting centers. By consolidating approvals across agencies into a single physical or digital location, these centers reduce duplication, minimize delays, and enhance transparency. Honolulu's Department of Planning and Permitting has experimented with this model, yet gaps in interagency integration and underinvestment in technological tools have limited its potential. Full realization of this model requires automated tracking systems, comprehensive staffing plans, and applicant-facing digital services. POSSE (Public One-Stop Service), the software chosen to streamline permitting, showed initial promise but needs full implementation and support to deliver the intended efficiencies.

Regulatory sandboxes offer another avenue for progress. These frameworks allow for controlled experimentation with novel solutions in fields like housing, energy, and mobility. Within a sandbox, regulations may be temporarily relaxed to enable pilot programs, as long as key protections remain. For example, Hawai'i could trial modular housing on state land, flexible grid technologies for clean energy integration, or micro-transit solutions tailored to rural areas. Sandboxes work best when paired with performance metrics and third-party evaluations to ensure accountability and scale successful innovations responsibly. The Federal Transit Administration's Enhancing Mobility Innovation (EMI) program funds projects that improve transit accessibility, reliability, and equity through technological innovation [43]. In 2025, EMI awarded $1.25 million to projects focused on automated buses and contactless payment systems. This program supports innovative service models and software development for demand-response transit, targeting improved mobility experiences and climate-smart transportation. Eligible applicants include transit agencies, nonprofits, and tech developers.

Finance remains a persistent barrier to transformative infrastructure, but a state-level Public Infrastructure Bank could help bridge this gap. Such a bank would use revolving loan funds and credit assistance to leverage public and private capital for projects aligned with community priorities, including affordable housing, climate-ready infrastructure, and digital equity. Many U.S. states already operate infrastructure banks that offer below-market interest loans and financing guarantees. By institutionalizing such a mechanism, Hawai'i could ensure that critical projects are not stalled by funding gaps, while aligning investments with public benefit goals. Streamlining delivery models is also essential. Design-build contracts, which integrate design and construction responsibilities under a single contractor, can reduce project timelines, costs, and legal disputes. They promote innovation by enabling more flexible, performance-based specifications. This approach has already gained traction in transportation and public works projects on the mainland and could be expanded in Hawai'i with appropriate procurement reforms.

Perhaps most importantly, institutional innovation must engage citizens from the outset. Citizen engagement platforms, including participatory budgeting, digital town halls, and mobile planning apps, empower residents to co-design infrastructure that reflects local needs. These platforms not only surface community wisdom but also reduce opposition by fostering transparency and trust. The experience of cities like San Jose, which uses online platforms to collect input on capital improvement projects, demonstrates how digital engagement can improve project alignment and speed. San Jose's Smart City Vision outlines a bold initiative to integrate technology and data-driven decision-making into all aspects of city governance [44]. It emphasizes goals such as becoming a safe, inclusive, user-friendly, sustainable, and innovative city. Strategies include leveraging AI, digital dashboards, and open data to improve safety, service delivery, transparency, and civic engagement. Special focus is given to digital inclusion in underserved communities, streamlining public services, and using sensors and broadband technologies to address housing, mobility, and environmental challenges. The San Jose city also promotes partnerships, experimentation, and performance-based governance to continuously improve public services and quality of life.

Looking abroad, Singapore's Housing Development Board (HDB) offers a compelling model. The HDB combines planning, financing, and construction functions under one agency and integrates housing with transit, education, and green spaces. The result is not only efficient delivery but also high-quality, community-oriented environments. While Hawai'i's context differs, the principles of integration and alignment remain highly relevant. Phang & Helble (2016) analyze Singapore's public housing system as a globally unique model of integration and scale [45]. Combining land acquisition, financing through the Central Provident Fund (CPF), and centralized planning via the HDB, Singapore has achieved over 90% homeownership and efficient housing delivery. This paper details policies like the Ethnic Integration Policy, macroprudential measures to curb speculation, and programs for housing equity monetization. It concludes that Singapore's success stems from a highly coordinated, state-led approach integrating housing, finance, and urban planning, offering key lessons for other high-density, land-scarce regions or nations.

Domestically, Oregon's streamlined land use system balances development with environmental protection by aligning local plans with state goals. Sullivan (2012) examines the development and evolution of Oregon's land use planning system from 1961 to 2011, highlighting the foundational influence of The Quiet Revolution in Land Use Control (1971) [46]. He traces how Oregon's unique political and social conditions enabled the adoption of Senate Bill 100 in 1973, which established a statewide planning program grounded in clear goals, urban growth boundaries, and state-local plan alignment. This system significantly reduced land use litigation, preserved farmland, and created a model for managing growth while protecting environmental resources. Sullivan emphasizes Oregon's success in achieving planning consistency and robust state oversight. Hawai'i could adapt similar frameworks to accelerate housing and infrastructure in priority areas while safeguarding natural and cultural resources.

California's efforts to modernize the California Environmental Quality Act (CEQA) also offer lessons. Recent reforms target duplicative reviews, mandate faster timelines, and support infill development. The Little Hoover Commission (2024) examines the CEQA, acknowledging its historic role in protecting natural resources while identifying areas for improvement [47]. This report notes CEQA's potential to delay housing and infrastructure due to litigation, procedural complexity, and misuse. The Commission recommends reforms including streamlining infill housing approvals, limiting "late hits" and "data dumps," aligning litigation standing with National Environmental Policy Act (NEPA) standards, enhancing judicial training, and clarifying thresholds for environmental significance. While affirming CEQA's importance, the report urges targeted changes to accelerate development without compromising environmental protections, offering valuable guidance for states like Hawai'i pursuing balanced policy models.

None of these innovations will succeed without trust, among agencies, between government and communities, and between present and future generations. Trust is built through transparency, accountability, and inclusive governance. Institutions must commit to shared goals, minimize bureaucratic turf wars, and create forums for continuous learning and adaptation. Moreover, equity must be central to institutional design. Innovation must not bypass those who need it most. Agencies should embed equity impact assessments into project selection, funding allocations, and performance evaluations. Community Benefit Agreements (CBAs) and inclusive procurement policies can ensure that infrastructure investments generate shared prosperity.

In Hawai'i, this means centering Native Hawaiian values and voices. It means creating space for youth leadership in planning decisions. It means treating resilience and equity as inseparable goals, not trade-offs. And it means holding institutions accountable not just for outputs, but for outcomes that matter: affordable homes, clean energy access, safe streets, and thriving communities. In the end, building better, smarter, faster is not merely a technical challenge, it is an institutional transformation. It requires breaking down silos, investing in capacity, and reimagining the relationship between government and people. If Hawai'i rises to this challenge, it can pioneer a new model of infrastructure governance rooted in trust, equity, and innovation.

10 Conclusion: The Cost of Inaction

Every delay in infrastructure carries a hidden tax: on families waiting for housing, on workers stuck in traffic, on students without broadband, on businesses without permits.

Hawai'i can't afford to keep kicking projects down the road. Smart infrastructure is not just about concrete and wires; it is about enabling the kind of society we want to become.

To compete, to thrive, and to care for future generations, we must build better. And we must start now. The next chapter explores Hawai'i's global footprint, examining how trade, diplomacy, migration, and climate position the islands in the broader Pacific and global economy.

References

[1]. Hawai'i Department of Business, Economic Development & Tourism. (2024, March). Marine Cargo and Waterborne Commerce in Hawai'i's Economy: Trends and Patterns in Hawai'i Marine Cargo 2001–2021. Retrieved From https://files.hawaii.gov/dbedt/economic/reports/Marine_Cargo_Report_3_24.pdf.

[2]. Derr, J. (2025, March 31). Hawaiian company challenges the constitutionality of the Jones Act. Reason Foundation. Retrieved From https://reason.org/commentary/hawaiian-company-challenges-constitutionality-jones-act/.

[3]. Case, E. (2025, February). Enough is enough, says Case regarding Jones Act and Hawaii. Grassroot Institute of Hawaii. Retrieved From https://www.grassrootinstitute.org/2025/02/enough-is-enough-says-case-regarding-jones-act-and-hawaii/.

[4]. Kapalama Container Terminal (KCT). (2023). About the Project. Retrieved from https://www.kctinfo.com/.
[5]. U.S. Energy Information Administration. (2024, April 18). Hawaii state energy profile. Retrieved from https://www.eia.gov/state/analysis.php?sid=HI.
[6]. University of Hawaii Economic Research Organization (UHERO) (2024). Hawaiʻi Housing Factbook. Retrieved from https://uhero.hawaii.edu/the-hawaii-housing-factbook-2025/.
[7]. Inafuku, R., Tyndall, J., & Bonham, C. (2022, April 14). Measuring the burden of housing regulation in Hawaii [UHERO Brief]. University of Hawaiʻi Economic Research Organization. Retrieved from https://uhero.hawaii.edu/wp-content/uploads/2022/04/MeasuringTheBurdenOfHousingRegulationInHawaii.pdf.
[8]. City and County of Honolulu. (2025). 2025–2028 Strategic Housing Plan. Retrieved from https://www4.honolulu.gov/docushare/dsweb/Get/Document-347776/2025-2028%20Strategic%20Housing%20Plan.pdf.
[9]. Bipartisan Policy Center. (2024). Finding the Goldilocks Zone for Permitting Reform. Retrieved from https://bipartisanpolicy.org/wp-content/uploads/2024/01/BPC_Report_Goldilocks-Zone-Permitting-Reform.pdf.
[10]. Grassroot Institute of Hawaiʻi. (2025, February). Provide permit applicants certainty via 60-day 'shot clock'. Retrieved from https://www.grassrootinstitute.org/2025/02/provide-permit-applicants-certainty-via-60-day-shot-clock/.
[11]. Office of the City Auditor. (2004, June). Review and assessment of the Department of Planning and Permitting's One-Stop Permit Centers (Report No. 04-02). City and County of Honolulu. Retrieved from https://www8.honolulu.gov/oca/wp-content/uploads/sites/39/2024/03/dpp_one-stop_permit_centers_final_report.pdf.
[12]. Bauer, I. (2024, March 28). AI a part of major upgrades to Honolulu permitting process. GovTech. Retrieved from https://www.govtech.com/artificial-intelligence/ai-a-part-of-major-upgrades-to-honolulu-permitting-process.
[13]. Jedra, C. (2025, October 20). 'Complete failure': Honolulu permit workers say tech upgrade is a bust. Honolulu Civil Beat. Retrieved from https://www.civilbeat.org/2025/10/complete-failure-honolulu-permit-workers-say-tech-upgrade-is-a-bust.
[14]. Administrative Conference of the United States. (2023, May 25). Virtual Public Engagement in Agency Rulemaking (Final Report). Retrieved from https://www.acus.gov/document/virtual-public-engagement-agency-rulemaking-final-report.
[15]. Higa, S. (2024, January 10). Opinion: Five ways to build more housing in Hawaiʻi. Hawaii Business Magazine. Retrieved from https://www.hawaiibusiness.com/hawaii-housing-crisis-barriers-and-solutions/.

[16]. Dayton, K. (2024, January 3). Hawaii construction boom will require workers from the mainland. Honolulu Civil Beat. Retrieved from https://www.civilbeat.org/2024/01/hawaii-construction-boom-will-require-workers-from-the-mainland/.
[17]. Spangler, S. (2022, July 27). NIMBY worsening Hawaii's housing crisis. KHON2. Retrieved from https://www.khon2.com/local-news/nimby-worsening-hawaiis-housing-crisis/.
[18]. Ward Research. (2024). 2024 Hawai'i Housing Planning Study. Hawai'i Housing Finance and Development Corporation. Retrieved from https://www.dropbox.com/scl/fi/0bvtcb2yao55ntm5ndsz9/FINAL_2024-HHPS-State-Report_Ward-Research.pdf?rlkey=cdfcjsa16u9dburzxvc2nwfh2&e=1&st=ra6hxgt6&dl=0.
[19]. World Population Review. (2025). Homeless Population by State 2025. Retrieved from https://worldpopulationreview.com/state-rankings/homeless-population-by-state.
[20]. City and County of Honolulu. (2025). Honolulu Strategic Housing Plan 2025–2028. Mayor's Office of Housing. Retrieved from https://hnldoc.ehawaii.gov/hnldoc/document-download?id=23423.
[21]. Bhagwati, P., & Kumar, M. (2024). Transit-oriented development: Learnings from global examples. LOGI – Scientific Journal on Transport and Logistics, 15(1). Retrieved from https://www.researchgate.net/publication/377199738_Transit-Oriented_Development_Learnings_from_Global_Examples.
[22]. U.S. Environmental Protection Agency. (2013). Infrastructure financing options for transit-oriented development. Retrieved from https://www.epa.gov/sites/default/files/2014-02/documents/infrastructure_financing_options_for_transit-oriented_development.pdf.
[23]. Edmonds, L. (2018). Financing the development in transit-oriented development: CDFI case study on the Denver Regional TOD Fund. Urban Institute. Retrieved from https://www.urban.org/sites/default/files/publication/98056/financing_the_development_in_transit_oriented_development_0.pdf.
[24]. City and County of Honolulu. (2025). 2025 Annual Sustainability Report of the City and County of Honolulu. Retrieved from https://public.tableau.com/app/profile/city.county.of.honolulu.ccsr/viz/AnnualSustainabilityReport-CityandCountyofHonolulu/Home?publish=yes.
[25]. Frank, L. D., Fox, E. H., Ulmer, J. M., Chapman, J. E., & Braun, L. M. (2022). Quantifying the health benefits of transit-oriented development: Creation and application of the San Diego Public Health Assessment Model (SD-PHAM). Transport Policy, 115, 14–26. Retrieved from https://doi.org/10.1016/j.tranpol.2021.10.005.
[26]. U.S. Department of Energy. (2015). Hawai'i Clean Energy Final Programmatic Environmental Impact Statement: Summary (DOE/EIS-0459). Office

of Electricity Delivery and Energy Reliability & Office of Energy Efficiency and Renewable Energy. Retrieved from https://www.energy.gov/sites/default/files/2015/09/f26/DOE-EIS-0529%20Hawaii%20Clean%20Energy%20FPEIS%2001%20Summary.pdf.
[27]. Hawaiʻi Public Utilities Commission. (2024). Annual Report for Fiscal Year 2023. Retrieved from https://puc.hawaii.gov/wp-content/uploads/2024/01/Final-PUC-Annual-Report-FY23-01.16.2024-v1.pdf.
[28]. Hawaiʻi Public Utilities Commission. (2020). Performance-Based Regulation Framework: Decision and Order No. 37507. Retrieved from https://puc.hawaii.gov/wp-content/uploads/2020/12/2018-0088.PBR_.Phase-2-DO.Final_.mk_.12-22-2020.E-FILED.pdf.
[29]. McCoy, M. (2021, May 19). Greetings From Hawaii, Where Utility Profit Depends on Performance [Audio podcast episode].In J. Farrell (Host), Local Energy Rules. Institute for Local Self-Reliance. Retrieved from https://ilsr.org/articles/hawaii-performance-based-regulation-ler-130/.
[30]. Carlisle, K., & Yugawa, J. (2022). Kūpuna Digital Inclusion Roadmap: Improving Access to Technology for Hawaiʻi's Kūpuna. Hawaiʻi Public Health Institute & AARP Hawaiʻi. Retrieved from https://www.hiphi.org/wp-content/uploads/2022/06/KupunaDigitalRoadmap-Final-June-2022.pdf.
[31]. National Telecommunications and Information Administration (NTIA). (2023). Broadband Equity, Access, and Deployment (BEAD) Program Overview. Retrieved from https://www.internetforall.gov/program/broadband-equity-access-and-deployment-bead-program.
[32]. Federal Communications Commission. (2024). Affordable Connectivity Program: Helping Households Connect. Retrieved from https://www.fcc.gov/acp.
[33]. National Digital Inclusion Alliance. (2021). Digital Navigator Model. Retrieved from https://www.digitalinclusion.org/digital-navigator-model/.
[34]. Gevelber, L. (2025, February 26). How Google is helping to close the digital divide in Hawaii and the Pacific. Retrieved from https://blog.google/outreach-initiatives/grow-with-google/how-google-is-helping-to-close-the-digital-divide-in-hawaii-and-the-pacific/.
[35]. World Economic Forum. (2025, January 6). Powering resilient communities through technology. Retrieved from https://www.weforum.org/agenda/2025/01/powering-resilient-communities-through-technology/.
[36]. Hawaii Department of Business, Economic Development & Tourism (DBEDT). (2023).State of Hawaiʻi Begins Work to Develop Digital Equity Plan to Bridge Digital Divide. Retrieved from https://broadband.hawaii.gov/digitalequityplan.
[37]. Fletcher, C. H., Romine, B. M., Genz, A. S., Barbee, M. M., Dyer, M., Anderson, T. R., Lim, S. C., Vitousek, S., Bochicchio, C., & Richmond, B. M. (2012). National assessment of shoreline change: Historical shoreline

change in the Hawaiian Islands (U.S. Geological Survey Open-File Report 2011–1051). Retrieved from https://pubs.usgs.gov/of/2011/1051/pdf/ofr2011-1051_report_508_rev052512.pdf.
[38]. Hawai'i State Climate Commission. (2022). Hawai'i Sea Level Rise Vulnerability and Adaptation Report: 2022 Update. Retrieved from https://climate.hawaii.gov/wp-content/uploads/2023/04/Sea-Level-Rise-Adaptation-and-Vulnerability-2022-Update_Final2-1.pdf.
[39]. Office of Planning and Sustainable Development – Coastal Zone Management Program. (2022). Sea Level Rise Adaptation and Vulnerability 2022 Update. Retrieved from https://files.hawaii.gov/dbedt/op/czm/ormp/assessing_the_feasibility_and_implications_of_managed_retreat_strategies_for_vulnerable_coastal_areas_in_hawaii.pdf.
[40]. Hawai'i Emergency Management Agency. (2020). Strategic Plan 2020–2025. Retrieved from https://dod.hawaii.gov/hiema/files/2020/06/2018-State-HI-HMP-Update-100218.pdf.
[41]. Federal Emergency Management Agency. (2024). Building Codes Save: Fire Hazards Pilot Study. Retrieved from https://www.fema.gov/sites/default/files/documents/fema_building-codes-save_study_12162024.pdf.
[42]. McMillen, H. L., 'Āina of Ka'ōnohi, Deluze, A. K., Enos, K., Mossman, K., Gunasekera, I., Espiritu, D., Jay, C., Jackson, P., Connelly, S., Han, M. H., Giardina, C. P., & Meyer, M. A. (2023). Urban 'Āina: An Indigenous, biocultural pathway to transforming urban spaces. Sustainability, 15(13), 9937. Retrieved from https://doi.org/10.3390/su15139937.
[43]. Federal Transit Administration. (2025, January 17). Enhancing Mobility Innovation. U.S. Department of Transportation. Retrieved from https://www.transit.dot.gov/research-innovation/enhancing-mobility-innovation.
[44]. City of San José. Smart City Vision. San José Office of Information Technology. Retrieved May 19, 2025, Retrieved from https://www.sanjoseca.gov/your-government/departments-offices/information-technology/smart-city-vision.
[45]. Phang, S.-Y., & Helble, M. (2016). Housing policies in Singapore (ADBI Working Paper No. 559). Asian Development Bank Institute. Retrieved from https://www.adb.org/sites/default/files/publication/181599/adbi-wp559.pdf.
[46]. Sullivan, E. J. (2012). The quiet revolution goes west: The Oregon planning program 1961–2011. The John Marshall Law Review, 45(2), 357–420. Retrieved from https://www.foster.com/assets/htmldocuments/pdfs/Quiet_Revolution_062312.pdf.
[47]. Little Hoover Commission. (2024). CEQA: Targeted reforms for California's core environmental law (Report No. 279). Retrieved from https://lhc.ca.gov/wp-content/uploads/Report279.pdf.

CHAPTER 7

Island at the Crossroads: Hawaiʻi's Role in the Pacific and Global Economy

1 Introduction: Small State, Big Position

With fewer than 1.5 million residents and a land area smaller than many U.S. counties, Hawaiʻi might appear peripheral to global economic powerhouses. But geography tells a different story. Located in the middle of the Pacific, it is closer to Tokyo than to Washington, D.C. and plays a unique role as a bridge between East and West, North and South, developed and developing economies. This chapter explores Hawaiʻi's global footprint: as a military and geopolitical hub, a crossroads for migration and trade, a potential leader in climate diplomacy, and a cultural influencer. Far from being just a remote outpost, Hawaiʻi stands at the nexus of some of the world's most pressing economic and strategic developments.

2 Hawaiʻi as a Strategic Geopolitical Hub

Hawaiʻi occupies a uniquely strategic position in the world, not just geographically but also politically, economically, and militarily. As the physical midpoint between the continental United States and Asia, Hawaiʻi has long been recognized as a critical node in America's engagement with the Indo-Pacific region. At the heart of this strategic relevance lies the presence of the U.S. Indo-Pacific Command (INDOPACOM), headquartered at Camp H.M. Smith on Oʻahu. As the oldest and largest of the

P. Yu, *Economic Development in Hawaiʻi*,
https://doi.org/10.1007/978-3-032-15689-1_7

U.S. military's unified combatant commands, INDOPACOM has jurisdiction over an area encompassing more than half the globe, from the western shores of the U.S. mainland to the Indian Ocean.

U.S. Department of Defense (2024) outlines that defense spending in Hawai'i totaled $10.0 billion in fiscal year 2023, comprising 9.2% of the state's GDP [1]. This included $6.2 billion in payroll for over 73,000 active-duty personnel, civilians, and reservists, and $3.6 billion in contracts awarded to local firms. This report reveals Hawai'i's critical role in U.S. Indo-Pacific strategy, emphasizing its function as a base for more than 100,000 military-affiliated individuals. Through the Readiness and Environmental Protection Integration (REPI) Program, the Department also supports efforts to conserve natural resources while maintaining operational readiness. Overall, defense spending is a foundational driver of Hawai'i's economy, influencing construction, logistics, and services across the islands, especially on O'ahu where military infrastructure is most concentrated.

Hawai'i's geopolitical significance is tied first and foremost to its proximity to key flashpoints in the Asia-Pacific. The island chain sits roughly 5,000 miles west of Washington, D.C., and just around 5,000 miles east of major Asian capitals such as Tokyo, Seoul, and Beijing. This centrality enables rapid deployment capabilities and offers a critical staging ground for projecting naval and air power across the Pacific.

Three rising arenas of strategic tension reveal Hawai'i's enduring importance to the United States. Rising tensions between China and Taiwan have elevated the Taiwan Strait to one of the world's most volatile geopolitical theaters. Chinese military conflict in the region would likely require U.S. intervention, and Hawai'i would be a key logistical and operational base for such a response. The contested waters of the South China Sea have become a flashpoint for regional disputes involving China, the Philippines, Vietnam, and Malaysia, among others. Freedom of navigation operations, as well as regional deterrence strategies, are often coordinated from INDOPACOM headquarters. The unpredictable nature of North Korea's regime and its growing nuclear capabilities ensure the continued strategic relevance of U.S. forces in the Pacific. In January 2018, Hawai'i experienced a stark reminder of this vulnerability when a false ballistic missile alert issued by the state's emergency management system was mistakenly sent to residents' phones, triggering widespread panic. For nearly forty minutes, residents believed an attack was imminent, exposing gaps in emergency preparedness and the psychological weight of living within range of nuclear threats. This episode, coupled with Pyongyang's advancing missile technology, reinforces the enduring necessity of Hawai'i's military facilities for U.S. surveillance, intelligence, and rapid-response operations across the Pacific theater.

In addition to geographic proximity, Hawai'i is a major host of multinational military exercises, most notably the Rim of the Pacific (RIMPAC), the world's largest international maritime warfare exercise. RIMPAC, held biennially and coordinated by the U.S. Pacific Fleet headquartered at Pearl Harbor, brings together over two dozen countries for joint training and cooperation. U.S. Pacific Fleet (2024) provides an overview of RIMPAC 2024, the world's largest international maritime exercise, hosted in Hawai'i with participation from 29 nations, 40 ships, 3 submarines, 150 aircraft, and over 25,000 personnel [2]. This exercise enhances interoperability and regional security through integrated training in maritime warfare, humanitarian aid, and disaster response, reinforcing Hawai'i's role as a hub for multinational military cooperation and Indo-Pacific peacekeeping efforts.

Furthermore, Hawai'i is critical to U.S. naval and air dominance projection. Pearl Harbor is one of the largest naval bases in the world, and nearby Hickam Air Force Base (now part of Joint Base Pearl Harbor-Hickam) serves as a critical node for air mobility, reconnaissance, and strategic deterrence missions. This infrastructure allows the U.S. to maintain a credible deterrent posture across the Pacific and respond quickly to crises from natural disasters to military conflict. U.S. Pacific Fleet (2025) provides a comprehensive update on the strategic importance of Joint Base Pearl Harbor-Hickam (JBPHH) as a cornerstone of U.S. naval and air dominance across the Indo-Pacific [3]. JBPHH supports submarine maintenance, strategic deterrence patrols, logistics, and force generation, particularly as the U.S. responds to growing maritime competition with China. The base plays a critical role in maintaining 80% combat-surge readiness, enhancing regional logistics, and supporting alliances through exercises like RIMPAC. Investments in shipyard infrastructure at Pearl Harbor are central to ensuring submarines and carriers remain operational, strengthening America's strategic posture and crisis responsiveness throughout the Pacific region.

The military presence in Hawai'i is not only strategic; it is deeply economic. Hawaii Defense Economy (2021) shows the central role of the military in Hawai'i's economy, second only to tourism [4]. Defense-related expenditures exceed $7 billion annually, supporting tens of thousands of jobs and injecting funds into local businesses and communities. Hawai'i ranks second nationally in defense spending as a share of GDP. This report offers interactive tools that analyze trends in defense procurement, industry sectors, and subcontractor flows, showing how changes in defense budgets can affect economic output, employment, and supply chains across the state. These data-driven insights are vital for planning, policy, and business development in a state where military activity is both a strategic and economic cornerstone.

Key areas of economic impact include construction. Military bases across Hawai'i are constantly undergoing upgrades, expansion, and maintenance, requiring a steady demand for construction labor and materials. Projects such as the upgrade of the Red Hill Bulk Fuel Storage Facility and ongoing improvements at JBPHH provide long-term employment opportunities for local contractors. The rise of cyber warfare has made digital infrastructure a top priority for INDOPACOM, which is undergoing a significant technological transformation to enhance its operational capabilities across the vast Indo-Pacific region [5]. Key initiatives include bolstering cyber defense mechanisms, integrating artificial intelligence (AI) for improved decision-making, and modernizing logistics and supply chain operations. Hawai'i plays a pivotal role in this transformation, serving as a strategic hub for secure communications and advanced technological deployments. Collaborations with local universities and institutions are fostering innovation and workforce development, particularly in STEM fields. These efforts aim to ensure that INDOPACOM remains agile and responsive to emerging threats and challenges in the region.

The State of Hawai'i is the largest employer, followed by the U.S. federal government—primarily through the Department of Defense (DoD)—and The Queen's Health System, which ranks third (Table 4).

Table 4 shows that Hawai'i's employment landscape is anchored by public service and private sector dominated by health care [6]. The State of Hawai'i remains the single largest employer, reflecting the central role of government in the islands' labor market. The U.S. Federal Government—largely through defense, postal, and administrative operations—is the second largest, reflecting the state's strategic importance. The Queen's Health Systems, Hawai'i Pacific Health, and Kaiser Foundation Health Plan & Hospitals round out the top five, showing that healthcare is not only an economic pillar but also a vital source of local stability and resilience. These rankings highlight how Hawai'i's workforce structure differs

Table 4 Top Five Biggest Employers in Hawai'i. The State of Hawai'i is the largest employer, with 88,585 workers statewide. The U.S. Federal Government follows with 24,804 employees. In the private sector, The Queen's Health Systems employs 9,537 people, Hawai'i Pacific Health 7,705, and Kaiser Foundation Health Plan & Hospitals 4,579 locally (out of 141,640 nationwide). Together, these organizations represent the core of Hawai'i's public and healthcare workforce, illustrating how government and healthcare dominate local employment

Name of Employer	*Local Employment*	*Total Employment*	*Organization Description*
State of Hawai'i	88,585	88,585	State Government
U.S. Federal Government	24,804	NA	Federal Government
The Queen's Health Systems	9,537	9,537	Health Care
Hawaii Pacific Health	7,705	7,705	Health Care
Kaiser Foundation Health Plan & Hospitals	4,579	141,640	Health Care

from many mainland states, with public-sector employment and healthcare services driving most job opportunities.

Hawai'i DoD (2025) outlines the critical role the state plays in supporting national security, emergency response, and community resilience through its multifaceted defense infrastructure [7]. In FY2024, the Department managed over $578 million in federal and state funds, with nearly $400 million in federal expenditure alone. This funding supported disaster response, notably the Maui wildfires, where over 1,100 personnel were mobilized. The National Guard provided aviation, medical, security, and logistical support during the crisis. Additionally, the Command, Control, Communications, and Cyber Directorate advanced cybersecurity capabilities, while international partnerships were strengthened through 50+ military exchanges with Indonesia and the Philippines. The Department's programs also fostered youth development, family readiness, and workforce integration across Hawai'i.

Military investments also stimulate demand for housing, education, retail, and healthcare services, creating a multiplier effect across the local economy. In many rural or underserved communities, defense-related spending serves as a critical economic lifeline. Despite its benefits, the military presence in Hawai'i is not without controversy. Some communities, especially Native Hawaiian groups, have long raised concerns about militarization, land use, and environmental degradation. Issues such as the contamination at Red Hill, the historical seizure of land, and noise pollution from military training exercises have fueled resistance and calls for reform. Compoc & Enomoto (2022) reports that RIMPAC, the world's largest international maritime military exercise, exemplifies the devastating environmental and social impacts of U.S. militarization in Hawai'i [8]. The authors argue that the exercise assaults Hawaiian land, water, and Indigenous communities, especially through the destruction of marine habitats and increased violence against women. RIMPAC reinforces what they call "Militourism", a problematic convergence of military presence and tourism industries. With over 140 military installations occupying vast Hawaiian lands, resistance movements rooted in kapu aloha and aloha 'āina have emerged, advocating demilitarization and Indigenous sovereignty. This essay calls for reimagining security through Indigenous values, rejecting endless war and environmental desecration in the name of U.S. national defense.

Activists argue that defense-related land use often limits access to traditional or sacred lands and imposes risks to the environment and public health. For example, protests over the use of Pohakuloa Training Area (PTA)[1] on Hawai'i Island reveal the tension between military readiness and cultural preservation. Watson (2022) reports that the proposed continued military use of approximately 23,000 acres at PTA on Hawai'i Island raises significant cultural concerns, particularly for Native Hawaiian communities [9]. The Cultural Impact Assessment reveals a wide range of traditional practices, both historical and ongoing, that are deeply tied to the land, such as mo'olelo, stone tool making, hula, and ceremonial rites, all of which face disruption when military operations limit access. Despite the Army's efforts to manage physical impacts, the assessment concludes that access limitations significantly hinder the exercise of cultural traditions, constituting a substantial adverse effect. These findings highlight tensions between national defense goals and cultural preservation in Hawai'i. Fernandez-Akamine (2024) reports that for 75 years, the PTA has been used for live-fire military exercises, resulting in environmental degradation and cultural desecration [10]. The area, rich in spiritual significance and rare ecosystems, has been contaminated by munitions and

[1] https://home.army.mil/pohakuloa/.

depleted uranium. Critics argue that the military presence threatens the sacred landscape, its water sources, and traditional practices. This article highlights efforts by cultural practitioners and activists to protect and restore Pōhakuloa, framing the struggle as part of a broader movement for environmental justice, cultural preservation, and Hawaiian sovereignty.

These concerns have prompted efforts to increase community engagement, improve environmental stewardship, and promote accountability within the defense establishment. INDOPACOM and related agencies have increasingly invested in community relations, environmental impact assessments, and partnerships with local educational and cultural institutions to improve dialogue and reduce tensions. In November 2025, Governor Josh Green named an Advisory Committee for Military Leased Lands to guide state discussions with the U.S. Army over leases on O'ahu and Hawai'i Island set to expire in 2029 [11]. Comprised mostly of Native Hawaiians, the committee advises on cultural, environmental, and economic strategies following the Board of Land and Natural Resources' rejection of the Army's final environmental statement. Emphasizing transparency and accountability, Green stated, "Hawai'i stands at an important crossroads—between national security and cultural stewardship; between federal authority and our responsibility to care for cultural and natural resources. We respect the role of the U.S. military in defending our islands and our entire nation, but that role must coexist with our values and our commitment to the people who call these islands home." This initiative reflects Hawai'i's effort to ensure defense activities align with local values and oversight. Looking ahead, Hawai'i's role as a strategic hub is poised to deepen. The rise of great-power competition, the shift in global economic power toward Asia, and the increasing risks of climate-related disasters all underscore the need for a robust U.S. presence in the Indo-Pacific.

Hawai'i is already being reimagined as a center not just for military might, but for regional diplomacy, disaster response coordination, and humanitarian assistance. Its strategic position allows it to serve as a bridge between the United States and key partners such as Japan, South Korea, Australia, India, and the Pacific Island nations. Moreover, its multicultural population and long-standing relationships across the region provide a unique platform for soft power diplomacy.

In the realm of defense innovation, Hawai'i is emerging as a testbed for new technologies, including unmanned systems, AI-enhanced decision-making tools, and climate-resilient infrastructure. Initiatives such as the Pacific Deterrence Initiative (PDI) are channeling new investments into enhancing Hawai'i's strategic infrastructure, including missile defense systems and cyber readiness. The National Security Innovation Network (2023) reports that the U.S. DoD has launched Defense Innovation OnRamp Hubs in five states, including Hawai'i, to strengthen national security by connecting local talent, startups, and academia with military needs [12]. Operated by Pacific Impact Zone, Hawai'i's hub will foster innovation and dual-use technologies to address critical defense challenges and support service members. Roberts (2024) reports that ManTech has launched the Kumaumau Center in Hawai'i, an innovation and partnership hub aimed at advancing U.S. military capabilities across the Indo-Pacific [13]. The center will support cyber defense, missile systems, secure communications, and C5ISR functions (Command, Control, Communications, Computers, Combat Systems, Intelligence, Surveillance, and Reconnaissance). It is designed to enhance technological dominance in both physical and digital combat environments through rapid development and deployment.

Hawai'i's role as a strategic crossroads in the Pacific is impossible to overlook. As home to U.S. Indo-Pacific Command, the islands anchor America's pursuit of peace, stability, and shared prosperity across the Asia-Pacific. Its geographical proximity to emerging flashpoints, its central role in multinational exercises, and its capacity to host forward-deployed forces make it indispensable to U.S. military strategy. At the same time, the economic spillovers from defense spending provide a crucial pillar of support to Hawai'i's economy, particularly on O'ahu. While concerns around militarization and environmental impact are valid and must be addressed, the strategic benefits of Hawai'i's military presence remain clear. As global dynamics continue to shift, Hawai'i will not merely be a bystander but an active and central player in shaping the future of the Indo-Pacific. It will do so not only through hard power but also through regional diplomacy, innovation, and resilience, reflecting both its enduring legacy and evolving promise as a gateway between East and West.

3 Trade, Logistics, and Economic Exchange

Hawai'i stands as a unique bridge between East and West, not only geographically but economically. Though often perceived as isolated due to its location in the middle of the Pacific Ocean, Hawai'i plays an integral role in the broader trans-Pacific trade, logistics, and economic exchange networks. Its status as a logistical crossroads, a destination for global travelers, and a conduit for strategic defense and diplomatic engagement presents multifaceted opportunities for the state's economic development.

Hawai'i is not a major exporter by volume when compared to industrial or agricultural powerhouses in the continental United States. However, the state's importance lies in its strategic location and capacity to serve as a central node in trans-Pacific logistics. The state's economic structure is heavily influenced by trade dynamics that are asymmetrical, imports significantly outweigh exports, reflecting both the consumption needs of Hawai'i's residents and the limits of its domestic production capabilities. Most of Hawai'i's trade flows are inbound. The islands import vast quantities of food, fuel, vehicles, and machinery. The geographic isolation and limited arable land mean that Hawai'i must rely on imports to meet the daily needs of its population. DBEDT (2024) reports that Hawai'i remains heavily dependent on food imports, with estimates suggesting 85%–90% of all food consumed is shipped in from outside the state [14]. This high reliance on imported food reflects both limited agricultural capacity and high consumption needs. It exposes the fragility of our supply chains and the deeper links between economic sustainability and food security. Given Hawai'i's geographic isolation, any disruption in shipping or global supply chains poses significant risks to local communities. These statistics reinforce the importance of efforts to strengthen local agriculture, invest in food production technologies, and build strategic reserves to increase self-sufficiency.

In contrast, Hawai'i's export profile is modest but distinctively specialized. Key exports include high-value agricultural products such as Kona coffee, macadamia nuts, tropical flowers, and chocolate. While the total volume may be limited, these products command premium prices in niche markets across Asia, North America, and Europe. In addition to goods, Hawai'i exports a variety of services with tourism, higher education, and military-related operations among the most prominent. DBEDT (2024) reports that in 2023, Hawai'i welcomed nearly 9.5 million visitors by air, generating $20.66 billion in spending, with tourism acting as a primary service export [15]. While domestic travel remained strong, international markets showed signs of recovery. Visitor satisfaction remained high as regenerative tourism efforts emphasizing sustainability and cultural preservation, continued to gain momentum. Challenges included workforce shortages and managing visitor impacts on communities and the environment. O'ahu remained the most visited island, while Maui saw declines following the wildfires. The report emphasizes balancing tourism's economic value with responsible, community-driven practices.

Higher education and cultural exchange programs also play an underappreciated role as export services. Universities such as UH Mānoa have actively engaged in enrolling international students, particularly from the Asia-Pacific region. DBEDT (2024) reports that in 2023, Hawai'i hosted 8,311 international students, generating an estimated $188 million in direct spending through tuition, fees, and living expenses [16]. The overall economic impact, including indirect and induced effects, totaled $370.4 million, supporting 4,645 local jobs and generating $26.1 million in state taxes. Long-term students contributed $139.2 million, while short-term students added $48.8 million. Japan remained the top source of international students, followed by South Korea and the Philippines. These students not only bolster educational institutions but also stimulate housing, retail, and service sectors. When combined with study-abroad and cultural immersion programs, Hawai'i's institutions can be strategically positioned as providers of global education in a culturally rich environment.

Logistics infrastructure forms the backbone of Hawai'i's role in regional trade. Honolulu Harbor remains the state's largest commercial harbor and the principal entry point for containerized cargo. Hawai'i's Department of Transportation (2023) outlines the Honolulu Harbor 2050 Master Plan, emphasizing the harbor's role as the state's primary commercial port, handling over 12 million tons of cargo annually [17]. Approximately 85% of goods consumed in Hawai'i are imported, with 91% arriving through the harbor system. The plan details long-term strategic infrastructure improvements to enhance cargo, passenger, fishing, and maritime support operations. A key focus is on increasing climate resilience and adapting to sea level rise through upgraded port infrastructure and disaster preparedness. Collaborative input from stakeholders ensures the harbor meets evolving economic and environmental demands, affirming its role as a logistical and economic lifeline for Hawai'i. Parallel to this, the Daniel K. Inouye International Airport in Honolulu functions as a vital aviation hub in the Pacific. Hawai'i's Department of Transportation, Airports Division (2023) reports that the state's airport system, led by Daniel K. Inouye International Airport, supports both domestic and international routes [18]. The airport system is self-sustaining and funded through user charges, bond revenues, and federal grants. In FY2023, total operating revenue rose to $490 million, with a $124 million increase in net position, indicating post-pandemic recovery. Capital improvement efforts included terminal renovations, runway resurfacing, and biometric upgrades. The airport system handled over half of the state's passenger traffic through Honolulu and played a critical role in logistics and economic connectivity for the region. Together, the harbor and airport solidify Hawai'i's standing as a regional logistics center.

An emerging trend is the increasing interest in establishing direct air and maritime routes to Pacific Island nations and Southeast Asia. This regional connectivity has strategic and economic dimensions. Economically, it opens doors for Hawai'i-based firms to engage in two-way trade with growing markets in Fiji, Samoa, the Philippines, and Indonesia. Strategically, enhancing connectivity positions Hawai'i as a convening ground for multilateral cooperation in disaster relief, education, renewable energy, and public health initiatives. Novak and Imai (2024) report that the Quad, an informal strategic partnership among Australia, India, Japan, and the United States, is increasing engagement with Pacific Island countries to address shared challenges in climate resilience, infrastructure, cybersecurity, and public health [19]. The report points to Hawai'i's rising importance as both a logistical hub and a diplomatic connector in the Indo-Pacific, advancing cooperation in undersea infrastructure, disaster relief, and health resilience. As a U.S. territory, Hawai'i offers proximity, facilities, and cultural linkages valuable for advancing Quad initiatives. The Quad aims to complement regional institutions and promote Pacific priorities while recognizing the importance of Indigenous sovereignty, sustainable development, and culturally grounded diplomacy in forming durable regional partnerships. The Quad nations conducted a tabletop exercise in Honolulu in 2025 to simulate the launch of the Indo-Pacific Logistics Network (IPLN) [20]. This initiative seeks to build a shared logistics framework for coordinated civilian disaster response and humanitarian aid across the region. Emphasizing interoperability, digital mapping, and joint planning, IPLN enhances regional readiness for cyclones, tsunamis, and health crises. It complements other Quad efforts such as the Indo-Pacific Partnership for Maritime Domain Awareness and the Pandemic Preparedness Program, reinforcing the Quad's image as a cooperative force for resilience, sustainability, and shared security in the Indo-Pacific.

According to the World Bank (2023), improving maritime connectivity across the Pacific Islands is central to regional resilience, with Hawai'i emerging as a key node for sustainable logistics and cooperative development [21]. This report advocates for a "blue transformation" of Pacific transport systems through decarbonization, digital innovation, and regional coordination. Hawai'i's port infrastructure and geographic location are seen as vital assets in linking Pacific Island nations with global markets. By investing in cleaner, more resilient maritime routes, including potential links to Honolulu, it envisions Hawai'i playing a greater role in fostering sustainable development, climate adaptation, and economic integration in the Blue Pacific.

Despite its small size, Hawai'i has the potential to develop export niches in emerging sectors such as agri-tech, climate technology, and value-added food products. The state's research institutions, including the UH system, are already engaged in cutting-edge research on sustainable agriculture, ocean sciences, and clean energy. Translating this research into commercial products and services can help diversify Hawai'i's export portfolio and reduce dependence on imports. UH News (2024) reports that UH Mānoa is leading the next phase of a $40 million U.S. Department of Agriculture (USDA)-funded climate-smart agriculture project, enrolling nearly 6,000 acres and over 50 producers across five islands [22]. This initiative focuses on implementing sustainable practices like composting, cover cropping, and biochar to enhance soil health and carbon sequestration. Supported by UH graduates, the research incorporates equity, Indigenous knowledge, and local well-being. Soil sampling data and climate-smart metrics aim to build a resilient local food system. With new enrollment underway, UH seeks to expand its vision of climate-smart agriculture rooted in both science and place-based cultural values.

Value-added food products are another promising area. Hawai'i-grown coffee, macadamia nuts, honey, and tropical fruits can be transformed into branded consumer goods with high export potential. O'ahu-based branding firm Omnitrak Group (2023) conducted a comprehensive study for the Hawai'i DBEDT to evaluate the potential of the "Made in Hawai'i" (MIH) brand [23]. This study found strong support from both consumers and manufacturers for a unified, official MIH brand that assures authenticity and boosts economic diversification. It showed that a MIH seal significantly increases consumer willingness to buy Hawai'i-made products and has high brand equity associated with quality, trust, and local culture. Recommendations included prioritizing online distribution channels, expanding MIH criteria to include local expenditures, and developing incentives for manufacturers. It also urged enforcement mechanisms and suggested using tourism-related taxes to fund the branding program.

By investing in branding, certification (e.g., organic or geographic indicators), and direct-to-consumer e-commerce, Hawai'i can elevate its position in global specialty food markets. These niche exports not only bring in revenue but also reinforce the state's cultural identity and soft power.

Rebranding higher education and cultural training as export services offers a novel pathway for economic expansion. Hawai'i's geographic proximity to Asia, combined with its multicultural environment and U.S.-accredited institutions, makes it a natural hub for international education. Joint degree programs, executive training in hospitality and tourism, and short-term language or cultural immersion courses could be marketed to students and professionals across the Asia-Pacific. Such programs can also serve as bridges for long-term partnerships in research, business, and public policy.

Trade diplomacy will play a key role in Hawai'i's future as a regional economic actor. Institutions and leaders in the state should seek active engagement in frameworks such as the Asia-Pacific Economic Cooperation (APEC) and the Pacific Islands Forum (PIF). These platforms offer opportunities to shape policy, facilitate people-to-people exchanges, and secure investment for infrastructure and innovation. Hawai'i can serve as both a participant and a host for APEC meetings, trade summits, and environmental dialogues, thereby enhancing its visibility and influence in regional affairs. Congressional Research Service (2024) outlines that the Pacific Islands region, including Hawai'i, spans a vast area critical to U.S. strategic interests [24]. The United States has significantly expanded engagement with Pacific Island nations through initiatives like increased development aid, new embassies, and defense agreements. Hawai'i, as the base of U.S. Indo-Pacific Command, plays a pivotal role in these efforts, anchoring U.S. defense and diplomatic strategies in the region. Forums such as the Pacific Islands Forum (PIF) foster regional cooperation, where Hawai'i could strengthen its leadership in multilateral platforms. The Honolulu Defense Forum (HDF) is an annual conference organized by Pacific Forum International, a non-partisan think tank based in Honolulu. Distinct from the intergovernmental Pacific Islands Forum, which unites sovereign Pacific nations, the Pacific Forum fosters Track 1.5[2] and Track

[2] Track 1.5 diplomacy refers to semi-official dialogue that brings together government officials (often in an unofficial capacity) and non-governmental experts to discuss sensitive policy issues, test new ideas, and build consensus outside formal negotiation channels.

2[3] security dialogues among policymakers, defense leaders, and researchers. HDF 2026, themed "Operationalizing Indo-Pacific Readiness and Deterrence," convened over 400 U.S. and allied officials to advance concrete solutions for strengthening deterrence, alliances, and defense innovation [25]. By leveraging Hawai'i's strategic location, the forum aims to close Indo-Pacific capability gaps and build an integrated, resilient security architecture.

Harding (2024) argues that the Pacific Islands are emerging as a critical arena in the geopolitical competition between the United States and China [26]. This report points to the islands as vital anchors of U.S. security, economic connectivity, and diplomatic presence in the Indo-Pacific. It outlines a comprehensive American strategy focused on strengthening relationships with island nations, reinforcing security alliances, and enhancing economic engagement through infrastructure and development support. Hawai'i is positioned as a central player in facilitating regional cooperation, military logistics, and diplomatic outreach. It specifically recommends utilizing Hawai'i's proximity and resources to bolster initiatives like the Compact of Free Association (COFA) and U.S. Indo-Pacific Command (USINDOPACOM) operations. Emphasizing Hawai'i's ability to serve as a hub for democratic engagement and trade diplomacy, the report calls for deeper investment in people-to-people ties, capacity building, and shared values to counterbalance Chinese influence in the region.

Another important vector is the development of dual-use infrastructure that serves both civilian and military purposes. With the presence of the U.S. Indo-Pacific Command, investments in ports, airfields, and communications infrastructure often receive federal support. These facilities can also serve commercial logistics needs, such as container transshipment, warehousing, and emergency response. Congressional Research Service (2023) reports that Hawai'i plays a critical role in the U.S. Indo-Pacific defense infrastructure, housing major installations such as JBPHH, Schofield Barracks, and Marine Corps Base Hawai'i [27]. These sites function not only as strategic military hubs but also as integral components of dual-use infrastructure that support both national security and civilian economic activity. Federal investments, especially through the Pacific Deterrence Initiative, have focused on modernizing port facilities, enhancing airfield

[3] Track 2 diplomacy involves informal, non-governmental discussions among scholars, think-tank analysts, retired officials, and civil society leaders. These dialogues aim to build trust, exchange perspectives, and generate policy recommendations that may later inform official Track 1 processes.

capabilities, and upgrading communications systems to ensure resilience against natural disasters and military threats. These improvements also have commercial benefits, such as supporting maritime trade, cargo handling, and emergency logistics. It highlights how infrastructure development in Hawaiʻi often aligns military readiness with broader economic goals. However, it also raises concerns about environmental risks, citing the Red Hill fuel leak as an example of why integrated planning and sustainability are crucial for long-term success and community trust.

Equity and inclusion must also be part of Hawaiʻi's trade and logistics strategy. The benefits of increased trade and innovation should be distributed fairly across islands and communities. This includes ensuring that Native Hawaiian businesses, rural cooperatives, and small-scale producers have access to export support programs, training, and financing. Community-led models, such as cooperative branding or shared logistics networks, can help local producers reach international markets while retaining economic control. Hawaiʻi Business Development & Support Division (2025) explains that the Hawaiʻi State Trade Expansion Program (HiSTEP), partially funded by the U.S. Small Business Administration, is designed to help small businesses grow through exporting [28]. Recognizing that Hawaiʻi's small market limits in-state growth, HiSTEP aims to equip local companies with the tools, knowledge, and support needed to enter global markets. The program includes three integrated components: Export Readiness (HiSTEP-ERP), Go Global! (HiSTEP-GG), and Company Assistance (HiSTEP-CA), each addressing specific stages of export development. HiSTEP helps participants increase export revenue, access new international markets, and expand their customer base. In 2022 alone, Hawaiʻi's exports (excluding tourism) generated $1.64 billion in sales, $400 million in household income, and $70 million in state taxes, while supporting 8,100 jobs. HiSTEP emphasizes the importance of diversifying Hawaiʻi's economy by leveraging global demand, especially since 95% of the world's consumers live outside the United States. It serves as a strategic avenue for sustainable economic expansion.

Finally, climate resilience must be embedded in all aspects of Hawaiʻi's trade and logistics planning. Rising sea levels, intensifying storms, and global supply chain disruptions necessitate a rethinking of how goods and services move across the islands and the Pacific. Investments in renewable energy at ports, green aviation fuel, and sustainable packaging for exports will not only enhance resilience but also align Hawaiʻi with global sustainability standards. The Climate Ready Oʻahu strategy, published by the City and County of Honolulu's Office of Climate Change, Sustainability and Resiliency (2023), lays out a comprehensive roadmap for preparing the island for the impacts of climate change [29]. With increasing threats from sea level rise, coastal erosion, flooding, extreme heat, and hurricanes, this plan outlines four key goals: reducing exposure to climate hazards, enhancing equity in adaptation, building resilient infrastructure and communities, and improving governance and funding mechanisms to support resilience. The strategy was shaped by input from over 1,400 community members and 80 partner organizations, integrating traditional Hawaiian ecological knowledge with the latest climate science. It includes more than 40 prioritized actions such as zoning updates to reduce development in high-risk areas, implementing green infrastructure like rain gardens and permeable pavement, protecting and restoring ecosystems, and establishing new funding tools for climate adaptation. A major emphasis is placed on equity, ensuring frontline communities—those most vulnerable to climate change impacts—are centered in decision-making and benefit first from adaptation investments. Nature-based solutions and community engagement are pillars of the approach, with initiatives that promote shoreline protection, urban tree planting, and culturally grounded practices. The plan promotes collaboration across city departments, state agencies, and community-based organizations, recognizing the need for collective action.

The strategy also establishes a framework for adaptive management, including performance metrics to track progress and allow for iterative improvements. Ultimately, Climate Ready O'ahu aims to safeguard the island's people, cultural heritage, and natural resources while guiding a just and inclusive transition toward a climate-resilient future. While Hawai'i may not match continental states in terms of export volume or industrial output, its strategic value in trade, logistics, and economic exchange is significant. By leveraging its geographic location, cultural assets, research institutions, and diplomatic connections, Hawai'i can carve out a unique role in the trans-Pacific economy. Focused investment in export niches, rebranded education services, and inclusive trade diplomacy will help the state transition from a passive node to an active architect of regional economic networks.

4 Hawai'i and the Pacific Islands: A Responsibility and a Relationship

As a Pacific Island itself, Hawai'i is intricately tied to the broader Pacific region through deep-rooted cultural, historical, and ecological interconnections. While Hawai'i functions as the 50th state of the United

States and operates within the legal, economic, and political systems of the U.S. mainland, it also retains a profound relational identity as part of Oceania. This duality endows Hawai'i with a unique capacity to act as both a bridge and a beacon in Pacific regional affairs. It holds not only a strategic geographic position, but a moral responsibility and cultural affinity that compel deeper, more meaningful engagement with its island neighbors.

The shared genealogy among Pacific peoples is more than symbolic; it is lived and experienced in language, tradition, and spirituality. Hawaiians trace their ancestry to seafaring Polynesians who navigated across vast ocean distances in double-hulled canoes, guided by stars, ocean currents, and oral wisdom. This heritage is mirrored in the stories of Samoans, Tongans, Micronesians, and other island nations, whose ancestral migrations knit the Pacific into a vast cultural continuum. These ties form the moral basis for modern-day solidarity and partnership. As a state with strong Indigenous foundations and contemporary governance, Hawai'i is uniquely positioned to operationalize its shared identity with the region into collaborative diplomacy and development initiatives. Through a spirit of aloha, which encompasses compassion, mutual respect, and collective responsibility, Hawai'i can champion a Pacific-centered model of international engagement.

One of the most impactful and enduring forms of Hawai'i's engagement with the Pacific lies in education. The University of Hawai'i system is a hub for Pacific Islands studies. Through its Center for Pacific Islands Studies (CPIS), the university offers robust academic programming, research, and community outreach that affirms and amplifies Pacific voices [30]. CPIS has served as a training ground for regional leaders in government, education, culture, and non-profit work. By centering Indigenous epistemologies, fostering inter-island student networks, and producing cutting-edge scholarship, the University of Hawai'i exemplifies the educational diplomacy Hawai'i can wield in service to the region. Expanding scholarships for Pacific Islanders, integrating traditional ecological knowledge in curriculum, and facilitating inter-university partnerships throughout Oceania are practical ways to deepen these ties.

The COFA agreements between the United States and the Federated States of Micronesia, the Republic of the Marshall Islands, and the Republic of Palau grant these nations a unique geopolitical relationship with the U.S., including the right for their citizens to live and work in the United States. Hawai'i, as one of the primary destinations for COFA migrants, plays an outsized role in hosting these communities. While the contributions of COFA citizens to Hawai'i's labor force, culture, and community fabric are significant, they often face systemic challenges: lack of access to affordable housing, healthcare gaps, educational inequities, and legal ambiguities. Federal underfunding and policy inconsistency have left state and local agencies to fill the void, often without adequate resources or authority. Mitchell-Eaton (2023) explores the COFA as a mechanism of "imperial mobility" that allows migration from Micronesia, the Marshall Islands, and Palau to the U.S. without offering full rights or protections [31]. While COFA migrants can live and work in the U.S. indefinitely, they often face exclusion from federal benefits, legal ambiguity, and systemic discrimination. Drawing on ethnographic research in Arkansas, Hawai'i, and across the Pacific, the author argues that COFA's structure reflects enduring U.S. imperial relationships and racial hierarchies. COFA citizens are frequently positioned as both strategic allies and second-class residents—integral to U.S. geopolitical interests yet marginalized in domestic policy. It draws attention to community-led movements across the Pacific Islands that continue to press for recognition, better healthcare access, and fairer laws. The author ultimately calls for a reimagining of COFA not merely as a legal arrangement but as a terrain of struggle for migrant justice, sovereignty, and decolonization.

Hawai'i can and should lead efforts to reform COFA-related policies. This includes expanding state-level support services, advocating for federal reimbursement of social service costs, and ensuring that COFA migrants have equal access to public education, healthcare, and housing programs. Beyond legal rights, it is essential to cultivate a cultural ethos of welcome and solidarity. True regional leadership requires introspection. Hawai'i must ensure that Pacific Islanders residing within its borders experience equity and belonging. This includes inclusive policymaking that incorporates Pacific Islander voices in state governance, community development, and public service delivery.

One promising model is the creation of a Pacific Islander Affairs Office, akin to those that exist for Native Hawaiian Affairs or immigrant integration in other states. Such an office could coordinate services, advocate for community needs, and serve as a conduit between the government and Pacific Islander populations. Executive Order 14031 (2021) establishes the President's Advisory Commission and the White House Initiative on Asian American, Native Hawaiian, and Pacific Islander (AA and NHPI) to advance equity, justice, and opportunity for these communities [32].

It points to the deep-rooted disparities in education, health, and income, while confronting the resurgence of anti-Asian violence and xenophobic sentiment. The initiative emphasizes data disaggregation, equitable resource allocation, improved language access, and expanded civic and economic participation. With interagency coordination, the order seeks systemic change through inclusive policymaking and federal accountability, reaffirming the administration's commitment to racial justice and community empowerment across AA and NHPI populations.

Many Pacific Island nations struggle with limited access to healthcare infrastructure, medical supplies, and trained personnel. Hawai'i's medical institutions can offer valuable support through training, telemedicine partnerships, and mobile clinics. For example, the John A. Burns School of Medicine (JABSOM) has opportunities to develop fellowships and outreach programs specifically tailored to Pacific Islander health priorities, such as diabetes, maternal health, and mental wellness [33]. Sinclair et al. (2020) evaluate the implementation of a culturally adapted diabetes self-management education and support (DSMES) program called Partners in Care, designed specifically for Native Hawaiians and Pacific Islanders (NHPIs) in Honolulu [34]. The intervention used trained peer educators and incorporated culturally relevant materials and analogies. Participants reported high satisfaction, improved diabetes knowledge, and enhanced self-management behaviors. The study shows that the program is both feasible and sustainable, with several community clinics now integrating it as part of their regular DSMES services. The culturally tailored, peer-led model presents a replicable and cost-effective strategy to improve health outcomes for NHPIs.

In education, beyond enrolling students from the Pacific, Hawai'i can support curriculum development, teacher training, and language revitalization efforts across the region. It can also serve as a pilot site for multilingual, place-based education models that can be adapted by other islands. Rather than replicating extractive or transactional models of foreign aid, Hawai'i is poised to develop a more relational approach grounded in mutual respect and reciprocity. In doing so, it can align its diplomatic philosophy with Indigenous values of responsibility (kuleana) and shared abundance (pono). This approach recognizes that development is not merely the transfer of resources or technology, but the co-creation of sustainable futures. Hawai'i's leadership can help facilitate regional dialogues, joint ventures, and culturally rooted initiatives that elevate Pacific ways of knowing and doing.

5 Climate Diplomacy and Sustainability Leadership

If the frontlines of climate change have a zip code, it's likely in the Pacific. Hawai'i, situated at the nexus of cultural heritage, ecological sensitivity, and geostrategic importance, exemplifies both the risks posed by climate change and the potential for regional climate leadership. Rising sea levels, coral bleaching, prolonged droughts, and extreme weather events are no longer distant threats—they are part of everyday life. But Hawai'i's distinct assets position it not as a passive victim of global warming, but as a bold innovator in climate diplomacy and sustainability leadership.

Hawai'i's scientific and institutional infrastructure is already internationally recognized. UH Mānoa, together with the Hawai'i Natural Energy Institute (HNEI), leads cutting-edge research on climate modeling, renewable energy deployment, and marine ecosystem dynamics [35]. These institutions contribute not only to scientific understanding but also to applied solutions, such as grid stabilization using renewable energy, coral restoration technologies, and predictive modeling of sea-level rise impacts. The Honolulu Climate Change Commission (2023) presents a comprehensive overview of climate change impacts and adaptation strategies for O'ahu and Hawai'i [36]. The report points to greenhouse gas emissions, rising temperatures, sea level rise, and extreme weather as defining challenges, noting that O'ahu accounts for roughly 80% of the state's emissions, driven primarily by electricity use and transportation. It outlines observed and projected local climate changes, including higher temperatures, drier seasons, sea level rise, and marine heatwaves. Honolulu's climate strategy includes transitioning to 100% renewable energy by 2045, closing its last coal plant, and incorporating sea level rise projections into planning. It emphasizes integrating climate science into city policies and investing in resilience across energy, transportation, and public infrastructure. The brief is grounded in global data from the Intergovernmental Panel on Climate Change (IPCC) and the National Oceanic and Atmospheric Administration (NOAA), and includes locally tailored adaptation steps, such as flood readiness tools, coastal setback laws, and renewable energy expansions to safeguard O'ahu's future.

Such capacity extends beyond conventional science. Hawai'i is rich in indigenous ecological knowledge rooted in centuries of adaptive stewardship. Traditional systems like the ahupua'a—a land division model that integrates mountain, land, freshwater, and ocean management—demonstrate how environmental planning can be holistically structured. Revived loko i'a (fishponds) strengthen ecosystems and food security alike, reflecting the enduring ingenuity of indigenous design. These models offer frameworks that bridge cultural relevance with contemporary resilience goals.

At the governmental level, the City and County of Honolulu has set a new bar for subnational climate action. Through its Office of Climate Change, Sustainability and Resiliency, Honolulu has committed to carbon neutrality by 2045, integrating climate adaptation into zoning, transportation, and infrastructure planning. City and County of Honolulu (2023) reports that Climate Ready O'ahu serves as a comprehensive adaptation strategy for addressing the island's growing climate challenges [37]. It outlines 12 strategies and 57 specific actions to reduce the risks from sea level rise, extreme heat, hurricanes, flooding, and drought. Developed through broad community engagement, this plan emphasizes public education, protection of cultural resources, infrastructure resilience, water security, and urban cooling. It prioritizes equity by focusing on the needs of vulnerable communities and Indigenous knowledge systems. It integrates natural systems with infrastructure planning and encourages community-led solutions, aiming to safeguard O'ahu's environment and residents for generations. It represents a blueprint for how coastal urban centers can prepare for climate impacts while enhancing livability and social cohesion. The strategy demonstrates Honolulu's commitment to integrating science, culture, and inclusive governance to build a climate-ready future.

With these assets in hand, Hawai'i is uniquely equipped to take on a larger role on the global stage. One avenue is through diplomacy by convening. Hawai'i is geographically and culturally situated to host regional climate adaptation conferences that engage Pacific Island nations, U.S. territories, Indigenous communities, and international climate organizations. Visioning Hawai'i's Adaptation to Climate Change documents a 2011 workshop that brought together 60 stakeholders from diverse sectors, including government, academia, nonprofits, and local communities, to collectively explore Hawai'i's future under climate change [3]. Organized by the University of Hawai'i's Center for Futures Studies and the State Office of Planning, the workshop used scenario planning and appreciative inquiry to shift perspectives from fear-based responses to opportunity-driven adaptation. Participants envisioned resilient communities that integrate traditional knowledge, environmental stewardship, and sustainable development. Key priorities included public education, coordinated climate governance, infrastructure investment, food and water security, and preserving cultural values. The report concludes that

Hawai'i's successful response to climate change requires long-term thinking, innovation, and inclusive collaboration rooted in shared values like justice, equity, and sustainability.

Beyond convening, Hawai'i can become an exporter of expertise. The knowledge generated at UH Mānoa and HNEI, combined with the practical lessons of local stewardship systems, can inform green tech consulting services to other island economies and coastal regions. As global demand increases for climate-smart agriculture, off-grid renewable energy systems, coastal adaptation planning, and sustainable tourism practices, Hawai'i's institutions and entrepreneurs can supply tested models and technologies. The Hawai'i Statewide Decarbonization Strategy (2023) presents a comprehensive roadmap for achieving net-negative carbon emissions by 2045, as mandated by Act 238[4] [39]. This report outlines actionable strategies across key sectors including energy, transportation, buildings, land use, and agriculture. It emphasizes cost-effective measures such as renewable energy deployment, energy efficiency, and reducing vehicle miles traveled. The strategy integrates equity, Indigenous knowledge, and public engagement, promoting just transitions for all communities. It also proposes emissions tracking, carbon intensity standards, and updated inventories.

Hawai'i also has the potential to lead by example through its own urban development. Climate-resilient urbanism involves integrating green infrastructure, smart transportation, sustainable housing, and robust disaster-preparedness systems. By prioritizing low-impact development, stormwater reuse, heat-reducing landscaping, and distributed solar microgrids, cities like Honolulu can become laboratories of climate-resilient design. These urban experiments will provide globally relevant lessons in how to thrive amid uncertainty. Yet, leadership on climate issues requires more than technical solutions; it demands narrative power. Hawai'i can articulate a vision of climate adaptation that is deeply relational, grounded in the values of aloha 'āina (love for the land) and mālama (care and stewardship). This narrative can counter technocratic and extractive approaches to sustainability with one that centers equity, culture, and community-led governance. The use of storytelling, place-based education, and cultural

[4] Hawai'i Act 238 (2022) established a statewide greenhouse gas emissions reduction limit—at least 50 % below 2005 levels by 2030—and required the Hawai'i State Energy Office to analyze pathways toward full economy-wide decarbonization by 2045, including measures across electricity, transportation, land use, and carbon-sequestration.

diplomacy can enhance Hawai'i's credibility as a moral leader in climate resilience.

In advancing this vision, partnerships are essential. Hawai'i should deepen its ties with Pacific Island nations through formal agreements on environmental cooperation, shared research agendas, and mutual disaster preparedness initiatives. Institutions like the Pacific Islands Development Program (PIDP) and the Pacific Regional Integrated Sciences and Assessments (RISA) program provide infrastructure for this kind of cooperation. As an established institution based in Hawai'i, PIDP is a vital bridge for formal agreements and knowledge exchange among Pacific Island nations, aligning with Hawai'i's environmental diplomacy goals [40]. Through transdisciplinary research and stakeholder engagement, Pacific RISA strengthens climate resilience across Hawai'i and neighboring Pacific Island nations—making it a foundational infrastructure for long-term cooperation and shared disaster preparedness planning [41]. Through research, education, and outreach, Pacific RISA translates climate data into actionable tools for sectors such as water, agriculture, fisheries, health, and disaster management. Its leadership in the Pacific Islands Regional Climate Assessment (PIRCA) fosters dialogue among governments, scientists, and community groups to identify knowledge gaps, share best practices, and guide adaptation strategies. Initiatives like Pacific Regional Invasive Species and Climate Change (RISCC) and Climate Matters Documoments[5] further connect science with local experience and policy [42]. Hawai'i should also leverage its relationships with federal agencies to ensure continued investment in climate research and adaptation funding for island communities.

Another pathway is through education and training. Hawai'i can establish fellowships, certificate programs, and capacity-building workshops tailored to Pacific climate leaders, municipal planners, and indigenous knowledge holders. Programs hosted at UH Mānoa or community colleges can provide technical training in resilience planning, green infrastructure, and community-based adaptation while also creating pathways for cultural exchange and mutual learning. To amplify its influence, Hawai'i can strategically engage in international platforms. Participation in networks like the Under2 Coalition, the Global Island Partnership (GLISPA), and island-focused United Nations Development Programme (UNDP) allows Hawai'i to shape climate policy, access funding, and share best practices.

[5] https://www.pacificrisa.org/education-outreach/documoments/.

Under2 Coalition[6] is the largest global network of states and regions committed to achieving net zero emissions by 2050—at the latest.

The 2023 Under2 Coalition Highlights Report outlines the collective progress of the coalition's more than 170 subnational governments toward achieving net-zero emissions by 2050 [43]. Key achievements include enhanced emissions data transparency, the expansion of the Net Zero Futures policy tool, and deeper integration of climate justice principles. In 2023, over 80 member governments committed to the Net Zero Futures initiative, working to align their targets with climate science. The coalition emphasized the need to embed equity into policymaking, particularly through the "Climate Justice Playbook" and the new Climate Justice Peer Learning Network, which supports underrepresented voices. This report also showcases regional collaboration and knowledge-sharing platforms that empower local governments to implement bold, customized policies. Examples include clean transport initiatives in Latin America, climate finance strategies in Africa, and just transition planning in Europe and North America. Members are encouraged to adopt science-based targets, support nature-based solutions, and foster community engagement. Moreover, the coalition strengthened its role in international climate diplomacy, contributing to COP28[7] through subnational voices and advocating for multilevel governance in global climate strategies. With a renewed call to action, the report urges continued collaboration and stronger political commitment to ensure a just and resilient future.

Hawai'i's participation signals subnational leadership and enhances its ability to access global climate finance, influence climate negotiations, and share its experiences with other island and coastal jurisdictions pursuing decarbonization. The Global Island Partnership (GLISPA)C[8] connects island leaders to advance sustainable development and climate resilience. GLISPA (2024) Strategy outlines a robust framework for advancing sustainable and resilient island communities worldwide [44]. Founded in 2006, GLISPA connects island governments, NGOs, and development partners to support and accelerate commitments aligned with biodiversity conservation, climate adaptation, and sustainable development. The 2024 strategy builds on years of success with initiatives like the Micronesia

[6] https://www.theclimategroup.org/under2-coalition.

[7] COP28 was the 28th annual United Nations climate summit, held in 2023 in Dubai, where global leaders gathered to assess progress on the Paris Agreement and negotiate new commitments to combat climate change.

[8] https://globalislandpartnership.org/.

Challenge, Caribbean Challenge Initiative, and Aloha+ Challenge, by reinforcing GLISPA's role as a catalyst, convener, and capacity builder. GLISPA operates on principles of inclusivity, voluntary collaboration, and adding value to existing networks. Its main goals include fostering durable partnerships, promoting conservation trust funds and high-leverage finance mechanisms, expanding communication efforts, and strengthening its organizational capacity. Through the Local2030 Islands Network, GLISPA acts as co-chair and co-secretariat to promote SDG implementation in island communities, spotlighting grassroots leadership and locally driven solutions. The strategy's key actions include incubating visionary commitments, telling impactful island stories, and developing a "Think and Do Tank" to elevate innovative finance and policy models. GLISPA also emphasizes leadership succession, expanding staffing, and securing long-term funding. It introduced the GLISPA Resilience Award to honor excellence in island sustainability. By 2024, GLISPA had mobilized over $150 million for island initiatives, supported more than 35 countries, and facilitated strategic global dialogues. Its evolution from biodiversity-focused advocacy to a broader sustainability platform exemplifies how small islands can lead in resilience and innovation on the global stage.

United Nations Development Programme (UNDP)[9] focuses on resilience-building in Pacific Island nations, addressing issues from disaster preparedness to sustainable livelihoods. The UNDP (2023) report titled Community-Based Resilience Building: Guidance Note provides a comprehensive framework for empowering local communities to adapt to climate change, natural hazards, and other systemic shocks [45]. It emphasizes that resilience is best achieved when communities lead and co-design interventions grounded in local knowledge, values, and governance structures. The guidance focuses on integrating disaster risk reduction, climate adaptation, and ecosystem management through inclusive processes that ensure marginalized and vulnerable groups are involved at all stages. It outlines a step-by-step approach to community-based resilience programming, including context analysis, stakeholder engagement, co-creation of solutions, and participatory monitoring and evaluation. It also encourages investment in social capital, indigenous knowledge systems, and nature-based solutions to enhance adaptive capacities. Additionally, it highlights the importance of multi-level governance, linking grassroots efforts to national and global resilience agendas. Case studies from various regions

[9] https://www.undp.org/.

illustrate how community-led initiatives have led to improved livelihoods, better disaster preparedness, and stronger social cohesion. This report concludes by stressing the need for flexible funding, long-term support, and policy coherence to sustain these efforts. Overall, the guidance promotes a shift from top-down interventions to locally anchored, systems-based resilience-building models.

Economic development must also align with this sustainability vision. Emerging sectors such as sustainable aquaculture, green construction, ecotourism, and climate finance can become engines of economic diversification. Incentivizing climate-aligned entrepreneurship through grants, tax benefits, and incubator programs can help foster a new generation of businesses that thrive within ecological limits. By embedding resilience into its economic DNA, Hawai'i reduces its vulnerability to external shocks and enhances its leadership credibility. Importantly, climate diplomacy must be inclusive. Marginalized communities, including Native Hawaiians, rural residents, and frontline workers, should be active participants in shaping policy, receiving benefits, and stewarding resources. Public processes must include culturally competent consultation, community-based monitoring, and citizen science. Climate justice cannot be an afterthought; it must be embedded in all planning, funding, and implementation strategies. Climate Counts Pocketbook (UNDP 2025) presents thirty key statistics that distill the global climate crisis into clear, actionable insights [46]. Each figure illustrates how climate change affects every region, sector, and generation—from rising sea levels and biodiversity loss to health impacts, education inequality, and economic costs. The booklet reveals that damages from inaction could reduce global GDP by 19% by 2050, while every $1 invested in adaptation yields over $10 in benefits. It calls attention to the moral imbalance of climate impacts: those least responsible, particularly in Africa and across small island nations, are the ones most vulnerable to its consequences. The publication stresses the urgency of limiting warming to 1.5°C, accelerating renewable energy, and promoting circular economies and carbon pricing to cut emissions. Interwoven throughout is the conviction that solutions already exist in community resilience, youth leadership, Indigenous stewardship, and sustainable finance.

Advancing meaningful climate action begins with stronger, more connected data systems. Decision-makers require access to timely, disaggregated, and locally relevant climate data. Expanding climate monitoring stations, improving geospatial data integration, and increasing public access to information will strengthen the knowledge base for action. Integrating traditional ecological knowledge into these data systems can create richer, more actionable insights. The Hawai'i Climate Data Portal (HCDP)[10] provides open access to high-resolution climate datasets, including rainfall, temperature, and projections across the islands. It integrates rainfall, temperature, and meteorological observations from numerous agencies to overcome Hawai'i's historically fragmented data landscape [47]. Given the state's extraordinary climatic diversity—spanning four of the five Köppen[11] climate zones—accurate and accessible data are essential for research and resource management. The portal's interactive tools allow users to visualize and download gridded maps, explore an extensive reference library, and access indigenous climate knowledge resources. By streamlining access to reliable climate information, HCDP enhances Hawai'i's capacity for water management, ecosystem protection, and climate adaptation while strengthening collaboration among scientists, policymakers, and local communities.

Longman et al. (2022) report that climate adaptation for tropical islands like Hawai'i requires approaches that integrate cultural knowledge, place-based experience, and collaborative learning to support effective land stewardship [48]. The authors describe a pilot workshop held in Hawai'i that brought together natural resource managers, cultural practitioners, and scientists to co-develop climate adaptation strategies grounded in Indigenous knowledge and community values. The workshop emphasized relationship-building, storytelling, and traditional ecological understanding as central components of climate education. Rather than focusing solely on scientific modeling or top-down directives, the approach facilitated dialogue across knowledge systems, strengthening both local capacity and climate resilience. Participants reported increased confidence in applying climate tools and heightened awareness of how cultural values can inform climate decision-making. The authors argue that such culturally grounded, community-centered training is essential in tropical island contexts where climate risks are high, ecosystems are fragile, and cultural ties to the land run deep. This model offers a promising blueprint for adaptation education that is both effective and respectful of local heritage.

[10] https://www.hawaii.edu/climate-data-portal/.

[11] The Köppen climate classification is one of the most widely used systems for categorizing global climates based on temperature and precipitation patterns. Developed by German climatologist Wladimir Köppen, it divides the world into five main groups—tropical (A), arid (B), temperate (C), continental (D), and polar (E)—with further subcategories describing variations in rainfall and temperature.

Finally, Hawai'i must continue to invest in leadership development. Supporting the next generation of climate professionals, cultural practitioners, scientists, and civic leaders through mentorship, scholarships, and public service fellowships will ensure continuity and innovation. Building a cadre of leaders who are fluent in both climate science and community organizing will solidify Hawai'i's role as a pioneering force in Pacific sustainability. In the face of rising seas and rising stakes, Hawai'i has a rare opportunity: to be both a sentinel and a source of solutions. Its geographic isolation becomes an advantage, offering a microcosm for testing innovations that can be scaled elsewhere. Its cultural depth becomes a resource, informing sustainability practices rooted in reciprocity and care. And its institutions, from universities to nonprofits to government agencies, become engines for global impact.

6 Tourism and Cultural Diplomacy

As we all know, tourism is both a challenge and an opportunity. Hawai'i receives global attention as a brand, a symbol, and an experience. This soft power can be directed toward more intentional cultural diplomacy. The visibility of Hawai'i in international consciousness presents an opportunity for the state to project more than sandy beaches and luxury resorts. It allows Hawai'i to become a conduit of cultural narratives, Indigenous resilience, and shared Pacific identity. In a time when global audiences are increasingly attuned to issues of cultural authenticity, Indigenous rights, and sustainability, Hawai'i can lead with values rooted in its own cultural traditions.

One effective pathway to deepen Hawai'i's role in cultural diplomacy is through international cultural exchanges and storytelling projects. These exchanges can transcend conventional tourism marketing by emphasizing genuine cross-cultural dialogue. Through artist residencies, music collaborations, joint museum exhibitions, and educational exchanges, Hawai'i can highlight its unique cultural assets, from mele and oli (song and chant) to mo'ōlelo (narrative traditions) and Hawaiian language revitalization. Storytelling is an ancient Hawaiian practice, a mechanism not just for entertainment but for education, cultural continuity, and community building. Sharing these stories with international audiences builds emotional resonance and mutual understanding, laying the groundwork for meaningful diplomacy.

Central to Hawai'i's cultural diplomacy strategy is the leveraging of its most iconic and authentic cultural elements. Hula, for instance, is a profound form of artistic expression and historical record, a dance form that encodes genealogies, cosmologies, and political history. Presenting hula not as mere performance but as a respected cultural tradition in international venues asserts Hawai'i's cultural sovereignty and reshapes global perceptions. Similarly, the Hawaiian language, once suppressed during colonial eras, is undergoing a powerful revival. Its inclusion in official exchanges, academic collaborations, and public performances underscores the vibrancy and legitimacy of Hawaiian epistemologies. Indigenous art, from kapa-making to carving and tattooing, can also serve as visual ambassadors that articulate worldviews centered on balance, land stewardship, and communal ties.

In concert with its creative and linguistic traditions, Hawai'i can advance regional diplomacy by hosting dialogues grounded in cultural intelligence and place-based insight. Pacific-wide conferences, symposia, and cultural festivals can be organized to foreground shared regional issues such as climate change, cultural preservation, food security, and post-colonial development. These events become more than spectacles; they become gatherings of thought leaders, elders, youth, and change-makers. By investing in the curation of these events with indigenous leadership and protocol at the center, Hawai'i positions itself as a convening space for Pacific resilience and innovation. It moves from being a tourist destination to becoming a diplomatic stage where culture is the medium and message.

The strategic engagement of foreign universities, museums, and cultural institutions is also a vital component of Hawai'i's cultural diplomacy. These partnerships offer platforms for sustained dialogue and knowledge co-production. Joint exhibitions that trace the migration routes of Pacific peoples, bilingual publications that explore decolonial thought, or academic symposia that bring together indigenous scholars from across Oceania serve to both amplify Hawai'i's voice and enrich global discourse. They also disrupt the asymmetries in traditional academic knowledge production by asserting localized, indigenous frameworks as legitimate and necessary. The Bishop Museum[12], for example, can collaborate with institutions like the Smithsonian or the British Museum to repatriate narratives along with objects, fostering deeper conversations on colonial legacies and restorative justice.

Hawai'i's cultural diplomacy efforts can also intersect with economic development. Culturally grounded creative industries, such as film,

[12] https://www.bishopmuseum.org/.

fashion, publishing, and heritage-based tourism, can generate income while promoting ethical representation. Investment in these sectors supports local entrepreneurs and cultural practitioners, ensuring that the benefits of cultural capital remain in the community. For example, supporting Native Hawaiian designers who integrate moʻolelo and traditional symbolism into their work can create high-value cultural exports while also educating global consumers. Similarly, encouraging the production and international distribution of Hawaiian-language films or documentaries on indigenous governance fosters both economic and diplomatic returns.

Cultural diplomacy must also reckon with the legacies of colonization and the ongoing political realities faced by Native Hawaiians. International engagement offers a stage not only for showcasing beauty and tradition but for truth-telling. Through formal partnerships, Hawaiʻi can initiate dialogues on reconciliation, historical trauma, and indigenous futures. These conversations can align with global movements for decolonization and indigenous rights, connecting Hawaiʻi with First Nations in Canada, Aboriginal communities in Australia, and tribal nations in the United States. Sharing experiences in language revitalization, cultural education, and legal recognition can yield mutual benefits and reinforce Hawaiʻi's role as a knowledge leader.

Moreover, these diplomatic engagements should be guided by the principles of kuleana (responsibility), pono (justice), and aloha ʻāina (love for the land). These values are not only cultural cornerstones but political orientations. When embedded in diplomacy, they inform a Hawaiʻi-led ethic of global cooperation that prioritizes equity, sustainability, and human dignity. International partners can learn from Hawaiʻi's land-based epistemologies and community-centric approaches to governance. In this way, Hawaiʻi contributes not just content but a model for how culture and diplomacy can co-create more just global systems.

In addition, the growing recognition of climate change as a cultural crisis positions Hawaiʻi as a key voice in global negotiations. Pacific Island nations have long articulated climate issues as existential, connecting sea level rise and ecosystem collapse with the loss of identity, place, and ancestral connection. Hawaiʻi, with its institutional capacity and cultural authority, can elevate these perspectives in international fora such as the United Nations Framework Convention on Climate Change (UNFCCC) or the Global Island Partnership. By framing climate action as a cultural imperative, not just a technical one, Hawaiʻi can push for more holistic and humane solutions.

Ultimately, cultural diplomacy allows Hawai'i to engage with the world not from the margins, but from a place of leadership grounded in indigenous intelligence and global relevance. It requires a strategic blend of investment, coordination, and authenticity. It demands that institutions work collaboratively with cultural practitioners, that education systems prioritize intercultural competence, and that tourism models are restructured to serve community-defined goals. It calls for humility and clarity, a willingness to speak truthfully about Hawai'i's complex histories while envisioning a future rooted in dignity and abundance.

7 The Hawaiian Diaspora and Global Talent Flows

Migration has always played a formative role in the development of Hawai'i's economy, society, and identity. In the twenty-first century, these patterns have placed Hawai'i within an increasingly complex and dynamic global web. As people move across borders for education, employment, family, and opportunity, they generate talent flows that challenge static notions of population and residence. Hawai'i's role in this network is defined by three intersecting trends: sustained outmigration to the continental United States, continued in-migration from Asia and the Pacific, and the maintenance of robust diaspora networks that span the globe. This positioning opens not only questions of demographic change but also vast possibilities for economic revitalization, cultural continuity, and global influence.

Outmigration, particularly among young professionals and college graduates, has long been a concern for Hawai'i. Brain drain narratives are often cited in policy discussions about workforce shortages, housing affordability, and generational sustainability. Census data consistently show net outmigration from Hawai'i to the continental U.S., especially to states such as California, Nevada, Washington, and Texas. Many of these migrants leave in search of lower costs of living, greater career mobility, and more affordable homeownership opportunities. This pattern is not simply a matter of economics but reflects a deeper friction between aspiration and opportunity. Hawai'i produces highly educated, culturally grounded young people who, facing systemic constraints at home, contribute their skills and energy to other economies. The loss is felt not only in the public sector—where educators, healthcare workers, and civil servants are sorely needed—but also in the entrepreneurial ecosystem, where fresh ideas and local insight are essential for innovation.

Yet, outmigration does not sever ties. The Hawaiian diaspora, which includes not only Native Hawaiians but also long-term residents, multiethnic families, and island-born individuals, maintains a palpable connection to home. These connections manifest in remittances, social media engagement, return visits, and community organizing abroad. Trask (1999) presents a powerful critique of the historical and ongoing colonization of Hawai'i, grounding her analysis in Native Hawaiian epistemology and lived experience [49]. Through essays that blend personal narrative, political commentary, and academic critique, she exposes the economic, cultural, and political forces that have dispossessed Native Hawaiians of land, autonomy, and identity. Trask also explores how resistance takes shape both within the islands and across the diaspora, where Hawaiians continue to engage in cultural revitalization, sovereignty movements, and international solidarity efforts. Her work serves as a rallying call for decolonization and Indigenous self-determination, offering a critical framework for understanding how connections to home are preserved through activism, education, and collective memory, even when Native Hawaiians are physically displaced.

In-migration into Hawai'i also shapes the state's demographic and economic profile. Immigrants from Japan, China, Korea, the Philippines, Micronesia, and other parts of Oceania have contributed to the state's rich multicultural society. These flows bring with them languages, cuisines, entrepreneurial spirit, and transnational family networks. The Philippines remains a major source of migration, with many Filipino migrants working in healthcare, hospitality, education, and domestic labor. Pacific Islander communities, such as those from the Federated States of Micronesia, face complex migration realities linked to U.S. Compact of Free Association agreements, with implications for housing, healthcare, and education systems. These in-migrants are not passive recipients of opportunities but active participants in Hawai'i's evolving identity and workforce. Their presence raises important questions about inclusion, equity, and policy support, especially as climate change and geopolitical shifts drive new waves of mobility in the Pacific.

What connects these migration flows is the concept of the diaspora as both a challenge and a resource. Diaspora networks are more than geographic dispersals; they are living systems of exchange, identity, and potential. These networks link Hawai'i residents to global markets, professional communities, philanthropic channels, and cultural institutions. Alumni associations, professional affinity groups, and social media platforms are increasingly used to mobilize Hawai'i-connected individuals for investment, mentorship, and policy advocacy. For instance, graduates of the University of Hawai'i and Kamehameha Schools who live abroad often return to mentor students, fund scholarships, or advocate for Native Hawaiian priorities in national forums. These efforts demonstrate the latent capacity of diaspora communities to influence home-region development, provided that there are institutional mechanisms to support sustained engagement.

One promising strategy is the development of virtual platforms for cultural exchange and business incubation. With the growth of digital connectivity, diaspora engagement no longer requires physical return. Web-based initiatives can facilitate intergenerational storytelling, language learning, and collaborative entrepreneurship. Online cultural festivals, Zoom-based lecture series, and collaborative design platforms allow Hawai'i-connected individuals to contribute creatively and intellectually from afar. Such programs can be particularly impactful for diaspora youth, who may feel culturally distant but are eager to reconnect. Virtual co-working spaces, mentor-matching apps, and investment platforms can also foster business partnerships between Hawai'i-based entrepreneurs and those with global capital, skills, or networks. These virtual bridges can democratize opportunity and create a more expansive definition of community.

At the same time, the return of diaspora members to Hawai'i—whether temporary or permanent—offers another avenue for talent circulation. Returnees often bring with them expanded professional networks, global perspectives, and new skill sets. These individuals can serve as conduits of innovation, helping to localize global best practices in education, public policy, technology, and sustainability. Encouraging return migration through targeted incentives, fellowship programs, and public service recruitment can help re-anchor this talent locally. Some of the most dynamic leaders in Hawai'i's nonprofit, business, and government sectors are individuals who left, grew professionally, and returned with renewed purpose. Supporting their transition home through housing assistance, business grants, or social reintegration programs ensures that their contributions are not lost to bureaucracy or burnout.

Returnees also play a powerful narrative role. Their stories disrupt the binary of "leavers" and "stayers," suggesting instead that mobility can be cyclical and generative. They offer living proof that belonging is not erased by departure and that commitment to place can be exercised from many locations. This perspective is especially important for younger generations who are often pressured to choose between personal ambition and loyalty to home. Highlighting returnee successes through public storytelling campaigns, school partnerships, or leadership development initiatives can help shift the cultural narrative from brain drain to brain circulation.

Migration should be seen as a cultural process, not just an economic or demographic one. Movements of people entail movements of stories, songs, practices, and paradigms. The Hawaiian diaspora carries with it a rich archive of cultural memory, adaptation, and resilience. Supporting cultural practitioners in the diaspora, whether through funding, partnerships, or visibility, helps ensure the continuity of Hawaiian epistemologies. Hālau hula abroad, Hawaiian language schools on the continent, and Pacific Islander cultural centers in diasporic hubs serve as sites of cultural production and healing. Their work contributes not only to diaspora identity but to global conversations on Indigenous knowledge, cultural sustainability, and decolonization. Goodyear-Ka'ōpua (2013) presents an in-depth ethnography of a Native Hawaiian charter school grounded in Indigenous values, language, and educational practices [50]. Through rich narratives and critical analysis, she shows how the school serves as both an educational institution and a site of cultural regeneration, fostering student empowerment, community engagement, and resistance to colonial educational models. It highlights how Hawaiian language immersion and place-based pedagogy create space for Indigenous sovereignty and self-determination. Although centered in Hawai'i, the pedagogical principles and community-rooted frameworks she explores are applicable to diasporic settings, where cultural continuity and identity formation often rely on educational innovation. This work provides a powerful example of how schools can be agents of decolonization and cultural resilience.

Engaging the diaspora strategically also means cultivating political relationships. Hawai'i-based policymakers, nonprofit leaders, and business associations can build alliances with Hawai'i-connected individuals in federal agencies, national foundations, and multinational corporations. These connections can open doors to funding, policy influence, and international partnerships. The diaspora can advocate for Hawai'i's interests in climate negotiations, educational reform, immigration policy, and Indigenous rights. For example, Hawai'i-born professionals in Washington, D.C., or international organizations like the UN or World Bank can be powerful allies if appropriately engaged. Diaspora diplomacy is not just symbolic; it is a strategic resource that can enhance Hawai'i's voice on the global stage.

Furthermore, the potential of migration and diaspora engagement must be reflected in education and workforce development systems. Students should be encouraged to see global mobility not as a loss but as a learning journey. Schools and universities can incorporate global Hawai'i curricula, intercultural communication training, and overseas internships. These programs equip young people to navigate multiple worlds while remaining grounded in local values. Workforce development initiatives can likewise integrate returnee recruitment, transnational skills recognition, and diaspora engagement strategies. In doing so, Hawai'i can prepare its future leaders to thrive in an interconnected world without feeling forced to abandon their roots.

Ultimately, migration is not merely a demographic issue, it is a bridge to global talent, knowledge, and exchange. Hawai'i's strategic location in the Pacific, its multicultural foundations, and its expansive diaspora position it uniquely to lead in rethinking migration as a force for connection rather than division. Tapping into the Hawaiian diaspora and global talent flows requires vision, coordination, and trust. But the rewards are profound: a revitalized economy, a more inclusive society, and a Hawai'i that is both deeply rooted and globally engaged.

8 Risks and Responsibilities in Globalization

As Hawai'i becomes increasingly intertwined with global systems of trade, tourism, information, and governance, the benefits of globalization are clear: enhanced access to markets, ideas, and innovation; expanded tourism revenue; and deeper international collaboration. Yet with these benefits come profound vulnerabilities. Global integration brings exposure to economic volatility, geopolitical tensions, public health crises, and cyber threats. The COVID-19 pandemic was not merely a health emergency but a full-spectrum stress test of globalization itself, exposing structural weaknesses and prompting renewed discussions about sovereignty, resilience, and ethical responsibility. For Hawai'i, situated at the crossroads of the Pacific, the stakes are especially high. The challenge lies in not only mitigating the risks associated with globalization but also in defining a pathway that upholds local values, promotes systemic resilience, and contributes responsibly to the global commons.

Among the most immediate vulnerabilities are disruptions to supply chains. The COVID-19 era underscored Hawai'i's dependence on external sources for food, fuel, medical supplies, and essential goods. As container ships were delayed, warehouses emptied, and local inventories dwindled, residents and policymakers confronted a sobering reality: globalization has created a just-in-time economy that fails under conditions of shock. With approximately 85–90% of Hawai'i's food imported; the risk of prolonged supply chain interruptions is not hypothetical but ongoing. These dependencies are exacerbated by energy insecurity, as Hawai'i imports most of its petroleum for transportation and electricity, tying its economic stability to global oil markets and maritime logistics.

Equally pressing are threats in the digital realm. Cybersecurity has become a cornerstone of national and regional resilience. Yet critical infrastructure in Hawai'i, from power grids and water systems to hospitals and airports, faces growing exposure to malicious attacks. As remote work and cloud-based services become more prevalent, the risks of ransomware, data breaches, and operational sabotage increase. Hawai'i, with its military installations, university research centers, and telecom nodes, is a strategic target. Cyber vulnerabilities can cascade quickly, disrupting everything from emergency communications to financial systems, and compromising public trust. Protecting these assets requires not only technical defenses but also cross-sector coordination, public education, and real-time response mechanisms. State of Hawaii Office of Homeland Security (2024) presents the Hawai'i Homeland Security Strategy 2022–2025 as a comprehensive framework to address emerging threats and vulnerabilities specific to Hawai'i's geography, infrastructure, and socio-political landscape [51]. This strategy identifies critical vulnerabilities, such as military base exposure, cyberattacks, over-reliance on tourism, and potential extremist activity. It emphasizes resilience through improved governance, expanded public-private partnerships, cybersecurity readiness, professional development, and multi-sector coordination. Key goals include building homeland security capacity, codifying intelligence processes, preparing a skilled security workforce, and promoting proactive vigilance. The document outlines mechanisms for response, recovery, and community engagement, all while safeguarding civil liberties and aligning local action with national security priorities.

Tourism, while economically central, also illustrates the double-edged nature of globalization. As visitor arrivals surged pre-pandemic to over 10 million annually, the social, cultural, and environmental costs became increasingly visible. Strain on natural resources, erosion of cultural sites, traffic congestion, housing pressure, and workforce exploitation all highlight the downsides of over-tourism. Beyond the physical impacts, cultural dilution is a growing concern. When Hawaiian traditions, language, and spirituality are commodified for mass consumption, the result is often distortion or erasure. Global exposure invites admiration but also appropriation, and without ethical guardrails, Hawai'i risks becoming a product rather than a place. The tension between economic gain and cultural integrity is at the heart of the globalization dilemma.

To address these challenges, Hawai'i must invest in resilience strategies that reduce dependency and enhance adaptive capacity. First and foremost is the need to build local capacity in key sectors such as food, energy, and data infrastructure. Strengthening agricultural self-sufficiency involves supporting local farmers, streamlining land-use regulations, and investing in agroecological practices that restore soil health and biodiversity. Innovations in urban farming, aquaponics, and traditional practices like loko i'a (fishpond systems) can also be scaled for both sustainability and cultural relevance. On the energy front, accelerated development of renewables such as solar, wind, and geothermal must be paired with energy storage, microgrids, and demand-response programs to enhance reliability and local control. In the digital sphere, Hawai'i must develop its own secure data centers, invest in cybersecurity training, and forge public-private partnerships that safeguard critical systems without overreliance on mainland or foreign providers.

Second, Hawai'i can benefit from international contingency protocols and mutual aid networks. These frameworks, modeled on disaster response systems, allow for coordinated sharing of resources, personnel, and expertise across borders in times of need. Regional compacts with Pacific Island nations, West Coast states, and international partners can support supply chain continuity, medical mobilization, and technology assistance during crises. For example, establishing pre-cleared emergency shipping routes, cross-trained personnel rosters, and multilingual communication protocols would reduce response times and logistical friction. Moreover, developing diplomatic and economic ties based on reciprocity rather than dependency can strengthen Hawai'i's standing as both a contributor to and beneficiary of global cooperation.

Third, globalization in Hawai'i must be guided by ethical principles that safeguard culture and environment. Exporting Hawaiian culture through tourism, media, or branding should not come at the cost of authenticity or community agency. Ethical guidelines developed in collaboration with cultural practitioners, educators, and community leaders can define what respectful representation looks like. These could include protocols for cultural tourism, consent standards for imagery and storytelling, and reinvestment commitments for cultural preservation. Similarly, environmental stewardship should be embedded in any initiative that seeks to scale or commercialize Hawai‘i-based models. Whether promoting regenerative agriculture, native ecological restoration, or renewable energy technologies, Hawai‘i must ensure that what is exported upholds the values of sustainability, equity, and aloha ‘āina.

The globalization debate in Hawai‘i is also deeply tied to questions of sovereignty and self-determination. As Native Hawaiian movements continue to assert claims to land, governance, and cultural rights, any resilience strategy must engage with these demands. Globalization, if left unchecked, can reproduce colonial dynamics under new guises. But if consciously navigated, it can also offer platforms for Indigenous diplomacy, international solidarity, and knowledge exchange. Participation in global forums such as the United Nations Permanent Forum on Indigenous Issues, the Global Island Partnership, or international climate negotiations can elevate Hawaiian voices and affirm the political agency of the lāhui (nation). Cultural diplomacy, in this context, becomes a tool for both visibility and advocacy.

Education is another vital dimension of Hawai‘i's globalization strategy. Preparing future generations to thrive in a globally connected world requires curricula that are both globally informed and locally grounded. Students should be equipped with intercultural communication skills, global citizenship awareness, and digital literacy. At the same time, they must be rooted in Hawaiian values, history, and epistemology. Programs such as international exchanges, study abroad with local reciprocity, and virtual partnerships with diaspora communities can expand worldviews while strengthening identity. Educational institutions, from K-12 to university levels, have a responsibility to foster global competence without promoting cultural detachment.

The private sector, too, has a role to play in ensuring ethical and resilient globalization. Businesses can adopt environmental, social, and governance (ESG) standards that reflect Hawai‘i's unique context. Corporate investment in local supply chains, workforce development, and cultural programming can yield long-term benefits. For tourism operators, this might mean transitioning from volume-based metrics to impact-based assessments—measuring success not by numbers of arrivals but by quality of experience, cultural contribution, and community benefit. Tech companies operating in Hawai'i can commit to data sovereignty principles and collaborate with local institutions on secure, locally managed platforms. Across sectors, leadership that prioritizes place-based ethics over short-term gains will shape a globalization model that aligns with Hawai'i's aspirations.

Ultimately, navigating globalization requires both strategic defense and cultural integrity. It is not enough to resist external pressures; Hawai'i must define its own terms of engagement. This means reclaiming narratives, building institutional capacity, and forging alliances that reflect shared values. It also requires ongoing dialogue within the community: what kind of future do we envision, and how do we ensure that globalization serves that vision rather than distorts it? The answers to these questions are not static. They must evolve with changing global dynamics, technological advancements, and generational shifts. But by anchoring its approach in aloha 'āina, kuleana, and pono, Hawai'i can model a form of globalization that is not extractive but regenerative—one that enriches both the local and the global.

9 Conclusion: From Outpost to Outlier to Influencer

Hawai'i is not peripheral. It is pivotal. In an era defined by Pacific realignment, climate urgency, and cultural resurgence, Hawai'i's position between Asia and North America, its Indigenous knowledge systems, and its innovation in sustainability place it at the forefront of global relevance. To move from outlier to influencer, Hawai'i must fully embrace this role. First, Hawai'i should treat its geographic location as an advantage, serving as a bridge for diplomacy, regional trade, and knowledge exchange. Building deeper ties with Asia-Pacific partners through education, cultural collaboration, and environmental initiatives will strengthen its international standing. Second, sustainability and culture must be recognized as export assets. Hawai'i can lead by example through regenerative tourism, traditional agriculture, and climate adaptation models rooted in Indigenous values. Third, Hawai'i's people are its greatest resource. By investing in education, global mobility, and leadership development, the state can empower a generation ready to represent local values on a global stage. This book's final chapter will turn these ideas into actionable strategy, outlining how Hawai'i can shape the future by amplifying what makes it unique. Hawai'i's path forward is not about fitting in; it's about leading with integrity, resilience, and aloha.

References

[1]. U.S. Department of Defense. (2024). Hawai'i State Fact Sheet – Readiness and Environmental Protection Integration (REPI) Program. Retrieved from https://www.repi.mil/Portals/44/Documents/State_Fact_Sheets/Hawaii_StateFacts.pdf.

[2]. U.S. Pacific Fleet. (2024, June 28). RIMPAC 2024 kicks off in Hawaii. Retrieved from https://www.cpf.navy.mil/Newsroom/News/Article/3822005/rimpac-2024-kicks-off-in-hawaii/.

[3]. U.S. Navy. (2025, May 14). Statement of Vice Admiral James Kilby Before the House Appropriations Committee on Navy Readiness. Retrieved from https://www.congress.gov/119/meeting/house/118229/witnesses/HHRG-119-AP02-Wstate-KilbyJ-20250514.pdf.

[4]. Hawaii Defense Economy. (2021). Economic Impact of Defense Spending. Retrieved from https://defenseeconomy.hawaii.gov/economic-impact/.

[5]. BizClik Media. (2024). INDOPACOM: Digital transformation in defense logistics and cyber operations. Retrieved from https://publication.bizclikmedia.com/cQsd.

[6]. Pacific Business News (2025). Hawai'i's Largest Employers by Local Workers, 2025. Retrieved from https://www.bizjournals.com/pacific/subscriber-only/2025/10/17/here-are-the-biggest-employers-in-hawaii.html.

[7]. Hawai'i Department of Defense. (2025). Annual Report for Fiscal Year 2024. Retrieved from https://dod.hawaii.gov/wp-content/uploads/2025/03/2024-DOD-Annual-Report.pdf.

[8]. Compoc, K., & Enomoto, J. L. (2022, July 26). A call to cancel RIMPAC in Hawai'i. Foreign Policy in Focus. Retrieved from https://fpif.org/a-call-to-cancel-rimpac-in-hawai%CA%BBi/.

[9]. Watson, T. K. (2022, April 1). Cultural Impact Assessment for the Army Training Land Retention at Pohakuloa Training Area. ResearchGate. Retrieved from https://www.researchgate.net/publication/361412177_Cultural_Impact_Assessment_for_the_Army_Training_Land_Retention_at_Pohakuloa_Training_Area.

[10]. Fernandez-Akamine, P. (2024, September 1). Pōhakuloa: A Land Besieged. Ka Wai Ola. Retrieved from https://kawaiola.news/cover/pohakuloa-a-land-besieged/.

[11]. Office of the Governor, State of Hawai'i. (2025, November 13). Gov. Green names advisory committee for military leased lands [Press release]. Governor Josh Green M.D. Retrieved from https://governor.hawaii.gov/newsroom/office-of-the-governor-news-release-gov-green-names-advisory-committee-for-leased-military-lands/.

[12]. National Security Innovation Network. (2023, October 2). Defense Innovation OnRamp Hubs to open in Arizona, Hawaii, Kansas, Ohio and

Washington. Retrieved from https://www.nsin.mil/news/2023-10-02-defense-innovation-onramp-hubs/.
[13]. Roberts, K. (2024, October 22). ManTech opens new partnership and innovation hub in Hawaii. ExecutiveBiz. Retrieved from https://executivebiz.com/2024/10/mantech-opens-new-partnership-and-innovation-hub-in-hawaii/.
[14]. Hawaii Department of Business, Economic Development & Tourism. (2024). Quarterly Statistical and Economic Report, Q4 2024. Retrieved from https://files.hawaii.gov/dbedt/economic/data_reports/qser/qser-2024q4.pdf.
[15]. Department of Business, Economic Development & Tourism. (2024). 2023 annual visitor research report. State of Hawaiʻi. Retrieved from https://files.hawaii.gov/dbedt/visitor/visitor-research/2023-annual-visitor.pdf.
[16]. Department of Business, Economic Development & Tourism. (2024). The Economic Impact of International Students in Hawaiʻi – Calendar Year 2023. Retrieved from https://files.hawaii.gov/dbedt/economic/reports/2024-11-foreign-student.pdf.
[17]. Hawaiʻi Department of Transportation, Harbors Division. (2023). Honolulu Harbor 2050 Master Plan. Retrieved from https://hidot.hawaii.gov/harbors/files/2023/01/VOL-I_HHMP-2050.pdf.
[18]. Hawaiʻi Department of Transportation, Airports Division. (2023). Daniel K. Inouye International Airport Audit Report. Retrieved from https://files.hawaii.gov/auditor/Reports/2023_Audit/DOT_Airports_2023.pdf.
[19]. Novak, P., & Imai, K. (2024). Bolstering cooperation among Quad and Pacific Island countries. Atlantic Council. Retrieved from https://www.atlanticcouncil.org/wp-content/uploads/2024/04/Bolstering-cooperation-among-Quad-and-Pacific-Island-countries.pdf.
[20]. Insights IAS. (2025, May 8). Indo-Pacific Logistics Network (IPLN). InsightsIAS. Retrieved from https://www.insightsonindia.com/2025/05/08/indo-pacific-logistics-network-ipln/.
[21]. World Bank. (2023). A blue transformation for Pacific maritime transport. Retrieved from https://documents1.worldbank.org/curated/en/099062723183020066/pdf/P1749900249d300fa0910307401e677b5ae.pdf.
[22]. University of Hawaiʻi News. (2024, September 19). Q&A: UH climate-smart agriculture project prepares for next phase. Retrieved from https://www.hawaii.edu/news/2024/09/19/climate-smart-agriculture/.
[23]. Omnitrak Group. (2023). Made in Hawaiʻi brand development plan. Hawaiʻi Department of Business, Economic Development and Tourism (DBEDT). Retrieved from https://invest.hawaii.gov/wp-content/uploads/2024/09/Made-in-Hawaii-Brand-Development-Plan-June-2023_upload.pdf.
[24]. Congressional Research Service. (2024, November 7). The Pacific Islands: Background and issues for Congress (CRS Report No. IF11208,

Version 16). Retrieved from https://crsreports.congress.gov/product/pdf/IF/IF11208/16.
[25]. Pacific Forum International. (2025). Honolulu Defense Forum 2026. Retrieved from https://pacforum.swoogo.com/HDF26.
[26]. Harding, A. J. (2024, October 1). The Pacific Pivot: An American Strategy for the Pacific Islands (Special Report No. 296). The Heritage Foundation. Retrieved from https://report.heritage.org/sr296.
[27]. Nicastro, L. A. (2023, June 6). U.S. Defense Infrastructure in the Indo-Pacific: Background and Issues for Congress (CRS Report No. R47589). Congressional Research Service. Retrieved from https://www.congress.gov/crs-product/R47589.
[28]. Department of Business, Economic Development & Tourism. Hawai'i State Trade Expansion Program (HiSTEP). Retrieved from https://invest.hawaii.gov/exporting-programs/hawaii-state-trade-expansion-program-histep/.
[29]. City and County of Honolulu. (2024). Climate Ready O'ahu: A Strategy for a Resilient Island. Office of Climate Change, Sustainability and Resiliency. Retrieved from https://www.cakex.org/sites/default/files/documents/Climate%20Ready%20Oahu_Final.pdf.
[30]. University of Hawai'i at Mānoa. Center for Pacific Islands Studies. Retrieved from https://www.hawaii.edu/cpis/.
[31]. Mitchell-Eaton, E. (2023). Compact of Free Association (COFA) Status: An Imperial Policy on the Move. Asian-Pacific Law & Policy Journal, 24(3), 1–24. Retrieved from https://manoa.hawaii.edu/aplpj/wp-content/uploads/sites/120/2023/05/APLPJ_Column_MITCHELL-EATON-Emily_Compact-of-free-association-cofa-status-an-imperial-policy-on-the-move.pdf.
[32]. Executive Office of the President. (2021, June 3). Executive Order 14031: Advancing equity, justice, and opportunity for Asian Americans, Native Hawaiians, and Pacific Islanders. Federal Register, 86(105), 29675–29681. Retrieved from https://www.federalregister.gov/documents/2021/06/03/2021-11792/advancing-equity-justice-and-opportunity-for-asian-americans-native-hawaiians-and-pacific-islanders.
[33]. John A. Burns School of Medicine. Hawai'i/Pacific Basin Area Health Education Center (AHEC). Retrieved from https://ahec.hawaii.edu/.
[34]. Sinclair, K. A., Zamora-Kapoor, A., Townsend-Ing, C., McElfish, P. A., & Kaholokula, J. K. (2020). Implementation outcomes of a culturally adapted diabetes self-management education intervention for Native Hawaiians and Pacific Islanders. BMC Public Health, 20, 1579. Retrieved from https://doi.org/10.1186/s12889-020-09690-6.
[35]. Hawai'i Natural Energy Institute. (2022). University of Hawai'i at Manoa. Retrieved from https://www.hnei.hawaii.edu.
[36]. Climate Change Commission. (2023). Climate Change Brief 2023. City and County of Honolulu. Retrieved from https://static1.squarespace.com/

static/5e3885654a153a6ef84e6c9c/t/64374370c0631e3ac922692a/1681343347345/Climate+Change+Brief+2023.pdf.
[37]. City and County of Honolulu. (2023). Climate Ready O'ahu: Climate Adaptation Strategy – Executive Summary. Office of Climate Change, Sustainability, and Resiliency. Retrieved from https://resilientoahu.org/climatereadyoahu.
[38]. Dator, J., & Ching, D. R. (2011). Visioning Hawai'i's adaptation to climate change: Final report of the alternative futures exercise at the 2011 planning meeting with the Hawai'i Ocean Resources Management Plan Partners. State of Hawai'i Office of Planning, Coastal Zone Management Program. Retrieved from https://files.hawaii.gov/dbedt/op/czm/ormp/reports/visioning_hawaii_adaptation_to_climate_change_aug_2011.pdf.
[39]. Hawai'i State Energy Office. (2023). Hawai'i pathways to decarbonization: Act 238, Session Laws of Hawai'i 2022 – Final report to the 2024 Hawai'i State Legislature. Retrieved from https://energy.hawaii.gov/wp-content/uploads/2022/10/Act-238_HSEO_Decarbonization_FinalReport_2023.pdf.
[40]. Pacific Islands Development Program (PIDP). East-West Center. Retrieved from https://pidp.eastwestcenter.org.
[41]. Pacific Regional Integrated Sciences and Assessments (Pacific RISA). University of Hawai'i at Mānoa. Retrieved from https://www.pacificrisa.org.
[42]. Pacific RISA. (2025). Managing climate risk in Pacific Islands. Pacific Regional Integrated Sciences and Assessments. Retrieved from https://www.pacificrisa.org/education-outreach/.
[43]. Under2 Coalition. (2023). Under2 Coalition Highlights Report 2023. The Climate Group. Retrieved from https://www.theclimategroup.org/our-work/resources/under2-coalition-2023-impact-report.
[44]. Global Island Partnership (GLISPA). (2024). Sustainable and resilient island communities through partnerships: GLISPA Strategy Booklet 2024. Retrieved from https://globalislandpartnership.org/media/attachments/2024/05/21/glispa_strategybooklet_2024-1.pdf.
[45]. United Nations Development Programme. (2023). Community-based resilience building: Guidance note. Retrieved from https://www.undp.org/publications/community-based-resilience-building-undp-guidance-note.
[46]. United Nations Development Programme. (2025). Climate counts pocketbook. UNDP. Retrieved from https://climatepromise.undp.org/sites/default/files/research_report_document/Climate%20Counts%20pocketbook.pdf.
[47]. Hawai'i Climate Data Portal. (2025). About the Hawai'i Climate Data Portal. Retrieved from https://www.hawaii.edu/climate-data-portal/2339-2/.
[48]. Longman, R. J., Peterson, C. L., Baroli, M., Frazier, A. G., Cook, Z., Parsons, E. W., Dinan, M., Kamelamela, K. L., Steele, C., Burnett, R., Swanston,

C., & Giardina, C. P. (2022). Climate adaptation training for tropical island land stewardship: Lessons from a collaborative, culturally grounded workshop in Hawai'i. Bulletin of the American Meteorological Society, 103(2), E428–E444. https://doi.org/10.1175/BAMS-D-21-0163.1.
[49]. Trask, H.-K. (1999). From a Native Daughter: Colonialism and Sovereignty in Hawai'i (Rev. ed.). University of Hawai'i Press. Retrieved from https://uhpress.hawaii.edu/title/from-a-native-daughter-colonialism-and-sovereignty-in-hawaii-revised-edition/.
[50]. Goodyear-Ka'ōpua, N. (2013). The Seeds We Planted: Portraits of a Native Hawaiian Charter School. University of Minnesota Press. Retrieved from https://www.upress.umn.edu/book-division/books/the-seeds-we-planted.
[51]. State of Hawai'i Office of Homeland Security. (2024). Hawai'i Homeland Security Strategy. Retrieved from https://law.hawaii.gov/ohs/wp-content/uploads/sites/2/2024/01/HSS-Final-Digital-1.pdf.

CHAPTER 8

Competing on Aloha—A Strategy for Hawai'i's Economic Future

1 Introduction: Beyond Growth, Toward Belonging

Hawai'i stands at a pivotal crossroads. Global crises such as climate change, widening inequality, geopolitical shifts, and digital disruption intersect with urgent local realities: a housing crisis that displaces residents, youth outmigration that drains future talent, and economic models that leave too many behind. These overlapping pressures demand more than policy tweaks. They require a fundamental reimagining of what economic success looks like. This final chapter draws from the themes explored throughout the book to offer a guiding framework: Hawai'i must move beyond measuring success by GDP alone and toward an economy rooted in belonging. The state's unique strength is not in replicating tech hubs or chasing cost competition, but in offering a value-based approach to prosperity. Competing on Aloha, an economy grounded in aloha (affection and care), kuleana (responsibility), and lōkahi (unity), is not only culturally authentic but globally relevant.

An aloha-driven economy recognizes that resilience is more than redundancy; it is relationship. It sees sustainability not as a trend but as a tradition. And it values people—not just as labor inputs or consumers, but as stewards, storytellers, and citizens. From regenerative tourism to climate-smart agriculture, from culturally grounded education to inclusive workforce development, Hawai'i has the tools to lead—not despite its size, but because of its clarity of purpose. Competing on Aloha invites Hawai'i to

P. Yu, *Economic Development in Hawai'i*,
https://doi.org/10.1007/978-3-032-15689-1_8

be a model for place-based economic transformation. This chapter will turn insights into strategy, articulating how belonging in its social, cultural, ecological dimensions can become a measurable economic advantage. In a world searching for connection, trust, and purpose, Hawai‘i's greatest asset is not just its brand or beauty; it is its ability to lead with meaning. The future lies not in scaling what others do, but in deepening what makes Hawai‘i different.

2 What Does It Mean to Compete on Aloha?

To speak of Hawai‘i's future is to speak of tension: between growth and stewardship, markets and mana, speed and sustainability. "Competing on aloha" offers a way to reconcile those tensions without flattening what makes the islands distinct. Aloha is often reduced in tourist brochures to a smile or a slogan. Yet for residents, it embodies a disciplined ethic of looking out for one another—an economy of belonging rather than a hospitality brand. By placing well-being, equity, and ecological integrity at the center of development, aloha redefines prosperity to include cultural vitality, environmental health, and intergenerational care. It does not reject markets; it reframes them around shared value, reminding us that price alone never captures real worth, and that any ledger detached from place cannot account for true wealth.

Every economy originates in a geography, yet most modern development erases that fact by defaulting to abstract metrics such as GDP per capita, labor productivity, and return on investment, without asking whose land, whose labor, and whose return. Aloha economics begins with the ‘āina, the living land that shelters and feeds, and with the people who have shaped and been shaped by it for centuries. In practice, place-based economics favors agricultural systems adapted to microclimates; housing typologies that reflect multi-generational living; and supply chains that trace accountability back to soil and sea. A coffee cooperative in Kona, for example, can capture more value locally when beans are roasted, packaged, and branded under a geographic indication that protects both quality and cultural story. Likewise, infrastructure that honors ahupua‘a boundaries, extending from mountain to reef, better aligns watershed management with flood resilience and coral-reef health than parcel-by-parcel permitting ever could. Place-based means exporting what is uniquely rooted rather than importing what is cheaply generic.

Classical economics prizes efficiency: the quickest throughput, the thinnest inventory, the cheapest source. Island economies reveal the fragility of that logic. A shipping delay can empty grocery shelves within days; a cyberattack on energy or water can paralyze entire counties. Competing on aloha therefore privileges redundancy, adaptability, and community capacity. Microgrids that allow neighborhoods to island from the main grid during outages sacrifice some economies of scale but gain life-saving autonomy during hurricanes. Local food systems, school gardens, cooperative aquaculture, rooftop farms may never displace all imports, yet they provide nutritional security, cultural continuity, and a buffer against global supply shocks. Resilience investments often look inefficient on spreadsheets until the first crisis strikes; then they look priceless.

Hawai'i's knowledge economy need not mimic Silicon Valley's winner-take-all model. Inclusive innovation braids Indigenous wisdom with emergent technology, positioning cultural practitioners and engineers as co-inventors rather than competitors. Examples abound: sensors that monitor lo'i kalo water levels in real time; AI tools that accelerate translation of Hawaiian-language newspapers; blockchain systems that trace fish catch to support both food safety and kūpuna fishers' livelihoods. By rooting R&D in community priorities such as climate-smart agriculture, culturally informed mental health platforms, bio-char enhanced soils, Hawai'i attracts researchers who see the islands not as a test market to extract from but as a living laboratory whose people co-define success. Inclusivity also means widening access to capital: revolving loan funds for Native Hawaiian enterprises, impact-investing pools that reward social and ecological performance metrics, and diaspora bonds that allow expatriates to channel savings into home -grown ventures.

Top-down policymaking often misses the daily realities of residents; bottom-up activism can stall without pathways to implementation. Aloha governance seeks the middle ground of deliberative democracy through citizen assemblies, participatory budgeting, and kūpuna advisory councils that invites broad input while maintaining the rigor of strategic planning. When Maui residents co-design their wildfire recovery plan, for instance, they bring ancestral knowledge of rain-belt planting and cultural protocols for clearing invasive grasses, alongside architects' expertise in fire-resistant materials. U.S. Environmental Protection Agency (EPA) (2023) outlines a culturally grounded approach to wildfire recovery in Maui, emphasizing respect for Native Hawaiian traditions during the cleanup and response efforts following the August 2023 fires in Lāhainā and Kula [1]. In partnership with FEMA and local leaders, the EPA integrated cultural monitors or trained community members, into field operations to ensure that environmental remediation respected sacred and historically significant sites. These monitors guided activities such as hazardous material removal, offering real-time input rooted in ancestral knowledge. Additionally, all EPA field staff received cultural training to align their technical work with community expectations and spiritual practices. This approach exemplifies a shift toward culturally responsive disaster management, in which environmental protection and cultural preservation are treated as interdependent. The case offers a valuable precedent for weaving Indigenous perspectives into recovery planning, showing that true resilience grows stronger when local cultural expertise is not merely recognized but placed at the center of the process.

Skeptics may label aloha economics as sentimental. Yet each principle maps onto competitive advantage in an era of turbulence. Risk mitigation through diversified local production and distributed infrastructure reduces exposure to supply chain shocks, cyberattacks, and extreme weather, all of which are now factored into capital costs by insurers and credit-rating agencies. Market differentiation built on products and services shaped by authentic place-based stories often commands premium prices, especially among consumers who value meaning as much as utility. Talent retention through workplaces that honor kuleana and lōkahi appeal to younger generations who weigh belonging as heavily as salary. Policy alignment through global frameworks such as the United Nations Sustainable Development Goals and the Paris Climate Agreement increasingly reward regions that integrate social justice and ecological stewardship into development. Hawai'i's values position it to capture those incentives. The 2024 UN report underscores the urgency of integrating climate policies and Sustainable Development Goals (SDGs) through synergistic approaches tailored to national contexts [2]. It stresses breaking down silos, aligning local development with global goals, and using participatory approaches to achieve just and transformative outcomes. Hawai'i can draw from this by embedding climate resilience and social equity into its economic planning. By coordinating state-level sustainability goals with national and international frameworks, Hawai'i can boost funding access, policy coherence, and long-term climate adaptation. This approach positions Hawai'i as a global model for integrating Indigenous values, inclusive governance, and ecological stewardship into sustainable development pathways.

Establishing a Hawai'i Resilience Fund that braids federal grants, impact-investor capital, green bonds, and hotel occupancy surcharges into patient financing for climate-adaptive housing and regenerative tourism upgrades would be transformative. Every county should nurture a community resilience hub that combines microgrid power, telehealth kiosks, job-training labs, and culture rooms, places that operate daily as makerspaces and pivot to shelters during disasters. Replace single-indicator success measures with a composite index that tracks ecological health, social equity, cultural vitality, and economic resilience. Zone coastal and mauka lands into corridors where regenerative enterprises receive expedited permitting, tax incentives, and technical assistance, provided they hire locally and report on ecosystem outcomes. Partner with chambers of commerce in Las Vegas, Seattle, and Tokyo to host virtual hackathons centered on Hawai'i's challenges, offering return fellowships and equity opportunities in spin-offs that choose to relocate or bring their intellectual property back home.

Competing on aloha does not promise frictionless consensus or utopian self-sufficiency. It acknowledges the unavoidable tensions of a tourist - dependent, geographically isolated, U.S.-state-yet-indigenous-homeland economy. What it does promise is coherence. Policies that speak the same ethical language as the communities they affect. Innovations that heal as they grow. Markets that remember the hands and hills behind every transaction. In an era when the world's largest economies are scrambling to redefine progress beyond GDP by incorporating happiness indexes, social capital measures, and carbon budgets, Hawai'i need not look outward for models. It can look inward, to a worldview that has for centuries regarded prosperity as a collective state of well -being where no one is left outside the circle.

That worldview has always been more pragmatic than romantic. Hawaiian voyagers read subtle swells, star lines, and cloud reflections for survival. Today's navigators of the island economy face new seas shaped by data, deregulation, and demographic shifts, but the principle remains the same. Steer by values you trust, adapt with every swell, and keep the crew in sight. Competing on aloha is strategic realism dressed in cultural clarity. It is Hawai'i's invitation to itself and to the world to measure wealth in relationships restored, ecosystems revived, and futures shared.

3 Strategic Pillars for a Future-Ready Hawai'i

Hawai'i's economic transformation must grow from soil and sea, from memory and modernity, from crises endured and possibilities glimpsed. If the chapters that preceded mapped challenges and assets, the task now is to weave their threads into a coherent cloth of strategic intent. Six pillars arise as intertwining roots that anchor a living ecosystem of prosperity.

First is the commitment to diversified, regenerative industries. The islands know too well the brittleness of single-sector dependence, whether it was sugar a century ago or mass tourism today. A future-ready Hawai'i channels its abundant sun, wind, and geothermal resources into a renewable energy portfolio that lowers utility bills, curbs emissions, and attracts cleantech research. It revitalizes regenerative agriculture, blending traditional lo'i kalo and agroforestry with climate-smart seed banks and vertical farms, so that school lunches feature food grown within sight of the cafeteria. The surrounding ocean becomes both larder and laboratory: seaweed farms that sequester carbon while feeding livestock, coral nurseries that restore reefs and supply biomedical compounds, seafloor mapping enterprises that guide sustainable mineral policy.

The creative and cultural sectors receive equal billing, turning mele, kapa, and augmented-reality storytelling into export revenue without commodifying spirit. Health and wellness entrepreneurs, from lā'au lapa'au (Hawaiian herbal medicine) herbalists to digital therapeutics startups, position the islands as a global center for whole-person care. Atkinson (2020) presents the Lā'au Lapa'au Preservation Project, a 3-year master class led by Kahuna Roddy Akau aimed at restoring Native Hawaiian healing traditions [3]. Rooted in spiritual, cultural, and environmental principles, this program immerses 30 students in ancestral practices, emphasizing cultural competency, deep connection to 'āina, and lifestyle transformation. Through teachings in Moanalua Valley, once home to Hawaiian priesthood, the project fosters a holistic healthcare model grounded in Hawaiian identity. It addresses urgent health disparities in the Native Hawaiian community by cultivating future healers who practice in alignment with spiritual and ecological wisdom, ensuring the continuity of lā'au lapa'au for future generations.

None of this flourish without a deliberate cultivation of human capital calibrated for tomorrow's economy. Apprenticeships that once centered on carpentry and plumbing now add photovoltaic maintenance, drone piloting, and Hawaiian language immersion teaching. Micro-credentials stack like coral polyps, allowing a hotel housekeeper to become an energy auditor or a fisherman to pivot into marine robotics. Place-based education returns classrooms to ahupua'a logic: math in the taro patch, chemistry in the fishpond, civics at the neighborhood board. The University of Hawai'i emerges as a testbed where Indigenous knowledge informs quantum computing algorithms designed for climate modeling. Broadband equity stops being a grant-proposal buzzword and becomes a constitutional promise—so a Moloka'i teen has the same gigabit canvas as a prodigy in Silicon Valley. Retention and return of local talent depend on affordable housing, wages aligned with the real cost of living, and meaningful enterprises that allow kama'āina to choose Hawai'i not out of sacrifice, but out of purpose and mission.

Infrastructure must rise to the scale of our vision while still honoring the humility of islands. Permitting and construction processes shed layers of duplication that have turned homebuilding into a decade-long marathon. Housing rises in walkable mixed-use clusters, cooled by passive design and powered by rooftop solar microgrids that island themselves during storms. Mobility evolves from car dependency to networks of electric shuttles, bikeways shaded by ulu trees, and ferries that link islands in a low-carbon archipelago. Broadband fiber traces highway corridors and submarine cables alike, with redundancy routes that screen against earthquakes and sabotage. Green infrastructure doubles as public space: wetlands restored as flood sponges and bird sanctuaries, seawalls traded for living shorelines of mangrove and oyster reef. Public capital such as pension funds, municipal bonds, and tourist tax flows through social impact screens so that every dollar of investment returns measurable community benefit alongside financial yield.

Governance ultimately determines whether these investments foster real inclusion or simply mask persistent inequality. Equity becomes the baseline, not the afterthought. Some decisions devolve to neighborhood boards where residents can shape zoning variances or park programming; others elevate Native Hawaiian councils whose ancestral stewardship rights guide land-use ethics. Community-based nonprofits receive multi-year core funding instead of one-off contracts, allowing long-term planning rather than crisis chasing. Data dashboards lay out budget outlays and climate metrics in plain language, while public agencies submit to citizen audits that track which commitments have been honored and which have been left behind. Participatory budgeting allows high-school civics classes to allocate small capital projects, teaching democratic muscle memory long before voting age. Trust, eroded by opaque deals and extractive development, gradually rebuilds as communities see their imprint reflected in policy decisions.

A future-ready Hawai'i does not retreat into insularity; it steps confidently onto regional and global stages. As climate impacts intensify across the Pacific, the islands lead adaptation summits in which atoll nations jointly design relocation financing mechanisms and coral genome banks. U.S. Global Change Research Program (2023) reports that climate change poses significant threats to the Hawai'i and U.S.-Affiliated Pacific Islands region through sea level rise, changing rainfall patterns, extreme weather, and warming temperatures [4]. These threats undermine food and water security, human health, infrastructure, cultural heritage, and biodiversity. Indigenous Knowledge systems, coupled with scientific research and community-based adaptation strategies, are essential for enhancing resilience. This report emphasizes regional collaboration, relocation planning for atoll nations, and innovations such as coral genome conservation and ecosystem restoration to support long-term sustainability and adaptive capacity across the Pacific.

Through it all is the insistence that cultural integrity remains our most enduring competitive advantage. Language revitalization is funded not as nostalgia but as strategic infrastructure: each new preschool immersion cohort expands the universe of thought available to solve complex problems. Land stewardship transcends conservation by extraction of cultural value; instead, it is woven into city budgets and private covenants so that every development sets aside space for native flora, events honoring kupuna, and public shoreline access. Cultural practitioners such as carvers, kumu hula, and navigators receive living-wage fellowships and health coverage, recognizing their knowledge as intellectual property vital to nation-building. Tourism operators adopt regenerative metrics, paying royalties to host communities, capping visitation at sacred sites, and employing storytellers who situate visitors within living culture rather than staged fantasy. In global forums, Hawai'i trades on authenticity: a small polity that has reconciled economic ambition with the humility of limited land and the sovereignty of Indigenous memory.

Skeptics may doubt whether such a model can outcompete regions chasing scale and speed. Yet the turbulence of the twenty-first century rewards systems that are adaptive, trusted, and meaningful. Investors already price climate risk; customers already pay premiums for transparent supply chains; employees already choose workplaces aligned with purpose.

Hawai'i's strategic pillars convert moral imperatives into market differentiators. Renewable energy attracts cleantech funds eager for real-world testing across microgrids. Regenerative agriculture supplies chefs and grocers who are marketing provenance, stewardship, and carbon neutrality. Cultural assets underpin creative industries whose intellectual property cannot be offshored. Broadband equity and stunning landscapes lure remote workers who contribute income without swelling commuter traffic. Governance reforms lower transaction costs by reducing litigation and protest delays. Pacific diplomacy opens grant and defense channels tied to climate security.

The greatest risk is fragmentation—initiatives launched in isolation, values invoked for branding but ignored in practice, cultural guardians consulted too late. Integration is therefore the discipline running through every pillar. Universities embed climate resilience internships within construction majors; tourism authorities require cultural certification before marketing new attractions; energy cooperatives reserve board seats for local fishers whose reefs host turbine cables. Metrics matter: dashboards that display reef health alongside visitor counts, household wage share alongside GDP, cultural practitioner income alongside venture-capital inflows. When outcomes conflict, aloha becomes the guide: Does this decision enhance community well-being, honor our kuleana to land and ancestors, and strengthen lōkahi among residents? If not, it is revised or rejected.

Hawai'i competes not by out-scaling Singapore or out-coding California but by offering the world a model of prosperity calibrated to limits and relationships. In doing so, it transforms its historic crossroads into a crucible of possibility: where regenerative industries flourish beside intact reefs, where classrooms speak ancestral languages while programming quantum software, where governance invites participation rather than protest, and where every economic metric traces back to the health of the people and the land that sustains them. Competing on aloha, Hawai'i stands ready not only to survive the storms of the century but to navigate them with purpose, inviting others to follow the stars it sets in motion.

4 Indicators for a New Economy

Competing on aloha is less a slogan than an accounting revolution. Every society takes the measure of what it cherishes most. For more than half a century, Hawai'i has defaulted to the same yardsticks that guide mainland decision-makers: GDP, per-capita income, seasonally adjusted unemployment. Those numbers tell a story of visitor arrivals, military payrolls, and retail receipts. They do not chronicle the other Hawai'i, the one where teachers hold two jobs, where reefs bleach after record heat, where a Maui family waits a decade for a home lot and a Moloka'i kupuna loses her dialect because there is no neighbor to speak it with. If the state is serious about an economy rooted in well-being, equity, and ecological integrity, it must renovate its dashboard. The task is not to abandon growth metrics but to surround them with indicators that reveal whether growth nourishes or corrodes the common good.

A first, unavoidable lens is housing affordability for residents. Economists track median sales price and apartment rents, yet those numbers float unanchored unless compared with local wages. A meaningful indicator expresses the share of households able to purchase or rent at least a two-bedroom unit while spending no more than 30% of income on shelter and utilities. Joint Center for Housing Studies of Harvard University (2024) reports that Hawaii continues to face one of the most severe rental affordability crises in the United States [5]. Over 55% of renter households in the state are cost-burdened, meaning they spend more than 30% of their income on rent and utilities. Honolulu ranks among the top three U.S. metro areas with the highest cost burdens, alongside Miami and Orlando. The affordability challenges have worsened since the pandemic, with the limited affordable rental supply failing to meet rising demand. Even in non-metro regions, low-income residents struggle to secure adequate housing.

Civic participation and trust in institutions form the bedrock upon which every market transaction rests. Social scientists once assumed that voter turnout and volunteer hours sufficed as proxies. Yet digital life has spawned new arenas of engagement and distrust. A Hawai'i civic index would combine classic measures such as voting rates in local elections, attendance at neighborhood boards with modern ones like the percentage of residents interacting with public budgeting platforms, survey-based confidence in police fairness, diversity of language access at city hearings, and the speed at which agencies fulfill open-record requests. Institute for Citizens & Scholars (2024) reports that civic measurement in the U.S. is evolving beyond traditional indicators like voting and volunteerism to include modern, equity-aware metrics [6]. While this report does not focus exclusively on Hawai'i, its framework is highly relevant to the state's diverse and multilingual communities. The authors highlight the importance of assessing civic readiness through new tools such as engagement in participatory budgeting platforms, language access at public hearings, and digital interaction with government services. These approaches offer practical guidance for developing a Hawai‘i Civic Index that reflects both classic and contemporary forms of civic participation and institutional trust, especially in a culturally pluralistic and geographically unique setting like Hawai‘i.

Ecological health must migrate from environmental impact statements buried in permit filings to the front page of economic briefings. Scientists already monitor coral cover, fish biomass, native forest canopy, aquifer recharge, soil carbon, and endangered-bird fledglings. What remains is to translate these metrics into a composite eco-integrity score updated annually and tied to budget triggers. If reef condition in Waikīkī drops below a resilience threshold, a portion of hotel-room taxes automatically flows to runoff-mitigation projects. If soil organic matter on former plantation lands rises, agricultural tax incentives kick in for the farmers responsible. Linking money arrows to ecological arrows transforms stewardship from moral plea to financial logic. Gross and Rodriguez (2017) report that Hawai‘i’s natural capital, including its forests, wetlands, and biodiversity, provides essential ecosystem services such as freshwater provisioning, climate regulation, and cultural preservation [7]. These services support the well-being of 1.4 million residents and 8 million annual visitors. However, investment in conservation has lagged behind the scale of environmental threats. This report evaluates Hawai‘i’s readiness to implement a Payment for Ecosystem Services (PES) approach that aligns ecological stewardship with financial incentives. It emphasizes the importance of creating a shared problem narrative, leveraging existing public-private partnerships, and adopting flexible PES tools such as carbon offsets and watershed protection fees. Gross and Rodriguez highlight the state’s unique biodiversity, vulnerability to climate change, and dependency on natural systems, proposing PES as a viable, equity-aware financial mechanism to strengthen conservation efforts while supporting economic sustainability.

Community wealth building shifts attention from income flows to asset accumulation. A headline metric could track the percentage of small and mid-size enterprises locally owned and the share of profits retained in Hawai‘i rather than expatriated. The Aspen Institute Financial Security Program (2022) outlines 101 evidence-based solutions to support inclusive wealth building across the United States, with principles highly applicable to Hawai‘i’s local economic landscape [8]. The report emphasizes five conditions for building wealth: financial stability, access to investable funds, affordable assets, consumer-friendly financing, and wealth protection. It recognizes systemic barriers such as income stagnation, high living costs, and racial inequities that disproportionately affect Native and marginalized communities. While the document does not single out Hawai'i-specific data, many of its proposals such as expanding cooperative ownership models, supporting Native-led financial institutions, and promoting reparative financial policies resonate with ongoing Hawaiian efforts to foster community wealth, support Native Hawaiian entrepreneurs, and ensure equitable access to housing and education. Implementing such targeted, asset-based strategies could help Hawai'i circulate more wealth locally, support Indigenous prosperity, and reduce structural financial inequality.

Education-to-career pathways and local talent retention provide the human dimension. Instead of merely graduating classes, the University of Hawai'i and community colleges would report how many alumni remain in the islands three- and five-years post-graduation and whether they are employed in fields aligned with their studies. High schools would log internship placements within regenerative agriculture, renewable energy, cultural resource management, and digital trade. The labor department would release an annual "brain circulation" index: number of kama'āina who return after working or studying abroad, the sectors they enter, and wage differentials they capture. The Hawaii Migration Flows: 2013–2017 report by Kim (2019), produced by DBEDT, analyzes migration trends and characteristics in Hawai'i [9]. It shows a net domestic out-migration of 7,600 residents per year, and when military-related flows are excluded, civilian losses increase to about 13,200 annually. Young adults (ages 18–34), highly educated individuals, and those in labor force transitions are the most mobile. California remains both the top origin and destination state, and international in-migration primarily comes from Asia, especially the Philippines and Japan. Migration is shown to be a crucial factor in Hawai'i's population dynamics, especially as natural increase slows. Understanding who leaves and who returns, especially kama'āina returning with new skills, can inform a "brain circulation" index that tracks economic reintegration and sectoral contributions. This information is vital for shaping policies that support talent retention, economic diversification, and targeted development.

Critics will caution that more data will not automatically fix structural inequities. True, numbers alone cannot build housing or restore reefs. But what is not measured is neglected; what is neglected decays. The alternative indicators proposed here integrate well-being into economic metrics, making it harder for decision-makers to hide behind aggregate growth as communities fray. Adopting a new dashboard does not displace conventional statistics; it expands the aperture. GDP still matters for bond ratings, but if it rises while reef health collapses and teacher outmigration spikes, leaders will confront that contradiction in real time. Job growth still impresses national rankings, yet if those jobs go to mainland contractors while cooperative ownership stalls, the imbalance will be visible.

Ultimately, measuring what matters is an act of sovereignty. Hawaiʻi declares that prosperity is not merely the sum of transactions but the quality of relationships between people and place, present and future, heritage and innovation. By aligning indicators with aloha, kuleana, and lōkahi, the state charts a course where growth supports flourishing rather than undermining it. The dashboard becomes both mirror and compass: reflecting where the islands stand and pointing toward the collective horizon they choose to sail.

5 Risks, Realism, and Resilience

Hawaiʻi's pathway toward an economy anchored in well-being, equity, and sustainability is both visionary and fraught. The ideals behind competing on aloha, centering culture, restoring ecological integrity, and building a regenerative economy are compelling because they promise to reconcile prosperity with justice. Yet the road from vision to realization is steep. Structural barriers, institutional inertia, and external shocks all threaten to derail transformation. It is necessary, then, to approach this moment with clear-eyed realism. Romanticizing the future will not help it arrive. Resilience begins with the honest appraisal of risk.

Among the most immediate and formidable challenges is resistance from industries invested in the status quo. Tourism, defense, and real estate are not just economic sectors; they are deeply entrenched power structures with influence over policy, land use, and labor markets. Moving toward a regenerative model that frees growth from extraction or overdependence calls on incumbents to evolve or accept that they may be left behind. However, industries accustomed to privileged incentives, regulatory exceptions, and market dominance rarely relinquish such advantages easily. Efforts to regulate visitor impact, impose green fees, cap short-term rentals, or require cultural consultation often provoke backlash. Proposals to redirect investment from resort construction to affordable housing, or from military procurement to renewable infrastructure, face well-funded opposition. Even the introduction of alternative metrics that de-emphasize visitor arrivals or defense spending may be resisted on the grounds of threatening economic stability.

These tensions are compounded by political fragmentation and short election cycles. The scale of economic transformation envisioned demands policy continuity over decades, yet Hawai'i's political system is not always designed for long-term alignment. Leadership changes, legislative turnover, and shifting priorities can interrupt momentum. Projects that depend on long-term investment such as watershed restoration, language immersion teacher training, or cooperative enterprise incubation, often outlast political tenures. Mayors and governors are judged by quarterly economic indicators and yearly budget battles, not generational progress. Without institutional mechanisms to protect long-term strategies from political whiplash, bold ideas risk stagnation or reversal. This is especially concerning in sectors where private actors will only invest if public commitment appears stable and reliable.

Another core vulnerability is the chronic underinvestment in public institutions and innovation ecosystems. A future-ready economy demands schools, universities, permitting agencies, planning departments, public health systems, and cultural institutions that are resourced and resilient. Yet austerity cycles, revenue shortfalls, and bureaucratic silos have weakened public capacity. Teachers are underpaid, regulatory processes are backlogged, and aging infrastructure crumbles under strain. Meanwhile, startup ecosystems, research labs, and innovation hubs often lack the capital, policy support, and market connections needed to scale. When public and civic systems are starved of investment, the burden shifts to philanthropy or volunteerism, neither of which can substitute for structural adequacy. The result is a fragmented economy where pilots stall before scaling, and where systemic transformation becomes language without structure.

Cultural integrity itself is at risk, not only from neglect but from commodification. As Hawai'i leans into cultural diplomacy and creative industries, the temptation grows to package heritage for consumption. This over-commercialization can flatten complexity, distort traditions, and sever practices from their spiritual or ecological roots. Hula performed for entertainment but devoid of protocol, Hawaiian language used for branding but not spoken at home, or sacred sites opened for recreation but stripped of ceremony—all constitute forms of erosion. If cultural assets are reduced to economic inputs without protective boundaries, the very foundation of competing on aloha begins to crumble. It is one thing to celebrate culture as an asset; it is another to safeguard its sovereignty from dilution and exploitation.

Overlaying these internal challenges are exogenous risks that Hawai'i cannot control but must prepare for. Climate change is the most pressing. Rising seas threaten coastal infrastructure and ecosystems. Droughts and hurricanes imperil food systems and public safety. Ocean acidification weakens fisheries and coral reefs. Climate migration reshapes regional geopolitics, while insurance markets retreat from high-risk zones, raising the cost of living. Global market volatility presents parallel dangers. Supply chain shocks, inflation, interest rate swings, and geopolitical instability all have disproportionate effects on island economies reliant on imports and vulnerable to tourism downturns. Pandemics, cyberattacks, and energy shocks expose just how fragile interdependence can be.

Recognizing these risks is not a call to retreat into fatalism. On the contrary, resilience is defined by preparation, alignment, and resolve. A resilient Hawai'i does not wait for risk to manifest before acting. It acknowledges that the old model, built on land speculation, mass tourism, fossil fuel imports, and colonial assumptions, is already unraveling. The costs of inaction, once abstract, now arrive as floods, displacement, teacher shortages, and community exhaustion. Denial is not a strategy; realism is. It is no longer enough to say that change is needed. It must be made structurally, institutionally, and narratively irreversible.

This begins with anchoring transformation in collective purpose. When sectors, communities, and leaders align around shared values such as aloha 'āina, kuleana, and pono, decision-making becomes more coherent even amid turbulence. Resilience is less about building walls and more about weaving networks. A neighborhood energy microgrid, a food co-op supplied by local farmers, or a school whose curriculum blends science with cultural wisdom all represent investments in systems that bounce back because they are deeply rooted. Redundancy, cooperation, and localization are not inefficiencies; they are adaptive strategies. Cohn (2024) discusses how the aftermath of the 2023 Lahaina wildfire in Maui presents a rare opportunity to rebuild with sustainable, community-driven energy systems [10]. John Sarter, whose home was destroyed, is pioneering a model involving solar panels, energy storage, and bidirectional EVs to form personal microgrids—demonstrating a scalable solution for resilience and affordability. Working alongside former Hawai'i Public Utilities Commission (PUC) Commissioner Jennifer Potter, the Maui PowerBack project seeks to implement distributed renewable energy infrastructure across the island, prioritizing equity, job creation, and grid independence. Their vision emphasizes replacing polluting diesel generators with solar-based microgrids and submitting a resident-informed energy plan to the Hawai'i Legislature.

At the institutional level, resilience means building muscle for foresight and coordination. Agencies must adopt scenario planning, interdepartmental task forces, and data systems that detect early warning signs across sectors. Universities can become resilience research hubs, training the next generation of planners, health workers, engineers, and educators in systems thinking. Philanthropy must fund ecosystem-level innovation, not just one-off programs. Government budgets must include resilience scoring, so that projects enhancing long-term capacity receive preference. Critical infrastructure, from water catchments and port facilities to data centers and healthcare clinics, must be hardened for tomorrow's compound shocks. The Hawai'i Critical Infrastructure Security & Resilience Program (CISRP) outlines a proactive and collaborative approach to safeguarding the state's critical infrastructure [11]. This program, led by the Office of Homeland Security (2023), adopts a strategic "Defend Today, Secure Tomorrow" model. It emphasizes risk management, stakeholder collaboration, and resilience planning across all sectors, including energy, water, transportation, healthcare, and cybersecurity. CISRP promotes a structured planning framework involving identification of infrastructure, assessment of risks and interdependencies, and development of mitigation strategies. For Hawai'i, this approach is vital due to geographic isolation, aging infrastructure, and climate threats. Benefits include improved emergency preparedness, prioritized investments, and enhanced ability to withstand disruptions. The framework also supports integration with existing local and federal plans, making it an essential tool for guiding infrastructure investments and ensuring long-term community resilience across the islands.

Policy reform is essential. Hawai'i's permitting systems must be redesigned for speed, transparency, and climate compatibility. Zoning codes must allow mixed-use, multi-generational housing close to transit and green infrastructure. The 2024 Hawai'i Community Development Authority (HCDA) Annual Report emphasizes the agency's efforts to support affordable housing and mixed-use, transit-oriented development (TOD) across multiple districts [12]. HCDA advanced projects like the Reserved Housing Program, targeting residents earning 80–140% of the area median income, and launched a 99-year leasehold pilot project to develop low-cost condominiums. Transit-oriented infrastructure was planned or constructed in East Kapolei, Iwilei-Kapālama, and UH West O'ahu to support up to 6,400 new housing units. In Kaka'ako, zoning reforms encourage affordable and climate-resilient development by removing minimum parking requirements and promoting public benefits. These initiatives illustrate how zoning flexibility and public investment in infrastructure can catalyze inclusive, sustainable housing in Hawai'i.

Tax policy must reward regenerative practices and penalize extractive ones. Procurement systems must favor local cooperatives and Indigenous vendors. Hawai'i State Procurement Office (2023) reports that consolidating procurement functions statewide would improve efficiency, equity, and consistency across agencies [13]. This report outlines a phased, 5-year plan to centralize procurement authority under the State Procurement Office while embedding procurement staff within departments. This hybrid model strengthens local agency support and builds professional capacity through standardized training and certification. Importantly, this report emphasizes that modernizing procurement systems, especially through eProcurement and shared services, can enhance participation by small, local, and Indigenous vendors, aligning purchasing practices with Hawai'i's broader economic and social priorities.

Emergency response systems must be integrated with cultural protocols and community trust networks. FEMA (2024) reports that effective risk and crisis communications, integrated with community engagement, are essential to building resilience before, during, and after disasters [14]. The inaugural FEMA Summit brought together over 1,200 communicators to exchange strategies on how to improve messaging clarity, trust, and cultural relevance in times of crisis. A key takeaway was the importance of two-way community engagement, recognizing diverse audience needs, and using trusted local messengers, including artists, nonprofits, and culturally aware communicators. Notably, the summit featured insights from Hawai'i-based participants, such as Mahina Martin from Maui County, emphasizing how trust-building and local engagement play a vital role in disaster preparedness and recovery. This report highlights practical tools like the Integrated Public Alert and Warning System (IPAWS) and the Message Design Dashboard that can be applied locally to enhance emergency communication in Hawaii's diverse communities. These frameworks support culturally competent, inclusive, and community-informed messaging strategies.

Resilience also requires narrative. People need to believe that transformation is not only possible but underway. This means lifting up stories of success: a village that restored its fishpond and now supplies local schools, a youth program that trained solar installers and helped families cut bills in half, an artist collective that revitalized a town square while teaching cultural history. When residents see evidence that new systems work, when they taste the taro, walk the reef, or listen to the chant, they become agents of the future rather than casualties of the past. Narrative resilience resists cynicism, the subtle erosion of faith in our collective capacity to change. Coons (2022) discusses SMALL TOWN * BIG ART[1], a creative placemaking initiative in Wailuku, Maui, supported by a $75,000 National Endowment for the Arts grant [15]. This project celebrates Wailuku's cultural identity through public art installations rooted in oral histories, intergenerational dialogue, and ʻōlelo noʻeau (Hawaiian proverbs). It emphasizes community engagement by involving local elders, artists, and cultural practitioners in every stage, from idea selection to creation. Project coordinator McHugh-White points to the project's power to foster trust, protect heritage, and deepen social capital. The program's success has inspired a countywide expansion, aiming to maintain cultural integrity while resisting pressures of gentrification.

In this work, timing matters. Windows of opportunity open briefly, whether in the aftermath of disaster, during leadership transitions, or as global norms shift. Hawaiʻi must be ready to act boldly when such windows open. That means pre-approving climate-ready capital projects, pre-negotiating community benefit agreements, pre-training civic leaders in rapid mobilization. It means investing in what policy scholars call "shovel-ready" and "shovel-worthy" initiatives—those that not only meet regulatory checklists but embody ethical vision. The Hawaiʻi Priority Climate Action Plan (PCAP) (2024) outlines 17 shovel-ready measures targeting greenhouse gas (GHG) reductions across key sectors like energy, transportation, waste, agriculture, and land use [16]. Developed collaboratively by state agencies, counties, and community stakeholders, this plan prioritizes actions that align with equity, resilience, and cost-effectiveness. Each initiative is designed to advance Hawaiʻi's statutory goals of reducing GHG emissions by 50% below 2005 levels by 2030 and achieving net-negative emissions by 2045. The PCAP emphasizes benefits for disadvantaged

[1] https://www.smalltownbig.org/.

communities, such as improved air quality, job creation, and lower living costs through energy-efficient housing and transit reforms.

None of this denies the difficulty of the task. Hawaiʻi's small scale, isolation, and economic dependencies are real constraints. But so too are its assets: an Indigenous worldview that values interconnection over domination, a globally recognized brand that can open markets and minds, a deep bench of community leaders and practitioners ready to build. If risk is everywhere, so is readiness. What remains is resolve. That resolve will be tested again and again. Projects will fail. Progress will stall. Opposition will organize. Yet resilience is not linear; it spirals. What matters is the capacity to reflect, adapt, and continue. Competing on aloha is not a five-year plan. It is a generational commitment, rooted in love of place and belief in each other. It asks of everyone, not just policy makers but business owners, teachers, artists, students, and kupuna, the courage to imagine systems worthy of the land we live on and the ancestors we honor.

The stakes are high, but so is the reward: a Hawaiʻi that moves beyond reacting to crisis and instead shapes an economy and society where well-being, dignity, and sustainability are not byproducts of success, but its very definition. In that Hawaiʻi, risk is acknowledged and faced with integrity. Realism is understood not as resignation, but as recognition. And resilience stands not as contingency, but as cornerstone.

6 Calls to Action

To move from strategy to practice requires a clear and coordinated set of commitments from every sector of society. Transformation on the scale Hawaiʻi requires cannot be driven by one institution or actor alone. It must be owned by the collective, rooted in collaboration, and guided by a shared sense of responsibility to future generations. This moment calls for action that is not symbolic, but structural. It demands courage from leaders, creativity from innovators, and consistency from communities.

Government must lead with bold policy, not incremental reform. Permitting processes for housing and clean energy need to be drastically simplified and accelerated, not only to unlock economic potential but to meet climate and affordability imperatives. Inafuku et al. (2022) report that Hawaii's exceptionally high home prices, more than double the national median, are partly driven by strict housing regulations that constrain supply [17]. To measure the regulatory burden, the authors implemented the Wharton Residential Land Use Regulatory Index (Wharton

Index[2]) across Hawaii's counties in 2021, filling a data gap left by previous national surveys. Their findings reveal that all four counties in Hawaii rank above the national average in regulatory restrictiveness, with Hawaii County ranking in the top 1% nationally. Key regulatory barriers include long permitting delays, extensive affordable housing requirements, and intense political and judicial involvement. These rules increase costs and discourage multifamily development, further tightening housing supply. For example, permitting delays in Hawai'i average between 14 and 18 months and affordable housing mandates in the state are seven times higher than the national average. The authors note that such regulations can unintentionally favor large developers with the resources to navigate complex bureaucratic processes, reducing competition and innovation in housing production. They argue that easing regulatory constraints, such as allowing more "as-of-right" development, could expand housing supply, improve affordability, and make the development landscape more equitable and responsive to housing needs in Hawai'i.

Business leaders must also shift their metrics of success. Profit is not the enemy, but profit without purpose is a liability. Investing in workforce pipelines from local schools and colleges ensures that economic opportunity is rooted in the community. Regenerative business models that prioritize ecological balance, fair labor, and circular design are no longer fringe experiments; they are becoming competitive advantages. Companies must move from extractive to contributive practices, embedding community impact into supply chains, operations, and ownership models. Partnering with place-based organizations brings not only legitimacy but also local intelligence, helping firms design products and services that meet real needs.

Educators and institutions sit at the heart of long-term change. Schools, colleges, and research centers must not only transfer knowledge but co-create it with the communities they serve. Integrating indigenous knowledge systems with STEM education produces graduates who can solve problems with both rigor and rootedness. Community-research partnerships can ensure that inquiry is not abstract but applied, addressing real issues in housing, health, agriculture, and culture. Curricula that reflect emerging industries—from climate adaptation to cultural

[2] The Wharton Index, or Wharton Residential Land Use Regulatory Index, is a standardized measure that quantifies the restrictiveness of land use regulations across U.S. jurisdictions, based on survey responses about zoning, permitting processes, and development constraints.

restoration—and that emphasize civic engagement help develop leaders who are not only employable but accountable. These institutions must see themselves not as neutral providers of credentials but as active agents of justice and regeneration.

Philanthropy has the potential to catalyze systems change, but only if it moves beyond programmatic funding to invest in the conditions for transformation. This means providing long-term, flexible support to rural and Native Hawaiian-led organizations, whose work is often undercapitalized despite being closest to the ground. Funding must prioritize relationships over deliverables, resilience over scalability. Philanthropy must also use its convening power to create cross-sector dialogues where influence is shared, and new ideas can emerge without gatekeeping. When philanthropy centers equity and embraces experimentation, it can serve as a bridge between vision and viability.

This is a collective undertaking. Each call to action represents a thread in a larger fabric. Only when woven together with trust, clarity, and persistence can Hawai‘i truly move from vision to transformation. A future grounded in aloha is not a slogan. It is a commitment to shared stewardship, across all roles and responsibilities.

7 Imagining Hawai‘i in 2050

Let us imagine a Hawai‘i in 2050, a place transformed by intention, equity, and vision. A child wakes up in a neighborhood where solar panels gleam on rooftops, where her school curriculum blends coding and climate science with Hawaiian language, mele, and mo‘ōlelo. She learns from educators rooted in their communities and from global mentors who connect virtually across oceans. Her classroom is powered not only by clean energy, but by a sense of place, history, and purpose. Education is not preparation for departure, but an invitation to deepen roots and broaden horizons.

Across the islands, local farms thrive as the backbone of food sovereignty. Regenerative practices restore soil health, sequester carbon, and honor ancestral methods of cultivation. Lo‘i kalo and loko i‘a are no longer novelties but central to community food systems. Agricultural cooperatives owned by local families supply produce to school cafeterias, neighborhood stores, and inter-island trade networks. Farming is no longer an economic afterthought; it is a respected and supported career path interwoven with land stewardship.

Tourism has evolved from mass extraction to meaningful exchange. Visitors no longer flood fragile ecosystems or drive-up housing costs. Instead, they are hosted in ways that honor cultural protocols and ecological limits. Community-based tourism enterprises flourish, offering authentic experiences led by kamaʻāina who retain control over their stories, their resources, and their futures. The economy is no longer built on volume but on values. Sustainability and host-community benefit define the new tourism paradigm.

Young adults no longer face the wrenching choice between leaving to succeed or staying to struggle. Affordable housing, career pathways in education, healthcare, and climate resilience, and a vibrant civic life make it possible to stay, thrive, and give back. For those who left, return is welcomed and supported. Networks of innovation, mentorship, and investment span from Hilo to San Francisco to Tokyo, forming a dynamic web of talent circulation. Hawaiʻi does not lose its best minds; it welcomes them home.

Elders are cherished as living archives of wisdom. Intergenerational homes bring together keiki and kupuna in mutual care. Social services are not fragmented but holistic, rooted in community health, traditional knowledge, and modern medicine. Aging is not feared but embraced as part of the life cycle. Programs support caregivers, and policies value time spent in service to family and community. Public spaces reflect the values of inclusion, beauty, and connection. Parks are designed with universal access in mind, integrating cultural landmarks, green infrastructure, and gathering spaces for art, ceremony, and play. Transportation is seamless, affordable, and low emission. Broadband connects even the most remote valleys, and public libraries double as co-working hubs and civic commons.

The economy has expanded its definition of contribution. Artists, caregivers, scientists, farmers, and storytellers are valued alongside engineers and entrepreneurs. Labor is dignified, and wages are sufficient for a decent life. Cooperatives, social enterprises, and circular economy models thrive. The University of Hawaiʻi's Pōʻai ke Aloha ʻĀina Center[3], led by Professor Kamanamaikalani Beamer, is pioneering a global model rooted in Hawaiʻi's ancestral circular economy, emphasizing regenerative, place-based practices like fishpond restoration and taro farming [18]. The center integrates cultural values, ecological sustainability, and social equity to

[3] https://www.kamakakuokalani.org/research/p%C5%8D%CA%BBai-ke-aloha-%CA%BB%C4%81ina.

confront today's climate and economic crises. Through community-led efforts at sites like He'eia and collaborations with international thought leaders such as Kate Raworth, UH promotes the revival of Indigenous economic systems as viable global alternatives to linear, extractive models. These initiatives demonstrate how ancestral knowledge can guide resilient, inclusive economies both locally and globally.

The climate crisis has not vanished, but it is met with courage, collaboration, and cultural wisdom. Sea walls and mangroves protect coastlines. Renewable energy powers homes and electric canoes. Schools teach keiki to track rainfall patterns and care for watersheds. Policy decisions are made with the input of scientists and cultural practitioners alike. Hawai'i stands not only as a survivor of climate change, but as a global leader in adaptation and resilience. None of this is unattainable. These images are not utopian dreams, but plausible futures born of community labor, political will, and shared imagination. This vision is within reach if we choose it, if we invest in it, and if we align our institutions with the values of aloha, kuleana, and lōkahi. The path forward requires courage, not only to innovate but to remember. It demands systems change, but also a reweaving of relationships: to land, to each other, and to the generations yet to come.

This is not merely about the future of Hawai'i. It is about the future from Hawai'i. In an era of global uncertainty, the islands can model what it means to thrive without extraction, to lead with cultural intelligence, and to define prosperity in human and ecological terms. The world is watching. The opportunity is here. The time is now.

8 Final Word: The Island Way Forward

Hawai'i is often portrayed in popular imagination as a tranquil paradise, suspended in time and space, buffered from the turbulence of the modern world. But that image, however alluring, obscures a deeper and more urgent truth: Hawai'i is not merely a place apart. It is, increasingly, a place ahead. A place where global crises arrive early, but so too do the seeds of solutions. A place where the wisdom of the past is not merely remembered but actively practiced to shape the future. As the world navigates the crises of climate change, economic precarity, cultural dislocation, and political fragmentation, Hawai'i stands as a living laboratory for how to survive and thrive with grace, ingenuity, and collective spirit.

To understand the island way forward, we must first confront the conditions that compel change. Hawai'i faces no shortage of daunting realities: skyrocketing housing costs that displace families, rising seas that threaten coastlines, an over-dependence on tourism that exhausts both land and labor, and a brain drain that sends young people away in search of opportunity. These challenges are not unique, but they are more concentrated, more visible, and more intimate in an island context. When resources are finite, when relationships are face-to-face, when nature is not an abstraction but a neighbor, the costs of dysfunction are immediate and personal. But so too are the rewards of change.

In Hawai‘i, it is possible to see with stark precision the difference between extractive and regenerative practices, between short-term profits and long-term well-being, between imported models and homegrown solutions. The path forward begins by embracing this clarity: recognizing that economic development cannot be separated from ecological health, that cultural preservation is not a luxury but a necessity, and that equity is not a political slogan but a daily practice rooted in community design.

To compete on aloha is to assert a different paradigm of prosperity. It is not to dominate markets but to dignify relationships. It is to shift the question from "How much can we grow?" to "How well can we live?" In this vision, the economy is not an engine to be maximized but a garden to be cultivated. Every investment, every policy, every innovation must be evaluated by its ability to nourish people, restore land, and strengthen bonds of reciprocity. This is not a rejection of ambition. It is an invitation to redefine it. Hawai‘i can and should lead by modeling a humane, place-based, and future-facing economy. An economy that measures success not just by income or output, but by the presence of meaning, the resilience of systems, and the depth of belonging. It is an economy that prizes circularity over linearity, sufficiency over excess, and stewardship over speculation.

This approach calls upon every sector of society to reorient. Policymakers must design with inclusion, accountability, and generational impact in mind. Businesses must evolve from extractive enterprises to regenerative partners, grounded in values that extend beyond the bottom line. Educational institutions must equip learners not only with skills but with a sense of kuleana, a recognition that knowledge is a privilege that carries responsibility. Community organizations must be empowered not as service providers of last resort, but as architects of collective care. And residents, in all their diversity, must be invited into shared authorship of Hawai‘i's future.

Crucially, this future must be navigated with humility. Hawai‘i's history includes profound trauma: colonization, cultural suppression, environmental desecration, and the displacement of Native Hawaiians from their ancestral lands. Any vision for the future must reckon with these legacies, not as distant footnotes but as active ingredients in present-day conditions. To move forward with integrity means centering the voices, leadership, and rights of Kānaka Maoli in all areas of policy, planning, and prosperity. It means recognizing that aloha is not a brand or a greeting; it is a practice of deep relationality that binds people to land, to ancestors, and to each other.

In many ways, Hawai'i is already modeling this path. Efforts to restore loko i'a (fishponds), revive 'Ōlelo Hawai'i (Hawaiian language), and implement ahupua'a-based land stewardship reflect a profound commitment to indigenous resilience. Programs that integrate STEM and traditional knowledge, that create regenerative tourism models, and that align entrepreneurship with social good are already underway. The question is not whether transformation is possible. The question is how to scale, sustain, and protect it.

This is where the concept of strategic patience becomes vital. Systemic change is not linear. It is cyclical, iterative, and often fragile. The island way forward requires institutions that are adaptive, policies that are coherent across administrations, and leaders who can hold complexity without defaulting to false choices. It requires long-term investment in civic infrastructure, public trust, and youth leadership. Hawai'i's competitive edge lies not in chasing the next trend, but in honoring what it already knows. The values of aloha, kuleana, and lōkahi are not nostalgic slogans. They are strategic assets in an era of fragmentation. They offer a compass when metrics fail. They invite a way of being that is as rigorous as it is relational. When embedded in economic development, they create enterprises that endure. When infused into governance, they produce legitimacy. When expressed through education, they prepare the next generation not only to succeed, but to serve.

To see Hawai'i as a place ahead is to release it from nostalgia and recognize it as a living prototype of a future that endures. A future where well-being is measured by health, connection, and dignity. A future where economic systems are in harmony with ecosystems. A future where diversity is not managed but celebrated. A future where land is not just property, but ancestor and teacher. A future where every keiki grows up believing that their gifts matter, that their culture is sacred, and that their home is worth fighting for. This is not utopia. It is rigorous hope. It is disciplined imagination. It is the everyday labor of people who love this place and are willing to protect it. The work ahead will be hard. It will require coalitions, compromises, and constant course correction. But the vision is clear: Hawai'i can lead by being most itself.

That is the promise of competing on aloha. Not to extract, but to elevate. Not to conform, but to create. Not to dominate, but to dignify. It is a calling that challenges easy answers and quick fixes. It is a calling that insists on integrity, rootedness, and resilience. And it is a calling that Hawai'i—in all its complexity, capacity, and courage—is ready to answer.

References

[1]. U.S. Environmental Protection Agency. (2023, October 19). Maui Wildfire Recovery: Respect for Cultural Significance. Retrieved from https://www.epa.gov/system/files/documents/2023-11/maui-wildfire-factsheet-respect-for-cultural-significance.pdf.

[2]. United Nations Department of Economic and Social Affairs (UNDESA) & United Nations Framework Convention on Climate Change (UNFCCC). (2024). Synergy solutions for climate and SDG action: Bridging the ambition gap for the future we want (2nd ed.). Retrieved from https://sdgs.un.org/sites/default/files/2023-09/UN%20Climate%20SDG%20Synergies%20Report-091223B_0.pdf.

[3]. Atkinson, Z. (2020). Lā'au Lapa'au Preservation Project. MIT Solve. Retrieved from https://solve.mit.edu/challenges/2020-indigenous-communities-fellowship/solutions/33038.

[4]. U.S. Global Change Research Program. (2023). Chapter 30: Hawai'i and U.S.-Affiliated Pacific Islands. In Fifth National Climate Assessment. Retrieved from https://nca2023.globalchange.gov/chapter/30.

[5]. Harvard Joint Center for Housing Studies. (2024). America's Rental Housing 2024. Retrieved from https://www.jchs.harvard.edu/sites/default/files/reports/files/Harvard_JCHS_Americas_Rental_Housing_2024.pdf.

[6]. Institute for Citizens & Scholars. (2024). Mapping civic measurement: How are we assessing readiness and opportunities for an engaged citizenry? Retrieved from https://citizensandscholars.org/wp-content/uploads/2024/05/Citizens-Scholars-Mapping-Civic-Measurement-Report-2024-update.pdf.

[7]. Gross, A. F., & Rodriguez, C. M. (2017). Hawai'i Carbon + Natural Capital: A Policy + Institutional Analysis for Payment for Ecosystem Services (PES) Approaches in Hawai'i. Conservation International. Retrieved from https://www.conservation.org/docs/default-source/publication-pdfs/ci_hawaii-carbon-natural-capital.pdf.

[8]. Aspen Institute Financial Security Program. (2022). 101 solutions for inclusive wealth building. Aspen Institute. Retrieved from https://www.aspenin

stitute.org/wp-content/uploads/2022/04/ASP-FSW_101Solutions_FINAL_Single1.pdf.

[9]. Department of Business, Economic Development & Tourism (DBEDT). (2019, December). Hawai'i migration flows: 2013–2017. Retrieved from https://files.hawaii.gov/dbedt/economic/reports/Hawaii_Migration_Flows_2013-2017_Dec2019.pdf.

[10]. Cohn, L. (2024, January 15). Creating a solar, EV and microgrid-based distributed energy system from the 'blank slate' created by the Maui wildfire. Microgrid Knowledge. Retrieved from https://www.microgridknowledge.com/residential-microgrids/article/33017574/creating-a-solar-ev-and-microgrid-based-distributed-energy-system-from-the-blank-slate-created-by-the-maui-wildfire.

[11]. Hawai'i Department of Defense. (2023). Hawai'i Critical Infrastructure Security & Resilience Program (CISRP). Retrieved from https://dod.hawaii.gov/hieng/files/2023/03/Hawaii-Critical-Infrastructure-Security-and-Resilience-Program_Add-2.pdf.

[12]. Hawai'i Community Development Authority (HCDA). (2024). 2024 HCDA Annual Report. Retrieved from https://dbedt.hawaii.gov/hcda/files/2025/01/2024_HCDA_Annual-_Report_Final.pdf.

[13]. Hawai'i State Procurement Office. (2023, December 28). Procurement Consolidation Working Group Final Report: Act 282, SLH 2022. Retrieved from https://spo.hawaii.gov/wp-content/uploads/2023/04/Procurement-Consolidation-Working-Group-Final-Report_Act-282-SLH-2022_2023-1228.pdf.

[14]. FEMA. (2024). Risk Communications, Crisis Communications, and Community Engagement Summit Report. Retrieved from https://www.fema.gov/sites/default/files/documents/fema_risk-communications-crisis-communications-community-engagement-summit-report-2024.pdf.

[15]. Coons, C. (2022, September 7). Our Town Grant Spotlight: SMALL TOWN * BIG ART. National Endowment for the Arts. Retrieved from https://www.arts.gov/stories/blog/2022/our-town-grant-spotlight-small-town-big-art.

[16]. Hawai'i Climate Change Mitigation and Adaptation Commission. (2024, March 1). Hawai'i Priority Climate Action Plan. Retrieved from https://www.epa.gov/system/files/documents/2024-03/hawaii-pcap-final-.pdf.

[17]. Janis Magin Meierdiercks, J. (2022, May 3). Hawai'i's building permit delays top the nation, study shows. Hawaii Business Magazine. Retrieved from https://www.hawaiibusiness.com/hawaii-building-permit-delays-top-nation-uhero-study-real-estate-carl-bonham/.

[18]. Beamer, K. (2024). A first-of-its-kind: Pō'ai ke Aloha 'Āina Center for the Ancestral Circular Economy & Justice. Noelo. Retrieved from https://research.hawaii.edu/noelo/a-first-of-its-kind/.

Discussion Questions

Chapter 1 Discussion Questions: The Island Economy at a Crossroads

1. What are the key factors contributing to the economic paradox in Hawai'i, where high life quality indicators coexist with financial insecurity?
2. How does the ALICE threshold reveal deeper economic struggles not captured by traditional poverty measures?
3. In what ways does Hawai'i's geographic isolation both hinder and foster innovation in its economy?
4. How can Hawai'i leverage its isolation to build a more resilient, self-sufficient economy?
5. What are the economic and environmental trade-offs associated with Hawai'i's dependence on tourism?
6. How might policies targeting short-term vacation rentals (STRs) impact housing affordability in Hawai'i?
7. What lessons can be drawn from workforce development strategies to reduce brain drain and increase economic inclusion?
8. Why is remote work seen as a potential solution to economic inequality and outmigration in Hawai'i?

P. Yu, *Economic Development in Hawai'i*,
https://doi.org/10.1007/978-3-032-15689-1

Chapter 2 Discussion Questions: Measuring Productivity in the Pacific

1. What sectors of Hawai'i's economy contribute most to its productivity challenges? How might workforce development or innovation change this dynamic?
2. How does the concept of "brain drain" relate to the mismatch between Hawai'i's educated workforce and its economic structure? What policy solutions could reverse this trend?
3. Compare Hawai'i's reliance on tourism and public sector employment to other island economies. What lessons can be learned, and what strategies should Hawai'i pursue to build a more resilient economy?
4. How do regulatory barriers—such as zoning laws or permitting delays—impact economic productivity and innovation in Hawai'i?
5. What role can indigenous knowledge systems play in reshaping Hawai'i's economic model toward sustainability and community well-being?

Chapter 3 Discussion Questions: Tourism and Transformation

1. How has tourism functioned both as Hawai'i's economic backbone and a source of social and environmental strain?
2. How can regenerative tourism be used as a tool for cultural revitalization and economic equity?
3. In what ways can community-led tourism initiatives create more sustainable and resilient local economies?
4. What specific policies could help shift tourism revenues toward local businesses and long-term investments in Hawai'i's people and environment?

Chapter 4 Discussion Questions: Diversify or Decline?

1. Why has economic diversification been so difficult to achieve in Hawai'i, despite decades of political and academic advocacy?
2. What are the key differences between economic diversification and economic replacement, and why does that matter for Hawai'i?
3. How did the COVID-19 pandemic expose the risks of Hawai'i's overreliance on tourism and defense?
4. Why are high-wage, low-carbon jobs considered essential for Hawai'i's future? What are examples of such jobs?

5. How can value-added agriculture improve both food security and economic stability in Hawai‘i?
6. What role do traditional Hawaiian practices play in shaping modern sustainable sectors like aquaculture and regenerative farming?
7. How can public policy and education reform better support emerging industries that align with Hawai‘i's values and strengths?

Chapter 5 Discussion Questions: People First

1. What are the key barriers that contribute to the "brain drain" from Hawai‘i, and how can public policy address them?
2. How can culturally responsive education improve both academic performance and economic opportunity for Native Hawaiian students?
3. In what ways can the University of Hawai‘i system become more effective in aligning education with workforce needs?
4. What are the strengths and weaknesses of a centralized education system, such as Hawai‘i's single statewide district model?
5. How can Hawai‘i better support non-traditional students, including returning adults and those from rural islands?
6. How can remote work be leveraged to reverse outmigration trends while maintaining local affordability?
7. Why is work-based learning considered essential in bridging the gap between education and employment?
8. What steps can be taken to ensure equity and inclusion across education-to-employment pathways in Hawai‘i?

Chapter 6 Discussion Questions: Building Smart

1. What is the "geographic premium" and how does it shape Hawai‘i's economic development and infrastructure costs?
2. How does the Jones Act affect Hawai‘i differently from mainland states, and what are the arguments for and against its reform?
3. In what ways can smarter supply chain planning help mitigate Hawai‘i's logistical vulnerabilities?
4. How does permitting complexity contribute to the housing crisis in Hawai‘i, and what reforms could streamline the process without sacrificing oversight?
5. What institutional innovations—like "one-stop shops" or regulatory sandboxes—hold the most promise for Hawai‘i, and why?

6. How does public opposition (e.g., NIMBYism) affect housing development in Hawai‘i, and how can community engagement be improved?
7. What role should the state play in aligning infrastructure investments with equity, resilience, and sustainability goals?
8. How can Hawai‘i turn geographic isolation from a disadvantage into a driver of innovation and resilience?

Chapter 7 Discuss Questions: Island at the Crossroads

1. In what ways does Hawai‘i's geographic location shape its strategic importance in the Indo-Pacific region, and how has this influenced U.S. military policy?
2. What are the economic trade-offs of Hawai‘i's heavy reliance on military spending? How might diversification reduce this dependency while preserving strategic relevance?
3. How can Hawai‘i leverage its location and logistics infrastructure to become a more influential actor in trans-Pacific trade and economic exchange?
4. Given the high level of imports, what policies or innovations could help strengthen Hawai‘i's economic resilience and reduce vulnerability to global supply chain disruptions?
5. What role should Hawai‘i play in advancing regional diplomacy and development among Pacific Island nations, given its shared cultural roots and political position as a U.S. state?
6. How can Hawai‘i turn its soft power—via tourism, cultural diplomacy, and climate leadership—into lasting influence in global policy, rather than relying primarily on its strategic military role?

Chapter 8 Discussion Questions

1. How does the concept of ‘competing on aloha’ redefine traditional economic metrics like GDP?
2. What are the benefits and challenges of adopting a place-based economic model in Hawai‘i?
3. In what ways can indigenous knowledge systems be integrated into STEM education and innovation?
4. How can Hawai‘i balance economic growth with ecological sustainability and cultural preservation?

5. What specific indicators should be included in a new economic dashboard for Hawai'i?
6. How can Hawai'i's procurement and tax systems be reformed to support regenerative and inclusive economic models?
7. How can public and private sectors collaborate to address systemic housing and infrastructure challenges?
8. How might the strategic pillars outlined in 'Competing on Aloha' serve as a model for other island or Indigenous communities globally?

Glossary

Agri-Entrepreneurs: Agri-entrepreneurs are individuals or businesses that engage in agriculture-related enterprises, applying innovation and entrepreneurial strategies to improve productivity, sustainability, and value-added processing in the agricultural sector.

Agri-tech: Technology applied to agricultural processes to increase productivity, sustainability, and efficiency.

Ahupuaʻa: A traditional land division system extending from mountain to sea, emphasizing integrated resource management.

ʻĀina: Land, but more deeply, that which feeds. Central to Hawaiian identity, reflecting a reciprocal relationship between people and the environment.

Aloha ʻĀina: A Hawaiian concept meaning love of the land, often tied to cultural and environmental care.

Aloha Economics: An economic framework rooted in Hawaiian values such as aloha (mutual care), kuleana (responsibility), and lōkahi (unity), prioritizing well-being and ecological integrity.

Aquaculture: The farming of fish, shellfish, and other aquatic organisms in controlled environments, often used as a strategy for sustainable food production.

Blue economy: Economic activities related to oceans and waterways that promote environmental sustainability and ecosystem health.

P. Yu, *Economic Development in Hawaiʻi*,
https://doi.org/10.1007/978-3-032-15689-1

Brain Circulation: A concept that tracks the movement of skilled local individuals who leave to study or work abroad and then return, contributing to their home communities.

Brain Drain: The emigration of educated or talented individuals from one location (such as Hawai'i) to another for better opportunities.

Brain Drain: The emigration of educated or talented individuals to other regions due to lack of opportunities at home.

Carrying Capacity: The maximum number of visitors an area can sustain without causing environmental or social degradation.

Circular Economy: An economic system aimed at eliminating waste and the continual use of resources through reuse, repair, and recycling.

Circular Economy: An economic system aimed at eliminating waste and the continual use of resources by reusing, repairing, refurbishing, and recycling existing materials and products.

Climate-smart agriculture: Agricultural practices designed to increase productivity, enhance resilience, and reduce greenhouse gas emissions.

Community Land Trust: A nonprofit model for housing that separates land ownership from homeownership to maintain affordability long-term.

Community Wealth Building: Strategies that prioritize local ownership, cooperative enterprises, and the retention of wealth within communities to promote long-term economic stability.

Cost of Living Index: A measure that compares the average cost of essential goods and services across different geographic areas.

Creative industries: Economic sectors that generate income through the creation of cultural products and services such as music, film, design, and art.

Cultural diplomacy: The use of cultural practices and exchanges to promote mutual understanding and strengthen international relationships.

Culturally Responsive Education: An educational approach that respects and incorporates students' cultural backgrounds, languages, and learning styles.

Diaspora: A population that lives outside its ancestral homeland but maintains emotional and cultural ties to it.

Digital Economy: The digital economy refers to economic activities that result from billions of everyday online connections among people, businesses, devices, data, and processes. It encompasses e-commerce, digital services, and the use of digital technologies to transform traditional business models.

Digital Navigator: A community-based digital literacy assistant who helps individuals gain access to and effectively use digital tools and services.

Economic Diversification: The process of expanding an economy to include a wider array of industries and reduce dependency on a single sector.

Economic diversification: he process of broadening the range of economic activities in a region to reduce reliance on a few dominant sectors.

Economic Mobility: The ability of individuals or families to improve their economic status, often measured by income or education.

Economic Multiplier: The additional economic activity generated from an initial spending. In tourism, it reflects how money circulates through local businesses, jobs, and services.

Economic Resilience: Economic resilience is the ability of an economy to withstand or recover quickly from external shocks, such as natural disasters, pandemics, or financial crises, while maintaining or quickly regaining functionality and prosperity.

Economic vulnerability: The susceptibility of an economy to external shocks, often due to overdependence on a limited number of industries.

Eco-Tourism: Responsible travel to natural areas that conserves the environment and improves the well-being of local people.

Externalities: Costs or benefits from an economic activity that affect third parties and are not accounted for in the market transactions such as environmental degradation from mass tourism.

Extractive Economy: A system that extracts resources without regard for environmental or social sustainability, leading to degradation over time.

GDP: Gross Domestic Product: the total monetary value of all final goods and services produced within a country's borders in a specific period of time.

Gentrification: The process by which urban neighborhoods are transformed through an influx of more affluent residents, often displacing lower-income families and small businesses.

Geographic Premium: An economic term describing the higher cost of goods, services, and infrastructure development due to a location's physical remoteness, such as Hawai'i's isolation from mainland supply chains.

Hale: House or building; used in names of civic buildings or homes.

High-wage, low-carbon jobs: Employment opportunities that offer good salaries while contributing minimally to greenhouse gas emissions.

Ho'omau: To perpetuate or sustain; often used to refer to the continuity of traditions.

Human Capital: The collective skills, knowledge, and experience possessed by a population, viewed in terms of their value to the economy.

Human Capital: The economic value of a worker's experience and skills, including education, training, intelligence, and health.

Innovation hub: A physical or virtual space designed to foster creativity, collaboration, and entrepreneurial development.

Innovation Index: A metric that evaluates a region's innovation capabilities, often including factors such as Research & Development (R&D) investment and startup activity.

Intercultural communication: The exchange of information across different cultures and social groups.

Kuleana: A Hawaiian value meaning responsibility or privilege, often used in the context of community and environmental stewardship.

Kuleana: Responsibility or privilege; often used to describe one's duty to care for land, community, or role within society.

Kumu hula: Master teacher of hula; also a cultural guide and source of knowledge.

Kūpuna: Elders or ancestors; respected sources of wisdom and knowledge, integral to intergenerational learning and community cohesion.

Labor Productivity: The amount of goods and services produced by one hour of labor. Used to gauge workforce efficiency.

Living Wage: A wage that is high enough to maintain a normal standard of living in a given location.

Lo'i kalo: Irrigated taro patch; a symbol of sustainable agricultural productivity in Hawaiian tradition.

Lōkahi: Unity, harmony, and balance; used as a pillar of social and ecological integration.

Loko i'a: Fishpond; ancient Hawaiian aquaculture system used to raise fish sustainably.

Longitudinal Data Systems: Data systems that track student progress from early education through postsecondary education and into the workforce.

'Ōlelo Hawai'i: Hawaiian language; revitalization efforts are central to cultural preservation.

Mele: Chant or song; used to transmit knowledge, genealogy, and values.

Microcredentials: Short, focused credentials that certify mastery of specific skills or competencies, often aligned with industry needs.

Mo'ōlelo: Story or history; narratives passed down through generations to preserve cultural knowledge.

Per Capita Income: The average income earned per person in a given area, calculated by dividing total income by the population.

Performance-Based Regulation (PBR): A utility regulation framework linking company earnings to performance outcomes like clean energy adoption, rather than capital investment.

Permitting Bottleneck: Delays caused by complex, multilayered regulatory approval processes that increase costs and uncertainty for developers.

Pilina: Relationship or connection; emphasizes interdependence and community ties.

Place-Based Economics: An economic approach that tailors policies and practices to the unique cultural, ecological, and geographic characteristics of a specific region.

Pono: Righteousness, morality, or balance; often invoked as a value guiding ethical behavior.

Productivity: The measure of output per unit of input, such as labor or capital. Often used to assess economic efficiency.

Public-Private Partnership: A cooperative arrangement between government and private sector entities to fund, build, and operate projects such as public services or infrastructure.

Regenerative agriculture: A type of farming that focuses on restoring soil health, biodiversity, and ecosystem function.

Regenerative Economy: An economic model that restores and renews natural and social systems, emphasizing environmental sustainability and community well-being.

Regulatory Sandbox: A policy tool that allows temporary regulatory flexibility to pilot new solutions in housing, energy, or mobility sectors.

Remittance: Money sent back home by migrants to support their families and communities.

Resilience: The capacity of a system or community to withstand and adapt to disruptions, maintaining essential functions and structures.

Shot Clock: A rule requiring government agencies to issue permit decisions within a set time frame to avoid project delays.

Shovel-Ready Projects: Projects that are fully designed, permitted, and ready to be implemented as soon as funding becomes available.

Skilled Trades: Occupations that require specialized training or apprenticeships, often in construction, clean energy, or manufacturing.

Skills Mismatch: A situation where available jobs do not align with the qualifications of the workforce, leading to unfilled roles and underemployment.

Soft power: A country or state's ability to influence others through cultural or ideological means rather than military force.

Stackable Credentials: Modular educational certifications that build upon each other toward a degree or advanced credential.

Supply Chain: The network of production, shipping, and distribution that brings goods and services to market.

Supply chain: The sequence of processes involved in the production and distribution of goods.

Talent Pipeline: A system or process designed to cultivate and prepare skilled individuals for employment in specific sectors.

Tourism Impact Zone: A designated area where tourism is regulated or limited to prevent overuse and to manage its effects on residents and the environment.

Transit-Oriented Development (TOD): Urban development approach focusing on high-density, mixed-use neighborhoods centered around public transportation to reduce car dependency.

Underemployment: A situation in which workers are employed below their skill level or are working part-time when full-time work is desired.

Urban Growth Boundaries: Zoning tools used to limit urban sprawl and protect agricultural or conservation lands, often used to guide development in areas like Oregon.

Value-added agriculture: Agricultural practices that increase the economic value of a product through processing, branding, or innovation (e.g., taro chips from raw taro).

Value-Added: The net output of a sector after adding up all outputs and subtracting intermediate inputs; often used to assess a sector's contribution to GDP.

Wage Competitiveness: The ability of an economy or employer to offer salaries that match or exceed those available in competing regions.

Wai: Water; a sacred and life-giving element in Hawaiian culture.

Work-Based Learning (WBL): Educational experiences that integrate real work environments with classroom learning.

Index

P. Yu, *Economic Development in Hawai'i*,
https://doi.org/10.1007/978-3-032-15689-1

www.ingramcontent.com/pod-product-compliance
Lightning Source LLC
Chambersburg PA
CBHW060848200126
38456CB00004B/458
* 9 7 8 3 0 3 2 1 5 6 8 8 4 *